SOCIAL AWAKENING

SOCIAL AWAKENING

ADOLESCENT BEHAVIOR AS ADULTHOOD APPROACHES

ROBERT T. MICHAEL
EDITOR

RUSSELL SAGE FOUNDATION / NEW YORK

The Russell Sage Foundation

The Russell Sage Foundation, one of the oldest of America's general purpose foundations, was established in 1907 by Mrs. Margaret Olivia Sage for "the improvement of social and living conditions in the United States." The Foundation seeks to fulfill this mandate by fostering the development and dissemination of knowledge about the country's political, social, and economic problems. While the Foundation endeavors to assure the accuracy and objectivity of each book it publishes, the conclusions and interpretations in Russell Sage Foundation publications are those of the authors and not of the Foundation, its Trustees, or its staff. Publication by Russell Sage, therefore, does not imply Foundation endorsement.

Library of Congress Cataloging-in-Publication Data

Social awakening : adolescent behavior as adulthood approaches / Robert T. Michael, editor.
    p. cm.
    Based on a conference held at the United States Bureau of Labor Statistics, Nov. 18-19, 1999. The conference was co-sponsored by the Bureau of Labor Statistics and Northwestern University/University of Chicago Joint Center for Poverty Research.
    Includes bibliographical references and index.
    ISBN 0-87154-616-7
    1. Adolescence—United States—Congresses. 2. Adolescent psychology—United States—Congresses. 3. Family—United States—Congresses. I. Michael, Robert T. II. United States. Bureau of Labor Statistics. III. Joint Center for Poverty Research

HQ796.S5632 2001
305.235'0973—dc21

2001019333

Text design by Suzanne Nichols.

RUSSELL SAGE FOUNDATION
112 East 64th Street, New York, New York 10021
10 9 8 7 6 5 4 3 2 1

Contents

Contributors

ROBERT T. MICHAEL is the Eliakim Hastings Moore Distinguished Service Professor and dean of the Irving B. Harris Graduate School of Public Policy Studies at the University of Chicago.

YASUYO ABE is research affiliate at the Population Research Center, National Opinion Research Center, and senior analyst at Berkeley Policy Associates.

LAURA M. ARGYS is associate professor of economics at the University of Colorado at Denver.

COURTNEY BICKERT is a graduate student in the Irving B. Harris Graduate School of Public Policy Studies and the Graduate School of Business at the University of Chicago.

JOHN CAWLEY is assistant professor in the Department of Policy Analysis and Management at Cornell University.

PINKA CHATTERJI is assistant professor of health economics in the Department of Epidemiology and Social Medicine at Montefiore Medical Center/ Albert Einstein College of Medicine.

JEFF DOMINITZ is research scientist at the H. John Heinz III School of Public Policy and Management at Carnegie Mellon University, and research director of the Carnegie Mellon Census Research Data Center.

BARUCH FISCHHOFF is University Professor in the Department of Social and Decision Sciences and the Department of Engineering and Public Policy at Carnegie Mellon University.

DIANE GIBSON is assistant professor at the School of Public Affairs, Baruch College of the City University of New York.

CHARLES F. MANSKI is Board of Trustees Professor in Economics and fellow of the Institute for Policy Research at Northwestern University.

MIGNON R. MOORE is assistant professor of sociology and African American studies at Columbia University.

H. ELIZABETH PETERS is associate professor in the Department of Policy Analysis and Management at Cornell University.

CHARLES R. PIERRET is a research economist at the Bureau of Labor Statistics.

ROBIN L. TEPPER is a doctoral candidate at the Irving B. Harris School of Public Policy Studies at the University of Chicago.

JAMES R. WALKER is professor of economics at the University of Wisconsin at Madison, and the principal investigator of the NLSY97.

L. SUSAN WILLIAMS is assistant professor of sociology at Kansas State University.

Acknowledgments

This volume is one of three products from the NLSY97 Early Results Conference held at the Bureau of Labor Statistics, November 18 to 19, 1999. The conference was co-sponsored by the Bureau of Labor Statistics and Northwestern University/University of Chicago Joint Center for Poverty Research with supplemental funding from the Russell Sage Foundation, the Ford Foundation, the Spencer Foundation, the W.T. Grant Foundation, and the Foundation for Child Development.

The authors wish to thank our editors, Suzanne Nichols, Emily Chang, and Joe Brown, for excellent editorial assistance in the preparation of this book.

Michael Horrigan and James R. Walker co-organized the Conference of Early Results from the NLSY97 with the editor of this book; the authors in this volume thank them for their efforts and support. The National Opinion Research Center (NORC) at the University of Chicago and its fine staff deserve much credit for the excellent data set that is the basis of this volume. All of us associated with the NLSY97 wish to express our thanks to the nine thousand youths and their parents who cooperated in the survey, and who will, we hope, continue to do so for years to come.

Introduction

A Lens on Adolescence: The 1997 National Longitudinal Survey of Youth

Robert T. Michael

PROBABLY no other span of life is associated with greater personal or public angst than the teenage years—the years of transition from childhood to adulthood. With an inexorability that is much anticipated but not well controlled, the child's body changes. With these physical developments come associated changes in capabilities, interests, and sense of self as well as in social relationships with family members, peers, and authority figures. Communities, schools, and other social institutions as well as family members and friends attempt to guide the judgments and actions of adolescents as they explore new options and prepare for the responsibilities of adulthood. The early teen years can be a time of great danger, and much social policy is meant to help young people negotiate the challenges that they face—for example, avoid teen pregnancy, improve school performance, remain in school, and curb excessive physical and sexual risk taking as well as the abuse of drugs, alcohol, and tobacco. But these years can also be a time of extraordinary achievement—in learning, in sports, in leadership, and in commitment—and a great deal of social policy is also meant to encourage such positive activity. A principal motivation for much social research has been to understand the influences on these varied choices adolescents make, and to offer guidance to the youths, their families, and to social-policy makers about how best to encourage the potentials and avoid the dangers that some of those choices entail.

The essays in this volume represent an attempt to further our understanding of the early teen years by utilizing an important new resource—the data set known as the National Longitudinal Survey of Youth, 1997 Cohort (NLSY97). The NLSY97 is the newest data set in the federal government's arsenal of surveys designed to help us understand what factors influence and what consequences follow from the actions and aspirations of a whole age cohort of Americans. These new data on some nine thousand young men and women aged twelve to sixteen were collected by means of lengthy interviews (with the youth and one parent), and they will be updated periodically for years to come. The information thus obtained will allow social scientists to explore a wide range of influences on behavior and experience. Even with only the first round of data available, however, we can begin to tell the story of these youths' lives and to detail the circumstances associated with their behavior.

In this volume, we focus principally on the role that the family plays in teenagers' lives—how its characteristics are related to various aspects of their behavior (whether they date, become sexually active, use alcohol, tobacco, or other drugs, engage in criminal activity), their health, how they spend their free time, and their expectations about their own futures. One of the advantages of extensive, omnibus interviews like the NLSY97 is that a wide array of behaviors and experiences can be investigated. And an understanding of the linkages thus revealed can help us design social policies that promote a healthy and successful transition to adulthood. Before I describe the nature of the findings detailed in subsequent chapters, however, it will help to place the data set in context and describe its key features.

Since the mid-1960s, social scientists have had available to them the results of several national longitudinal surveys. These surveys report on many facets of behavior and have therefore allowed the testing of a wide range of theories and formal structural models. The Department of Labor's National Longitudinal Survey (NLS) Program began its first field survey in 1966, running four concurrent cohorts through the 1970s, and then in 1979 began a new youth cohort (the NLSY79) that continues to be followed. Also in the 1960s, the National Science Foundation began to support the Panel Study of Income Dynamics (PSID), another longitudinal survey of families that continues to this day. Both the NLS and the PSID have introduced innovations and special foci that have substantially augmented the ability of analysts to study and to understand what influences choices and outcomes. These, together with a half dozen key surveys conducted through the Bureau of the Census and the several longitudinal school-based surveys sponsored by the Department of Education, are the major sources of information used by social-science and social-policy researchers. They are the grist used in Ph.D. mills, the basis of innumerable findings presented in testimony before legislative bodies, and a key reason for the considerable success of the social sciences over these past four decades.

So it is a time of considerable excitement when a new national survey comes along. NLSY97—sponsored by the Bureau of Labor Statistics (BLS)— is the newest of these major omnibus, longitudinal surveys. There is the expectation that it will be up-dated annually for the next two or three decades, as were its predecessors. Thus, it provides the opportunity to study a whole new generation of teenagers as they make the transition from school to work and from childhood to adulthood in the face of a perplexing, demanding, and extraordinary future. The NLSY97 offers us the opportunity to confirm or refute what we think we know, to explore what we could not explore with older or less complex data sets.

In constructing the NLSY97, a large number of scholars crafted questionnaire modules in their various areas of expertise. These modules were then molded into a cohesive whole that met the constraints imposed both by the budget and by the patience of the randomly selected youths and their parents. The database that resulted is a national, stratified, clustered sample of households in the United States, selecting all persons residing therein who were age twelve through sixteen on December 31, 1996, who spoke either English or Spanish. The resulting cross-sectional sample was supplemented by oversamples of African American and Hispanic youths. The number of household addresses fielded totaled 90,957. This number was expected to locate some ten thousand youths. Although the National Opinion Research Center (NORC) found some 88 percent of these addresses eligible for screening, and although of those eligible addresses a remarkable 94 percent were successfully screened, only 9,808 youths were found, of whom 92 percent were successfully interviewed. The final result was a sample of 9,022 (for details about the sample, see Moore et al. 2000; for a description of the survey effort see Michael and Pergamit 2001).

The sample of 9,022 youths represents the teenage American population at the start of the twenty-first century–all were age fifteen to nineteen on the last day of 1999. The sample is described in table I.1 by age, gender, and race (panel A), separately by region, health status, and urban-rural residence (panel B), separately by religion, Hispanic ethnicity, and parents' education (panel C), and separately by family income and family structure (panel D). The oversampling of blacks and Hispanics is evident in table I.1, which shows simple, unweighted counts of cases. Most of the other chapters in this book use sampling weights so that the reported statistics represent estimates that pertain to the population of adolescents in the United States. I leave it to the reader to look over the description of this sample as reflected in table I.1. The goodwill and cooperation of the respondents—"rebellious" adolescents—is affirmed by the high response rate and the evident face validity of the answers they provided.

The survey protocol was complex and intended to yield an exceptionally rich amount of information about the youths. There were three distinct components to Round 1 of the field effort. The first component was a screening of all targeted households to determine whether eligible youths were living there. If an eligible youth was found in a household, an extensive rostering was undertaken of all family members and basic demographic

TABLE I.1   *Characteristics of Youths in Round 1 of the NLSY97*

A. Number of Cases by Age, Gender, and Race

	Males				Females				
Age	All	White	Black	Other[a]	All	White	Black	Other[a]	Total
Twelve	160	108	34	17	171	107	45	17	331
Thirteen	885	528	226	123	832	481	215	125	1,717
Fourteen	923	557	230	126	845	477	241	123	1,768
Fifteen	976	547	279	144	901	543	211	137	1,877
Sixteen	944	550	254	134	936	540	256	126	1,880
Seventeen	692	402	168	115	690	377	221	88	1,382
Eighteen	39	20	12	6	28	14	9	5	67
Total	4,619	2,712	1,203	665	4,403	2,539	1,198	621	9,022

B. Number of Cases by Region, Health Status, and Urban-Rural Residence, Separately

Region		Health		Urban-Rural	
North	1,588	Excellent	3,497	Rural	3,808
North-Central	2,061	Very good	3,037	Urban	5,214
South	3,243	Good	2,025	Total	9,022
West	2,130	Fair	430		
Total	9,022	Poor	28		
		Total	9,017		

C. Number of Cases by Religion, Hispanic Ethnicity, Parent's Education, Separately

Current Religion		Hispanic Ethnicity		Parent's Education[b]	
Protestant	5,027	Hispanic	1,904	None	25
Catholic	2,532	Non-Hispanic	7,091	Less than high school	1,528
Jewish	83	Total	8,995	High school	2,614
Muslim	55			Some college	2,103
Other	119			College graduate	1,133
None	1,083			Postcollege	928
Total	8,899			Total	8,331

D. Number of Cases by Family Income and Family Structure, Separately

Family Income		Family Structure			
< $15,000	1,788	Intact (both biological parents)	4,419	Biological mother only	2,561
$15,000 to $30,000	1,570	Biological mother and spouse	975	Biological father only	311

TABLE I.1   *Continued*

Family Income		Family Structure			
$30,000 to $50,000	1,883	Biological father and spouse	211	No parent	414
$50,000 to $100,000	2,235	Cohabiting parent	131	Total	9,022
> $100,000	618				
Total	8,094				

Source: Author's compilation.
Note: If numbers do not sum to 9,022, the remaining cases are not specified for that category.
[a] Includes 61 American Indians, Eskimos, or Aleuts, 160 Asian or Pacific Islanders, and 1,065 others.
[b] If two parents, the higher level achieved by either of the two parents.

information collected. Information was also obtained about key nonresident family members, in particular biological parents, siblings, and offspring. Depending on the complexity of the family structure, that rostering exercise could take as little as a few minutes (if an eligible youth was not found) or as much as half an hour or more (if the family involved was large or their relationships complex). The detailed information thus obtained about family structure is one of the many strengths of this new data set. Several chapters in this volume—particularly chapters 1, 2, and 4—make special use of it, combined with information provided later in the interview about transitions in living arrangements over the youth's lifetime.

The second component was an hour-long interview with one of the youth's parents, usually the mother or mother figure in the home. This interview was designed to collect information usually available only to the adults in a household—source and amount of family income; assets and debts; marital, residential, and employment histories of the adults in the family; social-program participation; certain assessments of the youth in question—as well as family background and the youth's health status. More sensitive issues were handled by means of a self-administered questionnaire (SAQ). This parent interview was one important difference between the NLSY97 and earlier surveys, including the NLSY79. Previously, there was no extensive parental interview, and, while the young people surveyed were asked to provide some basic financial information, much less detail about the family's history and circumstances was available in the NLSY79. Moreover, the new survey included even younger youths (aged twelve and thirteen) than had been included in NLSY79 and they, especially, would not have been expected to be able to provide this detailed information. Such information is vital, however, when studying certain public-policy issues, and the NLSY97 therefore represents an important new source of evidence about the effects of social-welfare programs. Several of the later chapters in this volume—particularly chapter 9—demonstrate the potential inherent for this type of analysis.

The third component was an interview with the youth. The interview covered education, job training and employment history, health status, peer relationships, time use, social behavior, attitudes and expectations, and a characterization of the relationship with each parent. Again, more sensitive issues were handled by means of an SAQ. The duration of interviews varied, depending on the complexity of the life of the youth in question, but the average interview lasted seventy-five minutes. An exceptional amount of information was obtained about schooling—both the social and the curricular dimensions. The survey focused particularly on math education, including a short math test so that skill level could be evaluated and compared to courses taken and grades received. Also included were innovative questions about expectations one year from the interview date, by age twenty, and by age thirty. Chapters 7 and 8 make special use of this information and show how useful such a line of questioning can be.

The survey was conducted, from beginning to end, by means of a laptop computer, including the SAQ which featured an audio-assisted capability in English and Spanish. One of the key differences between this survey and most other large-scale surveys is that the NLSY97 was designed from the start as a computer-assisted interview. This means that the questions were couched in terms of the context of previous responses. It also implies that, while the flow of the interview was thereby more conversational and natural, the information obtained was more complex and rich—and more difficult to analyze. Details that might previously have been captured in the response to a single question are now spread throughout the interview and more elaborated. Consider, for example, how much more information can be obtained about *family income* when instead of asking simply "What was your family's income last year?" the interviewer poses some two dozen very specific questions about each relevant family member's wages, fringe benefits, interest, dividend, and transfer payments. (There will always, of course, be the occasional piece of missing information with which the analyst must contend.)

Since the first round of the NLSY97 became available for public use in January 1999, an "early results" conference was held in November 1999 to begin exploring the data.[1] Following the conference, its organizers—Michael Horrigan of the BLS, who oversees the NLS Program; Robert Michael, the project director of the NLSY97 for the first several years; and James Walker, the current project director—arranged to publish three collections of papers disseminating the results of the conference. Those papers dealing with employment issues will appear in a special issue of the *Monthly Labor Review* (see Horrigan 2001). Those papers dealing with schooling will appear in a special issue of the *Journal of Human Resources* (see Walker 2001). Those papers dealing with social-relationship issues appear in the present volume.

It should be noted that, while each of the essays in this volume can stand on its own—each presents hypotheses, findings, and suggestions for further research worth reflection in their own right—in this introduction I attempt, not just to highlight the more interesting results of each essay, but to illustrate the potential that the NLSY97 holds for future research. The characterization of authors' results that follows may therefore differ in emphasis from their own. The volume is organized around four general topics: family background; dating and sexual behavior; adolescents' expectations; and antisocial behavior. In what follows, I review each chapter in turn.

Adolescents' Families and Their Influences on Youths
The Effect of Family Structure on Youth Outcomes in the NLSY97

Charles R. Pierret examines the relation between family structure and the transition to adulthood and attempts to determine why "the transition to adulthood appears to be much more difficult for youths who come from broken families" (23). His study offers us an overview of the range of living situations experienced by adolescents in the United States today: overall, only about half (51 percent) have lived their whole lives in intact families; when the figures are broken down by race, that proportion is slightly higher for whites (58 percent) and dramatically lower for blacks (22 percent). Pierret divides the sample into eight distinct subgroups on the basis of family-structure history. For the African Americans, the modal experience shared by 28 percent is always to have lived with a single mother. Table 1.2 details the full array of these eight patterns for youths by race-ethnicity. Table 1.3 offers a very interesting breakdown of the amount of the youth's lifetime spent living in the various family arrangements, reminding us that the current description of family arrangement often does not reflect the full experience. For example, those currently living with a remarried mother are estimated to have spent more than a quarter of their life with both biological parents, about one-third with their mother only, and a bit more than one-third with their mother and a stepfather.

Pierret's work emphasizes how valuable an extensive interview with a parent can be when it comes to eliciting information about family-structure history. He provides "a first glimpse at the relation between family structure and the successful transition to adulthood" (24) by examining grade-point average in the eighth grade and the incidence of five "potentially troubling behaviors" (24)—smoking cigarettes, drinking alcohol, smoking marijuana, engaging in sexual activity, and getting arrested. In his reduced-form estimates of these behaviors, Pierret finds a strong and consistent relation with family structure: in comparison with living in an intact family, "all the family-structure variables except having been adopted significantly predict a lower grade-point average and a greater probability of problem behaviors" (36). The implied magnitude of many of these effects is quite large. Compared to the effect of gender, for example, the family-structure effect is typically twice as large.

Building on his thoughtful discussion of the relation of family structure to child outcomes, Pierret returns to the issue of causation and tries to go behind the strong ordinary least squares (OLS) effects to explore why these correlations with family structure are so strong. He suggests several mechanisms. One is the *instability* introduced into youths' lives by family-structure changes. A second is the *conflict* that prevails in most disrupted families. A third is unobserved *economic and social* factors that accompany divorce. Some of these mechanisms can be measured directly, some can be instrumented, but the resulting analyses prove unsatisfactory. Pierret concludes by suggesting strategies for further, more sophisticated analyses, the results of which, he emphasizes, will become increasingly powerful as additional survey rounds are completed and researchers are able to exploit the longitudinal feature of the data set, a theme often repeated in this volume, as befits essays that began life as part of an "early results" conference.

Patterns of Nonresident-Father Involvement

Like Pierret's essay, this essay, by Laura M. Argys and H. Elizabeth Peters, is motivated by negative youth outcomes, approaching the problem via the issue of the father-child relationship. Argys and Peters focus on children with a nonresident father, their initial analysis distinguishing among those fathers who are absent because they are divorced from the child's mother, those who are absent because they are separated from her, and those who are absent because they never married her. Subsequent analysis distinguishes among absent fathers in terms of the method by which paternity was established. Unlike Pierret, who examines youth outcomes directly, Argys and Peters investigate both the reasons for and the nature of father-child involvement and the relation between the level of involvement and the amount of child support received, but they do not extend the analysis to measures of child behavior or outcomes. While theirs is the only analysis presented in this volume that remains at the background level, their through exploration of the subject provides a solid basis on which subsequent analyses can build.

Also like Pierret's essay, this essay reveals how complex the task of characterizing the child's circumstances is. Consider but one example. On average, the length of time that the father has been absent from the home ranges from as little as five years for those parents who are separated, to nine years for those parents who are divorced, to as long as twelve years for those parents who never married (and the reader should keep in mind that, in these data, the child is on average age fourteen). If an analyst does not control for the length of time that the father has been absent, it might erroneously be inferred that it is type of separation that affects child outcomes. Conversely, if type of separation is not controlled for, it might erroneously be inferred that it is length of separation that affects child outcomes.

Argys and Peters consider only a subset of the NLSY97 sample, the nearly 2,500 adolescents whose biological father is alive, identified, but nonresident: about 1,100 whose parents are divorced, another 1,100 whose parents never married, and about 250 whose parents are separated. They characterize the extent of father-child involvement, the amount of child support provided by the father, the nature of the father-child relationship as described by the youth, and the nature of the parents' interactions as described by the youth. These relationships are defined in terms of the father's supportiveness, his habits of offering praise or criticism, and whether he knows the youth's friends, for example.

Among the conclusions drawn from this analysis are the following: Both the extent and the quality of the father-child relationship are greater if the parents had at one point been married. An interesting pattern is also revealed regarding financial support—the amount of court-ordered child support is greater where the parents had previously been married, but the actually receipt of child support, conditional on an award, is more likely if the parents never married. Among African Americans, the payment of child support is less likely and the amount of father-child contact is less if the parents had been married, whereas the amount of contact is likely to be greater if the parents never married. There appears to be less communication between parents who never married than between those who were previously married.

Argys and Peters have previously researched the issue of paternity establishment, and they pursue that topic with these new data. They classify families in the never-married sample into four categories: both parents on the birth certificate; voluntary paternity; involuntary paternity; and no paternity. Tables 2.6 and 2.7 reveal the dramatic effect that paternity type has on child custody as well as the close relation that it has to both father-child contact and financial support. As might be expected, the fact that paternity has been established greatly influences whether child support has been awarded. Also, the extent of father-child contact is greater if paternity has been established voluntarily.

There are many papers each of us can probably recall that claim to control for family structure with one or two variables. Argys and Peters's work represents a strong rebuke of that practice. It emphasizes—as does Pierret's—

that family structure has many dimensions, financial as well as social, and that both past and present circumstances must be taken account of, even when the focus of study is a young child. Changing family relationships, past legal agreements, and various other negotiations between the parents all surely influence many youth outcomes.

Parental Regulation and Adolescent Discretionary Time-Use Decisions: Findings from the NLSY97

Round 1 of the NLSY97 contained a small survey module on adolescent time use, and Robin L. Tepper exploits that information in her essay. She offers the basic descriptive information that one would expect to find: focusing on twenty-four hundred youths aged twelve to thirteen, she reports that, on average, only 5.5 hours per week are devoted to homework and even less time, 3.1 hours, to reading for pleasure but a whopping 17.5 hours to television viewing. So much for the "Too Much Homework" headlines!

Tepper's essay, however, goes well beyond a simple description of time use and fits well in this section dealing with the influence of families on adolescent behavior. Tepper uses the time-use information to explore the role that parents play in the socialization and developmental experiences of their children. She discusses three types of parental regulation: regulation through rules, through monitoring, and through what she calls *structure.* (Structure is measured in terms of whether the family eats dinner together each night [45 percent of the families of those youths surveyed did], whether the adolescent participates in religious activities each week [66 percent of those surveyed did], and whether he or she takes any extra classes or lessons during the week [31 percent did].) And she constructs indices of regulation through rules and regulation through monitoring and uses these as well as the three indicators of structure in her separate multivariate OLS analyses of time spent on homework, watching television, and reading for pleasure.

Controlling for several youth personal characteristics, Tepper finds that monitoring and structure, but not rules per se, seem to be the ways parents influence the time allocation of their adolescents. As one would expect, parental guidance is associated with more time spent doing homework and reading for pleasure and less time watching television. Tepper also documents other relationships: girls report spending more time doing homework and reading for pleasure and less time watching television than do boys, and blacks report spending more time doing homework and watching television. Tepper pursues her point further by fully interacting the parenting styles and background factors with several key pairs of attributes: race (black versus white), parent's education (more highly versus less highly educated), and family type (single versus two parent). The pattern that emerges suggests that regulation through structure has a greater effect on white than on black adolescents, on adolescents in two-parent families than on those in single-parent families, and on adolescents whose parents are more highly educated than on those whose parents are less highly educated. Throughout, monitoring is relatively consistently correlated with time use, while the indicator *rules* per se seldom exhibits statistical significance.

Tepper's essay is but one way the time-use module can be used, but in it she shows the value of measuring the psychologists' notion of parenting style and exploring it in these data. Her concept of family structure is a real contribution, I think—one that others will probably want to explore further.

Adolescents' Dating and Sexual Behavior
Family Environment and Adolescent Sexual Debut in Alternative Household Structures

With Mignon Moore's essay, the focus of the volume narrows to particular important adolescent behaviors, in this case the beginning of partnered sexual activity, which she terms *sexual debut.* Moore use sexual debut as a vehicle with which to investigate the influence of family structure, the concept *family* here being refined so as to capture the distinctions between two-biological-parent families, remarried stepfamilies, first-marriage stepfamilies, cohabiting households, maritally disrupted single-parent families, and never-married single-parent families. She is interested in documenting how family structure is related to sexual debut—what differences there are among whites and blacks, and whether the observed differences are associated with the nature of parental support and discipline, characterized as parenting style.

Moore's sample is between the ages of fourteen and sixteen, and her focus is on a dummy variable indicating whether the youth has had intercourse; a weighted logistic regression model is used. Confirming previous results, Moore initially shows that youths in intact families are much less likely to have had sex than are those in any of the other family-structure types. A more refined analysis, one fully interacting these effects by race, finds a similar association with family structure for whites and blacks, but only for some types of family structure—that is, for maritally disrupted and never-married single-parent families compared to intact families but not for remarried black stepfamilies or cohabiting black households. Her decomposition of the white-black results reveals gender differences among the two races: among the blacks, but not among the whites, girls are much less likely to have had intercourse than are boys (see table 4.3).

Moore also introduces measures of parenting style, in particular the strictness and the supportiveness of each parent, and she does so taking account of family structure. The results are complicated, differing by race and family structure. One of the complications is that the influence of a biological father and that of a stepfather are quite distinct, causing Moore to suggest that "it appears as though most parenting efforts by stepfathers in remarried stepfamilies are likely to be rebuffed, at least initially" (125). Moore's essay shows again how important a full elaboration of family structure can be in investigating the influence of families on adolescents.

Exploring Determinants of Adolescents' Early Sexual Behavior

This essay takes a direct look at the information provided in the NLSY97 about dating and sexual behavior. Descriptive tables show the distributions of behaviors measured in the survey, including age at first sex, number of sex partners, and frequency of sex in the past year. The survey also contains somewhat comparable information about dating behavior, allowing parallel analyses to be conducted of both dating and sexual behavior. While there are steep age gradients over the age range considered (fourteen to seventeen years), the overall prevalence of social dating is 72 percent (with boys reporting a rate seven points higher than that of girls), that of partnered sexual activity 30 percent (with boys reporting a rate two points higher). As is typically found in similar studies, the sexually active boys report having more sex partners than do the sexually active girls: 34 percent of the boys and 20 percent of the girls report having had five or more sex partners ever.

The gender-specific multivariate models of ever having had sex and ever having dated show several similar relations: both behaviors increase dramatically with age and with earlier age at puberty, both show a strong positive relation with the absence of the father, and both occur more frequently among those who have no religious affiliation. Many other characteristics show quite different relations with these two behaviors.

The central concern of the essay is an exploration of the widely observed negative relation between parent's education and the onset of adolescent sexual activity. The authors argue that parent's education proxies youth career aspirations and that those with strong aspirations (that is, those with more highly educated parents) have a strong motivation to avoid sexual activity and thus pregnancy and other associated risks. The evidence is presented in two steps: first, the effect of parent's education on age at first sex is demonstrated; then, direct indicators of career prospects are introduced, diminishing the effect of parent's education dramatically.

Further evidence supporting this hypothesis is revealed in the analysis of dating behavior. Since dating per se does not present the same risks as sexual activity, the same relations should not be observed, and they are not.

For the girls, there is even a positive relation between parent's education and dating.

Body Weight and the Dating and Sexual Behaviors of Young Adolescents

John Cawley's essay takes yet another look at the onset of sexual activity and dating, but with a quite narrow and focused perspective: he is interested in whether being overweight influences dating and sexual behavior. Many adolescents.are obsessively concerned with their weight, and Cawley, who has worked extensively with data on obesity from the National Health and Nutrition Examination Survey, seeks evidence here about the effects of being overweight on these social behaviors. He wants to go beyond simple correlation to say something about causality. To do so, he uses an instrumental-variables approach and offers a clear discussion of this methodology for any reader who is not familiar with it.

The instrumental variable used is the youth's biological father's body mass index (BMI). Cawley explains that, if the father's BMI is correlated with the youth's BMI but not with the youth's dating or sexual behavior, he can proceed statistically to determine whether it is the youth's weight per se that affects dating and sexual behavior.

Cawley finds that weight (specifically, being overweight) does not affect boys' likelihood or frequency of dating. (He notes that taller boys are more likely to date.) He also finds slight evidence that heavier boys are less likely to engage in sexual activity and stronger evidence that they are less likely to have sex frequently. Different patterns emerge for girls. Heavier girls are less likely to date and less likely to do so frequently. Among girls, however, there is no association between weight and reported sexual behavior.

Adolescents' Expectations and Their Well-Being

Adolescents' Expectations Regarding Birth Outcomes: A Comparison of the NLSY79 and NLSY97 Cohorts

James R. Walker uses the expectations questions asked of the youths—one of the novel features of the NLSY97—to explore adolescent fertility. The scope of his essay is broad, and he addresses issues of both methodology and behavior.

Walker delves deeply and instructively into the problems involved in analyzing the answers to expectations questions—questions about "the percent chance" that something will happen by some specific point in the future. His discussion of the "heaping" of answers is particularly interesting (see table 7.2). He performs a convincing assessment of the internal consistency of the answers provided, in terms of both strict logic (for example, for a fifteen-year-old, the likelihood of dying in the next year must be lower than that of dying by age twenty) and contextual relevance (those who are already sexually active are objectively more likely to get pregnant within the next year than are those who are not yet sexually active) (see table 7.3). He also argues that youths' answers to expectations questions are more sensible if the content of those questions is salient to their lives, demonstrating the better consistency found among answers to questions about fertility than among answers to questions about mortality.

Walker makes informative comparisons between the NLSY79 and the NLSY97 data. Since the fertility-expectations questions—and therefore the responses—differ between surveys, one of Walker's most useful contributions is a demonstration of how to transform the information available in one survey into a form comparable to that available in the other. Walker also exploits the longitudinal nature of the NLSY, comparing NLSY79 fertility expectations with subsequent actual fertility behavior. Overall, he finds that, although most teens can reliably assess short-term fertility outcomes, there are important exceptions, particularly among poor black women, who experience many more teen births than anticipated.

Perhaps his most substantive and important finding, however, is that fertility expectations remained essentially unchanged in the interval between the two surveys: 15 percent of the youths surveyed in 1979 and 17 percent of those surveyed in 1997 expected to become a parent before age twenty. There is, of course, much left to study regarding this interesting stability over time, as Walker notes.

Who Are Youth "At Risk"?
Expectations Evidence in the NLSY97

Jeff Dominitz, Charles F. Manski, and Baruch Fischhoff also use the expectations questions—in this case to explore which youths are "at risk," an attribute commonly found in social-welfare analysis. Typically, the designation at risk is assigned on the basis of demographic attributes or of experiences usually associated with adverse outcomes. Dominitz, Manski, and Fischhoff, however, take a different tack, exploiting information in the NLSY97 about expectations of completing high school by age twenty, serving jail or prison time by age twenty, and becoming a parent by age twenty. They consider a youth to be at risk if his or her assessed chance of receiving a high school diploma is less than 90 percent, of serving jail time is 5 percent or higher, and of becoming a parent is 10 percent or higher. Three levels of severity of risk are presented, based on these criteria.

Applying this algorithm to information collected from both the youths and their parents, Dominitz, Manski, and Fischhoff calculate that 6.2 percent of the youths are at risk by their own assessment and that 4.8 percent are at risk by their parents'. They go on to characterize risk status by gender and by race-ethnicity. And they also show that the pattern of risk is positively associated with living in a single-parent family and negatively associated with family income. Finally, they show that risk status is quite strongly associated with whether a youth has smoked cigarettes, used marijuana, carried a handgun, dealt drugs, repeated a grade in school, or engaged in sexual activity.

Since both youths' self-assessments and parents' assessments of the youths were collected, Dominitz, Manski, and Fischhoff compare the two. While youth and parent assessments are closely correlated, it turns out that a larger percentage of the parents than of the youths themselves see no chance at all of the three target adverse outcomes. This is, as the authors comment, counter to the common wisdom that adolescents see themselves as invulnerable.

Dominitz, Manski, and Fischhoff offer us an important, innovative way of identifying those youths who are at risk. As they themselves emphasize, this first-wave data will become even more valuable as the youths are tracked over time. We can then see whether their own and their parent's predictions are borne out.

Food Stamp Program Participation and Health: Estimates from the NLSY97

Diane Gibson begins her essay with an investigation of the relation between four measures of the youth's health and the family's use of Food Stamps if impoverished. The theory motivating the essay suggests that the added resources made available through the Food Stamp Program should improve youth health. The challenge of the empirical study undertaken is, of course, controlling adequately for health status in the absence of Food Stamps. As Gibson points out, her controls are incomplete because currently available data allow her to control only for current income levels and a few past years of Food Stamp receipt, not for the family's complete income and program-participation history.

The measures of health that Gibson uses are indicators of whether a youth is underweight or obese, a youth's self-reported health status, and chronic-illness status as reported by a youth's parent, all obtained from the NLSY97. (Note that Gibson's measure of obesity is more stringent than Cawley's—BMI over thirty rather than BMI over twenty-five.) The NLSY97 data also contain information about the receipt of Food Stamps in the most recent complete year (1996) and the number of years over the past five in which Food Stamps were received.

Gibson shows that, in these data at least, the receipt of Food Stamps is not systematically associated with the measures of youth health that she investigates. As she stresses, however, strong conclusions should not be drawn from these early results since the controls for the counter-factual comparisons are not as adequate as she would like, and subsequent waves of the data will offer a much richer statistical opportunity to control for some of these.

Gibson also shows that among those personal characteristics that are associated with health status, girls are less likely than boys to report themselves as underweight or in good health and more likely to be obese and (by parent assessment) to have a chronic illness.

Adolescents' Antisocial Behavior

What Determines Adolescent Demand for Alcohol and Marijuana? A Comparison of Findings from the NLSY79 and the NLSY97

The three chapters in this section share a common focus on the prevalence and the determinants of several illegal, dangerous, or inappropriate behaviors by the adolescents. All three make comparisons of the information in the new NLSY97 with information obtained in the NLSY in 1980 and subsequently, and so these chapters speak to the differences in these antisocial behaviors over the past two decades.

Pinka Chatterji uses information contained in the NLSY79 and the NLSY97 to examine differences in substance-use patterns over the last two decades. She also brings to bear information obtained from other sources—data on price as well as on other determinants of substance use (for example, minimum drinking age and legal penalties for possession). (Incidentally, a very useful feature of the NLSY data set is that, under certain, restricted conditions, researchers can obtain information about state and county of residence of the respondent, thereby permitting the researcher to import into the analysis additional relevant information.) Not many would have thought to include the price of beer by year and state, but that is a piece of information Chatterji uses effectively in this chapter.

Chatterji first tackles the important issue of underreporting, showing some indication of underreporting in the NLSY97, but less than what has been documented as occurring the NLSY79. The probability of greater underreporting in the earlier data set somewhat clouds the evidence of a trend in smoking and drinking among adolescents. That said, a much higher proportion of youths today report having used marijuana and alcohol by age seventeen than did so in the early 1980s.

Chatterji next presents a series of multivariate models showing the correlates of alcohol and marijuana use before age seventeen for both the new 1997 data and the earlier data; she also estimates models on the frequency of alcohol and marijuana use both ever and within the last month. Many patterns found in this analysis confirm previous evidence. For example, girls are less likely to report using alcohol or marijuana and, among those who do drink, to report drinking less in the past month, although both boys and girls report about the same rates of binge drinking in the past month. Whites appear to be more likely to use alcohol and marijuana, as are youths living in single-parent families. Those with an alcoholic relative are much more likely to use both alcohol and marijuana.

The results of the analysis using price information are mixed. The money prices of substances—beer, cigarettes, and cocaine—do not show the expected relations, which is puzzling since other data sets do show price responsiveness in youth demand. Chatterji points out that her 1979 analysis is not able to link the price and behavior information fully and that that fact may help explain the absence of price sensitivity for that era, but she is not yet able to explain the lack of a price effect in the 1997 data. By contrast, the legal penalties for marijuana possession seem to elicit the expected response of lower demand. There is, in fact, evidence of cross-price effects on binge drinking, suggesting that the two activities may be complements. Chatterji urges that caution be used, however, when drawing conclusions.

Changes in Gender and Racial Gaps in Adolescent Antisocial Behavior: The NLSY97 Versus the NLSY79

Yasuyo Abe addresses trends in antisocial behavior over the last two decades, using multivariate models to explore the effect of various demographic and economic characteristics. She distinguishes between two types of antisocial behavior: covert (including committing property crime and vandalism, stealing, and selling illegal drugs) and overt (including fighting, attacking, and strong-arming). The NLSY79 and the NLSY97 ask about similar, but not identical, sets of behaviors that can be fitted into these two categories.

While Chatterji shows that alcohol and marijuana use rose substantially over the last two decades, Abe's evidence is that the rates of antisocial behavior fell by nearly half, and that reduction is seen in both overt and covert activity and consistently across all age, gender, and racial/ethnic groups. But, as Abe emphasizes, the NLSY79 definitions of antisocial behavior are much looser than the NLSY97 definitions are, so some undetermined amount of that decline is only definitional, unfortunately. She therefore uses relative rates and finds quite similar patterns: for example, young men are more likely than young women to engage in all types of delinquent activity in both years, and whites more likely to engage in covert criminal behavior, African Americans in overt criminal behavior.

Abe also presents an interesting, detailed picture of specific behaviors by single year of age for the two time periods, allowing a simple comparison of rates over time as well as patterns across ages. According to her analysis, juvenile crime rates peak in the age range of fifteen to seventeen.

A multivariate analysis is performed as well, focusing on the two covert and overt sets of antisocial behavior and conducted in parallel for the 1980 and the 1997 data. It is striking how similar are the patterns of relations between family-background and socioeconomic factors and the target behaviors across the two years. As Abe summarizes, "the coefficient estimates for 1980 and 1997. . . appear to have the same signs and to be generally comparable in magnitude" (348). She also undertakes a standard decomposition of the white–African American differences in overall antisocial activity.

City Kids and Country Cousins: Rural and Urban Youths, Deviance, and Labor Market Ties

L. Susan Williams also examines deviant behavior, this time with an emphasis on urban-rural differences. She offers a strong defense for studying rural adolescent behavior and notes how little attention the topic receives. She focuses on both the differential levels of deviance in the two contexts and the interaction of rural-urban setting with race and gender patterns of deviant behavior.

Williams points out that FBI statistics on juvenile arrests suggest that rates of *property* crime have declined over the period from 1980 to 1997, with the urban-rural rates converging toward the lower, rural levels. There has been a convergence in rates of violent crime as well, with a decline in urban but a noticeable increase in rural crime. Williams looks to the NLSY79 for 1980 and the NLSY97 for 1997 for youths aged fifteen to seventeen to check on these trends and rural-urban gaps in the survey responses. Like Abe, she notes that the differences in the definitions of behaviors across the two survey questionnaires make the comparison of absolute levels difficult. She shows, however, that the sizable urban-rural gaps revealed in 1980 have mostly disappeared in the 1997 data, qualitatively reflecting the same trends as seen in the FBI's Uniform Crime Reports (UCR) on arrests. Also consistent with UCR reports, NLSY data reveal that rural arrest rates rose and that the ratio of urban-to-rural rates declined. However, while, according to the UCR, urban arrest rates fell, according to the NLSY data they rose.

Williams estimates a multivariate logistic regression on a composite of any of seven relatively severe deviant or criminal acts. That model shows that the rate of criminal activity is higher among young men and those who have had what she identifies as *bad experiences* (for example, being bullied, being threatened, seeing someone shot, having one's house burglarized) and lower among blacks, those in good schools, and, importantly for her focus, youths in urban areas. So, for this composite indicator of deviance, rural youths have a higher rate when controls are included. Using her multivariate model for a subset of the younger youths and including additional controls for family and personal attributes, Williams also shows that the rates on the composite index are quite high—10 to 20 percent higher in rural than in urban areas for both the boys and the girls in several specific social conditions.

There are systematic differences in reported crime-victimization rates as well as in reported crime-commission rates. Williams documents the patterns by gender and rural-urban residence, revealing some interesting differences. Notably, and somewhat surprisingly, I think, she reports that rural women are more likely to be threatened at school than are their urban counterparts.

This final chapter also looks at several separate additional issues. Williams shows a very strong positive association between reported criminal acts and reported arrests; interestingly, when the incidence of criminal acts is controlled for, arrest rates are higher among young men and urban youths. She also addresses the issue of whether engaging in antisocial acts is statistically associated with youths' self-assessment of the chance of completing college, finding a strong negative association, other things held constant. She addresses as well the alleged deterioration of parental influence and social control in rural areas as more women enter the workforce, contending that "the evidence lends some support to the notion that there still exists a rural culture that exerts influence via the family" (392).

While I will not attempt to summarize the results presented in this volume, I think that a few general reflections are in order. The NLSY97 makes available a wide range of detailed information about some nine thousand young men and women across the United States, all collected from the youths themselves and their parents. Unfortunately, not all youths and parents responded to all the questions, so subsets of respondents must occasionally be used. Since this is, as yet, a one-time or cross-sectional survey, there is not much opportunity to structure longitudinal analyses and thereby get at real causal relations. Researchers will be able to undertake such analyses shortly, however, as new waves of data become available. Current limitations aside, the essays in this volume show the wonderful strength of the NLSY97 data and give us some very important early results.

One conclusion that readers will surely draw from these essays is how complex is family structure and how strongly it affects the lives of these adolescents. We see the varied experiences of youths in terms of the proportions of their short lives spent in one or another family circumstance and the subtlety of the nature of their interactions with noncustodial fathers. We see the varied nature of parental discipline and regulation and the strong association with adolescents' actions. We see much evidence of a strong association between family characteristics and the expectations, aspirations, and behaviors of the youths and indications that family structure can predispose youths to favorable or adverse outcomes. While the mechanisms or routes of influence are not always clarified, one cannot read these essays and doubt the importance and breadth of family influence on these adolescents.

It is not only the structure of the family that matters, of course. There is much evidence here of the strong influence of parent's education, family income, race, and place of residence as well. And the gender differences observed in various behaviors and attributes are fascinating, if not bewildering. As the youths age, and as new rounds of data become available, the role of other, nonfamily influences—peer groups, social institutions (including schools), religious institutions, job markets, communities—will be made increasingly clear. And, as the youths make key decisions that define their adult behavior and affect their overall well-being—decisions about education level and content, career, marital status, family size and structure, and location—the early results reported here will provide a fine basis on which to build a growing understanding.

The temptation to offer a litany of the fascinating and important "facts" reported here is almost too great to be resisted. As a compromise, I offer just a few.

We learn that about two-thirds of the life of the average youth in the study have been spent with both parents, about a quarter with the mother only, and the rest in a variety of other arrangements. We learn that the average twelve- to fourteen-year-old spends only about five hours per week doing homework, three hours per week reading for pleasure, and seventeen hours per week watching television. We learn that three-quarters of the youths aged fourteen to seventeen have begun dating and that about one-third have also begun to have sex. We learn that one in six girls is overweight and one in six underweight and that one in seven boys is overweight and nearly one in three underweight. We learn that the median youth reports that he or she has a 5 percent chance of becoming a parent by age twenty, a 10 percent chance of not living to age twenty, and about an 85 percent chance of graduating from college by age thirty. (These are not the same youths, so cross-event consistency is not at issue here.) This does not imply that only 5 percent of the youths will have a baby before they reach twenty or that anything close to 10 percent will die before that age, but these expectations influence the youth's motivation and his or her calculation about behaviors of all sorts. We learn that 3 percent of girls and 7 to 8 percent of boys are at severe risk of adverse socioeconomic outcomes. And we learn that over 40 percent of the entire sample of twelve- to seventeen-year-olds report having used alcohol, that nearly 10 percent report binge drinking in the last thirty days, and that well over half report engaging in antisocial and even criminal activity.

No doubt readers will assemble their own sets of most interesting facts. But the importance of this volume lies, not just in the facts presented, but in the fact that the whole represents the beginning of an effort to document more thoroughly than has been done before the factors and circumstances that motivate teenagers and that constrain their behaviors. There is a payoff to be had now but a greater payoff to come as successive waves of data are collected. And an important part of the research effort will be to integrate the findings reported here with those reported in the two companion volumes that feature behavior pertaining to schooling and employment.

Overall, it is stunning, I think, how consistently the characteristics of the youth and his or her family that are associated with one aspect of behavior are also those associated with other aspects, whether substance abuse, criminal activity, sexual activity, self-image, or school achievement. Of course, such consistency is not news to the researcher. Still, it is reassuring to have it confirmed by new survey data. I do not mean to imply, of course, that collecting new data sets and conducting new analyses are redundant activities. Social-science research of necessity builds on prior work, honing interpretations and conducting more precise analyses. New efforts always offer the possibility of new insights as well as confirmation. And new insights are, after all, the motivation behind new data sets.

It is especially interesting, I think, to see what new strategies, measures, and methods different researchers use to exploit the same basic resources. It is these different approaches that will lead to far richer understandings of the data and more robust findings—and to an understanding of what further work must be undertaken. The several essays in this volume that approach similar topics with different techniques and emphases surely underscore this point. I think that, in the end, readers will agree that the essays collected in this volume affirm the value of this new data source and the contributions that it can make to our understanding of adolescent behavior at the turn of the century.

Note

1. In turning to these early results, I remind the reader that we are dealing with a longitudinal survey that has moved beyond the first round of interviewing. In the summer following the interviews that produced the data used in this volume, the youths were scheduled to take a battery of tests assessing their abilities, interests, and career potential, testing funded by the Department of Defense. (For those familiar with earlier NLSY data, these assessments included the modern version of the Armed Services Vocational Aptitude Battery.) By the conference date, the second round of surveying had been completed, the third round was about to commence, and preparations were being made for the fourth. In other words, the survey program is well under way.

References

Horrigan, Michael, ed. 2001. Special issue of *Monthly Labor Review* (summer).

Moore, Whitney, Steven Pedlow, Parvati Krishnamurty, and Kirk Wolter. 2000. *National Longitudinal Survey of Youth 1997(NLSY97): Technical Sampling Report.* Chicago: National Opinion Research Center (November).

Michael, Robert T., and Michael R. Pergamit. "The National Longitudinal Survey of Youth, 1997 Cohort." *Journal of Human Resources.* Forthcoming(summer).

Walker, James R., ed. Special issue of *Journal of Human Resources* (36)4. Forthcoming.

Part I

ADOLESCENTS' FAMILIES AND
THEIR INFLUENCES ON YOUTHS

1

The Effect of Family Structure on Youth Outcomes in the NLSY97

Charles R. Pierret

IT IS WELL established that children who spend part of their childhood in a single-parent family—either because they were born to an unwed mother or because their parents divorced—do worse on a number of measures of well-being than do those who grow up in two-parent families (McLanahan and Sandefur 1994). Among the problems experienced by children from single-parent households cited by Barbara D. Whitehead (1993) in her controversial article in the *Atlantic Monthly,* "Dan Quayle Was Right," are increased poverty, emotional and behavioral problems, teenage pregnancy, drug abuse, failure to complete high school, and trouble with the law. The transition to adulthood appears to be much more difficult for youths who come from broken families than for those from intact families.

But, although the consequences are well established, the causes and relative importance of the problems experienced by children of single parents remain the subject of controversy. Some of these problems are a direct result of the parents' separation. Divorce and single motherhood lead to greater poverty and residential mobility for children. Ties to one parent are often weakened, leaving the child economically and emotionally vulnerable (McLanahan and Sandefur 1994). But some of the causes may predate the parents' separation. Conflict between the parents may scar youths and lead to negative consequences, especially if that conflict results in abuse. In extreme cases, divorce may actually help children. Also, characteristics that make individuals unsuccessful marriage partners (immaturity, for example) may make them unsuccessful parents. The extent to which problems are the consequence of the breakup of the family and the extent to which they are the consequence of already-extant problems within the family remain open questions. Ultimately, what we want to know is whether particular children in a particular family situation would fare better if the parents were to stay together or to split up.

Making this kind of assessment is difficult for the social scientist. It is difficult to arrive at generalizations on the basis of case studies or small data sets, and large, longitudinal data sets often lack sufficient detail. The National Longitudinal Survey of Youth, 1997 Cohort (NLSY97), attempts to remedy some of the shortcomings of other longitudinal data sets by starting data collection at younger ages and collecting more extensive information about family history. Among its advantages over other data sets, it also collects information about the timing of problem behaviors (first use of drugs, first sexual activity, and so on) so that a relation, if there is one, between changes in family history and these behaviors can be established. Other related variables—such as the quality of the parents' marriage and the grandparents' marital status when the parent was young—are also available.

Unfortunately, there are also some drawbacks to the NLSY97, at least in its first round. At this point, the data are not longitudinal, so it is not yet possible to develop models that are based on changes in key variables. Also, the outcomes that can be measured at this point are limited. Ideally, information on educational attainment, employment status, marriage and child-bearing, and serious criminal behavior would be available. But such information will be available only after future rounds have been completed, and this essay must be satisfied with less-informative, intermediate outcome measures. It does, however, provide a first glimpse at the relation between family structure and the successful transition to adulthood by taking as outcomes grades in the eighth grade and participation in certain potentially troubling behaviors—smoking cigarettes, drinking alcohol, using marijuana, engaging in sexual activity, and engaging in criminal activity.

Theory

There are many reasons to believe that children from nonintact families will have worse outcomes than those from intact families. Parents provide myriad resources to children; divorce leads to a diminution of these resources (McLanahan and Sandefur 1994). Single parents may be less able to satisfy their children's emotional needs or to provide the kind of guidance and supervision that children require; children may feel responsible for their parents' divorce or abandoned afterward. Such feelings and unmet needs may manifest themselves as developmental or behavioral problems.

Divorce also affects a family's economic resources, changing the distribution of income. Even if no loss of income is experienced, after a divorce resources must be stretched to support two households where before they were supporting only one. And divorce almost always decreases the economic resources available to women and children (Duncan and Hoffman 1985): the father typically has more disposable income afterward, the mother and children less. Little wonder that, in 1998, the poverty rate among households headed by single mothers was 29.9 percent, while among two-parent households, it was only 5.3 percent (U.S. Census Bureau 1999).

Divorce may also result in a loss of community resources. Part of this loss is caused by a lack of economic resources. The communities in which single-parent households can afford to live often do not possess the level of resources that characterizes the more affluent communities in which two-parent households can afford to live. Children of single parents may also have less residential stability as mothers move to adapt to their new circumstances or to establish households with new boyfriends or spouses.[1]

Still, even if these losses result in poor child outcomes, it does not necessarily follow that divorce *causes* these outcomes. Strictly speaking, to prove causality we must show that children in broken families would have been better off if their families had remained intact. Given that we do not observe the counterfactual, this is extremely difficult to do.

Consider a child whose parents are deciding whether to separate. Assume that this couple has complete information about possible outcomes and weighs their own well-being and that of their child equally. Assume also that this well-being or utility can be transferred among the members of the family without diminishing the total utility available to the family. Under these conditions, couples would choose the alternative that maximizes total utility and then share it equally among all family members. Therefore, given these conditions, children whose parents decide to separate would do at least as well as they would have done had their parents decided to stay together.

This model demonstrates that adverse outcomes may not be caused by the family disruption per se. Children from nonintact families may do worse than children from intact families, but they do better than they would have done had the family stayed together. In this model, families are subject to unexpected shocks, both good and bad. On the margin, an adverse shock (a parent's unemployment, for instance) will be absorbed equally by all members of a family. Negative shocks are likely to lead to both divorce for the parents and poor outcomes for the children,[2] causing divorce and bad outcomes to be correlated. But divorce does not cause poor youth outcomes; rather, it acts as a marker of those families that have received adverse shocks.

Other factors can also lead to this correlation between divorce and poor outcomes. Unobserved characteristics, for example, can exacerbate the apparent difference in outcomes between children in intact and children in nonintact families. Let us say, for example, that there is a trait that makes one both a poor spouse and a poor parent but that this trait is difficult for social scientists to observe. Given otherwise identical families, people who possess this trait will be both more likely to divorce and more likely to have children with problems than people who do not. Again, divorce per se does not cause children's problems, but it will be strongly correlated with adverse outcomes.

The assumptions of the model are strong ones, and their failure to hold provides clues to the ways in which divorce actually can cause adverse child outcomes. For example, the model assumes perfectly informed parents. Therefore, one potential cause of real-life adverse child outcomes may be a lack of information about the negative effects of rearing a child in a single-parent household. Parents attempt to do what is best for their children, but they are simply misinformed.

A second assumption that may not hold is that parents fully consider the consequences of divorce (or a failure to marry) for their child. This is a classic agency problem. The parents decide whether to stay together, but the child, who is affected by the decision, does not get a voice in the decision. Even worse, each parent can act unilaterally; only one parent needs to miscalculate or ignore the damage to the child for a harmful separation to take place. It is not the couple that makes the decision but each of the partners individually.

A final problematic assumption is that individual well-being or utility can be transferred among family members. In theory, children who benefit from living in an intact family will be willing to share some of the utility gained with a parent who might otherwise prefer a divorce. In practice, however, it may be difficult to transfer the utility that a child will receive only in adulthood to a parent who wants to break up the family now. Also, given the painful circumstances surrounding the breakup of a marriage, it is difficult to expect the rational-utility calculation that this theory requires.

It should also be noted that causality sometimes runs in the opposite direction. Negative youth outcomes early in life may strain the parents' marriage. In some cases, these negative outcomes might lead to divorce not the other way around.

Data

The sample for this analysis is drawn from the first round of the NLSY97. It consists of all youths for whom a completed parent interview was available. Outcome measures include grade-point average in the eighth grade and indicator variables for certain negative behaviors: whether the youth smoked cigarettes, drank alcohol, or smoked marijuana on at least two days in the last month, had been arrested two or more times ever, and had had sex with three or more partners ever.[3] It is not clear how strongly these behaviors are correlated with success or failure in future life. However, one suspects that good grades will lead to increased educational opportunities and that continuation of these negative behaviors into adulthood will result in adverse consequences. Note that I have chosen to eliminate those who have simply experimented with these negative behaviors, limiting the analysis to those who have engaged in them with some regularity.[4] Table 1.1 shows the incidence of these behaviors, as well as grade-point average in the eighth grade, by race, gender, and family income.

Information about family structure was obtained from the parent interview. Respondents were asked to provide a family-structure history, starting with the family structure at the child's birth and going on to identify both the years in which the family structure changed and the new parent figures. To get a complete history, the responding parent's marital history must also be obtained. For example, a boy's biological mother may report simply that he has lived his entire life with her. It is then necessary to determine whether and when the mother was married or divorced to determine whether the youth was living in a single-parent family, with both biological parents, or in a stepfamily.

This process is fraught with difficulty. For one thing, the instrument did not include a way to check whether the current living situation as reported in the parent interview matched that reported during the screening process. For instance, say that in the screening process it had been reported that the youth was living with both biological parents but that in the parent interview the mother claimed to have been married when the child was born but to have been subsequently divorced and to have remarried. It is of course possible that the mother divorced and then remarried the biological father, but it is also possible that the father figure was mistakenly reported as the biological father when he was actually the stepfather. I primarily used the marital and family-structure histories obtained during the parent interviews and not information obtained during the screening process to code relationships. Thus, if the father figure had been reported as the biological father in the screening process and as the stepfather in the parent interview, I coded him as a stepfather.

Information obtained during the screening process did, however, take precedence when the father figure in question was the spouse of a woman whose child was born out of wedlock. No attempt was made in the parent interview to determine, when such women marry, whether the man they are marrying is their child's father. In some cases, women did not marry until eight years after the birth of the child but reported during the screening process that their spouse was the child's biological father. Since in such cases the information obtained during the parent interview was not informative on whether the new spouse was the child's biological father or stepfather, I used the information obtained during the screening process and coded the current spouse as the biological father. However, if the marriage later broke up and the father figure no longer lived with the mother and

TABLE 1.1 Mean Grade Point Average in the Eighth Grade and Percentage of Youths Engaging in Analysis Behaviors, by Race, Gender, and Family Income, NLSY97

		Percentage Engaging in Analysis Behaviors				
	Mean Grade-Point Average in Eighth Grade	Smoked Tobacco Two Times in Last Month	Drank Alcohol Two Times in Last Month	Smoked Marijuana Two Times in Last Month	Arrested Two or More Times Ever	Had Sex with at Least Three Partners Ever
Overall	2.90	16.7	13.8	6.9	2.9	11.7
Race						
White	2.97	19.4	15.0	7.4	2.5	9.1
Black	2.66	8.3	8.1	5.5	4.0	22.5
Hispanic	2.67	11.6	14.6	6.0	4.3	13.9
Other races	3.20	18.0	10.8	5.9	1.3	9.7
Gender						
Male	2.73	16.5	14.3	7.8	4.2	13.0
Female	3.07	17.0	13.3	6.0	1.5	10.4
Family income						
< $25,000	2.63	18.6	13.2	8.3	5.5	19.5
$25,000 to $50,000	2.80	16.4	13.2	6.1	2.7	11.6
> $50,000	3.12	15.9	14.1	7.0	1.8	8.0

Source: Author's compilation.
Note: All observations are weighted by NLSY97 sample weights.

child, there is no screener information to determine if he was the biological father or stepfather. In such cases, I identified him as a stepfather.

This points out one limitation of these histories. Cohabitors are not identified, only spouses. Thus, if a girl's parents have never married, she will be identified as living in a single-parent household even if her biological father has been resident her entire life.

Also problematic was determining the correct sequencing of marriages and changes in parent figures. When marital histories were collected, both the month and the year of changes in marital status were reported. But only the year in which a change in parent figures occurred was reported. Thus, it is not always clear whether a change in parent figures occurred before or after a change in marital status. Since the living situation at the end of a calendar year can be identified exactly, I take living situation at the end of the year to represent living situation throughout the year. It is therefore likely that I undercount changes in living situation for some youths since, if more than one change occurred during the calendar year, I count only the situation that prevailed at the end of the year. Variables indicating the percentage of time a particular living situation prevailed (for example, the percentage of time spent in a single-mother family) are calculated by dividing the number of times the youth was living in a single-mother family at the end of a calendar year by the total number of calendar year-ends she has been alive.

Figures 1.1 and 1.2 show the basic facts of family structure for NLSY97 youths by race-ethnicity.[5] By the end of the first calendar year of their lives, approximately 15 percent of whites, 29 percent of Hispanics, and 59 percent of blacks were not living in intact families, largely because they were born to single mothers. By the end of the twelfth calendar year, these figures had grown to approximately 35 percent of whites, 45 percent of Hispanics, and 73 percent of blacks. The smoothness of the curves in figure 1.1 actually hides some of the divorce activity that is apparent in figure 1.2. The probability of divorce is very low in the first year of a child's life, then increases through the next three or four years. The probability of divorce remains relatively constant between years seven and ten, declining after that for whites and Hispanics. Blacks have a higher probability of divorce regardless of the child's age, while the probability for whites and Hispanics is fairly comparable. The probability that the parents of children in intact families will divorce in a given year is somewhere around 3 percent throughout much of the preteen years.

Much of the literature on the effects of family structure has been forced to rely on very limited information on family structure itself. The standard measure is the type of family in which the youth lived at age fourteen— intact, single mother, or some other (Michael and Tuma 1985; Astone and McLanahan 1991; McLanahan and Bumpass 1988; McLanahan and Sande-

FIGURE 1.1   *Percentage of Youths in Intact Families by Age and Race*

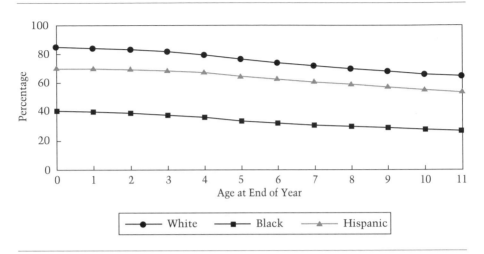

Source: Author's compilation.

FIGURE 1.2   *Probability of Divorce by Age of Child and Race*

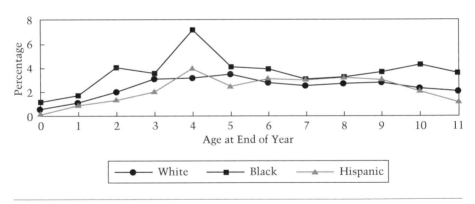

Source: Author's compilation.

fur 1994). Because of the rich family-background history that it makes available, the NLSY97 allows a more complicated delineation of family history. In some ways, it suffers from too much information. The analyst is faced with a great diversity of information—the different types of households, when and how long each type was lived in, the number and sequence of changes— and is therefore forced to develop a framework with which to make sense of the data.[6]

After a great deal of experimentation, I divided youths into eight groups on the basis of the family structure in which they lived from birth to the date of the parent interview. The first, and largest, group is children who live in an *intact family*—that is, those whose parents were married when they were born and who were still married at the time of the parent interview (regardless of whether the children have lived elsewhere—with grandparents or in an institution—on occasion). The second group is children who live with a *divorced mother*—that is, children whose parents were married when they were born but who afterward divorced, the children now living with the mother, who never remarried. The third group is children who live with a *divorced-remarried mother*—that is, children whose parents were married when they were born but who afterward divorced, the children living with the mother, who remarried. (Children remain classified in this group even if their remarried mother divorces again. The distinguishing characteristic of this group is that the children in it have spent some time as part of a stepfamily.) The fourth group is children who live with a *single mother*—that is, children whose mothers were unmarried when they were born and who have not subsequently married. The fifth group is children who live with a *single-married mother*—that is, children whose mothers were unmarried when they were born but who eventually married. The sixth group is children who live in *other biological parent* households—that is, children who have lived with at least one of their biological parents for at least two-thirds of their lives (including those who have lived with their biological father, with or without a stepmother, after a divorce). The seventh, and smallest, group is children who have been *adopted*—that is, those living with adoptive parents other than stepparents. The last group is all *other* children, those who do not fit into any of the other categories—for example, those who have lived more than a third of their lives with neither biological parent but instead with grandparents, other relatives, or foster parents.

Table 1.2 shows the breakdown of youths by family type, both overall and by race. Almost 58 percent of whites but only around 22 percent of blacks have lived in intact families throughout their lives. In fact, the black youths in our sample are more likely to have lived their whole lives with a single mother than in an intact family. It is interesting to note that only 25 percent of divorced black mothers have remarried, whereas 45 percent of divorced white mothers have done so. Blacks are also seven times more likely than whites to live in other family situations (8.7 versus 1.2 percent).

Table 1.3 shows other family-structure variables by family type. As expected, youths whose mothers have divorced and remarried experienced the most changes in parent figures—2.33. (This figure includes the change from living in an intact family to living with a divorced mother and the change from living with a divorced mother to living with a remarried mother.) This

TABLE 1.2   *Percentage of NLSY97 Youths by Family Type*

Family Type	Total	White	Black	Hispanic	Other
Intact family	51.4	57.7	21.8	50.7	55.8
Divorced mother	12.3	12.1	13.5	11.7	12.6
Divorced-remarried mother	8.4	9.8	4.6	5.8	6.0
Single mother	9.0	4.2	28.3	13.5	5.4
Single-married mother	7.6	6.1	15.0	8.5	5.0
Other biological parent	8.0	8.4	7.5	6.2	7.2
Adopted	0.7	0.6	0.6	0.3	3.5
Other	2.7	1.2	8.7	3.3	4.5
Observations	7,808	3,998	2,018	1,564	226

Source: Author's compilation.
Note: All observations are weighted by NLSY97 sample weights.

group also experienced the most residence changes, having lived at an average of 5.7 residences. (Since the average age of these children is slightly under fifteen years, this figure represents a move roughly every three years.) This is double the average number of residences for children living in an intact family.

The means, overall and by family-structure type, of each of the dependent variables as well as of other control variables are shown in table 1.4. It is immediately apparent how much better children in intact families do on every outcome measure than do children in every other group except those who have been adopted. Children living in intact families have eighth-grade grade-point averages 10 to 20 percent higher than those of children in the other groups, they are less likely to smoke, drink, or use marijuana regularly, and they are 50 to 80 percent less likely to have been arrested twice or to have had sex with three or more partners. They have higher household incomes—children living in intact families have household incomes more than twice that of those living with a divorced mother and more than three times that of those living with single mothers. And they also have more highly educated mothers—the mothers of children living in intact families have nearly two more years of education than do single mothers.

In this analysis, age is roughly equivalent across the eight family types. Since the incidence of some of these behaviors increases quite rapidly with age, I use age in months divided by twelve as the measure of age. Figure 1.3 shows the percentage of youths at a given age who have engaged in the analyzed behaviors. All the behaviors are five to ten times more prevalent among the oldest youths than among the youngest. For example, alcohol use, defined as at least two days of drinking in the last month, increases from 3 percent at age twelve to 28 percent at age seventeen.

TABLE 1.3   *Means of Family-Structure Variables by Family Type*

Type of Family	Overall	Intact Family	Divorced Mother	Divorced or Remarried Mother	Single Mother	Single or Married Mother	Other Biological Parent	Adoptive	Other
Percentage of time with									
Both parents	0.629 (0.005)	0.998 (0.000)	0.533 (0.009)	0.286 (0.008)	0.000	0.000	0.310 (0.013)	0.028 (0.011)	0.062 (0.008)
Mother only	0.228 (0.004)	0.000	0.464 (0.009)	0.319 (0.009)	0.982 (0.002)	0.524 (0.010)	0.166 (0.011)	0.042 (0.013)	0.108 (0.010)
Father only	0.22 (0.001)	0.000	0.000	0.000	0.000	0.000	0.269 (0.012)	0.000	0.011 (0.003)
Mother and stepfather	0.072 (0.002)	0.000	0.000	0.390 (0.008)	0.000	0.467 (0.010)	0.039 (0.005)	0.000	0.012 (0.003)
Father and stepmother	0.016 (0.001)	0.000	0.000	0.000	0.000	0.000	0.197 (0.013)	0.000	0.011 (0.003)
Grandparents	0.014 (0.001)	0.001 (0.000)	0.001 (0.000)	0.002 (0.001)	0.007 (0.001)	0.005 (0.001)	0.002 (0.001)	0.003 (0.003)	0.458 (0.026)
Adopted	0.006 (0.001)	0.000	0.000	0.000	0.000	0.000	0.000	0.868 (0.020)	0.001 (0.001)
Other situations	0.013 (0.001)	0.001 (0.000)	0.002 (0.000)	0.002 (0.001)	0.010 (0.001)	0.004 (0.001)	0.016 (0.002)	0.058 (0.016)	0.338 (0.024)
Number of family structure changes	0.660 (0.012)	0.018 (0.003)	1.077 (0.011)	2.328 (0.037)	0.186 (0.016)	1.611 (0.037)	1.894 (0.055)	0.827 (0.087)	1.043 (0.070)
Total residences	3.82 (0.04)	2.87 (0.04)	4.54 (0.12)	5.72 (0.17)	4.17 (0.11)	5.21 (0.18)	5.11 (0.18)	3.56 (0.40)	3.93 (0.27)

Source: Author's compilation.
Note: All observations are weighted by NLSY97 sample weights. Number in parentheses is the standard error of the mean.

TABLE 1.4　　*Variable Means by Family Type*

Type of Family	Overall	Intact Family	Divorced Mother	Divorced or Remarried Mother	Single Mother	Single or Married Mother	Other Biological Parent	Adoptive	Other
Grade-point average in eighth grade	2.898 (0.014)	3.067 (0.018)	2.764 (0.040)	2.793 (0.047)	2.547 (0.037)	2.691 (0.048)	2.712 (0.053)	3.113 (0.203)	2.711 (0.074)
Smoked tobacco two times in last month	0.167 (0.004)	0.133 (0.006)	0.202 (0.013)	0.239 (0.018)	0.171 (0.012)	0.162 (0.014)	0.275 (0.019)	0.108 (0.046)	0.149 (0.021)
Drank alcohol two times in last month	0.138 (0.004)	0.126 (0.005)	0.165 (0.012)	0.149 (0.015)	0.123 (0.010)	0.134 (0.013)	0.193 (0.016)	0.056 (0.034)	0.121 (0.019)
Smoked marijuana two times in last month	0.069 (0.003)	0.049 (0.004)	0.101 (0.010)	0.088 (0.012)	0.080 (0.009)	0.082 (0.010)	0.108 (0.013)	0.056 (0.034)	0.074 (0.016)
Had sex with at least three partners ever	0.117 (0.005)	0.068 (0.005)	0.131 (0.014)	0.134 (0.019)	0.222 (0.017)	0.191 (0.020)	0.175 (0.020)	0.066 (0.042)	0.214 (0.031)
Arrested two or more times ever	0.029 (0.002)	0.014 (0.002)	0.039 (0.006)	0.028 (0.007)	0.057 (0.007)	0.034 (0.007)	0.052 (0.009)	0.049 (0.032)	0.081 (0.016)
Age	14.83 (0.02)	14.82 (0.02)	14.78 (0.05)	14.84 (0.06)	14.82 (0.05)	14.83 (0.06)	14.99 (0.06)	15.27 (0.19)	14.89 (0.09)
Household income	52,342 (538)	66,596 (841)	29,975 (788)	52,769 (1,759)	20,917 (705)	36,720 (1,242)	50,183 (1,954)	55,105 (7,156)	31,610 (2,021)
Biological mother's highest grade completed	12.95 (0.03)	13.32 (0.05)	13.09 (0.09)	13.07 (0.10)	11.67 (0.08)	12.16 (0.09)	12.68 (0.11)	7.97 (2.37)	11.58 (0.19)
Black	0.149 (0.004)	0.063 (0.004)	0.164 (0.012)	0.081 (0.011)	0.470 (0.016)	0.293 (0.017)	0.140 (0.014)	0.142 (0.051)	0.479 (0.030)
Hispanic	0.123 (0.004)	0.121 (0.005)	0.118 (0.010)	0.085 (0.012)	0.185 (0.012)	0.137 (0.013)	0.096 (0.012)	0.059 (0.035)	0.152 (0.021)
Other race	0.039 (0.002)	0.043 (0.003)	0.040 (0.006)	0.028 (0.007)	0.024 (0.005)	0.026 (0.006)	0.035 (0.008)	0.207 (0.060)	0.066 (0.015)
Score on PIAT math test	51.77 (0.47)	58.98 (0.67)	50.32 (1.23)	50.71 (1.72)	34.11 (1.18)	43.30 (1.52)	47.38 (1.65)	39.82 (6.76)	29.84 (2.16)

Source: Author's compilation.
Note: All observations are weighted by NLSY97 sample weights. Number in parentheses in the standard error of the mean.

FIGURE 1.3   *Percentage of Youths Engaging in Target Activities by Age*

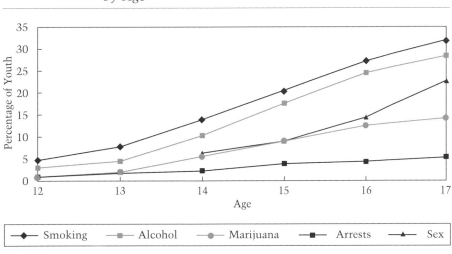

Source: Author's compilation.

Analysis Results

The basic analysis results are derived from an OLS regression of grade-point average in the eighth grade and five probit analyses conducted on the five target troubling behaviors (having smoked cigarettes, drunk alcohol, or smoked marijuana on at least two days in the last month, having been arrested at least two times ever, and having had sex with at least three partners ever). The independent variables are seven variables for family type (intact family is the omitted category); a cubic polynomial in age; last year's log household income; highest grade completed by the biological mother; and indicator variables for urban residence, being female, being black, Hispanic, or some other race. There are also indicator variables for not knowing income and not knowing highest grade completed by the biological mother.

Table 1.5 shows the results of this analysis. The first row shows the estimated grade-point average and probability of engaging in the target behaviors for a fourteen-year-old white, urban male who lives in an intact family with an income of $45,000 and whose mother has twelve years of education. The first column contains the OLS regression coefficients of the regression of eighth-grade grade-point average (as estimated by the youth) on family-structure variables and other control variables and their standard errors. The next five columns give the results of probit analyses on the prob-

TABLE 1.5   Marginal Effects of Family Structure on Grades and Probability of Engaging in Problem Behaviors

Model	Grade Point in Eighth Grade	Smoked Two Times a Month	Alcohol Two Times a Month	Marijuana Two Times a Month	Sex with Three Partners	Arrested Two or More Times Ever
Base value or probability	2.665	0.094	0.077	0.031	0.020	0.021
Family type						
Divorced mother	-0.253*	0.076*	0.040*	0.050*	0.028*	0.041*
	(0.041)	(0.014)	(0.012)	(0.011)	(0.012)	(0.012)
Divorced-remarried mother	-0.275*	0.080*	0.019	0.027*	0.023*	0.024*
	(0.049)	(0.017)	(0.013)	(0.010)	(0.012)	(0.012)
Single mother	-0.316*	0.075*	0.016	0.033*	0.039*	0.058*
	(0.045)	(0.017)	(0.012)	(0.010)	(0.016)	(0.014)
Single-remarried mother	-0.222*	0.048*	0.023	0.032*	0.039*	0.030*
	(0.049)	(0.016)	(0.013)	(0.011)	(0.017)	(0.012)
Other biological parent	-0.283*	0.110*	0.042*	0.044*	0.042*	0.038*
	(0.051)	(0.019)	(0.015)	(0.012)	(0.017)	(0.013)
Adoptive	0.064	-0.032	-0.047	0.003	-0.001	0.007
	(0.164)	(0.033)	(0.021)	(0.023)	(0.015)	(0.023)
Other	-0.201*	0.064*	0.020	0.029*	0.037*	0.055*
	(0.071)	(0.026)	(0.019)	(0.015)	(0.018)	(0.020)

	(1)	(2)	(3)	(4)	(5)	(6)
Urban	0.004	−0.016*	0.001	−0.001	0.001	0.008*
	(0.026)	(0.007)	(0.006)	(0.003)	(0.003)	(0.003)
Female	0.369*	−0.009	−0.012*	−0.013*	−0.012*	−0.016*
	(0.025)	(0.006)	(0.005)	(0.003)	(0.005)	(0.004)
Black	−0.161*	−0.073*	−0.048*	−0.015*	0.034*	−0.004
	(0.034)	(0.007)	(0.006)	(0.004)	(0.013)	(0.004)
Hispanic	−0.052	−0.057*	−0.010	−0.008	0.004	−0.002
	(0.037)	(0.007)	(0.008)	(0.004)	(0.004)	(0.004)
Other race	0.225*	−0.001	−0.021	−0.005	0.003	−0.012
	(0.074)	(0.017)	(0.014)	(0.009)	(0.009)	(0.007)
Log income	0.032*	−0.005*	−0.001	−0.001	−0.002*	−0.001
	(0.010)	(0.002)	(0.002)	(0.001)	(0.001)	(0.001)
Biological mother's highest grade completed	0.053*	−0.003*	0.001	0.000	−0.001*	−0.002*
	(0.005)	(0.001)	(0.001)	(0.001)	(0.001)	(0.001)
Observations	3,821	7,753	7,743	7,744	4,560	7,755

Source: Author's compilation.
Note: All models also include a cubic polynomial in age and indicators for the absence of income and mother's education. Base case is fourteen-year-old, white, urban male in an intact family with income of $45,000 and mother's education of twelve years. Standard errors are given in parenthesis.
* The underlying variable has $p < .05$.

ability of having engaged in each of the five target behaviors. Rather than report probit coefficients, which are difficult to interpret, I present the marginal effect of changes in the independent variables on the probability that a person with the baseline characteristics will have engaged in the specified behaviors.[7] Standard errors for the marginal effects are given in parentheses. It is easy to determine the magnitude of the estimated effects—simply compare the marginal effects to the baseline values. For example, the results indicate that the 9.4 percent base probability that the youth smokes cigarettes is increased 80 percent, or 7.6 percentage points, if the youth lives with a divorced mother.

With one exception, all the family-structure variables except having been adopted significantly predict a lower grade-point average and a greater probability of problem behaviors. The exception is the model for drinking alcohol, where only the variables for living with a divorced mother and living in some other biological parent household are significant. What is also striking is how similar the effects are across types of nonintact families (other than adoptive families). For example, all six family-structure variables are associated with a reduction in grade-point average from 0.20 to 0.32 points (a 7 to 12 percent reduction from the base case). While all the effects are statistically significant, none is statistically different from any of the others.

The relative size of these coefficients can be quite large, suggesting that, after other factors have been controlled for, being from a nonintact family raises the probability of smoking by 50 to 120 percent, of using marijuana by 80 to 160 percent, and of having been arrested by 100 to 250 percent. These effects are especially striking when compared to those of other variables. Income is not statistically significant except in the grade-point average, smoking, and sex models. The effect of changing household income from $20,000 to $100,000 is only a 2 percent increase in grade-point average, an 8 percent decline in the probability of smoking, and a 17 percent decline in the probability of having had sex with at least three partners. In other words, in these models, the effects of family structure are five to ten times greater than those of changing income by a factor of five.

One might object that current income is not the right variable for present purposes. Perhaps the problem is more fluctuations in income than income levels. In that case, what we may really want to know is how changes in family structure have changed income level. Of course, only one observation of income is available. One potential solution is to consider a measure of permanent income and let current income serve as a measure of transitory income. I have included mother's education as a measure of permanent income. It, too, has only modest effects on these variables compared to the effects of the family-structure variables. It is statistically significant in all but the alcohol and the marijuana models. However, the difference between having a mother with a tenth-grade education and having one who has completed college is a 12 percent decrease in grade-point average, a 20 percent increase in the probability of smoking, a 30 percent increase in the probability of having sex with three or more partners, and a 60 percent increase in the probability of being arrested.

The gender gap in these behaviors is consistent across models. Girls are much less likely to engage in all these behaviors except for smoking. The gender differential is about half the family-structure effect for all the other target behaviors, and it is slightly larger than the family-structure effects in the grade-point-average model. The race and ethnicity differences are also fairly consistent. After controlling for family structure, blacks are less likely to engage in all these behaviors except having sex with three or more partners, although the effect on arrests is insignificant. The effect of being Hispanic is also a consistently lower probability of engaging in all the problem behaviors except sex with three or more partners, although the coefficients are statistically significant only in the smoking model.

These initial models demonstrate how strong the correlation between family structure and the target behaviors is. The obvious question, of course, is why this correlation exists. One hypothesis is that changes in family structure cause a great deal of instability in the lives of children. I therefore examine two variables that measure instability in children's lives: number of family-structure changes and number of residence changes. Because of a concern with outliers, I truncate this variable at fifteen and create an indicator variable for more than fifteen residences. In general, these variables are significant and have the hypothesized effect—the more instability one has experienced, the lower one's grades, and the more likely one is to engage in the target behaviors (see table 1.6). These variables also tend to attenuate the family-structure effects. In fact, many of them are no longer statistically significant. Notably, only two of the stepfamily variables (living with a divorced or remarried mother and living with a single or married mother) are significant after controlling for the number of family-structure and residence changes. Admittedly, this may be a semantic distinction since one cannot live in these family structures without first going through at least one family-structure change. But it does suggest that the problem may be in the difficulty involved in making transitions, not in the state of living in a stepfamily. In general, the marginal effects of the other family-structure variables decrease by 30 percent or more when changes in residence and family structure are accounted for.

A second explanation for the adverse effect of family disruption is conflict within the household, not family breakdown. While we have no measure of conflict in households that had already dissolved by the first round of interviewing, we know something about the relationship between spouses

TABLE 1.6   Marginal Effects of Family Structure on Grades and Probability of Engaging in Problem Behaviors: Models with Residential Mobility and Family-Structure Changes

Model	Grade Point in Eighth Grade	Smoked Two Times a Month	Alcohol Two Times a Month	Marijuana Two Times a Month	Sex with Three Partners	Arrested Two or More Times Ever
Base value or probability	2.689	0.083	0.073	0.027	0.015	0.016
Family type						
Divorced mother	-0.171*	0.041*	0.026*	0.037*	0.013*	0.019*
	(0.046)	(0.013)	(0.012)	(0.010)	(0.008)	(0.008)
Divorced-remarried mother	-0.097	0.015	-0.005	0.012	0.004	0.000
	(0.069)	(0.017)	(0.014)	(0.010)	(0.006)	(0.007)
Single mother	-0.292*	0.059*	0.011	0.026*	0.026*	0.037*
	(0.045)	(0.015)	(0.011)	(0.009)	(0.012)	(0.011)
Single-remarried mother	-0.096	0.008	0.006	0.018*	0.017*	0.004
	(0.059)	(0.014)	(0.013)	(0.010)	(0.010)	(0.007)
Other biological parent	-0.141*	0.050*	0.020	0.029*	0.016*	0.009
	(0.064)	(0.019)	(0.016)	(0.012)	(0.010)	(0.008)
Adoptive	0.137	-0.037	-0.048	0.000	-0.004	-0.001
	(0.164)	(0.026)	(0.019)	(0.020)	(0.010)	(0.014)
Other	-0.118	0.033	0.012	0.019	0.020*	0.029*
	(0.074)	(0.022)	(0.019)	(0.013)	(0.012)	(0.014)
Total residences	-0.012*	0.004*	0.001	0.001*	0.001*	0.002*
	(0.005)	(0.001)	(0.001)	(0.001)	(0.001)	(0.000)
Number of family-structure changes	-0.062*	0.014*	0.008	0.002	0.002	0.004*
	(0.021)	(0.005)	(0.004)	(0.002)	(0.002)	(0.002)
Observations	3,788	7,681	7,671	7,672	4,521	7,682

Source: Author's compilation.

Note: All models also include a cubic polynomial in age and indicators for the absence of income and mother's education as well as the control variables in table 1.5 (urban, female, black, Hispanic, other race, log income, and highest grade completed by biological mother). Base case is fourteen-year-old, white, urban male in an intact family with income of $45,000, mother's education of twelve years, only one total residence, and no family-structure changes.

* The underlying variable has $p < .05$.

in intact families. For those born in 1982 or later, the self-administered portion of the parent interview contained a section asking how often the spouse compromised, insulted, screamed at, expressed affection for, encouraged, or blamed the respondent.[8] I added the score on each of these questions to create a scale with higher scores representing greater harmony within the relationship. I then standardized this scale to a mean of zero and a standard deviation of one. Those living in nonintact families were assigned a value of zero. I included only those born in 1982 or later in this analysis (table 1.7). Thus, the sample size for the grade-point and sex models was much lower. Also, because these youths were younger, the incidence of problem behaviors was much lower. In all cases, this variable had the expected sign—more family conflict within intact families led to lower grades and a higher incidence of problem behaviors. While in the smoking and sex models the coefficients were not statistically significant, the size of the effect was fairly large: a 1-standard-deviation reduction in the score on the parents' relationship scale increased the probability of problem behavior on the order of 15 to 45 percent.[9]

To this point, we have seen the strong correlation between family structure and the analyzed outcomes. We have also seen the relation of instability and conflict within the family to these outcomes. Still, we have not really answered the causality question: How different would the outcomes have been had the parents stayed together? To do this, we must control for the endogeneity of family dissolution.

Many unobserved variables that affect the likelihood that children will engage in problem behaviors may also affect the probability that they will live in nonintact families. Those unobserved variables, and not family structure itself, might cause the problem behaviors. To control for this possibility, I attempted to use an instrumental-variables approach. Doing so required finding variables that affect family structure but do not cause problem behaviors directly. This is a tall order. It is difficult to find any variables that we can be certain are exogenous to the child's behavior equation but affect the probability of divorce. However, I chose whether the mother was born in the United States, whether the mother's parents divorced when she was young, whether the mother is Catholic, whether the mother is non-Protestant, and the divorce rate and illegitimacy ratio in the current state of residence. Rather than instrumenting for each family type, I divided types into *disrupted* and *nondisrupted*. Intact families and adoptive families where adoption occurred before age three were considered nondisrupted families. All others were considered disrupted.

If instrumental variables worked well, I hoped to determine what part of the disruption effect was caused by the actual disruption and what part was caused by unobservables that were related to both marital disruption and the child's problem behavior. I felt that the effect of disruption after in-

TABLE 1.7   *Marginal Effect of Spouse Relationship Variable*

Model	Grade Point in Eighth Grade	Smoked Two Times a Month	Alcohol Two Times a Month	Marijuana Two Times a Month	Sex with Three Partners	Arrested Two or More Times Ever
Base value or probability	2.569	.092	.078	.029	.035	.013
Parents' relationship	.089*	-.012	-.014*	-.009*	-.009	-.006
	(.040)	(.007)	(.006)	(.004)	(.008)	(.003)
Percentage effect of 1-S.D. change in parents' relationship	3.5	-12.8	-18.0	-30.0	-24.1	-44.4
Observations	898	4,662	4,660	4,663	1,524	4,534

Source: Author's compilation.
Note: All models also include a cubic polynomial in age and indicators for the absence of income and mother's education as well as the control variables in table 1.5 (urban, female, black, Hispanic, other race, log income, and highest grade completed by biological mother). Base case is fourteen-year-old, white, urban male in an intact family with income of $45,000, mother's education of twelve years, and average parents' relationship.
* The underlying variable has $p < .05$.

strumenting would be less than the effect without instrumenting. However, the actual results turned out to be exactly counter to these expectations. In all cases, the coefficient on marital disruption doubled after instrumenting. At present, I cannot explain this result other than to note that the instruments were probably not exogenous to the child's behavior equations. Future research will examine this issue more closely.

Conclusions

There can be little doubt that children living in nonintact families earn lower grades in school and exhibit a greater propensity to engage in problem behaviors in their teen years. Even after controlling for income and mother's education, NLSY97 youths living in nonintact families are up to 120 percent more likely to be using marijuana regularly and 250 percent more likely to have been arrested two or more times. Family-structure effects prove to be larger and more consistent than the effects of income or mother's education. Interestingly, the effects vary much more between intact and nonintact families than among the various types of nonintact families.

Certainly, one major reason for the poorer outcomes is the increased instability that results from family disruption. This essay shows that greater numbers of residence and family-structure changes are correlated with poorer grades and more behavior problems. In fact, after controlling for these changes, the effect of certain family-structure variables often becomes insignificant.

Still, two major questions remain about these results. First, while family structure is correlated with problems in the teen years, its effect on serious adult problems remains unclear. It could be that family problems make these children more rebellious at these ages but that the effects will fade and the long-term damage will be minimal. As time passes, the longitudinal nature of the NLSY97 will allow us to see how problems within the family of origin affect adjustment to the adult world.

Second, the issue of causality remains murky. The ultimate question is whether the youth outcomes would have been different had the biological parents stayed together. It is clear that large differences between intact and nonintact families remain even after controlling for observables, and it is difficult to believe that none of these are a direct result of the family disruption. Still, divorce may be a marker for family problems that are not easily observed. This essay shows that, among children living in intact families, those whose parents' relationship is more contentious fare worse than those whose parents' relationship is less contentious. At what point is it better to dissolve the family? On average, people who divorce may be different from those who stay together in other unobservable ways, and these unobservable differences may be the cause of poor child outcomes. An attempt to disentangle this causality puzzle through instrumental-variables techniques did not work. It may simply prove too difficult to find any truly exogenous variation in family-structure decisions.

In closing, I would suggest that, since we know nothing about family-structure and residence changes for the over one thousand youths for whom no parent interview was conducted, the NLSY97 consider adding a retrospective module to collect this information.[10] Such a module would also clear up the confusion that exists where the relation between family-structure and residence changes (that is, which occurred first) is not clear. Since such changes are extremely significant parts of these youths' lives, chances are good that they will be easily and accurately recalled. The goal of the NLSY97 being to understand the forces that shape youths as they make the transition to adulthood, there can be little doubt that a clear understanding of their living situation is essential if that goal is to be achieved.

Notes

1. The role that stepparents play in the lives of stepchildren is ambiguous. On the one hand, they tend to bring additional economic resources to the family, and they may also contribute additional guidance and supervision. On the other hand, they appear to contribute less to stepchildren than to their own children (Case, Lin, and McLanahan 1999), and their presence also leads to additional disruption in the lives of children who have probably experienced too much disruption already.

2. In Becker's (1974) theory, since a positive shock to either spouse would make it possible for that individual to find a better match, positive and negative shocks are equally likely to lead to divorce. I am thinking, however, of a model in which the value of marriage to a particular person is not equal across all potential spouses (see Pierret 1997). In such a model, shocks to the match-specific utility component will affect only spouses' value to each other. Positive shocks will not lead to divorce since they do not make either spouse more desirable to other potential spouses.

3. Given that these behaviors are all seen as socially undesirable for children of this age, one should certainly be concerned about the veracity of responses to these questions. However, all these responses are gathered by means of a self-administered questionnaire, so the incentive to lie is minimized.

   Information about grade-point average in the eighth grade was obtained only from those who had completed the eighth grade. Information about number of sex partners was obtained only from those who had been born in 1982 or earlier. Sample sizes for the analyses of these outcomes are somewhat smaller than they are for other analyses.

4. Preliminary analysis with the less-restrictive indicators for ever engaging in these activities showed comparable results.

5. In these figures, as throughout this essay, *white* means non-Hispanic whites, and *black* means non-Hispanic blacks. Hispanics can be of any race. Those of Asian or Native American descent are separated into the category *other races*. Because of small sample sizes, this group is not reported separately in these figures. Also, these figures and all summary figures and tables are based on weighted data. The statistical analysis, however, is not weighted.

6. For a discussion of the problem of coding the information obtained through family histories in such a way that usable variables can be developed, see Wu and Martinson (1993).

7. For indicator variables, the reported effect is the difference between the probability when that variable is zero and the probability when it is one. These are calculated by the dprobit procedure in Stata.

8. The answers to these six questions ranged from never (0) to always (4).

9. Using the round 2 beta release, I examined those families that were intact at round 1 but had divorced before round 2. Their average standardized score on this scale was 0.904 below that of those families that remained intact at round 2.

10. The NLS program has experience in this area, having performed such a retrospective collection of family histories in the NLSY79. For an example of the use of these data, see Wu (1996).

References

Astone, Nan M., and Sara S. McLanahan. 1991. "Family Structure and High School Completion: The Role of Parental Practices." *American Sociological Review* 56(3): 309–20.

Becker, Gary S. 1974. "A Theory of Marriage." In *Economics of the Family: Marriage, Children, and Human Capital,* edited by Theodore W. Schultz. Chicago: University of Chicago Press.

Case, Anne, I-Fen Lin, and Sara McLanahan. 1999. "Household Resource Allocation in Stepfamilies: Darwin Reflects on the Plight of Cinderella." *American Economic Review* 89(2): 234–38.

Duncan, Greg J., and Saul D. Hoffman. 1985. "A Reconsideration of the Economic Consequences of Marital Disruption." *Demography* 22(4): 485–98.

McLanahan, Sara S., and Larry L. Bumpass. 1988. "Intergenerational Consequences of Family Disruption." *American Journal of Sociology* 94(1): 130–52.

McLanahan, Sara S., and Gary Sandefur. 1994. *Growing Up with a Single Parent: What Hurts, What Helps.* Cambridge, Mass.: Harvard University Press.

Michael, Robert T., and Nancy B. Tuma. 1985. "Entry into Marriage and Parenthood by Young Men and Women: The Influence of Family Background." *Demography* 22(4): 525–44.

Pierret, Charles R. 1997. "Why Has the Marriage Rate Declined in the United States? An Economic Analysis of the Marriage Market." Unpublished paper. Bureau of Labor Statistics.

U.S. Census Bureau. 1999. "Poverty in the United States, 1998." P60-207. Washington: U.S. Government Printing Office.

Whitehead, Barbara D. 1993. "Dan Quayle Was Right." *Atlantic Monthly* 93(4): 37–56.

Wu, Lawrence L. 1996. "Effects of Family Instability, Income, and Income Instability on the Risk of a Premarital Birth." *American Sociological Review* 61(3): 386–406.

Wu, Lawrence L., and Brian C. Martinson. 1993. "Family Structure and the Risk of a Premarital Birth." *American Sociological Review* 58(2): 210–32.

2

Patterns of Nonresident-Father Involvement

Laura M. Argys and H. Elizabeth Peters

HIGH rates of out-of-wedlock childbearing and marital disruption have increased the probability that children born in the United States will live apart from their biological father for some portion of their childhood. Although the consequences of living in a single-parent family are well documented (McLanahan and Sandefur 1994; Zill and Schoenborn 1990; Pierret, chapter 1 in this volume), there is considerable debate about the mechanisms that lead to negative outcomes for children and the factors that might mitigate these adverse outcomes.

Policy makers are beginning to emphasize the important role that fathers play in their children's lives. Many assert that what adversely affects children in single-parent households is the lack of attachment of the absent parent to the child, often evidenced by the minimal contact maintained and the inadequate financial and emotional support provided. One of the major goals of the 1996 Personal Responsibility and Work Opportunity Reconciliation Act (PRWORA) was to build on the provisions of the Family Support Act of 1988 and make nonresident fathers take greater responsibility for the support of their children. To achieve this goal, PRWORA included comprehensive child-support-enforcement provisions.

In response to the high proportion of out-of-wedlock births, recent policies have targeted the children of unmarried mothers. In 1980, 18 percent of all births were to unmarried mothers; by the mid-1990s, almost one-third of births were to unmarried mothers (National Center for Health Statistics 1999). Of primary concern is the fact that there is often no legal paternity determination (and thus no child-support order) and that many of these children will therefore wind up on the welfare rolls. The 1993 Omnibus Budget Reconciliation Act (OBRA) and PRWORA have resulted in changes in paternity-establishment policies at the state level, both by providing financial incentives for states to increase their paternity-establishment rates and by mandating certain practices, such as voluntary in-hospital paternity-acknowledgment programs.

Legal paternity gives the father rights (for example, visitation) as well as responsibilities (for example, child support). Increases in paternity establishment not only should reduce state welfare expenditures on children with an absent parent but may also benefit children by encouraging nonresident fathers to become more involved with their children. It has been suggested that greater levels of father-child involvement may benefit fathers as well (Lerman and Sorensen 2000).

To examine nonresident-father involvement, we analyze a cohort of adolescent children born between 1980 and 1984 from the National Longitudinal Survey of Youth, 1997 Cohort (NLSY97). We extract a sample of adolescents between the ages of twelve and sixteen who did not live full-time with their fathers in 1997. We use these data to address two issues. First, we compare father-involvement measures for youths whose fathers are absent because they either divorced, separated, or never married the child's mother, and we examine the determinants of these father-child-involvement measures. The specific measures of involvement on which we focus in the essay include amount of contact, level of child support, and quality of father-child and mother-father interaction. Second, we use the data to classify the children in nonmarital families into groups based on type of paternity establishment (for example, voluntary acknowledgment, involuntary acknowledgment, and no acknowledgment) and show how our different measures of father involvement vary by type of paternity establishment.

Research on Nonresident-Father Involvement

The bulk of the research on interactions between nonresident fathers and their children has focused on the involvement of these fathers in the aftermath of divorce. Studies have documented that a substantial minority of children whose parents divorce do not see their nonresident fathers regularly, although some research has suggested that the amount of contact may have increased in recent years (Furstenberg and Harris 1992; Seltzer and Bianchi 1988). Nearly half of all children with a father living elsewhere saw him less than once a month or not at all in the past year (Seltzer and Bianchi 1988).

More recent research has documented the patterns of father-child contact for children born outside marriage (Furstenberg and Harris 1993; Mott 1990). It has been found that frequent contact is more common than it had previously been thought to be. Estimates from the National Longitudinal

Survey of Youth, 1979 Cohort (NLSY79), child data show that the proportion of noncustodial fathers who see their children at least weekly ranges from 40 to 50 percent (Lerman 1993; Mott 1990; and Veum 1993). Note, however, that younger children are overrepresented in the NLSY child data. Estimates from the National Survey of Families and Households (NSFH) are that 30 percent of noncustodial fathers see their children at least weekly (Seltzer 1991).

Although substantial proportions of children born outside marriage have little contact with their nonresident fathers, the effect of such minimal interaction is not clear. Most studies have found that visitation or custody is unrelated to child well-being measured in a variety of ways. Increased visitation is found to have no significant effect on children's achievement scores (King 1994), parent-child affection (Donnelly and Finkelhor 1992), educational and employment attainment (Furstenberg and Harris 1993), or behavioral problems (King 1994). A few studies, however, have found beneficial effects on some aspects of child well-being (Pearson and Thoennes 1990). In particular, it has been suggested that the benefits of father-child contact depend, not just on the amount of contact, but rather on the quality of father-child interaction and the degree to which mother-father conflict is present (Buchanan, Maccoby, and Dornbusch 1991; Furstenberg and Harris 1993; McLanahan et al. 1994).

The negative effects of growing up without a father present may also be attributed to the resulting reduction in financial support. The poverty rate for single-parent female-headed households was 31.6 percent in 1997, compared to 5.7 percent for all other families (Council of Economic Advisors 1999, table B-33). Even though nonresident fathers may contribute to the child's financial well-being by paying child support, national statistics illustrate that child support is not provided to all eligible children. In 1995, nearly 75 percent of divorced mothers but only 52 percent of separated mothers and 44 percent of never-married mothers had been awarded child support (Current Population Report 1999). In addition, among those with awards, only half receive the full amount that they are owed each year, and nearly one-quarter receive no payments at all.

Family income is an important determinant of child well-being (Haveman and Wolfe 1995; Duncan and Brooks-Gunn 1997), but the contribution of child support to child well-being extends beyond the simple addition of money to the child's household. Recent studies have demonstrated that child support may have a positive effect on children's cognitive development over and above the effect of the additional income (Knox 1996; Argys et al. 1998). Child-support income has also been found to have beneficial effects on educational attainment (Graham, Beller, and Hernandez 1994; McLanahan et al. 1994; Knox and Bane 1994). Argys and Peters (1998) suggest that one reason that child support has greater benefits than income from other sources is that parents with voluntary awards can reach cooperative agreements regarding child support that tie larger payments to more money being spent to benefit the child. In this essay, we extend the model of cooperative child-support agreements to the methods of paternity establishment among unmarried parents.

Disentangling the effects of various types of father involvement on child well-being is complicated by the bidirectional relations between the variables. For example, the positive correlation between contact and the payment of child support can be explained in a variety of ways. It may be that both simply reflect the degree of commitment of the father to the child and that this commitment is what is associated with improved child well-being (Veum 1993). It is also possible that child support and contact are related to the level of conflict between the mother and the father, which ultimately affects child well-being (McLanahan et al. 1994; Veum 1993). Some have suggested that nonpayment of child support may be due to the inability of the nonresident parent to monitor or control how the money is spent. However, when there is regular contact between father and child, cooperative child-support agreements may result in larger child-support payments, which are in turn tied to more money being spent to benefit the child (Argys and Peters 1998; Weiss and Willis 1985).

Most previous studies that have examined the patterns and determinants of nonresident-father visitation, financial support, and emotional support have focused on parents who married and subsequently divorced. Current high levels of out-of-wedlock childbearing underscore the need to examine the full spectrum of children with absent fathers. Using data from the NLSY97, we are able to examine father-child interactions in three large samples of children: those whose parents are divorced; those whose parents are separated but not divorced; and those whose parents never married each other. These data afford us the opportunity to look at a wide range of father-involvement activities, from contact and overnight visits with the child to financial support. We also report measures of the child's assessment of the quality of the father-child relationship and measures of the mother's assessment of the mother-father relationship. The NLSY97 provides information that allows us to distinguish cooperative (voluntary) agreements regarding custody and paternity from noncooperative (court-ordered) agreements, and we compare differences in father involvement depending on the method of paternity establishment.

Data Description

In 1997, a new cohort of the NLSY was launched. Just over nine thousand adolescents born from 1980 through 1984 were first interviewed in 1997, when they were between the ages of twelve and sixteen. In this study, we use data from both parent and youth questionnaires. The information provided by the residential parent that is relevant to our study includes family income; family background (education, race, employment, religion, and marital history of the responding parent); child support, custody agreements, and paternity status of the youth; nature of current interactions (if any) with the absent biological father; and characteristics of the nonresident parent (age, race, education, and current employment status). In our analysis, we use information provided by the youth about the nature of the relationship with the absent parent, including amount of contact, how recent that contact was, and the youth's view of the father (for example, enjoys time with father, wants to be like father, and so on).

Our sample consists of respondents who live with their biological mother but not their biological father (and whose biological father is alive) and respondents who live part-time with their biological mother and part-time (in a different household) with their biological father. Thus, some of the respondents were born to married parents, and others were born outside marriage. To classify respondents into groups based on the reason the father is nonresident (because the parents divorced, separated, or never married each other), we compared the respondent's birth date with information about the dates of marriage, separation, and divorce reported by the mother. After deleting respondents living with both parents and respondents for whom data were missing or in some way inconsistent, we arrived at a final sample containing 1,132 respondents whose parents' marriage ended in divorce, 253 respondents whose parents' marriage ended in separation (but not divorce), and 1,084 respondents who were born outside marriage and whose parents never married each other.[1]

Socioeconomic Characteristics of the Sample

Mean characteristics of our three samples are reported in table 2.1. These averages are weighted to reflect population totals. Because of the cohort nature of the data, the average age of the adolescents in each of the samples is just over fourteen years. The proportion male varies little across the samples—although males are slightly overrepresented in the nonmarital sample. Other demographic differences between the groups are evident. In particular, children in the nonmarital sample are much more likely to have been born to teenage mothers and to live in an urban area. Separated women are most likely to have been raised Catholic, perhaps reflecting strong religious views regarding divorce. There are also significant racial and ethnic differences among our samples. Almost 47 percent of the nonmarital sample were born to African American mothers, while the proportion of Hispanic mothers is highest in the separated sample.

TABLE 2.1   *Characteristics by Reason for Father's Absence*

	Parents Divorced	Parents Separated	Parents Never Married to Each Other
Demographic characteristics			
Age of youth (years)	14.33	14.22	14.28
	(1.51)	(1.47)	(1.53)
Youth is male (percentage)	46.83	47.57	52.38
Teenage mother at youth's birth (percentage)	12.16	9.14	32.01
Number of children under eighteen	2.23	2.54	2.54
	(1.11)	(1.17)	(1.32)
Youth born out of wedlock (percentage)	3.44	2.38	100
Mother is black (percentage)	10.35	18.55	46.67
Mother is Hispanic (percentage)	8.14	19.16	12.39
Mother raised Catholic (percentage)	32.36	38.04	22.99
Mother currently married (percentage)	40.02	0	26.06
Father currently married (percentage)	33.13	3.62	20.89
Father's marital status missing (percentage)	12.61	6.86	35.34
Years since father left home	9.44	5.09	11.99
	(3.89)	(4.39)	(5.07)
Household residence (percentage)			
Live in Northeast region	17.25	21.76	18.71
Live in North Central region	27.79	15.03	19.86
Live in South region	32.77	38.03	44.21
Live in West region	22.19	25.18	17.22
Live in urban area	56.85	56.11	62.29
Socioeconomic characteristics			
Mother's education	13.34	12.53	11.68
	(2.51)	(2.85)	(2.53)
Father's education	12.58	12.02	11.74
	(2.65)	(2.75)	(2.55)
Father's education missing	33.12	42.13	50.98
Family income (dollars)	25,084	10,178	15,378
	(26,905)	(11,488)	(19,445)
Family income missing (percentage)	12.34	14.57	18.51
Mother currently receiving welfare (percentage)	9.74	20.68	28.18
Mother employed (percentage)	79.62	73.76	66.31

TABLE 2.1   *Continued*

	Parents Divorced	Parents Separated	Parents Never Married to Each Other
Father employed (percentage if reported)	88.68	84.49	73.74
Father's employment missing (percentage)	40.10	48.48	56.59
Sample size	1,132	253	1,084

Source: Authors' compilation.
Note: Means are weighted to population totals. Standard deviations for continuous variables are given in parentheses.

Our three samples also exhibit striking differences in the current marital status of both parents as reported by the mother. Parents whose marriage ended in divorce are those most likely to be currently married. This is consistent with statistics that indicate a higher probability of marriage among the previously married than among the never married (U.S. Bureau of the Census 1998, table 159). However, 26 percent of mothers who gave birth outside marriage are married in 1997 (to someone other than the biological father of the respondent). None of the separated mothers report being married, but, surprisingly, over 3 percent of fathers in the separated sample are reported to be currently married. Since separation without a subsequent divorce should preclude remarriage, this finding represents an inconsistency in the data.

We construct a variable that measures the number of years that the father has been absent. For children of divorced or separated parents, absence begins as of the date of separation or, if no separation date is reported, the date of divorce. For youth whose parents never married each other, absence begins with the child's birth date for cases where children never lived with their fathers and the last date the child lived with the father for the remaining cases. Since the average ages of children in each of the three samples are almost identical, any variation in average *years since father left home* reflects differences in how recent the parents' breakup was. On average, fathers in the separated sample left most recently (five years before the 1997 interview), then fathers in the divorced sample (just over nine years before the interview), then fathers in the never-married sample (nearly twelve years before the interview).

Our three samples also exhibit significant socioeconomic differences. Both parents' educational attainments are highest for the divorced sample, followed by the separated sample, then the nonmarital sample. Employment indicators, as reported by mothers, follow the same pattern. Employment is highest among the divorced sample and lowest among parents who never married each other. Not surprisingly, youths in the divorced sample experience the highest average 1996 annual family income ($25,084). However, family income for youths whose parents never married was higher than that for those in the separated sample. This apparent anomaly is explained by the higher prevalence of current marriage and the addition of a spouse's income among the nonmarital birth sample. For example, reported 1996 family income for youths in the nonmarital sample was $21,699 for those whose mothers were currently married and $10,992 for those whose mothers were currently unmarried.

Patterns of Father Involvement

Previous research examined the patterns and covariates of many dimensions of nonresident-father involvement. The NLSY97 allows us to capture aspects of visitation and custody arrangements and practices, financial support in the form of child-support awards and actual payments, the quality of father-child interaction, and conflict or cooperation between the biological parents. Weighted averages of our measures of father-child involvement are reported in table 2.2.

The custody information comes from a series of questions in the parent survey (completed by the resident mother in all our sample cases) regarding legal responsibility for the child. Because divorcing parents must participate in the legal process to dissolve their marriage, it is not surprising that the majority (83 percent) of mothers in this sample report the existence of a custody agreement. Only about one-quarter of mothers in both the separated and the nonmarital samples report such an agreement. Among those who have a custody agreement, nearly one-third of both the divorced and the separated samples report that the agreement provided for joint custody of the youth. Only 18 percent of the mothers in the nonmarital sample who had a custody agreement reported that it provided for joint custody. Unfortunately, the wording of the survey questions makes it impossible to determine whether the parent is reporting joint *legal* custody (where the absent parent has the right to participate in decisions that affect the health, education, and well-being of the child) or joint *physical* custody (where the child actually lives with both parents in separate residences).

Children were asked about any contact they *ever* had with their biological fathers and then about contact within the past year. For the most part, our measures of father-child contact tell a consistent story. Contact is highest among fathers who married and then were separated or divorced from their child's mother. This is reflected both in the proportion of children who report ever having had contact or ever having lived with their father and in the proportion who report any contact or overnight visits within the past year.

TABLE 2.2   *Father Involvement by Reason for Father's Absence*

	Parents Divorced	Parents Separated	Parents Never Married to Each Other
Custody agreement[a] (percentage)			
Any custody agreement	83.21	25.71	25.72
Joint custody, if any agreement	33.10	35.47	17.73
Father-child contact[b] (percentage)			
Ever any father-child contact	95.00	94.57	77.04
Father ever lived with youth	76.97	82.47	44.24
Any father-child contact last year	82.07	82.68	57.05
Any overnights in last year	37.50	37.79	24.20
Weekly contact	27.67	30.93	19.14
Weekly contact if any contact	33.31	36.56	32.79
Child support[a]			
Ever awarded child support (percentage)	83.43	47.39	45.51
Child support owed in 1996 (percentage)	79.31	39.64	42.15
Child support received in 1996 if owed (percentage)	83.03	87.34	82.65
Amount of child support received if owed (annual, dollars)	3,467 (3,391)	4,275 (4,961)	2,483 (3,650)
Father-child relationship[b] (percentage)			
Father was very supportive[c]	45.46	54.20	43.92
Father was permissive[c]	49.50	44.34	54.94
Wants to be like father[d]	37.04	44.42	25.75
Thinks highly of father[d]	62.13	71.38	58.54
Enjoys time with father[d]	72.53	73.82	65.82
Father usually or always praises youth[d]	57.20	66.66	52.98
Father usually or always critical[d]	7.16	3.27	11.20
Father usually or always helpful[d]	46.82	57.64	37.08
Father usually or always blames youth[d]	4.59	0	4.35
Father usually or always cancels[d]	8.53	13.01	18.27
Father knows youth's friends[d]	14.19	21.22	15.17
Father knows friends' parents[d]	9.86	20.52	8.37
Father knows who youth is with[d]	36.06	55.56	33.62
Father familiar with school issues[d]	43.52	59.17	34.12

(*Table continues on p. 58.*)

TABLE 2.2   *Continued*

	Parents Divorced	Parents Separated	Parents Never Married to Each Other
Mother-father relationship[a] (percentage)			
Mother and father talked last year	81.06	87.61	59.10
Mother friendly to father	39.05	41.81	48.33
Mother neutral to father	51.03	53.84	42.64
Mother hostile to father	9.92	4.35	9.03
Father friendly to mother	39.55	42.41	53.93
Father neutral to mother	44.85	47.36	36.61
Father hostile to mother	15.60	10.23	9.46
Sample size	1,132	253	1,084

Source: Authors' compilation.
Note: Means are weighted to population totals. Standard deviations for continuous variables are given in parentheses.
[a] Reported by mothers.
[b] Reported by youths.
[c] Asked of all youths who have had any contact with their father.
[d] Asked of all youths between the ages of twelve and fourteen who had any contact with their father.

A closer look at the percentages, however, raises some questions. The vast majority (95 percent) of youths in the divorced sample report ever having had contact with their father, but only 77 percent report ever having lived with their father. This is possible if the parents separated at or before the child's birth, but it would mean that 23 percent of the divorced sample followed this unusual pattern of divorce. To examine this issue further, we calculate the child's age when the father left the home. Although it is true that the fathers of youths who report never having lived with their father left home when the child was younger (a mean age of 3.6, compared to 6.0 for those who report ever having lived with their father), only 12 percent left before the child was six months old. This result suggests that children's reports of contact in the early years of their lives may be unreliable. Reports of contact within the past year, however, are likely to be more accurate.

Patterns of current contact reveal a similar pattern across the samples, although at lower levels. More than 80 percent of youths whose parents divorced had contact with their fathers in the last year, and over one-third stayed overnight at their father's house in the last year. A greater proportion of fathers in the nonmarital sample dropped out of their children's lives: only just over half the children reported some contact with their father in the past year, and 24 percent reported overnight visits. Similar patterns are observed for frequent contact. About one-quarter of respondents in the divorced sample saw their fathers weekly, compared to only 19 percent of the respondents in the nonmarital sample. The proportion with weekly contact is somewhat lower than what has been reported in other data sets. Note, however, that the average age of our respondents is fourteen, much older than either the NLSY79 children or the NSFH sample, and we know that contact declines over time.

The NLSY97 is unique in that it asks respondents to assess their relationship with and the quality of their interactions with their father. Respondents are asked whether their father knows their friends, whether he is familiar with school issues, whether he is usually critical or usually blames them, whether he is permissive, whether he is supportive or helpful, and whether they enjoy spending time with him and want to be like him. Table 2.2 shows that there is a surprising similarity in the average responses across the three different groups. Note, however, that these questions were asked only of respondents who had any contact with their biological fathers during the past twelve months. Thus, because contact is less frequent among the nonmarital sample, those in that sample who answered the questions are likely to be a more select group. Although the differences between the groups are small, the pattern is that the responses of those in the nonmarital sample are slightly more negative. Among those who have contact with their fathers, the largest differences between the divorced sample and the nonmarital sample are in the proportion of respondents reporting that they want to be like their father (37 and 26 percent, respectively), that the father usually cancels plans for no good reason (9 and 18 percent, respectively), and that the father is familiar with school issues (44 and 34 percent, respectively).

Another important difference across the samples is in the nature of the relationship between the respondent's biological parents. Slightly more than 80 percent of mothers in the divorced sample but only about 60 percent of mothers in the nonmarital sample spoke with the respondent's biological father in the past twelve months. Conditional on having talked with the biological father in the last year, mothers were asked to evaluate how friendly or hostile they acted toward the father and how friendly or hostile the father acted toward them. Just over 90 percent of mothers in the divorced sample and a similar proportion of mothers in the nonmarital sample reported being friendly with or neutral toward their child's father, although it is interesting to note that those in the nonmarital sample were a little more likely to report being friendly and a little less likely to report being neutral. A similar picture emerged for father's attitude, the vast majority of mothers in all samples reporting it to be either neutral or friendly; however, 16 percent of mothers in the divorced sample, compared to only 9 percent in the nonmarital sample, reported that the father was hostile.

Determinants of Father-Child Involvement

Tables 2.3, 2.4, and 2.5 present reduced-form regressions of a number of types of father involvement—both time and money. We report odds ratios from logit regressions of dichotomous variables indicating the presence of a child-support award, any child-support receipt, any contact ever between father and child, any contact with the father in the past year, and any overnight visits with the father in the past year. We also report coefficients from a tobit regression of the amount of child support received in 1996. Note that figures in all the columns except the third (which reports amount of child support) are given as odds ratios and that coefficients less than one therefore represent a lower probability.

Table 2.3 shows the results for our three samples combined. These regressions use dummy variables to capture differences between the samples. Many of the patterns seen in the means tables hold up in this multivariate analysis. Financial support—both awards and payments—is less for blacks and Hispanics and for mothers who never married the father of their child; this financial support is greater when mothers and fathers are more highly educated and have more children and when fathers are currently married. It is interesting to note that, while the families in the nonmarital sample are much less likely to have child-support awards, conditional on having an award they are more likely to receive child support than observationally similar divorced families in the divorced sample. Father-child contact is greater when parents are more highly educated and is generally lower among blacks, Hispanics, families with more children, male children, and the separated and nonmarital samples.

The results also show that the longer the father has been absent from the home, the less likely he is either to pay child support or to maintain contact. However, this finding can be interpreted in a number of different ways. One possibility is that fathers gradually lose interest in their children and that their involvement therefore drops off over time. The decline could also be due to a reduction in parent-child interaction that occurs as children grow older.[2] Alternatively, this finding could reflect unobserved differences in fathers and families. In our cohort-based sample, fathers who left home long ago also left when the child was young, which could indicate a father who is less interested in his children. Because time since leaving the home affects both the probability of father-child contact ever (most likely reflecting unobserved differences in the father's interest in the child or the mother's willingness to allow the father to become involved with the child) and the probability of father-child contact in the current year (reflecting age or duration effects), it is likely that several explanations are valid.

For a number of reasons, it is also important to analyze the samples separately, especially those whose parents' marriage ended in divorce versus those whose parents never married each other. (Note that, for ease of analysis, we have combined the divorced and the separated samples, creating what we call the *disrupted* sample.)[3] As discussed earlier, the socioeconomic characteristics of the the disrupted sample and the nonmarital sample differ markedly. In addition, divorce generally requires a legal determination of child support and custody or visitation rights. Thus, divorced parents have negotiated (or been forced into) an explicit agreement about time and money, and the agreement can be legally enforced. In contrast, fathers who never married the mother of their child have no legal rights (to visitation or custody) or obligations (to pay child support) until paternity has been legally established. Historically, paternity-establishment rates have been low. More recently, the state has developed an interest in establishing paternity, especially among those who rely on government support.

Tables 2.4 and 2.5 present the same regressions separately for the disrupted sample and the nonmarital sample. The results show some interesting contrasts between the two groups. One of the most striking differences is the effect of race. Compared to whites, blacks in both samples are less likely to have been awarded child support and, if they have been awarded child support, are likely to receive less. However, the effect of race on father-child contact differs between the disrupted and the nonmarital samples. Father-child contact in the disrupted sample is significantly higher among white families than among black, whereas the opposite is true in the nonmarital sample.

Another difference between the two samples is in the effect of being a boy on the amount of father-child contact. Among children in the nonmarital sample, the odds that boys will ever have had contact with their fathers are about two-thirds those of girls. But this gender difference is not found in the disrupted sample.

In both samples, families with more children are significantly more likely to have been awarded child support. However, only in the nonmarital sample is there some evidence that additional children significantly lower the probability of father-child contact. One possible explanation for this result is that unmarried mothers may have children born of different fathers.

Paternity Establishment and Father Involvement

National paternity-establishment rates have risen steadily throughout the 1980s and 1990s. The Office of Child Support Enforcement (1996) reports that IV-D (that is, child-support-enforcement) offices established paternity in fifty-seven of every one hundred out-of-wedlock births.[4] This increase

(Text continues on p. 68.)

TABLE 2.3   Regressions of the Determinants of Father's Involvement—Full Sample

	Ever Awarded Child Support[a]	Any Child Support Received 1996 If Owed[a]	Amount of Child Support Received 1996 If Owed[b]	Any Contact Ever[a]	Any Contact in Past Year[a]	Any Overnights in Past Year[a]
Mother is black	0.534*** (5.03)	0.560*** (2.85)	−1,596.12*** (5.45)	1.273 (1.26)	0.969 (0.22)	0.742** (2.37)
Mother is Hispanic	0.358*** (6.74)	0.894 (0.42)	−360.52 (0.99)	0.857 (0.71)	0.718** (2.03)	0.631*** (2.90)
Number of children in household	1.209*** (4.75)	1.104 (1.53)	183.57** (2.12)	0.911* (1.71)	1.006 (0.14)	0.924* (1.93)
Mother's education (years)	1.099*** (4.27)	1.121*** (3.24)	174.37*** (3.64)	1.060* (1.91)	1.060** (2.54)	1.041* (1.91)
Father's education (years)	1.114*** (4.00)	1.061 (1.39)	307.95*** (5.73)	1.104**** (2.60)	1.058** (2.07)	1.017 (0.70)
Mother currently married	0.655*** (3.55)	1.116 (0.62)	−362.48 (1.50)	0.809 (1.26)	0.868 (1.15)	1.067 (0.57)
Father currently married	1.341** (2.28)	1.971*** (3.39)	870.28*** (3.54)	0.751 (1.40)	1.115 (0.79)	0.943 (0.50)
Teenage mother	1.265* (1.91)	0.699* (1.87)	−654.67** (2.31)	1.133 (0.73)	0.900 (0.82)	1.081 (0.61)

Youth is male	1.031	0.993	−113.48	0.739**	0.756***	1.142
	(0.31)	(0.04)	(0.54)	(2.09)	(2.66)	(1.39)
Parents separated	0.190***	1.464	1,440.79***	0.380***	0.576***	0.868
	(9.30)	(1.09)	(3.16)	(2.87)	(2.60)	(0.82)
Parents never married to each other	0.281***	2.103****	471.76	0.503***	0.684***	0.959
	(10.12)	(3.49)	(1.62)	(3.47)	(2.80)	(0.33)
Years since father left home	0.986	0.951***	−142.90***	0.809***	0.875***	0.929***
	(1.26)	(2.73)	(5.83)	(8.73)	(10.10)	(6.92)
Northeast region	1.097	1.160	16.76	1.248	1.347*	1.340*
	(0.57)	(0.58)	(0.05)	(0.94)	(1.73)	(1.90)
North Central region	1.068	1.210	134.99	1.450	1.286	0.987
	(0.42)	(0.83)	(0.43)	(1.57)	(1.52)	(0.65)
South	1.171	1.315	−87.04	1.028	1.059	1.003
	(1.13)	(1.26)	(0.28)	(0.14)	(0.39)	(0.02)
−2 log likelihood	2,493.915	1,112.909	20,595.812	1,299.526	2,245.340	2,593.397
Sample size	2,253	1,274	1,274	2,253	2,253	2,253

Source: Authors' compilation.

[a] Dependent variable is a dichotomous variable. The estimates reported are odds ratios from the logit $P = 1/[1 + \exp(-X\beta)]$. *t*-statistics are given in parentheses.

[b] Dependent variable is a continuous variable censored at 0. Coefficients are from the lower-limit tobit (see Maddala 1983). *t*-statistics are given in parentheses.

* Odds ratio is different from 1 at the 10 percent level.

** Odds ratio is different from 1 at the 5 percent level.

*** Odds ratio is different from 1 at the 1 percent level.

TABLE 2.4   Regressions of the Determinants of Father's Involvement—Disrupted Sample

	Ever Awarded Child Support[a]	Any Child Support Received 1996 If Owed	Amount of Child Support Received 1996 If Owed[b]	Any Contact Ever[a]	Any Contact in Past Year[a]	Any Overnights in Past Year[a]
Mother is black	0.402*** (5.09)	0.662 (1.62)	-1,451.29*** (3.79)	0.478** (2.31)	0.524*** (3.27)	0.507*** (3.94)
Mother is Hispanic	0.322*** (5.84)	0.811 (0.71)	-98.02 (0.23)	0.523* (1.94)	0.532*** (2.98)	0.499*** (3.53)
Number of children in household	1.252*** (3.41)	1.127 (1.37)	251.26** (2.17)	0.919 (0.84)	0.997 (0.04)	0.915 (1.58)
Mother's education (years)	1.088*** (2.79)	1.136*** (3.08)	163.86*** (2.90)	1.043 (0.86)	1.018 (0.57)	1.028 (1.07)
Father's education (years)	1.162*** (3.94)	1.118** (2.07)	317.75*** (4.80)	1.094 (1.42)	1.087** (2.11)	1.029 (0.94)
Mother currently married	0.675** (2.34)	1.122 (0.55)	-414.89 (1.44)	0.858 (0.55)	0.944 (0.34)	1.073 (0.50)
Father currently married	1.170 (0.85)	2.769*** (4.07)	1,043.36*** (3.46)	0.939 (0.19)	1.366 (1.62)	1.017 (0.12)
Teenage mother	1.053 (0.23)	0.448*** (3.16)	-1,335.67*** (3.18)	1.046 (0.12)	0.738 (1.38)	0.964 (0.19)

Youth is male	0.927	1.082	26.45	0.868	0.896	1.176
	(0.54)	(0.42)	(0.10)	(0.58)	(0.73)	(1.34)
Parents separated	0.208***	1.509	1,133.35***	0.531*	0.654*	0.974
	(7.93)	(1.12)	(2.31)	(1.72)	(1.84)	(0.14)
Years since father left home	1.010	0.923***	−214.32***	0.838***	0.861***	0.932**
	(0.54)	(3.15)	(6.15)	(5.00)	(7.31)	(4.42)
Northeast region	1.049	0.955	−112.01	1.083	1.556*	1.256
	(0.22)	(0.15)	(0.27)	(0.26)	(1.84)	(1.19)
North Central region	1.034	1.333	208.64	1.192	1.479*	1.046
	(0.16)	(1.03)	(0.56)	(1.18)	(1.81)	(0.26)
South	0.971	1.061	−214.32	1.410	1.461*	1.098
	(0.22)	(0.23)	(0.62)	(1.00)	(1.91)	(0.56)
−2 log likelihood	1,270.005	742.869	14,662.978	519.448	1,141.969	1,613.905
Sample size	1,318	901	901	1,318	1,318	1,318

Source: Authors' compilation.

[a] Dependent variable is a dichotomous variable. The estimates reported are odds ratio from the logit $P = 1/[1 + \exp(-X\beta)]$. *t*-statistics are given in parentheses.

[b] Dependent variable is a continuous variable censored at 0. Coefficients are from the lower-limit tobit (see Maddala 1983). *t*-statistics are given in parentheses.

* Odds ratio is different from 1 at the 10 percent level.

** Odds ratio is different from 1 at the 5 percent level.

*** Odds ratio is different from 1 at the 1 percent level.

TABLE 2.5 Regressions of the Determinants of Father's Involvement—Nonmarital Sample

	Ever Awarded Child Support[a]	Any Child Support Received 1996 If Owed	Amount of Child Support Received 1996 If Owed[b]	Any Contact Ever[a]	Any Contact in Past Year[a]	Any Overnights in Past Year[a]
Mother is black	0.698** (2.00)	0.382** (2.44)	−1,900.84*** (4.32)	2.403*** (3.02)	1.722*** (2.75)	1.398 (1.55)
Mother is Hispanic	0.430*** (3.32)	1.420 (0.54)	−1,104.80* (1.71)	1.269 (0.81)	1.228 (0.78)	1.243 (0.74)
Number of children in household	1.168*** (3.05)	1.078 (0.74)	65.99 (0.55)	0.887* (1.82)	0.993 (0.13)	0.912 (1.51)
Mother's education (years)	1.101*** (2.90)	1.043 (0.57)	157.89* (1.75)	1.074* (1.78)	1.113*** (3.07)	1.062 (1.58)
Father's education (years)	1.060 (1.54)	0.921 (0.98)	229.74*** (2.63)	1.112** (2.18)	1.037 (0.92)	1.000 (0.01)
Mother currently married	0.619*** (2.74)	1.269 (0.62)	−116.36 (0.27)	0.804 (1.01)	0.822 (1.06)	1.097 (0.46)
Father currently married	1.528** (2.30)	1.127 (0.33)	886.84** (2.15)	0.613* (1.84)	0.920 (0.41)	0.796 (1.09)

	(1)	(2)	(3)	(4)	(5)	(6)
Teenage mother	1.386**	1.258	52.72	1.139	0.969	1.137
	(2.20)	(0.77)	(0.15)	(0.66)	(0.20)	(0.74)
Youth is male	1.118	0.893	−332.06	0.671**	0.630***	1.077
	(0.80)	(0.40)	(0.98)	(2.17)	(3.06)	(0.46)
Years since father left home	0.975*	0.994	−45.32	0.779***	0.878***	0.922***
	(1.82)	(0.21)	(1.45)	(6.94)	(7.45)	(5.53)
Northeast region	1.183	2.631*	616.27	1.262	1.086	1.407
	(0.70)	(1.75)	(0.97)	(0.76)	(0.32)	(1.26)
North Central region	1.149	1.692	82.85	1.641	1.102	0.921
	(0.58)	(1.10)	(0.14)	(1.56)	(0.38)	(0.29)
South	1.433*	2.888**	330.67	0.888	0.769	0.898
	(1.66)	(2.26)	(0.57)	(0.43)	(1.14)	(0.43)
−2 log likelihood	1,205.496	337.570	5,887.026	758.908	1,066.766	958.265
Sample size	935	373	373	935	935	935

Source: Author's compilation.

[a] Dependent variable is a dichotomous variable. The estimates reported are odds ratios from the logit $P = 1/([1 + \exp(-X\beta)])$. *t*-statistics are given in parentheses.

[b] Dependent variable is a continuous variable censored at 0. Coefficients are from the lower-limit tobit (see Maddala 1983). *t*-statistics are given in parentheses.

* Odds ratio is different from 1 at the 10 percent level.
** Odds ratio is different from 1 at the 5 percent level.
*** Odds ratio is different from 1 at the 1 percent level.

in paternity-establishment rates has been accomplished, in part, by means of policy changes. During the 1980s, the focus was on making it easier to establish paternity when the father was unwilling to acknowledge responsibility: for example, the statute of limitations in paternity cases was extended to the child's eighteenth birthday; the establishment of paternity and the enforcement of child-support orders across state lines were facilitated; and genetic testing (which determines paternity more accurately and convincingly) was made more widely available. Subsequently, the focus has been on encouraging the voluntary acknowledgment of paternity: paternity establishment is now encouraged in the hospital at the time of the child's birth, and the administrative process for couples who want to establish paternity has been simplified. (It should be noted that policies encouraging voluntary acknowledgment mostly postdate the birth dates of the youths in our sample.)[5] Since policies were adopted on a state-by-state basis, there is tremendous variation in paternity-establishment rates by state.

A unique feature of the NLSY97 data is that, for each respondent, there are indicators of whether paternity has been established and the method used to establish it. This type of information is only beginning to be collected in a few large-scale micro data sets, and there is little past experience on which to rely when designing questions about paternity.[6] In the NLSY97, the responding parent was first asked who was listed on the respondent's birth certificate (mother and father or mother only). If the father was not listed, the mother was asked whether paternity had been established by court order or whether the father had in any way legally acknowledged paternity. The responses to these questions indicate that paternity was established (either forcibly or voluntarily) in almost 80 percent of cases, a figure that is far higher than the paternity-establishment rate of 28 percent estimated from 1984 administrative records.

The most likely explanation of this discrepancy is that respondents gave inaccurate information when asked who is listed on the birth certificate. In cases where the child was born out of wedlock, almost 60 percent of mothers indicated that both the mother and the father were listed on the birth certificate. This figure is much higher than would be expected given information available from other sources. For example, recent reports from Massachusetts indicate that, as late as 1994, in cases of out-of-wedlock births the father's name appeared on the birth certificates only 50 percent of the time (Policy Studies 1995). In addition, in the 1980s, that the father's name appeared on the birth certificate was typically not sufficient to establish legal paternity, so the information collected in the NLSY97 cannot be used to determine legal paternity.

We use the survey responses to classify families in the nonmarital sample into four categories: both parents on birth certificate; voluntary paternity (including signing a legal document or other papers indicating paternity); involuntary paternity (court ordered or established by genetic testing); and no paternity. Table 2.6 presents means of some of our variables separately for each paternity group. Despite the limitations of the paternity data, the results in table 2.6 show meaningful distinctions across the groups. For example, as one might expect, those in the no-paternity group are very unlikely to have a custody or child-support agreement, and those in the involuntary-paternity group are more likely to have custody agreements that have been decided by a judge. It is interesting to note, however, that those in the involuntary-paternity group are the most likely to have been awarded child support (the desire for child support often being the motivating factor in establishing paternity) but that, conditional on receiving child support, the amount that they receive is substantially lower than that received by the both-parents-on-birth-certificate and voluntary-paternity groups.

The pattern of father-child contact also follows a logical progression, with most contact occurring in the both-parents-on-birth-certificate group, somewhat less contact occurring in the involuntary-paternity group, and the least contact occurring in the no-paternity group. Table 2.6 also includes more subjective information about the father-child relationship and mother-father interaction. Other than the fact that mothers are least likely to have any interaction with fathers in the no-paternity group, there does not seem to be any clear association between paternity type and quality of relationship given contact.

To confirm that the differences in father-child involvement by paternity type remain after controlling for observable family differences, we report in table 2.7 regressions for the nonmarital sample that include all variables in table 2.5. In addition, these regressions include dummy variables that indicate the effect of paternity type (both parents on birth certificate, voluntary paternity, and involuntary paternity) compared to the no-paternity group. (We report only the effects of the paternity variables in this table.) The multivariate results in table 2.7 reinforce the inferences made from the data in table 2.6. Specifically, we see that all types of paternity are associated with more father-child contact and a greater probability of receiving child support than are found in the no-paternity group. The greatest probability of having been awarded child support is found in the involuntary-paternity group. Conditional on having been awarded child support, the receipt of child-support payments is equally likely across all paternity types, but this comparison is complicated by the fact that very few in the comparison group (no paternity) have been awarded child support.

To see whether the higher award probability among the involuntary-paternity group results in greater financial support, we ran regressions of the *unconditional* probability of receiving child support and the amount paid. In these regressions, reported in the last two columns of table 2.7, the

TABLE 2.6   *Father Involvement by Method of Paternity Establishment—Nonmarital Sample*

	Both Parents on Birth Certificate[a]	Voluntary Paternity[b]	Involuntary Paternity[c]	No Paternity[d]
Custody agreement[e] (percentage)				
Any custody agreement	36.22	19.53	21.08	1.74
Joint custody if agreement	20.84	7.36	4.07	0
Custody decided by parents if agreement	41.06	49.51	31.74	50.50
Custody decided by judge if agreement	57.40	50.49	63.97	0
Father-child contact[f] (percentage)				
Ever any father-child contact	86.43	79.44	77.47	52.59
Father ever lived with youth	53.87	42.69	35.56	25.47
Any father-child contact last year	67.23	54.46	58.14	31.00
Any overnights last year	30.78	22.04	21.12	9.84
Weekly contact	23.48	18.19	15.51	9.66
Weekly contact if any contact	34.37	33.40	26.47	28.53
Child support[e]				
Ever awarded child support (percentage)	53.15	34.01	70.58	14.71
Child support owed in 1996 (percentage)	49.35	33.61	65.72	11.95
Child support received in 1996 if owed (percentage)	82.03	86.77	85.69	73.67
Amount of child support received if owed (annual, in dollars)	2,873 (4,197)	2,118 (2,785)	1,818 (1,887)	1,005 (1,173)
Father's education (years)	11.91 (2.42)	10.97 (2.48)	11.64 (2.79)	11.55 (2.80)
Father-child relationship[f] (percentage)				
Father was very supportive[g]	41.77	57.96	43.56	52.24
Father was permissive[g]	53.13	57.17	56.51	65.20
Wants to be like father[h]	23.07	41.59	28.29	33.28
Thinks highly of father[h]	58.23	51.88	52.55	72.62
Enjoys time with father[h]	65.98	58.98	63.22	72.68

sample consists of all children, regardless of award status, and it is assumed that no child support is received if no child support is currently owed. Clearly, all paternity types are more likely to receive child support, and to receive greater amounts of support on average, than is the no-paternity group. Statistical tests indicate that the increase in the probability of an award that occurs when paternity is established involuntarily (column 1) itself increases the likelihood of receiving any child-support payments (column 7). The odds ratio (5.67) of the involuntary-paternity group is significantly larger than those of the both-parents-on-birth-certificate and the voluntary-paternity groups. However, the amount of child support received by those in the involuntary-paternity group is not significantly greater (column 8).

There are two possible reasons for this result. First, fathers whose paternity was established by court order may have fewer financial resources. One way to evaluate this possibility would be to compare the amounts of the child-support awards. Unfortunately, award amounts are not available in the NLSY97. Another way would be to assess the ability of fathers to pay child support. In table 2.6, we report the average education levels for fathers in each group. The data do not show that these fathers have lower levels of education than fathers with voluntary types of paternity establishment. An examination of the average education levels of the fathers in each of the four groups indicates that those in the involuntary-paternity group are not necessarily the most poorly educated, although this measure may not reflect true differences between the groups since father's education is missing for half the nonmarital sample. Second, fathers in the involuntary-paternity group may be less motivated to provide financial or emotional support for their children. That the data reveal lower levels of reported father-child contact for this group supports this conjecture, but the data do not allow us to determine whether these fathers are meeting their child-support obligations.

Conclusions and Directions for Future Research

In this essay, we use data from the NLSY97 to measure various types of father-child involvement for respondents who do not live full-time with their biological fathers. This cohort was born during the period when nonmarital fertility rates were rising rapidly and when policy makers began to focus on ways to increase child-support payments from absent fathers and increase paternity establishments for children born outside marriage.

We first examine child-support receipt and the amount of contact between the biological father and the adolescent respondent. We look separately at families in which the father was absent because of a marital disruption and those in which the father was absent and the parents never married each other. Our findings are generally consistent with those of studies using other data. We do, however, document lower levels of father-child contact than do other studies, most likely because the adolescent respondents from the NLSY97 are, on average, older than the children who are the focus of most other studies of father involvement.

One finding that has previously been suggested by the ethnography literature is that black unwed fathers have more contact with their children than is commonly believed. Specifically, we find that, controlling for other factors, black unwed fathers pay less child support but have more contact with their children than do comparable whites. This finding raises important questions about differences by race in the nature of fathers' contributions to their children's lives and the relation between contact and child support. Do the NLSY97 data adequately capture racial differences in various dimensions of involvement (such as informal financial contributions)? Do blacks and whites have different parenting values? Does the high prevalence of out-of-wedlock childbearing among blacks lead to different parenting strategies?

One of the unique features of the NLSY97 data is the set of questions asking those youths who have contact with their fathers to assess the quality of their relationship. So far, we have presented only the means for these assessments, separately for the disrupted and the nonmarital samples and by our paternity classification. Surprisingly, respondents in the nonmarital sample rate their fathers only slightly lower than do respondents in the disrupted sample. However, it is important to recognize that the responses of the former are likely to be biased upward because only those who had any contact with their father in the past year were asked these questions.

Much more detailed analysis of these questions needs to be conducted. In particular, a factor analysis would identify the primary dimensions of the father-child relationship and allow the development of a scale that could summarize this information more efficiently. In addition, we would like to know about the father, child, and family factors that influence the father-child relationship and the child's assessment of that relationship. Finally, it is important to understand whether and how positive father-child interactions might lead to other beneficial youth outcomes, such as better and more responsible fathering or a smoother transition from child roles to adult education, family, and work roles. As the cohort that it samples ages into adulthood, the NLSY97 will be an ideal data set to use to address the latter question.

Another important feature of these data is the information that they provide on paternity establishment. Although the levels of paternity establishment that we infer from the data are higher than those reported in administrative records, the further classification of paternity establishment into voluntary and involuntary types shows patterns of father involvement that are intriguing. In particular, we find that adolescents whose paternity has been established (no matter what the means) receive more child support and experience more father-child contact than do those whose paternity has not been established. However, paternity establishment by means of a court order is more strongly associated with child support than with father-child contact. Specifically, compared to adolescents whose paternity has been established voluntarily, those whose paternity was established by means of a court order are more likely to have been awarded child support, are more likely actually to receive child support, but have slightly less contact with their fathers.

Our findings imply that it is important for policy makers to recognize that different type of families may require different policy treatments. In addition, our analysis suggests a number of unanswered questions. For example, what does it mean to have established paternity, and can increased paternity establishment lead to better long-term father-child interactions and later child well-being? Can policy by itself influence whether the establishment of paternity, the provision of child support, and other types of interactions are voluntary or involuntary? Does a punitive approach to paternity establishment and the provision of child support lead to hostile and disenfranchised fathers? Will the current emphasis on in-hospital and other more-cooperative methods of paternity establishment facilitate better father-child interactions? These questions will continue to be important in the years ahead, but very few data sets contain the necessary detailed information about economic, social, demographic, and legal behaviors and outcomes. Data from the NLSY97 may contribute to our understanding of these issues as these youths begin to transition into parenthood and other adult roles.

We would like to acknowledge support from the Ford Foundation and from the National Institute of Child Health and Human Development (NICHD) grant HD30944. We are grateful for the excellent computer programming of Suzann Eshleman.

Notes

1. Our sample-exclusion restrictions included the following: parent interview not collected ($N = 1,060$); responding parent not the biological mother ($N = 879$); youth adopted ($N = 176$); specified for deletion by CHRR ftp file ($N = 38$); biological father deceased ($N = 418$); biological father appears on respondent's household roster ($N = 3,354$); and unable to code as either divorced, separated, or nonmarital ($N = 245$). Note that the exclusion restrictions were implemented sequentially, so the N's reported above are conditional on not being excluded for any earlier reason.

The divorced and separated samples include 51 observations in which the respondent was born outside marriage but was reclassified because the biological parents later married each other and subsequently divorced or separated.

2. To see how sensitive this effect is to alternative specifications, we ran all regressions adding the child's age as an independent variable. The negative effect of *years since father left home* remains in all specifications.

3. The separated sample has intermediate characteristics and behaviors. Having combined the divorced and separated samples, however, we include a dummy indicating that in some cases the marriage has not been legally dissolved.

4. It should be noted that this is not an indicator of the number of out-of-wedlock births for which paternity is established. IV-D agencies may be establishing paternities for older children born in previous years, and this statistic does not capture paternities established outside the IV-D caseload.

5. Another important recent development—the 1996 welfare-reform legislation—may, however, hold some relevance for our sample members. That legislation—and its earlier manifestations, state welfare waivers—emphasized the importance of establishing paternity for children receiving welfare. Sanctions (reduced welfare benefits) were imposed on mothers who did not cooperate in identifying and locating the father of their child.

6. Several other data sets—such as the Survey of Income and Program Participation, the NSFH, and the Panel Study of Income Dynamics—have begun to include some information about paternity. The paternity data collected by these data sets have their own different limitations and biases.

References

Argys, Laura M., and H. Elizabeth Peters. 1998. "Can Adequate Child Support Be Legislated? A Model of Responses to Child Support Guidelines and Enforcement Efforts." Unpublished paper. University of Colorado at Denver.

Argys, Laura M., H. Elizabeth Peters, Jeanne Brooks-Gunn, and Judith Smith. 1998. "The Impact of Child Support on Cognitive Outcomes of Young Children." *Demography* 35(2): 159–73.

Buchanan, Christy M., Eleanor E. Maccoby, and Sanford M. Dornbusch. 1991. "Caught between Parents: Adolescents' Experience in Divorced Homes." *Child Development* 62(5): 1008–29.

Bumpass, Larry L. 1984. "Children and Marital Disruption: A Replication and Update." *Demography* 21(1): 71–82.

Council of Economic Advisors. 1999. *Economic Report of the President.* Washington: U.S. Government Printing Office.

Donnelly, Denise, and David Finkelhor. 1992. "Does Equality in Custody Arrangement Improve the Parent-Child Relationship?" *Journal of Marriage and the Family* 52(3): 636–42.

Duncan, Greg J. and Jeanne Brooks-Gunn, eds. 1997. *Consequences of Growing Up Poor.* New York: Russell Sage Foundation.

Furstenberg, Frank F., Jr., and Kathleen Mullan Harris. 1992. "The Disappearing American Father: Divorce and the Waning Significance of Biological Parenthood." In *The Changing American Family,* edited by S. J. South and S. E. Tolnay. Boulder, Colo.: Westview.

———. 1993. "When and Why Fathers Matter: Impacts of Father Involvement on the Children of Adolescent Mothers." In *Young Unwed Fathers: Changing Roles and Emerging Policies,* edited by Robert I. Lerman and T. J. Ooms. Philadelphia: Temple University Press.

Graham, John W., Andrea H. Beller, and Pedro Hernandez. 1994. "The Relationship between Child Support Payments and Offspring Educational Attainment." In *Child Support and Child Well-Being,* edited by I. Garfinkel, S. McLanahan, and P. Robins. Washington, D.C.: Urban Institute Press.

Haveman, Robert, and Barbara Wolfe. 1995. "The Determinants of Children's Attainments: A Review of Methods and Findings." *Journal of Economic Literature* 33(4): 1829–78.

King, Valerie. 1994. "Nonresident Father Involvement and Child Well-Being: Can Dads Make a Difference?" *Journal of Family Issues* 15(1): 78–96.

Knox, Virginia W. 1996. "The Effects of Child Support Payments on Developmental Outcomes for Elementary School Age Children." *Journal of Human Resources* 31(4): 816–40.

Knox, Virginia W., and Mary Jo Bane. 1994. "Child Support and Schooling." In *Child Support and Child Well-Being,* edited by I. Garfinkel, S. McLanahan, and P. Robins. Washington, D.C.: Urban Institute Press.

Lerman, Robert. 1993. "A National Profile of Young Unwed Fathers." In *Young Unwed Fathers: Changing Roles and Emerging Policies,* edited by Robert I. Lerman and Theodora J. Ooms. Philadelphia: Temple University Press.

Lerman, Robert, and Elaine Sorensen. 2000. "Father Involvement with Their Nonmarital Children: Patterns, Determinants, and Effects on Their Earnings." *Marriage and Family Review* 29(2–3): 137–58.

Maddala, G. S. 1983. *Limited Dependent and Qualitative Variables in Econometrics.* Cambridge: Cambridge University Press.

McLanahan, Sara, and Gary Sandefur. 1994. *Growing Up with a Single Parent: What Hurts, What Helps.* Cambridge, Mass.: Harvard University Press.

McLanahan, S., J. Seltzer, T. Hanson, and E. Thomson. 1994. "Child Support Enforcement and Child Well-Being: Greater Security or Greater

Conflict?" In *Child Support and Child Well-Being,* edited by I. Garfinkel, S. McLanahan, and P. Robins. Washington, D.C.: Urban Institute Press.

Mott, Frank. 1990. "When Is a Father Really Gone? Paternal-Child Contact in Father-Absent Homes." *Demography* 27(4): 499–517.

National Center for Health Statistics. 1999. "Number and Percent of Births to Unmarried Women, by Race: United States, 1940–97." Available at *www.cdc.gov/nchs/data/t1x1797.pdf.*

Office of Child Support Enforcement. 1996. *Child Support Enforcement: Twenty-first Annual Report to Congress.* Washington: Department of Health and Human Services, Administration for Children and Families.

Pearson, Jessica, and Nancy Thoennes. 1990. "Custody after Divorce: Demographic and Attitudinal Patterns." *American Journal of Orthopsychiatry* 60(2): 233–49.

Policy Studies, Inc. 1995. *Report to the Commonwealth of Massachusetts: Massachusetts Paternity Acknowledgment Program: Implementing Analysis and Program Review.* Denver, Colo.: Policy Studies, Inc.

Seltzer, Judith A. 1991. "Relationships Between Fathers and Children Who Live Apart: The Father's Role After Separation." *Journal of Marriage and the Family* 53(1): 79–101.

———. 1999. "Legal Fatherhood for Children Born Out of Wedlock." Paper presented at the Conference on Nonmarital Childbearing. Institute for Research on Poverty, University of Wisconsin (April).

Seltzer, Judith A., and Suzanne M. Bianchi. 1988. "Children's Contact with Absent Parents." *Journal of Marriage and the Family* 50(3): 663–77.

U.S. Department of Commerce, Bureau of the Census. 1998. *Statistical Abstract of the United States: 1998.* Washington: U.S. Department of Commerce, Economics and Statistics Administration.

———. 1999. *Current Population Reports* (March). "Child Support for Custodial Mothers and Fathers: 1995." Available at *www.census.gov/prod/99pubs/p60-196.pdf.*

Veum, Jonathan R. 1993. "The Relationship between Child Support and Visitation: Evidence from Longitudinal Data." *Social Science Research* 22(3): 229–44.

Weiss, Yorum, and R. J. Willis. 1985. "Children as Collective Goods in Divorce Settlements." *Journal of Labor Economics* 3(3): 268–92.

Zill, N., and C. A. Schoenborn. 1990. "Developmental, Learning, and Emotional Problems: Health of Our Nation's Children, 1988." *Advance Data* no. 1990. DHHS pub. no. (PHS)91-1250. Hyattsville, Md.: National Center for Health Statistics.

3

Parental Regulation and Adolescent Discretionary Time-Use Decisions: Findings from the NLSY97

Robin L. Tepper

Most American adolescents spend fewer than seven hours each day in school, which leaves them with considerable free time at their disposal. Previous studies have estimated that this discretionary time accounts for 40 to 50 percent of most adolescents' waking hours (Carnegie Council on Adolescent Development 1992; Larson and Richards 1989). Adolescents spend these nonschool hours in a variety of ways: doing homework, participating in sports, watching television, spending time with friends, and engaging in extracurricular activities. The way adolescents allocate their after-school and weekend time has an important effect on healthy development, academic achievement, and long-term productivity (Coleman, Hoffer, and Kilgore 1982; Eccles and Barber 1999; Gaddy 1986; Larson and Klciber 1993; Keith 1982; Keith et al. 1986). Young people who spend their discretionary time engaged in productive activities such as studying, working on hobbies, playing sports, or reading for pleasure have the opportunity to develop skills, increase competence, and establish a strong sense of identity—all attributes highly correlated with future success (Carnegie Council on Adolescent Development 1992; Larson and Kleiber 1993).

This essay uses data from the National Longitudinal Survey of Youth, 1997 Cohort (NLSY97), to explore parents' role in influencing adolescents' decisions regarding time use. Parental regulation, which involves placing fair and consistent limits on adolescent behavior, has been shown to contribute positively to adolescent socialization and functioning (Barber and Olsen 1997). Parental regulation has been shown to be associated with a number of youth outcomes, including achievement, school engagement, and antisocial or problem behavior (Eccles et al. 1997). In this essay, the link between parental regulation and adolescent time use will be examined, and the hypothesis that parents who regulate adolescent behavior will have a positive influence on time-use decisions will be tested. Three dimensions of parental regulation are identified: regulation through *structure*, regulation through *monitoring*, and regulation through *rules*. The analysis explores whether and how these aspects of parental regulation influence adolescent time use.

While most studies of parental influence have focused primarily on the extent to which parents can influence amount of time spent on homework, this essay explores three aspects of time use—time spent watching television, reading for pleasure, and doing homework—in an effort to gain a broader understanding of parental influence. In this study, parental regulation is found to have a significant influence on all three of these time-use activities, even after controlling for the child's background characteristics and prior achievement. Findings from this study also suggest that some methods of regulation may be more effective than others. Those parents who regulate via structure and monitoring are found to have a greater effect on adolescent's time-use decisions than do those who regulate their adolescents' behavior primarily through the use of rules.

This study also finds that parents from different backgrounds make differential use of these three methods of regulation. Highly educated parents and two-parent households use all three methods more frequently than do less educated parents and single-parent households. Similarly, the effectiveness of different methods of regulation varies depending on family background. For example, imposing structure appears to be more effective in reducing time spent watching television in African American families than in white families.

Literature Review
Time Use

Many have suggested that the productive use of time plays a positive role in successful adolescent development. A study by the Carnegie Corporation of New York, *A Matter of Time* (1992), argues that the productive use of nonschool hours both reduces the time available for adolescents to engage in less-desirable or delinquent activities and provides them with an opportunity to learn new skills and develop competencies. Similarly, Larson and Kleiber (1993) note that free-time activities can provide adolescents with the opportunity to set goals, learn skills, experience challenges, and develop a positive sense of identity. In general, the ways adolescents spend their time is likely to affect the skills, attitudes, and behavior patterns developed later in life (Huston et al. 1999).

As I note in my introductory remarks, three time-use activities are explored in this analysis: time spent on homework, time spent watching television, and time spent reading for pleasure. Previous research has begun to establish a link between these specific time-use activities and measurable outcomes. Several studies have shown that time spent on homework and time spent reading for pleasure are both positively related to grades and achievement test scores, even after controlling for students' prior achievement and for background characteristics (Coleman et al. 1982; Gaddy 1986; Keith 1982; Keith et al. 1986).

Contrary to expectations, little evidence has been found linking television viewing and academic achievement, either positive or negative (Gaddy 1986; Gortmaker et al. 1990). Unlike homework and reading for pleasure, however, television has been shown to contribute little to adolescent development. As a passive activity, television watching provides few challenges and limited opportunities to develop skills or competencies, especially for older children and adolescents (Huston et al. 1999; Larson and Kleiber 1993). There is also growing evidence that television violence can promote aggressive behavior (Rubinstein 1983).

While the productive use of discretionary time appears to have important implications for adolescent development and long-term achievement, there is little research exploring the potential determinants of after-school time use. The limited research available indicates that school environment may be one important predictor. The type of school a student attends and the amount of homework assigned has been shown to influence both time spent on homework and time spent watching television. Literature on Catholic schools, for example, has consistently shown that private school students spend far more time on homework than do their public school counterparts. This literature suggests that differences in school structure and climate may account for this phenomenon. It has been hypothesized that Catholic schools provide greater discipline and have more rigorous requirements than do public schools and in this way influence time spent on homework (Bryk, Lee, and Holland 1993; Coleman, Hoffer, and Kilgore 1982; Jensen 1986). A study by Natriello and McDill (1986) also supports the notion that school characteristics may matter. Their findings suggest that teachers who set high standards for their students have a positive influence on time devoted to homework.

Adolescent achievement has also been explored as a potential determinant of time use. In his study of television and achievement, Gaddy (1986) suggested that leisure-time activities are chosen on the basis of the ratio between the reward offered and the effort required. Students who find it difficult to read are less likely to spend time reading and more likely to spend time watching television. A similar argument can be made about homework. More-able students likely exert less effort and often receive a greater reward for homework completion than do less-able students. Thus, we would expect more-able students to devote more time to homework than do less-able students. Previous studies have supported a link between time use and prior achievement (for example, Keith et al. 1986).

Previous research has also begun to investigate the role that parents play in determining how their children spend discretionary time. A study by Keith et al. (1986) found that adolescents who report that their parents know a great deal about both their personal and their academic lives spend more time on homework than do their peers whose parents are less involved. This finding did not hold for time spent watching television, however. Natriello and McDill (1986) also found that parents who set high standards for their adolescents have a positive effect on time spent on homework.

Parenting Style

The hypothesis to be tested in this essay is that parental regulation is likely to influence adolescent time-use decisions in positive ways. The psychology literature indicates that parents who combine high levels of support and involvement with behavioral supervision and strictness have a positive influence on many developmental outcomes. Effective parenting has been shown to involve three components: connection (establishing consistent, positive emotional bonds with children); regulation (placing fair and consistent limits on adolescent behavior); and support for psychological autonomy (allowing children to experience, value, and express their own thoughts and emotions) (Barber and Olsen 1997). These behaviors have been shown to contribute to positive socialization and developmental experiences for adolescents, including academic achievement and measures of academic engagement such as time spent on homework (Dornbusch et al. 1987; Slicker 1998; Steinberg et al. 1992).

While all three components have been shown to be important predictors of behavior and achievement, this analysis focuses exclusively on parental regulation. Previous research has shown that discipline and control strategies are particularly important factors in influencing adolescent self-regulation and school achievement (Eccles et al. 1997; Hess and McDevitt 1984). For example, Eccles et al. (1997) found a positive relation between parental regulation and adolescents' ability to mobilize energies for learning and achievement. We would therefore expect parental regulation to be positively associated with youths' decisions to spend more time engaged in productive activities.

There are a number of ways that parental regulation might influence time use. On the one hand, parents who explicitly monitor time use, for example, by placing limits on television time or monitoring homework completion, will likely influence the time a child spends on these activities (Huston et al. 1999). However, parents may also influence adolescent time use indirectly by providing structured experiences and establishing clear expectations in other parts of a child's life. Parents who model and encourage the productive use of time, for example, will likely influence a child's independent time-use decisions in positive ways. Larson and Kleiber (1993) also argue that adults who provide structured environments for their children help facilitate initiative on the part of the adolescent, especially if those environments create challenging experiences.

Previous research has suggested a number of different ways to conceptualize parental regulation. Most researchers define *regulation* as monitoring and limit-setting behavior on the part of the parent (Barber and Olsen 1997; Eccles et al. 1997; Steinberg et al. 1992; Slicker 1998). Measures of parental regulation generally include how much the parent knows about the child's behavior and the kinds of rules and limits that are placed on the child. In attempts to extend this construct to other environments, such as the child's school or neighborhood, *regulation* has also been conceptualized as the presence of structure and social organization (Barber and Olsen 1997). Recently, Eccles et al. (1997) introduced the concept of *out-of-family management.* This conceptualization of parental regulation focuses on the behaviors that parents use to "organize and arrange their children's social environments" (Elder et al. 1995, 773).

In an attempt to combine these conceptualizations and to distinguish between rule setting and other methods of regulation and control that might influence time use more indirectly, this essay identifies three separate approaches to parental regulation: regulation through *monitoring;* regulation through *rules;* and regulation through *structure.* Parents who regulate through monitoring take an interest in what their children do and in those with whom their children interact in an effort to regulate their behavior. Parents who regulate through rules place explicit limits on adolescent behavior, for example, by setting a curfew or limiting television time. Parents who regulate through structure make efforts to organize and structure their children's environments. Specifically, they provide social organization within the household and also involve their children in outside organizations and activities that provide structure. The construct *regulation through structure* relates closely to the Eccles et al. (1997) conceptualization of out-of-family regulation and family management.

Methods and Data

The data collected in the first round of the NLSY97 provide an opportunity to explore the role that parental regulation plays in adolescent time-use decisions. The first round of the NLSY97 asked respondents (who ranged in age from twelve to fourteen years of age) whether they participate in, how many days per week they engage in, and how much time they spend each day on each of the following discretionary activities: watching television; doing homework; and reading for pleasure.[1] Approximately 5,300 adolescents answered these time-use questions.

For this analysis, only the responses of the twelve- to thirteen-year-olds were used since these respondents also answered the parenting-style questions. This reduced the sample size to approximately 3,200. The elimination of data missing because of participant nonresponse on items such as parents' education, income, and immigrant status reduced the final sample size to 2,318. A chi-square analysis testing for bias in the sample indicates that the reduced sample contains significantly more white respondents than the original sample (64.5 versus 56.7 percent), significantly fewer respondents from single-parent families (29.7 versus 32.6 percent), and significantly more parents with a college education (52.8 versus 48.7 percent).[2]

Participant responses were combined to obtain a measure of hours per week spent on each activity. Responses of more than twenty-four hours per day spent on any one activity were eliminated from the analysis. However, responses indicating more than twenty-four hours a day spent on two or more activities combined—for example, eighteen hours per day on television and seven hours per day on homework—were left in the analysis because television watching, homework, and reading for pleasure are not mutually exclusive activities. Many adolescents, for example, do their homework while watching television.

There is an extremely low correlation found between these three time-use activities.[3] The correlation between television viewing and reading is not statistically significant, and the highest correlation found is between reading and homework, which are positively and significantly correlated ($r = 0.10$). For these three time-use variables, it appears that time spent engaged in one activity does not detract from time spent on another. This finding is consistent with previous research on time use (Huston et al. 1999).

Adolescents spend significantly more time each week watching television than they do either reading for pleasure or working on homework. On average, they spend 17.53 hours per week watching television but only 5.48 hours per week on homework and 3.11 hours per week reading for pleasure. These findings are consistent with previous research on adolescent time use (Carnegie Council on Adolescent Development 1992; Huston et al. 1999; Bryk, Lee, and Holland 1993).

There is considerable variation in time use among the different respondents and between activity types. Table 3.1 shows frequency distributions for the four time-use variables in this study for all respondents sampled. It is interesting to note that, while most (49.09 percent) of the population sampled reported spending between one and five hours a week on homework, over 10 percent reported spending no time on homework during a typical week. On the other hand, a third of the sample (35 percent) reported

TABLE 3.1   *Frequency Distributions of Time-Use Activities*

Hours per Week	Frequency	Percentage	Cumulative
Homework			
Zero	619	11.61	11.61
One to five	2,618	49.09	60.70
Five to ten	1,353	25.37	86.07
Ten to fifteen	494	9.26	95.33
More than fifteen	249	4.67	100.00
Total	5,333	100.00	
Television			
Zero	228	4.25	4.25
One to ten	1,419	26.44	30.69
Ten to twenty	1,841	34.31	65.00
Twenty to thirty	988	18.41	83.41
Thirty to forty	493	9.19	92.60
More than forty	397	7.40	100.00
Total	5,366	100.00	
Reading			
Zero	2,098	40.08	40.08
One to five	2,232	42.64	82.71
Five to ten	617	11.79	94.50
More than ten	288	5.50	100.00
Total	5,235	100.00	

Source: Author's compilation.
Note: Frequency distributions are not weighted.

watching between ten and twenty hours of television per week while an additional third reported watching over twenty hours of television per week. Approximately 60 percent of the respondents indicated that they spent at least some time each week reading for pleasure.

There are significant differences in the way respondents use their time depending on gender, race, parents' education, and school type. As can be seen in table 3.2, girls spend significantly more time doing homework and reading for pleasure than do boys. Girls also spend significantly less time watching television. On average, black adolescents reported watching eight more hours of television a week more than did their white peers, yet they did not spend significantly less time reading for pleasure. As might be expected, the higher the parent's level of education, the more time the participant spends doing homework and reading for pleasure, and the less time he or she spends watching television. Finally, time use differed signifi-

TABLE 3.2   *Mean Hours per Week on Time-Use Activities by Gender, Race, Parents' Education and School Type*

	Homework	Television	Reading	N
Gender				
Male	4.79	18.52	2.54	1,195
	(4.42)***,a	(13.20)***	(5.73)***	
Female	6.20	16.49	3.71	1,123
	(6.73)	(12.62)	(5.26)	
Race				
White	5.43	16.18	3.07	1,495
	(5.37)**	(11.89)***	(5.69)	
Black	5.38	24.34	3.11	528
	(7.55)	(15.35)	(4.54)	
Other	6.01	18.91	3.41	295
	(5.34)	(14.37)	(5.57)	
Parents' education				
< High school	3.95	20.13	2.81	401
	(3.82)***	(15.12)***	(5.49)**	
High school	5.30	19.86	2.62	691
	(6.43)	(13.29)	(5.00)	
> Some college	5.89	15.87	3.41	1,226
	(5.60)	(12.03)	(5.77)	
School type				
Public	5.26	17.82	3.09	2,127
	(5.44)***	(13.14)*	(5.61)	
Catholic	8.25	16.43	2.88	108
	(8.28)	(11.08)	(4.88)	
All	5.48	17.53	3.11	2,318
	(5.71)	(12.96)	(5.54)	

Source: Author's compilation.
Note: Standard deviations are given in parentheses.
[a] Analysis of variance indicates statistically significant difference in means
* $p < .05$. ** $p < .01$. *** $p < .001$.

cantly by the type of school the respondent attended. As has been shown in previous research, Catholic school students spend significantly more time on homework than do their public school peers.

Measures of Parental Regulation

For this analysis, five measures of parental regulation were created: *regulation through monitoring, regulation through rules,* and three types of *regulation through structure.*

Regulation Through Monitoring   This measure—which will be referred to as *monitoring*—combines the responses of participants (aged twelve to thirteen) to four questions about how much their resident mother (the mother figure with whom they live) knows about their lives. Responses were coded on a scale from 0 to 4, where 0 is "knows nothing" and 4 is "knows everything." Items include "How much does your mother know about who your friends really are?" "How much does your mother know about who you are with when you are not at home?" "How much does your mother know about your teachers and school activities?" and "How much does she know about your close friends' parents, that is, who they are?" Participants' responses to these four items were combined into a single measure of parental monitoring using factor analysis ($\alpha = .71$).

Parents who rate high on this measure have children who believe them to be highly involved in and knowledgeable about their lives. This measure is intended to identify those parents who regulate their children by taking an interest in what they do and those with whom they interact. While not a direct measure of parental behavior, a child's perception of the level of parental involvement may, in this case, be more important than the actual behavior. Adolescents who believe that their parents know a great deal about their lives will likely behave accordingly. This measure is comparable to most researchers' conceptualization of parental regulation.

Regulation Through Rules   This measure—which will be referred to as *rules*—indicates the degree to which parents set explicit rules and limits on adolescents' behavior. It consists of six items about parents' limit-setting behavior.

Respondents (aged twelve to thirteen) were asked to answer the following three questions: "Who sets the limits on who you can hang out with?" "Who sets the limits on how late you stay out at night?" and "Who sets limits on what kinds of television shows and movies you watch?" Responses were coded on a scale from 1 to 3, where 1 = "My parent or parents set limits," 2 = "Parent lets me decide," and 3 = "My parents and I decide together."

The parents of these youths were also asked questions about who sets limits in the household. The questions were framed as follows: "I am going to talk to you about some things parents often make rules about. Please tell me if you make rules about these things or does the youth decide for himself or herself?" Items included "Who sets limits on who the youth hangs out with?" "Who decides how late this youth can stay out at night?" and "Who decides what kinds of TV shows and movies this youth can watch?" Responses were coded on a scale of 1 to 3, where 1 = "Parent makes rules," 2 = "Child decides for self," and 3 = "Child and parent decide jointly." Youth and parent responses were combined, using factor analysis, to create one measure of parental regulation ($\alpha = .54$).[4]

All responses were recoded (3 = parent decided; 2 = parent and child decide jointly; 1 = child decides) so that a higher score would indicate a greater degree of limit setting within a household. The correlation between the *rules* and the *monitor* variables is significant but low ($r = .11$), suggesting that these variables are related but that they measure different constructs.

One potential problem with this measure is its inability to distinguish between parents who impose explicit limits on principle and those who do so in response to a particular situation. For example, some parents may limit television viewing because they feel it to be harmful per se, while others limit it because their child tends to watch too much. This disadvantage is also inherent—although to a lesser degree—in the other measures of regulation described here.

Regulation Through Structure   *Structure* can be thought of as the behaviors that parents use to organize and arrange their children's social environments. As noted earlier, this construct relates closely to the concept of family management developed by the MacArthur Network on Successful Adolescent Development (see Elder et al. 1995). The three measures of structure used here were developed on the basis of responses to three questions about the child's activities.

The first measure of regulation through structure—which will be referred to as *lessons*—is a dummy variable indicating whether a child is enrolled in any extra classes or lessons during a typical week. The survey asks respondents whether they take any extra classes or lessons, such as music, dance, or foreign language, during a typical week. This question likely captures such things as piano lessons, ballet classes, and extra tutoring but not involvement in sports or other extracurricular activities. Over 30 percent of the survey respondents indicated that they were taking extra classes or lessons.

The second measure of structure through regulation—which will be referred to as *dinner*—is a dummy variable indicating whether the respondent eats dinner with his or her family seven nights a week. The survey asks respondents to indicate how many nights during a typical week they have dinner with their family. A large proportion of the sample (45 percent) indicated that they eat dinner with their family seven nights a week. This measure is dichotomous rather than continuous because, if a respondent eats dinner with his or her family seven nights a week, it is assumed that dinner is a regular, structured activity in that household. However, if the respondent reported eating dinner with his or her family only occasionally, it is less clear that the event is a regular, structured activity.

The third measure of structure through regulation—which will be referred to as *religious activity*—is a dummy variable indicating whether the respondent participates in religious activities one or more times a week.

(This is what Eccles et al. [1997] refer to as "religion as family regulation.") Almost 66 percent of the sample indicated that they participate in religious activities at least once a week.

Background Characteristics

The data contained in the NLSY97 provide the opportunity to control for and test the influence of a variety of background characteristics on adolescent time-use behavior. All analyses presented in this essay control for the race and gender of the youth, family income, and parents' education. In addition, these analyses control for the type of school the youth attended since studies have shown that Catholic school students spend more time on homework than do public school students. Since, as already discussed, student ability is also thought to be a determinant of time-use decisions, the student's standardized math Piat score is included in all analyses.

Also included in these analyses are control variables intended to capture the different time-use opportunities available to adolescents. Youths who live in rural areas, for example, may have a greater opportunity to engage in outdoor activities than those who live in urban areas, and, as a result, the latter may watch more television. Similarly, an adolescent with very poor health might be apt to watch more television than a healthier peer would. There may also be regional differences in time use—differences that depend on climate, for example.

Finally, a number of variables were included in this analysis to control for household environment, including the child's religion, whether the child is a first-generation American, the number of children in the family, and whether the child is growing up in a single-parent household. Descriptive statistics for all independent variables used in the analysis, including the five measures of regulation, are displayed in table 3.3.

Differential Use

A question of interest in this study is whether parents from different backgrounds use the three target methods of regulation (through monitoring, through rules, and through structure) differently. Means for the five measures of parental regulation are reported in table 3.4 by parents' education, race, and family structure. There appear to be significant differences in the methods of regulation that parents choose, differences based on their background.

More highly educated parents generally engage in more monitoring than do less-educated parents, although the former are less likely to impose rules. Highly educated parents are also more likely to enroll their children in extra classes and lessons. Only 24 percent of respondents

TABLE 3.3   *Descriptive Statistics for Independent Variables*

Variable (N = 2,318)	Mean	S.D.
Personal characteristics		
Female	0.49	0.50
Black	0.13	0.34
Other race	0.10	0.30
Hispanic	0.11	0.31
Poor health	0.04	0.19
Rural	0.51	0.50
Northeast	0.19	0.39
South	0.31	0.46
West	0.22	0.42
Catholic	0.30	0.46
No religion	0.10	0.31
Other religion	0.03	0.16
Standardized PIAT	103.45	17.83
School characteristics		
Catholic school	0.05	0.22
Private school	0.04	0.18
Other school	0.00	0.06
Family characteristics		
Single parent	0.25	0.43
First generation	0.10	0.30
Kids in family	2.46	1.14
Log (income)	10.51	1.04
< High school	0.12	0.33
High school	0.29	0.45
Measures of regulation		
Lessons	0.31	0.46
Religious activity	0.66	0.48
Dinner	0.45	0.50
Monitoring	0.12	0.78
Rules	−0.01	0.72

Source: Author's compilation.

TABLE 3.4   *Mean Levels of Regulation by Parents' Education, Race, and Family Structure*

	High School (N = 401)	High School (N = 691)	Some College (N = 1,226)
Monitoring	0.00 (0.86)	0.08 (0.80)	0.17 (0.74)***,[a]
Rules	0.07 (0.71)	0.05 (0.74)	−0.05 (0.70)***
Dinner	0.50 (0.50)	0.48 (0.50)	0.42 (0.49)**
Religious activity	0.64 (0.48)	0.58 (0.49)	0.69 (0.46)**
Lessons	0.24 (0.43)	0.22 (0.41)	0.37 (0.48)*

	White (N = 1,495)	Black (N = 529)	Other (N = 312)
Monitoring	0.16 (0.75)	−0.05 (0.87)	0.03 (0.81)**
Rules	−0.05 (0.71)	0.29 (0.68)	−0.09 (0.73)*
Dinner	0.45 (0.50)	0.46 (0.50)	0.46 (0.50)
Religious activity	0.63 (0.48)	0.78 (0.42)	0.67 (0.47)***
Lessons	0.32 (0.47)	0.29 (0.45)	0.27 (0.45)

	Two Parent (N = 1,630)	Single Parent (N = 688)	
Monitoring	0.16 (0.76)	0.01 (0.82)***	
Rules	0.01 (0.70)	−0.07 (0.77)*	
Dinner	0.46 (0.50)	0.41 (0.49)*	
Religious activity	0.67 (0.47)	0.60 (0.49)**	
Lessons	0.32 (0.47)	0.29 (0.45)	

Source: Author's compilation.
[a] Analysis of variance indicates statistically significant difference in means.
* $p < .05$. ** $p < .01$. *** $p < .001$.

whose parents had less than a high school education reported taking extra classes or lessons, while 37 percent of respondents whose parents had at least some college reported being enrolled in such classes. The most highly educated parents and those with the least education were more likely to have children who reported regular involvement in religious activities than were parents with a high school degree.

Respondents with the least-educated parents were the most likely to report eating dinner with their parents seven nights a week. Fifty percent of respondents whose parents had less than a high school degree, but 42 percent of those whose parents were more highly educated, reported eating dinner with their parents seven nights a week. This difference may reflect the fact that, among the more highly educated families, both parents are more likely to work and therefore less likely to be home for dinner. Children of highly educated parents may also be more likely to be involved in clubs, team sports, or other activities that cause them to miss dinner regularly.

Differences by racial background in the types of regulation in which parents engage can also be identified. White parents monitor their children more than do parents of other races. On the other hand, black parents are much more likely to have children who report regular involvement in religious activities than are parents of other races (78 percent of black respondents, compared to 63 and 66 percent of white and other-race respondents, respectively). Black parents also use explicit rules with their children much more often than do parents of other races. There were no significant differences by race in regularly eating dinner with parents or in enrollment in extra classes or lessons.

Finally, single parents are less likely than are two-parent families to engage in most types of regulatory activities. Single parents are less likely to use both rules and monitoring than are two-parent families. They are also less likely to dine regularly with their children (41 versus 46 percent) and less likely to have children who report regular involvement in religious activity (60 versus 67 percent), although they are not less likely to have children enrolled in extra classes or lessons.

Analysis and Results

To test the hypothesis that parents who provide consistent regulation of their adolescent's activities influence the way in which that child structures his or her own discretionary time, a model was estimated using ordinary least squares. Robust standard errors were used to correct for cases in which the standard deviation of the independent variables increased as the value of the variable increased (heteroskedasticity). The model is as follows:

$$Y = \beta_0 + \beta_1 X + \beta_1 R + \varepsilon,$$

where Y is, separately, one of three variables: time spent on homework; time spent watching television; or time spent reading for pleasure. The same regressors are used in all three models. X is a vector of the youth's background characteristics (listed in table 3.3), and R is a vector of the five measures of regulation discussed above: *monitoring, rules, lessons, dinner,* and *religious activity.*

Influence of Background Characteristics

Many of the background characteristics included in this analysis have a significant influence on adolescent time-use decisions, a finding consistent with the results of previous research.[5] Results are presented in table 3.5. The model presented in columns 1 and 2 of table 3.5 confirms that gender is an important predictor of time spent on homework: girls devote almost an hour and a half more to their homework per week than do boys. After controlling for important background characteristics, black students also appear to spend significantly more time on homework than do white students. Similarly, Catholic school students spend almost 2.5 hours more per week on their studies than do their public school peers. Achievement and parents' education also positively influence time spent on homework.

Gender and race are both predictors of time spent watching television, with girls watching significantly less television than boys and black adolescents watching significantly more than whites (columns 3 and 4 of table 3.5). The lower the income and education of the child's parents, the more television he or she is likely to watch in a typical week. As hypothesized, poor health has a strong and positive effect on hours of television watched. Interestingly, adolescents who have many siblings appear to watch less television. There may be several reasons for this finding. Children from large families may have limited access to the television or less freedom to watch the shows they like since, in theory, many individuals are competing for control of the television set. Children from large families may also have increased opportunities to engage in alternative activities since there are more children around with whom to interact. Attending a private school is also associated with lower levels of television watching, as is a high achievement score on the math Piat test.

Only a few background characteristics appear to influence time spent reading for pleasure (columns 5 and 6 of table 3.5). Girls spend more time reading for pleasure than do boys. Higher achievers also read more. Interestingly, in this model, family income is not significantly related to time spent reading for pleasure, although parents' education is. Young people who live in rural areas appear to read less, while young people from the South and the West appear to read more. These regional differences are difficult to explain.

TABLE 3.5   OLS Regressions with Robust Standard Errors on Time Spent on Homework

	Homework		Television		Reading	
	Coef.	S.E.	Coef.	S.E.	Coef.	S.E.
Background characteristics:						
Constant	-0.58	(1.74)	30.73	(3.82)	0.60	(1.71)
Female	1.35	(0.23)***	-1.95	(0.52)***	1.13	(0.23)***
Black	0.89	(0.39)**	6.44	(0.86)***	0.34	(0.39)
Other	0.41	(0.47)	1.35	(1.03)	0.09	(0.46)
Hispanic	0.43	(0.46)	0.05	(1.01)	0.20	(0.45)
Poor health	-0.39	(0.60)	4.30	(1.32)***	0.30	(0.59)
Rural	0.11	(0.24)	0.92	(0.54)*	-0.58	(0.24)**
Northeast	0.17	(0.35)	0.88	(0.78)	0.21	(0.35)
South	-0.37	(0.31)	1.45	(0.68)*	0.67	(0.31)**
West	0.13	(0.34)	-0.89	(0.75)	0.89	(0.34)***
Catholic	0.17	(0.30)	1.18	(0.65)*	-0.09	(0.29)
No religion	-0.38	(0.42)	0.39	(0.92)	0.63	(0.41)
Other religion	1.03	(0.73)	-0.07	(1.62)	0.26	(0.72)
Standardized piat	0.02	(0.01)***	-0.04	(0.02)**	0.02	(0.01)***
Catholic school	2.32	(0.55)***	0.11	(1.22)	0.00	(0.55)

	(1)		(2)		(3)	
Private school	1.24	(0.63)**	−4.29	(1.39)***	0.60	(0.62)
Other school	−0.40	(1.88)	−0.90	(4.13)	−0.16	(1.85)
Single parent	−0.06	(0.31)	0.96	(0.68)	0.18	(0.31)
First generation	0.77	(0.45)*	1.64	(0.99)*	0.81	(0.44)*
Kids in family	−0.06	(0.10)	−0.79	(0.23)***	−0.04	(0.10)
Log (income)	0.23	(0.14)*	−0.72	(0.30)**	−0.09	(0.14)
<High school	−1.28	(0.42)***	0.83	(0.93)	−0.55	(0.42)
High school	−0.05	(0.28)	1.79	(0.62)***	−0.66	(0.28)**
Measures of regulation:						
Lessons	0.87	(0.26)***	−1.71	(0.57)***	0.62	(0.25)**
Religious activity	0.16	(0.27)	−2.65	(0.60)***	−0.19	(0.27)
Dinner	0.55	(0.24)**	0.09	(0.52)	0.44	(0.23)*
Monitoring	0.46	(0.16)***	−1.38	(0.34)***	0.18	(0.15)
Rules	0.16	(0.17)	−0.30	(0.38)	0.23	(0.17)
Adjusted R^2	0.06		0.12		0.03	
N	2,318		2,318		2,318	

Source: Author's compilation.
*$p < .10$. **$p < .05$. ***$p < .01$.

The Influence of Parental Regulation

In general, parental regulation appears to have a significant influence on all three measures of adolescent time use, with structure having the most significant effect, especially for children whose parents enroll them in extra classes or lessons.[6] Adolescents whose parents enroll them in extra classes or lessons spend significantly more time doing homework and reading for pleasure and significantly less time watching television than do their peers whose parents do not enroll them in extra classes or lessons. Students enrolled in extra classes (the variable *lessons*) spend about fifty minutes more each week on homework (column 1 of table 3.5). Similarly, adolescents enrolled in extra lessons spend almost forty minutes more a week reading for pleasure (column 5 of table 3.5). These results hold despite the fact that activities such as taking piano lessons leave *fewer* hours free to devote to homework and pleasure reading.

Adolescents taking extra lessons also watch approximately an hour and three-quarters less television per week (column 3 of table 3.5). It is possible that this result merely reflects time displacement—the hour spent at an extra class or lesson leaves an hour's less time for television watching. However, the findings for homework and reading for pleasure are in the opposite direction, lending support to the notion that displacement may not be the only way in which regulation through structured activity influences television time.

Other measures of regulation through structure were also significantly related to adolescent time-use decisions. Adolescents who participate regularly in religious activities watch over 2.5 hours less television each week than those who do not (column 3 of table 3.5). Respondents who regularly dine with their family (the variable *dinner*) spend over half an hour more each week on homework and spend half an hour more reading for pleasure each week than do those who do not.

The variable *monitoring* also appears to have a positive effect on the way an adolescent spends his or her time. The more a parent knows about a child's friends and schoolwork, the more time that child spends on homework, and the less time he or she spends watching television. The results from the model displayed in columns 1 and 3 of table 3.5 indicate that a 1-standard-deviation increase in the involvement measure is associated with over an hour less television viewing per week and with twenty more minutes each week devoted to homework.

In general, while these results lend support to the hypothesis that parental regulation is positively associated with adolescent time-use decisions, they indicate that structure and monitoring may affect those decisions more significantly than does rule making. The variable *rules* was not significant in any of the three models, while *monitoring* was significantly related to both homework time and television time, and in each model two of the three measures of structure (*dinner, lessons,* and *religious activity*) were significantly related to the time-use activities measured.

Interactions

Given these results and the finding that different parents make differential use of various methods of regulation, the interaction between background characteristics and methods of regulating adolescent time use were explored. Separate analyses were conducted of time spent watching television and time spent on homework, running regressions separately by race (black versus white), family structure (single parent versus two parent), and parents' education level. These fully interacted models contain all the same covariates as the models already presented; however, for presentation purposes, only the coefficients on the regulation variables (*lessons, religious activity, dinner, monitoring,* and *rules*) are displayed in table 3.6.[7]

Some interesting findings emerge from these analyses. In general, it appears that, although more highly educated parents and two-parent families regulate their children at higher rates (as shown in table 3.4), regulation has a similar association with adolescent time use when less-educated parents or single-parent families engage in these behaviors. For each of the groups explored here, monitoring and the imposition of structure were related to more time being spent on homework and less time being spent watching television.

However, the same regulatory practices were not equally effective for all groups. Examining the interaction between parents' education and parental regulation in columns 1 and 2 of table 3.6, for example, we find that, while respondents whose parents had only a high school degree or less spent almost an hour and twenty minutes more each week on homework if they were enrolled in extra lessons, respondents whose parents had at least some college education spent less than an hour more each week on homework if they took extra lessons. This may reflect differences in the types of extra classes that respondents in these two groups are taking. It may also indicate that the same kinds of classes have a more significant effect on those adolescents whose parents are otherwise not able to provide them with significant intellectual stimulation at home.

Enrolling in extra classes or lessons does not appear to influence the time-use decisions of black adolescents significantly, while it does for whites (see the bottom panel of table 3.6). On the other hand, for black adolescents, having parents who monitor them positively influences time spent on

TABLE 3.6   *OLS Regressions with Robust Standard Errors on Homework and Television Separately by Parents' Education Level, Family Structure, and Race*

	Homework				Television			
	> High School		≤ High School		> High School		≤ High School	
	Coef.	S.E.	Coef.	S.E.	Coef.	S.E.	Coef.	S.E.
Lessons	0.71	(0.34)**	1.31	(0.41)***	-1.21	(0.70)*	-2.11	(0.99)**
Religious activity	-0.15	(0.39)	0.56	(0.38)	-2.61	(0.80)***	-2.77	(0.92)***
Dinner	0.50	(0.33)	0.42	(0.35)	-0.36	(0.67)	0.57	(0.84)
Monitoring	0.44	(0.22)**	0.46	(0.22)**	-1.01	(0.46)**	-1.67	(0.52)***
Rules	0.22	(0.24)	0.18	(0.25)	-0.75	(0.50)	0.17	(0.60)
Adjusted R^2	0.05		0.07		0.13		0.07	
N	1,226		1,092		1,226		1,092	

	Two Parent		Single Parent		Two Parent		Single Parent	
	Coef.	S.E.	Coef.	S.E.	Coef.	S.E.	Coef.	S.E.
Lessons	0.92	(0.30)***	0.57	(0.51)	-1.59	(0.62)**	-2.44	(1.30)*
Religious activity	-0.05	(0.33)	0.50	(0.51)	-3.33	(0.67)***	-0.48	(1.31)
Dinner	0.59	(0.28)**	0.40	(0.47)	0.16	(0.57)	-0.25	(1.19)
Monitoring	0.36	(0.19)*	0.70	(0.28)**	-1.49	(0.38)***	-0.91	(0.73)
Rules	0.39	(0.21)*	-0.32	(0.32)	-0.63	(0.43)	0.86	(0.82)
Adjusted R^2	0.06		0.05		0.11		0.08	
N	1,630		688		1,630		688	

	White		Black		White		Black	
	Coef.	S.E.	Coef.	S.E.	Coef.	S.E.	Coef.	S.E.
Lessons	0.95	(0.31)***	0.73	(0.72)	-1.74	(0.66)***	-0.79	(1.50)
Religious activity	0.18	(0.32)	0.43	(0.80)	-2.38	(0.69)***	-4.72	(1.67)***
Dinner	0.57	(0.28)**	0.50	(0.66)	0.10	(0.61)	-1.20	(1.38)
Monitoring	0.27	(0.19)	0.79	(0.38)**	-1.68	(0.41)***	0.07	(0.80)
Rules	0.18	(0.21)	-0.22	(0.50)	-0.73	(0.45)	1.36	(1.03)
Adjusted R^2	0.05		0.11		0.10		0.07	
N	1,495		528		1,495		528	

Source: Author's compilation.
*p < .10. **p < .05. ***p < .01.

homework, while this variable is not significant for whites. Although significant for both, participation in religious activities is more likely to reduce time spent watching television for black adolescents than for white adolescents (almost five hours for blacks versus approximately three hours for whites). Such differences may reflect cultural differences or the differential availability of opportunities. The extra classes in which black students are enrolled may be qualitatively different from the classes in which white students are enrolled.

Another interesting finding is that dining together regularly, which occurs equally across all races and only slightly more frequently in two-parent families (as shown in table 3.4), seems to influence time use only for white adolescents from two-parent families and is associated only with increased time spent on homework.

Discussion

The results reported in the previous section seem to support the initial hypothesis that parental regulation influences adolescent's time-use decisions. Parents who regulate their children's lives by providing them with opportunities to participate in structured and organized activities, especially extra classes and lessons, influence the time that children spend on all three areas explored here. Children of parents who monitor regularly also appear to spend more time doing homework and less time watching television, although these results did not hold for reading for pleasure. The importance of parental regulation persists for both black and white respondents, respondents whose parents have varying degrees of education and respondents from both single-parent and two-parent households.

The finding that monitoring has a positive influence on adolescents is not surprising. It is consistent with previous research about the importance of both parental regulation and parental involvement. On the other hand, the important role that structure seems to play in adolescent time-use decisions is particularly interesting. This is an aspect of parental regulation that has only recently begun to receive attention in the literature (Eccles et al. 1997). Of course, the results of this analysis cannot tell us how or why taking extra classes or lessons, being involved in religious activities, or having dinner regularly with one's family influences adolescent time-use decisions. We can speculate that such activities encourage the development of such skills as organization or time management or that they teach young people to value the productive use of time. However, it appears that involvement in these activities has a stronger positive influence on adolescent time use than does race, parents' income, or parents' education, those things usually assumed to affect adolescent time use. It is, therefore, a finding that warrants further attention.

At the same time, the imposition of rules generally appears to have little influence on the time-use decisions of adolescents. This result is somewhat surprising. It may indicate that adolescent time use is more a function of the general socialization processes that they experience in their family and less a function of their parents' explicit limit-setting behavior. This finding may also reflect the prior behavior of the adolescent whose parent feels compelled to place strict limits on him or her. For example, parents who indicate that they limit their child's television watching may be doing so because it had become excessive. Parents who monitor time spent on homework closely may do so because otherwise that homework would not be completed. Finally, the measure of regulation through rules constructed here did not have high reliability. A more reliable measure might yield different findings.

The analysis indicated that more highly educated parents are generally more likely to use all three types of regulatory practices. Many economists and much previous research have shown that parents' education is an extremely important predictor of a child's future achievement and success. Of course, there are many reasons why this may be so. However, this study sheds some light on one of the ways in which highly educated parents influence their children's success. Highly educated parents seem to place fair and consistent limits on adolescents' behavior. They tend to be involved in the lives of their children, to know their friends and teachers, and to be informed about school activities. They often provide their children with order and structure and seek out opportunities for involvement in structured activities. This study indicates that all these things are positively associated with the time-use decisions that adolescents make, which may in turn affect their achievement and future productivity. It is also likely that such parental regulation is directly associated with a wider range of important outcomes.

Despite the high correlation between parents' education and parental regulation, an initial exploration of the interaction between parental regulation and various family-background characteristics indicates that these regulatory practices can have a significant effect on adolescent time use for respondents from a variety of backgrounds. The finding that youths whose parents are not highly educated but enroll them in extra classes and lessons spend significantly more time on homework is especially interesting. Similarly interesting is the role that monitoring and involvement in religious activity seem to play in time devoted to homework and television watching for black adolescents.

The results presented here are primarily exploratory and far from conclusive. They fail to account for the endogenous nature of many of the variables of interest, and they leave much room for further analysis and exploration. Further analysis of the interactions between respondent background and the influence of parental regulation is certainly needed. What are the underlying factors that make these regulatory practices more effective for some adolescents and less so for others? Furthermore, the time-use activities examined here represent only a sampling of the ways in which adolescents spend their free time. Can a similar link be found between adolescent involvement in sports or extracurricular activities and the three approaches to parental regulation explored here?

Time use also represents only one outcome of interest. How might these three approaches to parental regulation influence such other outcomes as delinquency, achievement, or psychological adjustment? Finally, the family is only one context in which adolescent socialization occurs. How might similar kinds of regulatory practices in schools and other social institutions influence adolescent time-use decisions or other behaviors?

Conclusions

The results of this analysis seem to indicate that regulation has a generally positive influence on the way in which adolescents spend their discretionary time. Adolescents whose parents regulate their behavior spend more time engaged in productive activities and less time in nonproductive activities. The influence of such regulation appears to be independent of many of the background characteristics that we would normally associate with these activities.

These results have implications both for parents and for policy makers. They suggest that parents may be able to have a positive developmental influence on their children both by setting fair and consistent limits on behavior and by providing them with opportunities for structured involvement in activities. In fact, it appears that one of the most effective ways parents can influence their child's use of time is by involving him or her in structured activities. At the same time, if involvement in structured activities has a positive influence on a child, these findings may indicate a need to fund more after-school programs and provide other structured activities for children who otherwise would not have access to them.

I wish to thank Robert Michael, Robert LaLonde, Ariel Kalil, Mimi Engel, Carolyn Hill, Brian Jacob, and Dough Noonan for their helpful comments. This research was supported by a grant from the Spencer Foundation.

Notes

1. The NLSY97 also asked about time spent in extra classes and lessons. However, for this analysis, class time was not included as a dependent variable. While some adolescents may choose to spend time taking piano lessons, ballet lessons, or foreign-language classes, it is assumed that, for a large majority, these activities have been initiated and encouraged by parents. This is especially true since respondents are between twelve and fourteen years of age and are less likely to take the initiative in planning their after-school involvements than an older sample might be.

2. Calculations do not use sampling weights. Most of the missing data were for variables that were not central to this analysis. However, dropping these cases creates some problems in interpreting the coefficients on the variables of interest. In an effort to explore the magnitude of this problem, analyses were also conducted with a more complete data set, replacing missing responses with the mean response in that category. These analyses did not yield results with meaningful differences from the ones presented here.

3. Unless otherwise noted, all figures were calculated using 1997 sampling weights.

4. Although reliability was quite low, this scale was retained for conceptual reasons. Future research will attempt to construct a more reliable measure of regulation through rules.

5. Analyses were conducted both with and without the regulation variables included in the model. The coefficients on the background characteristics did not change significantly with the introduction of the regulation variables.

6. The five measures of regulation are jointly significant in all three models, as are the three measures of regulation through structure.

7. The full model is available from the author on request.

References

Barber, Brian K., and Joseph A. Olsen. 1997. "Socialization in Context: Connection, Regulation, and Autonomy in the Family, School, and Neighborhood and with Peers." *Journal of Adolescent Research* 12(2): 287–315.

Bryk, Anthony S., Valerie E. Lee, and Peter B. Holland. 1993. *Catholic Schools and the Common Good*. Cambridge, Mass.: Harvard University Press.

Carnegie Council on Adolescent Development. 1992. *A Matter of Time: Risk and Opportunity in the Nonschool Hours*. New York: Carnegie Corp.

Coleman, James S., Thomas Hoffer, and Sally Kilgore. 1982. *High School Achievement: Public, Catholic, and Other Private Schools Compared.* New York: Basic.

Dornbusch, Sanford M., Philip L. Ritter, P. Herbert Leiderman, Donald F. Roberts, and Michael J. Fraleigh. 1987. "The Relation of Parenting Style to Adolescent School Performance." *Child Development* 58(5): 1244–57.

Eccles, Jacquelynne S., and Bonnie L. Barber. 1999. "Student Council, Volunteering, Basketball, or Marching Band: What Kind of Extracurricular Involvement Matters?" *Journal of Adolescent Research* 14(1): 10–43.

Eccles, Jacquelynne S., Diane Early, Kari Frasier, Elaine Belansky, and Karen McCarthy. 1997. "The Relation of Connection, Regulation, and Support for Autonomy to Adolescents' Functioning." *Journal of Adolescent Research* 12(2): 263–86.

Elder, Glen H., Jacquelynne S. Eccles, Monika Ardelt, and Sarah Lord. 1995. "Inner-City Parents under Economic Pressure: Perspectives on the Strategies of Parenting." *Journal of Marriage and Family* 57(3): 771–84.

Gaddy, Gary D. 1986. "Television's Impact on High School Achievement." *Public Opinion Quarterly* 50(3): 340–59.

Gortmaker, Steven L., Charles A. Salter, Deborah K. Walker, and William H. Dietz Jr. 1990. "The Impact of Television Viewing on Mental Aptitude and Achievement: A Longitudinal Study." *Public Opinion Quarterly* 54(4): 594–604.

Hess, Robert D., and Theresa M. McDevitt. 1984. "Some Cognitive Consequences of Maternal Intervention Techniques: A Longitudinal Study." *Child Development* 55(6): 2017–30.

Huston, Aletha C., John C. Wright, Janet Marquis, and Samuel B. Green. 1999. "How Young Children Spend Their Time: Television and Other Activities." *Developmental Psychology* 35(4): 912–25.

Jensen, Gary F. 1986. "Explaining Differences in Academic Behavior between Public-School and Catholic-School Students: A Quantitative Case Study." *Sociology of Education* 59(1): 32–41.

Keith, Timothy Z. 1982. "Time Spent on Homework and High School Grades: A Large-Sample Path Analysis." *Journal of Educational Psychology* 74(5): 248–53.

Keith, Timothy Z., Thomas M. Reimers, Paul G. Fehrmann, Sheila M. Pottebaum, and Linda W. Aubey. 1986. "Parental Involvement, Homework, and TV Time: Direct and Indirect Effects on High School Achievement." *Journal of Educational Psychology* 78(5): 373–80.

Larson, Reed, and Douglas Kleiber. 1993. "Daily Experience of Adolescents." In *Handbook of Clinical Research and Practice with Adolescents*, edited by Patrick Tolan and Bertram Cohler. New York: Wiley.

Larson, Reed, and Maryse Richards. 1989. "Introduction: The Changing Life Space of Early Adolescents." *Journal of Youth and Adolescence* 18(6): 501–9.

Natriello, Gary, and Edward L. McDill. 1986. "Performance Standards, Student Effort on Homework, and Academic Achievement." *Sociology of Education* 59(1): 18–31.

Rubinstein, Eli A. 1983. "Television and Behavior: Research Conclusions of the 1982 NIMH Report and Their Policy Implications." *American Psychologist* 38(7): 820–25.

Slicker, Ellen K. 1998. "Relationship of Parenting Style to Behavioral Adjustment in Graduating High School Seniors." *Journal of Youth and Adolescence* 27(3): 345–72.

Steinberg, Laurence, Susie D. Lamborn, Sanford M. Dornbusch, and Nancy Darling. 1992. "Impact of Parenting Practices on Adolescent Achievement: Authoritative Parenting, School Involvement, and Encouragement to Succeed." *Child Development* 63(5): 1266–81.

Part II

Adolescents' Dating and Sexual Behavior

4

Family Environment and Adolescent Sexual Debut in Alternative Household Structures

Mignon R. Moore

THE PURPOSE of this study is to further our understanding of the relation between family structure, quality of parenting, and the onset of sexual activity among African American and white youths. While the literature on child well-being has noted the beneficial effects of living in a two-parent as opposed to a single-mother household, only recently have researchers begun to explore the association between family type and youth sexual behavior more rigorously, using refined concepts of family type. Moreover, sociologists have begun to investigate the way in which such developmental measures as parental support and discipline mediate the effect of family structure on adolescent outcomes once race and other demographic characteristics have been taken into account (Thomson, McLanahan, and Curtin 1992; Thomson, Hanson, and McLanahan 1994).

This essay addresses these issues through three research questions: How does the risk of teenage sexual debut vary by family structure?[1] Does a similar relation between family structure and sexual debut hold for black and white youths? Do mother's or father's support and discipline mediate the relation between family structure and sexual debut?

In answering these questions, the essay offers the following contributions to this line of research: First, it provides finer definitions of household structure than those used in most other work by including cohabiting households as a separate category, distinguishing between remarried stepfamilies (formed when a divorced mother remarries) and first-marriage stepfamilies (formed after a nonmarital birth),[2] and incorporating never-married single-mother households into the study design. Second, it presents discrete models to predict the onset of sexual intercourse by race since, while the few studies measuring the effects of family environment separately for black and white adolescents have produced inconsistent results, they have generally suggested a weaker relation among black youths (Steinberg et al. 1991; Avenevoli, Sessa, and Steinberg 1999). Also, rather than limiting analyses to the two-biological-parent reference group as is typically done, the essay tests for significant differences in the risk of sexual debut between family types to test competing hypotheses about the detrimental effects of cohabiting households versus remarried stepfamilies. Third, the study uses interaction terms to determine whether the father's parenting behaviors mediate the relation between family structure and adolescent transition to intercourse, particularly in households where the father is not the biological parent. The literature here suggests that white children in stepfamilies exhibit an increase in problem behavior during adolescence, regardless of father's behavior, because of difficulty adjusting to the stepfather as a parent figure (Bray 1999; Hetherington, Cox, and Cox 1982). The effect of cohabiting fathers' parenting behaviors is less studied. I argue the importance of incorporating nontraditional family forms into research designs that concentrate on adolescent behavioral outcomes and also suggest reasons why these alternative household structures might affect African American and white youths in different ways.

Overview
Family Structure: Old and Newer Family Forms

Researchers investigating child well-being have distinguished between two-parent households that contain both biological parents and those that contain a biological parent and a stepparent and have tended to define single-parent households as those that have experienced a marital disruption and are now headed by single mothers. However, the structure and dynamics of two-parent and single-parent families have changed (Bumpass and Raley 1995; Bumpass, Raley, and Sweet 1995). A demographic look at American households reveals a substantial number of alternative family structures that have been omitted from standard research designs examining adolescent sexual outcomes. This omission is particularly problematic when estimating the effect of family structure on African American youths, who initiate sexual activity at earlier ages and who are more likely to spend time in one of these alternative family structures (Mott 1990; Wojtkiewicz 1992; Manning and Lichter 1996; Bumpass, Raley, and Sweet 1995; Bumpass and Raley 1995). Thus, while we know that black youths are more likely to engage in intercourse when they live with one biological parent instead of two, we know less about the abilities of remarried stepfamilies and other alternative two-parent family structures to delay the onset of sexual activity.

Our understanding of the relation between alternative two-parent families and the sexual behavior of white adolescents is also limited. There are three important forms of the nontraditional two-parent family that have received little attention in the literature on family structure and the onset of sexual activity but that should be considered in any discussion of family structure and its influence on youth behavior: cohabiting households, remarried stepfamilies, and first-marriage stepfamilies. In addition, given the substantial proportion of single-parent families formed as a result of a nonmarital birth, the effect of living in a never-married as opposed to a maritally disrupted household should also be measured.

Cohabiting Households   Roughly 13.3 percent of unmarried U.S. households with children are cohabiting families (Manning and Lichter 1996). Moreover, 40 percent of all children will spend some time in a cohabiting household before adulthood (Smock 2000). However, few studies have examined the effect of living in a cohabiting household on the risk of onset of sexual activity in early adolescence, although there are reasons to suspect a relation (Bumpass and Sweet 1989). Researchers have only recently begun to view cohabitation as a legitimate family form, in part because of the ambiguity surrounding the role of the unmarried partner in relation to the other household members. The cohabiting partnership may be a precursor to marriage, a substitute for marriage, or a more serious boyfriend-girlfriend relationship (McLanahan and Casper 1995). For instance, while socialization or modeling hypotheses assert that the presence of a parent's sex partner in the home socializes the child toward a greater acceptance of nonmarital sexual activity (Moore and Chase-Lansdale 2001; Newcomer and Udry 1984, Thornton and Camburn 1987; McLanahan 1988), the presence of an additional adult in the home might discourage adolescent problem behavior because of increased supervision and monitoring (Hogan and Kitagawa 1985; Dornbusch et al. 1985).

Indeed, the relationship between the nonbiological partner and the children in the household is subjective and may vary significantly from one household to the next. Factors such as length of coresidence, presence of partner's biological children, adult individual human capital and personal characteristics may all be related to the quality of the cohabiting relationship and the partner's role in the household. Moreover, because marital relationships and nonmarital unions are embedded within the context of different cultures, norms, and expectations, the meaning of these relationships might vary across racial or ethnic groups (Bumpass and McLanahan 1989; Orbuch, Veroff, and Hunter 1999). Distinct patterns of entry into, exit from, and duration of cohabiting unions by race and ethnicity (Landale and Forste 1991; Manning and Smock 1995; Bumpass and Raley 1995; Smock 2000) have led some to suggest that cohabitation is more of a transitional or transient state for whites and a substitute for marriage for blacks (Manning and Smock

1995). Never-married blacks are more likely to enter into cohabiting rather than marital unions, maintain cohabiting relationships for longer durations, and have children in cohabiting relationships than are whites (Manning and Lichter 1996; Raley 1996; Schoen and Owens 1992).[3] That black cohabiting households are more likely to contain children also supports the idea of this union as a "marriage-like" state in black communities (McLanahan and Casper 1995). If it is true that, in terms of socialization and child rearing, black cohabiting households act similarly to black married households, the effect on youth behavior may also be the same—a lower likelihood of early sexual debut than in black single-parent families.

Stepfamilies: Remarriage Versus First Marriage During the past twenty years, increases in the rates of divorce, nonmarital childbearing, and remarriage have increased the proportion of children living in stepfamilies (Ihinger-Tallman 1988; Furstenberg and Cherlin 1991). Stepfamilies are usually considered to be new married family structures produced after a marital disruption, containing one or more children from one partner's previous marital relationship (Mott 1990; Amato 1994; Chase-Lansdale, Cherlin, and Kiernan 1995). Generally, youths in remarried stepfamilies exhibit more behavioral problems than do children who live with both biological parents, primarily because the multiple transitions and family upheavals that accompany divorce and remarriage are associated with disorganization and instability (Hetherington 1999; Chase-Lansdale and Hetherington 1990; Pierret, chapter 1 in this volume). However, for the adolescent, the transition from a never-married single-mother family to a first-marriage stepfamily is an experience both theoretically and empirically distinct from the transition to a maritally disrupted single-parent family or a remarried stepfamily. The instability associated with the disruption of a marriage and the replacement of a biological parent with a stepparent may not occur if the child was the result of a nonmarital birth and, until the transition to a stepfamily household, never experienced a father or a father figure living in the home.[4]

Little research compares the outcomes of black and white adolescents in remarried stepfamilies, and hardly any studies acknowledge the first-marriage stepfamily or examine youth outcomes in it, yet Bumpass, Raley, and Sweet (1995) found that black children were more than twice as likely as white children to live in first-marriage stepfamilies. One study of African American families in high-poverty urban neighborhoods found that, compared to girls in other family types, girls living in stepfamilies were significantly less likely to initiate sexual intercourse and to conceive a child in adolescence and significantly more likely to perform better in high school (Moore and Chase-Lansdale 2001).[5]

Such research supports the hypothesis that the effect of living in stepfamily households may vary with community and cultural context. For example, white families are more likely to live in an advantaged context, one in which most children live with both biological parents, and, in this context, living in a stepfamily or some other household type may be perceived negatively and may therefore contribute to a greater likelihood of problem behavior. But, when a family lives in a community with significant rates of unemployment, welfare receipt, nonmarital childbearing, and adolescent delinquency, as some black families do, the presence of an additional adult in the household may be a source of stability and discipline that may not be present in many other homes in the neighborhood. Children living in such households may experience a lower sense of "relative deprivation"—that is, perceive themselves to be better off economically and socially than their peers in single-parent households—and therefore be less likely to engage in problem behaviors. Since black children from all socioeconomic strata are significantly more likely to spend some time in single-parent families (Bumpass and Raley 1995; Wojtkiewicz 1992), the comparison group for youngsters in black cohabiting or stepfamily households is also more likely to come from single-parent families.

Never-Married Versus Maritally Disrupted Single-Mother Families
The effect of living in a single-mother family on sexual behavior in early adolescence has been attributed to one of two factors: the marital disruption assumed to produce this family form (Hetherington 1987; Chase-Lansdale and Hetherington 1990)[6] or the lack of supervision and parental support associated with having only one parent in the home (Thomson, McLanahan, and Curtin 1992). In the past, never-married and maritally disrupted families were collapsed into one single-parent category even though the family histories involved were very different. More recent work has begun to compare outcomes for children in different types of single-parent households (Astone and McLanahan 1991; Thomson, McLanahan, and Curtin 1992; McLanahan and Sandefur 1994). Research examining adolescent sexual behavior and family structure indicates that nonmarital childbearing is more likely to occur among young women in never-married households than among those in divorced or separated households. This is in part due to the poorer economic circumstances and fewer parental resources of the never-married (McLanahan and Sandefur 1994; Wu and Martinson 1993; Wu and Thomson 1998). Thus, we would expect the risk of intercourse to be higher for youths in never-married single-parent families.

Parent-Child Relationships:
Adolescent Perceptions of Parental Support and Strictness

In the past decade, sociologists have integrated family-process models used by developmental psychologists into their research designs, estimating the effect of family structure on parenting behaviors and parental support, and connecting the relationships thus established to child and adolescent well-being (Astone and McLanahan 1991; Thomson, McLanahan, and Curtin 1992; Thomson, Hanson, and McLanahan 1994; Pittman and Chase-Lansdale, in press). For example, researchers have found lower levels of parental support and strictness in stepfamilies and cohabiting families, a factor contributing significantly to more behavior problems in school, poorer academic performance, and more internalizing and externalizing behaviors (Hetherington, Cox, and Cox 1982; Thomson, Hanson, and McLanahan 1994; Astone and McLanahan 1991; Amato 1994). Also, noncoercive parental control in two-biological-parent families has been linked to a lower likelihood of girls engaging in sexual activity during adolescence (Hogan and Kitagawa 1985; Danziger 1995; Pittman and Chase-Lansdale, in press).

When the focus narrows from parents in general to the father or father figure in particular, the effect of parenting behavior is less clear. We do know that, after controlling for mother's parenting behavior and other characteristics, more social support from and more active involvement on the part of the biological father have weak to moderate effects on other aspects of child and adolescent well-being (Simons et al. 1994; Amato 1998). We also know that, while the quality of a stepfather's parenting behavior can affect long-term adjustment in remarried stepfamilies, it has little short-term effect on behavior during the teenage years as efforts at firm and supportive parenting on the part of the stepfather are rebuffed by youths struggling with identity issues made worse by the absence of the biological father (Hetherington, Cox, and Cox 1982; Bray 1999). But the role that the new father figure plays in the family varies significantly depending on whether he is a cohabiting partner, a second husband, or a first husband. And little is known about the quality of parenting displayed by men in cohabiting relationships or new fathers in first-marriage stepfamilies, especially in African American family structures.

In sum, given the increasing proportion of nontraditional families (that is, those other than two-biological-parent households) in recent years, the standard measures of family structure are inadequate when attempting to analyze behavior in the context of contemporary society. I therefore distinguish between two-biological-parent households, remarried stepfamilies, first-marriage stepfamilies, cohabiting households, maritally disrupted single-mother families, and never-married single-mother families. I then test for a mediating effect of parenting behavior in different family types by adding measures of the support and strictness provided by mothers and fathers or father figures within the household. I also present these effects in pooled and separate estimates by race.

Data and Measures

The analyses are based on data from round one of the National Longitudinal Study of Youth, 1997 Cohort (NLSY97), which includes 9,022 respondents aged twelve to sixteen as of December 31, 1996. The data are drawn from two subsamples: a cross-sectional sample designed to be representative of the noninstitutionalized segment of people living in the United States and born between 1980 and 1984 and an oversample of Hispanic and black people living in the United States and born during that same time period.[7] The larger data set consists of information gathered from a household screening interview (with a parent) and separate 1-hour personal interviews with the youth and a parent (usually the same the parent as in the screening interview). Parents' marital status is drawn from information collected during the screening interview. Parents' education and household income are gathered from the parent interview. All additional information is drawn from the youth interview, which was conducted entirely as a computer-assisted personal interview (CAPI). Further information and data documentation can be found in the *NLSY97 User's Guide* (Center for Human Resources 1998).

Sample

The initial sample of 9,022 youth respondents is reduced to individuals who were asked about their sexual history (those age fourteen and older, 60 percent of the sample). Because the analyses focus on black-white differences in predicting the risk of sexual debut, I exclude other racial groups (14 percent of the sample). Since the analyses examine refined measures of family structure, and since children who do not live in a single-parent household or experience a marital transition overwhelmingly reside with the biological mother (Cowan and Hetherington 1991), I also exclude individuals in single-parent families who do not live with the biological mother (12 percent of the sample). Finally, I omit respondents in single-mother households or stepfamilies for whom mother's marital history is missing (4 percent of the sample). These data reductions result in a final sample size of 3,727: 2,624 whites and 1,103 blacks.[8]

The dependent variable, *initiation of intercourse*, was obtained through the recoded response to the following question on the youth CAPI: "Have you ever had sexual intercourse, that is, made love, had sex, or gone all the way, with a person of the opposite sex?"

Family structure is the household living situation that existed at time of the interview. To measure family structure, the individual with whom the screening interview was conducted (usually the parent) was asked to identify each individual in the household and his or her relationship to the first five people named on the resulting household roster. Residence with a parent or parents was determined by the youth's response to the question, "Do you live with either your mother/father or a mother/father figure?" Thus, family structure is determined by the relationship of each parent figure listed on the household roster to the youth respondent as well as by the youth's indication of a parent figure in the household.

Two-biological-parent households (63 percent) are families where the youth respondent lists both the biological mother and the biological father in the household.[9] A broad *stepfamily* category was first created if the respondent listed a stepfather in the household or if a stepfather was listed on the household roster. Mother's marital history was then used to refine this classification: households were classified as *remarried stepfamilies* (9 percent) if the mother's marital history indicated a divorce and at least one remarriage after the child's birth and as *first-marriage stepfamilies* (2 percent) if the child was born out of wedlock and the mother had afterward married someone other than the child's biological father and not subsequently divorced.[10] *Cohabiting households* (3 percent) are identified in two ways: when the youth reports that the mother's live-in boyfriend acts as a "father-figure" and when the mother's relationship to an individual listed on the household roster is described as "lover/partner."[11] *Single-parent families* are those where no biological, step-, or adoptive father or mother's boyfriend is listed in the youth interview or on the household roster. These families are then separated into *never-married single-mother families* (8 percent) and *maritally disrupted single-mother families* (19 percent), according to mother's marital history.

To assess parental support and discipline, the NLSY97 asks respondents age fourteen and older the following questions about parental behavior: "Is your mother/father strict or permissive?" "Is your mother/father very supportive, somewhat supportive, or not very supportive?" The first question is recoded 1 if *strict*, 0 otherwise. The second question was recoded 1 if *very supportive*, 0 otherwise, such that a value of 1 is given for *highly supportive* parenting. Because the parenting questions are based only on the adolescent's report of parent behavior, they are defined as *perceptions* of parenting and social support.

Individual background characteristics include race (*black* = 1, 16 percent) and gender (*female* = 1, 50 percent), both shown to relate strongly to age at sexual debut. During adolescence, the probability of sexual initiation increases substantially with each year of age. Because the risk of sexual debut can differ significantly from one year to the next, it is more appropriate to consider each year of age as a separate indicator of intercourse rather than present age as a continuous variable assuming similar risk from one year to the next. This study uses three dummy variables measuring age: *age fourteen*, *age fifteen*, and *age sixteen*, with age fourteen as the omitted category. The literature also suggests an association between early physical maturity or pubertal development and age at sexual debut for girls and late physical maturation and age at sexual debut for boys (Katchadourian 1990; Udry and Cambell 1994; Brooks-Gunn 1988). Analyses therefore include a dummy variable for *early female pubertal development* if the female began menarche at an age more than 1 standard deviation below the mean age of menarche for the sample (11.07 years, 13 percent of women) and a variable for *late male pubertal development* if the male reports that the signs associated with puberty (developing pubic or facial hair, voice cracking or lowering) have not yet begun or have barely started (6 percent).

Family income is based on information collected from the responding parent and is measured using a ratio comparing total household income to the federal poverty level for the previous year. An income-needs ratio of 1 means that the family is living at or below the poverty level. This measure was then collapsed into three dummy variables: *poor* (0 to 1.00, 10 percent of the sample), *near poor* (1.01 to 3.00, 31 percent of the sample), and *not poor* (3.01 to 14.49, 36 percent of the sample).[12] Mother's years of education were obtained from the household roster information and recoded into the following dummy variables: *less than high school, high school, some college, college graduate or higher,* and *missing mother's education.*

Analyses and Procedure

Table 4.1 presents a descriptive look at the percentage distributions of sample demographic characteristics by race. Table 4.2 addresses the first research question (the relation between sexual debut and family structure) by reporting the risk of sexual debut by family structure. The logistic regression models here compare the odds of transition to first intercourse for adolescents living in two-biological-parent households with those of adolescents living in remarried stepfamilies, first-marriage stepfamilies, cohabiting households, maritally disrupted single-mother families, and never-married single-mother families. An interaction term for race and gender is also included. Table 4.3 addresses the second research question (differences between blacks and whites in the relation between sexual debut and family structure) by reporting regressions estimated separately for blacks and whites to compare the odds of sexual debut by family structure. Tables 4.4 and 4.5 address the third research question (the extent to which differences in parental support and discipline account for family-structure variation in the risk of sexual debut). The risk of sexual debut is estimated separately for two-parent and single-parent households to determine whether maternal and paternal support and control operate similarly in these households. Separate analyses for black and white adolescents are also presented to test whether the expected relations between family structure and sexual debut operate in a similar way for these groups.

FIGURE 4.1   *Percentage of Respondents Initiating Intercourse by Age, Race, and Gender, Weighted*

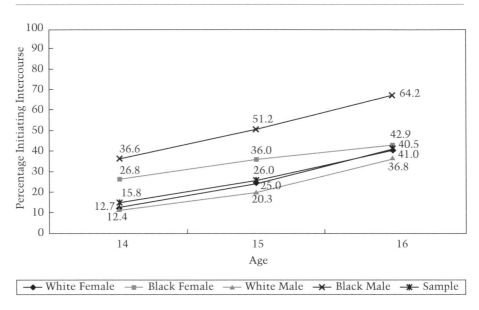

Source: Author's compilation.

Results

Twenty-seven percent of the sample initiated intercourse. The age-graded nature of sexual debut is illustrated in figure 4.1: with each age, the proportion of respondents initiating intercourse increases. Consistent with other research (Zelnick and Shah 1983; McLanahan and Sandefur 1994; Zabin et al. 1981; Michael and Bickert, chapter 5 in this volume), black adolescents report higher rates of initiation at earlier ages when compared to whites, but the proportion of white males and black and white females initiating sexual intercourse begins to converge at age sixteen, when youths approach late adolescence. However, for every age in the sample, black males report the highest rates of sexual debut, and these findings persist in logistic regression models controlling for family structure, household income, mother's education, and other background characteristics.

Looking at bivariate analyses by sexual debut in table 4.1, we see that respondents who have initiated sexual intercourse are less likely to live with two biological parents (49 versus 69 percent) and report less-strict and less-supportive parents. They are twice as likely to be black and poor (income-needs ratio less than or equal to one), to be older, and to have a less highly educated mother. Girls who have initiated sexual intercourse are also more likely to have experienced early pubertal maturation. When sample characteristics for blacks and whites are compared, blacks are significantly more likely to live in cohabiting households, first-marriage stepfamilies, and both types of single-parent families. They are more likely to report a strict mother (59 versus 50 percent) and less likely to report a highly supportive father (61 versus 67 percent). Black females are more likely to report early pubertal development while black boys are more likely to report later development. Blacks are more likely to be poor and to have mothers with less than a high school degree, although the proportion of mothers in black and white households with twelve years of schooling is slightly higher in black families.

The study's first main objective is to compare the risk of sexual debut by family structure, and table 4.2 shows this relation controlling for individual and family-background characteristics. In model 1, the control variables all relate to sexual debut in the expected direction. In addition, all family types are associated with increased odds of sexual debut when compared to households with two biological parents. For example, the probability of sexual debut is 90 percent greater for teenagers in remarried stepfamilies and 66 percent greater for those in never-married single-mother families. However, the odds of sexual debut are not *significantly* greater for adolescents in first-marriage stepfamilies, implying that their risk of sexual debut is statistically similar to that of youths living with two biological parents. Employing tests of equality between subsets of coefficients in model 1, the probability of sexual debut is significantly lower for youths in first-marriage stepfamilies than for those in cohabiting households ($p = .050$). None of the other coefficients are significantly different from each other or decrease in significance when the race by gender interaction term is incorporated into the model. However, the significance of this interaction in model 2 means that the odds of sexual debut are significantly lower for black females than for black males. In addition, the race variable indicates that the odds of sexual debut are 2.9 times greater for black males than for white males.

Table 4.3 presents models similar to those used in table 4.2, but it examines the family-structure relations separately for black and white youths. Beginning with the white sample, the odds of sexual debut are significantly higher for adolescents in every alternative household structure than they are for teenagers living with two biological parents. In particular, sexual debut is twice as likely for adolescents in remarried stepfamilies and three times as likely for those in cohabiting households compared to those in two-biological-parent households. Both never-married and maritally disrupted

(*Text continues on p. 124.*)

TABLE 4.1   Descriptive Sample Characteristics, by Sexual Debut and Race

	Sample (N = 3,727)	Percentage Initiated (N = 1,081)	Percentage Abstained (N = 2,646)	Whites (N = 2,624)	Blacks (N = 1,103)
Initiated intercourse	.27	.00	1.00***	.24	.43***
Family structure					
Two biological parents	.63	.49	.69***	.68	.40***
Remarried household	.09	.13	.08***	.09	.08
First-marriage stepfamily	.02	.03	.02	.02	.04***
Cohabiting household[a]	.03	.05	.02***	.02	.05***
Never married single parent	.05	.08	.04***	.03	.19***
Maritally disrupted single parent	.18	.23	.16***	.16	.25***
Parental support and discipline					
Mother is strict	.51	.45	.53***	.50	.59***
Father is strict[b]	.56	.51	.57**	.56	.59
Mother is highly supportive	.80	.74	.82***	.80	.80
Father is highly supportive[b]	.66	.52	.71***	.67	.61*
Background characteristics					
Black	.16	.26	.13***	.00	1.00
Female	.49	.49	.49	.50	.48
Age fourteen	.34	.19	.39***	.35	.33
Age fifteen	.34	.32	.35	.36	.34

Age sixteen	.32	.49	.26***	.29	.33*
Early pubertal development (females)	.13	.17	.11***	.11	.21***
Late pubertal development (males)	.06	.06	.06	.05	.12***
Income-need categories					
Poor (0 to 1.00)	.10	.16	.08***	.10	.23***
Near poor (1.01 to 3.00)	.31	.34	.30*	.31	.31
Not poor (3.01 to high)	.36	.29	.39***	.38	.18***
Missing income-needs ratio	.23	.21	.23	.21	.28***
Mother's education					
Less than high school	.15	.21	.13***	.17	.24***
High school graduate	.36	.41	.34***	.35	.39
Some college	.26	.22	.27***	.25	.22*
College graduate	.20	.13	.23***	.21	.10***
Missing mother's education	.03	.03	.02+	.02	.05***

Source: Author's compilation.
Note: Weighted percentages and unweighted N.
[a] No biological father in this household structure.
[b] Asked only of respondents living in two-parent households.
* $p < .05$. ** $p < .01$. *** $p < .001$.
+ $p < .10$.

TABLE 4.2   *Logistic Regressions Predicting Odds of Sexual Debut by Family Structure for Entire Sample (Weighted)*

Variables	Model 1 B (S.E.)	Model 1 Odds Ratios	Model 2 B (S.E.)	Model 2 Odds Ratios
Bio parents (omitted)				
Remarried	.6440 (.1288)	**1.90*****	.6371 (.1292)	**1.89*****
First-marriage step	.3206 (.2622)	1.38	.3524 (.2621)	1.42
Cohabiting	.8811 (.2166)	**2.41*****	.8665 (.2176)	**2.38*****
Never-married single	.5097 (.1713)	**1.66****	.5503 (.1726)	**1.73*****
Maritally disrupted single	.5833 (.1049)	**1.79*****	.5889 (.1054)	**1.80*****
Black	.6207 (.1049)	**1.86*****	1.0705 (.1404)	**2.92*****
Female × black	. . .		−.9610 (.2002)	0.38***
Female	−.1083 (.0831)	0.90	.0687 (.0909)	1.07
Age fifteen	.6483 (.1041)	1.91***	.6537 (.1045)	1.92***
Age sixteen	1.3741 (.1012)	3.95***	1.3807 (.1016)	3.98***
Early menstruation	.4107 (.1572)	1.51**	.4629 (.1564)	1.59**
Late puberty (males)	−.0159 (.2320)	0.98	−.1191 (.2393)	0.89
Poor	.3351 (.1441)	1.40*	.3480 (.1447)	1.42*
Near poor	.1279 (.1012)	1.14	.1345 (.1016)	1.14
Missing income	.0037 (.1111)	1.00	.0139 (.1115)	1.01
Mother < H.S.	.1776 (.1143)	1.19	.1872 (.1147)	1.21
Mother some college	−.3454 (.1026)	0.71***	−.3614 (.1031)	0.70***
Mother college grad.	−.5290 (.1195)	0.59***	−.5307 (.1198)	0.59***

TABLE 4.2   *Continued*

Variables	Model 1		Model 2	
	B (S.E.)	Odds Ratios	B (S.E.)	Odds Ratios
Missing mother ed.	.0888 (.2402)	1.09	.0728 (.2420)	1.08
Constant	−1.9743***		−2.0729***	
−2LL	3,938.735***		3,915.356***	
d.f.	18		19	
Change in −2LL			23.379***	
N	3,727		3,727	

Source: Author's compilation.
Note: Significant relations for family-structure variables are in boldface type.
* *p* < .05 (two tailed). ** *p* < .01 (two tailed). *** *p* < .001 (two tailed).

TABLE 4.3   *Logistic Regressions Predicting Odds of Sexual Debut by Family Structure for Whites and Blacks Separately (Weighted)*

Variables	Whites		Blacks	
	B (S.E.)	Odds Ratios	B (S.E.)	Odds Ratios
Bio parents (omitted)				
Remarried	.7229 (.1397)	**2.06***	.1052 (.3403)	1.11
First-marriage step.	.2010 (.3336)	1.22	.6400 (.4513)	1.90
Cohabiting	1.0980 (.2544)	**3.00***	.3424 (.4113)	1.41
Never-married single	.4912 (.2532)	**1.63***	.5243 (.2547)	**1.69***
Maritally disrup. single	.5712 (.1214)	**1.77***	.6960 (.2241)	**2.01***
Female	.0584 (.0928)	1.06	−.8653 (.1977)	0.42***
Age fifteen	.7022 (.1213)	2.02***	.4841 (.2191)	1.62*
Age sixteen	1.4878 (.1163)	4.43***	.9580 (.2210)	2.61***
Early menstruation	.4789 (.1818)	1.61**	.3297 (.3131)	1.39

(*Table continues on p. 124.*)

TABLE 4.3   *Continued*

Variables	Whites B (S.E.)	Whites Odds Ratios	Blacks B (S.E.)	Blacks Odds Ratios
Late puberty (males)	−.2750 (.3261)	0.76	.0201 (.3777)	1.02
Poor	.2258 (.1749)	1.25	.7373 (.3053)	2.09*
Near poor	.1062 (.1109)	1.11	.3350 (.2754)	1.40
Missing income	.0331 (.1233)	1.03	.0927 (.2774)	1.10
Mother < H.S.	.2071 (.1337)	1.23	.1459 (.2288)	1.16
Mother some college	−.3980 (.1151)	0.67***	−.1925 (.2391)	0.82
Mother college grad.	−.5615 (.1295)	0.57***	−.2818 (.3323)	0.75
Missing mother ed.	.5003 (.2888)	1.65†	−.5990 (.4284)	0.55
Constant	−2.1197***		−.9596**	
−2LL	3,139.939***		752.400***	
d.f.	17		17	
N	2,624		1,103	

Source: Author's compilation.
Note: Significant relations for family-structure variables are in boldface type.
* $p < .05$ (two tailed). ** $p < .01$ (two tailed). *** $p < .001$ (two tailed).
† $p < .10$ (two tailed).

single-parent households are also related to higher odds of sexual debut when compared to two-biological-parent households. In analyses employing tests of equality between coefficients, the risk of sexual debut is significantly greater for white adolescents in cohabiting households than for those in maritally disrupted single-parent families ($p = .026$), first-marriage step-families ($p = .014$), or remarried stepfamilies ($p = .026$). The risk of sexual debut was not significantly different when comparing youths in first-marriage stepfamilies with those in two-biological-parent households, and it was lower for adolescents in first-marriage stepfamilies than for those in remarried stepfamilies ($p = .069$) or cohabiting households ($p = .014$).

The relations between family structure and sexual debut are not as clear for black adolescents. Although the odds of sexual debut are significantly greater for teenagers in never-married and maritally disrupted single-parent families than they are for those living with two biological parents (1.69 and 2.01, respectively), the risk of sexual debut is not significantly greater for adolescents living in any of the alternative two-parent families. Moreover, the odds of sexual debut are significantly greater for youths in maritally disrupted single-parent families than they are for those in re-married stepfamilies ($p = .050$). That the risk of sexual debut is greater for whites in alternative two-parent family structures but not African Americans supports the hypothesis that, for the latter, living in a two-parent family, even one that does not consist of two biological parents, may be associated with a decreased risk of early adult transitions and acting-out behavior when compared to living in a single-parent household.

The final research objective is to see whether high levels of parental support and discipline reduce the effect of family structure on the risk of sexual debut. Table 4.4 presents the logistic regressions predicting sexual debut for adolescents in *two-parent households* only, with separate models by race.

Beginning with whites, family structure operates in a way similar to that in which it operates in table 4.3, with the risk of sexual debut significantly greater for teens in remarried stepfamilies and cohabiting households. Model 2 incorporates the four parenting measures and allows a first look at the mediating effect of the parenting variables on sexual debut. For white adolescents, having strict and highly supportive mothers and highly supportive fathers, but not strict fathers, is associated with reduced odds of sexual debut. While the introduction of these parenting measures reduces the effect of the alternative family structures on sexual debut, their significant negative association with sexual debut remains. Model 3 interacts the paternal parenting measures with family structure and shows the differential effect of paternal support and strictness on sexual debut for youth with different types of father figures. Among remarried stepfamilies, the odds of sexual debut are significantly higher for white adolescents living with step-fathers who are strict (2.82) and highly supportive (2.60) than for those living with stepfathers who are not strict and not very supportive. This finding is consistent with other research finding that children resist any type of parenting by stepfathers in remarried households, even when the parenting style is firm and supportive, a style considered optimal for white youths (Bray 1999; Avenevoli, Sessa, and Steinberg 1999). However, strict and supportive parenting by the stepfather appears to work well with youths in first-marriage stepfamilies, who are *less* likely to report sexual debut when they also report this type of parenting by their stepfathers. That this relationship operates in an opposite direction for stepfathers in remarried and first-marriage stepfamilies suggests a qualitative difference in the way parenting is received by youths in these two family forms.

The interactions between parenting style and sexual debut work differently for African American adolescents. In model 2 of table 4.4, the odds of

TABLE 4.4 Logistic Regressions Predicting the Odds of Sexual Debut in Two-Parent Households, Separate Models for Whites and Blacks (Weighted)

| | Whites | | | | | | Blacks | | | | | |
| | Model 1 | | Model 2 | | Model 3 | | Model 1 | | Model 2 | | Model 3 | |
Variables	B (S.E.)	Odds Ratio	B (S.E.)	Odds Ratio	B (S.E.)	Odds Ratio	B (S.E.)	Odds Ratio	B (S.E.)	Odds Ratio	B (S.E.)	Odds Ratio
Bio. parents (omitted)												
Remarried	.7426 (.1416)	2.10***	.5894 (.1447)	1.80***	-.4192 (.2691)	0.66	.0887 (.3534)	1.09	.0753 (.3711)	1.08	-.2820 (.6103)	0.75
First-marriage step.	.2625 (.3336)	1.30	.0113 (.3425)	1.01	1.1238 (.6738)	3.08†	.6863 (.4880)	1.99	.6758 (.4983)	1.97	.7674 (1.1122)	2.15
Cohabiting	.8595 (.3421)	2.36*	.7675 (.3459)	2.15*	-.2226 (.5631)	0.80	-.1740 (.4753)	1.19	-.0147 (.4972)	0.99	.5166 (.8645)	1.68
Mother strict	...		-.2236 (.1130)	0.80*	-.1798 (.1145)	0.84	...		-.7176 (.2902)	0.49*	-.7082 (.2949)	0.49*
Mother support	...		-.4565 (.1334)	0.63***	-.4417 (.1346)	0.64***	...		-.2978 (.3503)	0.74	-.2275 (.3568)	0.80
Father strict	...		-.1066 (.1132)	0.90	-.2741 (.1257)	0.76*	...		-.0129 (.2914)	0.99	.0416 (.3423)	1.04
Father support	...		-.6125 (.1147)	0.54***	-.7747 (.1270)	0.46***	...		-.6365 (.2790)	0.53*	-.7755 (.3311)	0.46*
Remarried × father strict	...		...		1.0360 (.2915)	2.82***	...		...		.5780 (.7455)	1.78

	(1)	(2)	(3)		(4)	(5)	(6)	
1st-marr. step. × father strict	…	…	-1.2591 (.8122)	.28	…	…	.4323 (.9895)	1.54
Cohab. × father strict	…	…	.6917 (.7135)	2.00	…	…	-.4404 (1.0849)	.64
Remarried × father support	…	…	.9540 (.2926)	**2.60**	…	…	.2688 (.7492)	1.31
1st-marr. step. × father support	…	…	-1.7578 (1.0197)	**.17†**	…	…	-.4867 (1.092)	.61
Cohab. × father support	…	…	1.3368 (.7020)	**3.81†**	…	…	-1.0965 (1.2008)	.33
Constant	-2.1660***	-1.2746***	-1.1318***		-.8454*	.2860	.2540	
-2LL	2,410.919***	2,344.422***	2,310.425***		384.685***	370.889***	368.779***	
d.f.	15	19	25		15	19	25	
Change in model chi-square	66.497***		33.997***			13.796***	2.11	
N	2,082	2,082	2,082		578	578	578	

Source: Author's compilation.

Note: Significant relations for family-structure variables are in boldface types. Models control for gender, age, pubertal development, income-needs ratio, and mothers' education.

* $p < .05$ (two tailed). ** $p < .01$ (two tailed). *** $p < .05$ (two tailed).
† $p < .10$ (two tailed).

sexual debut are reduced for youths who report having strict mothers and highly supportive fathers. Model 3 indicates a 54 percent lower probability of sexual debut for youths with biological fathers who are highly supportive. However, none of the interactions between father type and paternal support and strictness in alternative households are significantly related to the onset of sexual activity. These results suggest that the existing measures of parental support and discipline may not adequately capture the relation between parenting style and sexual debut for African American youths in alternative two-parent families. Alternatively, paternal support may be most protective when received from the biological father.

Table 4.5 addresses the effect of highly supportive mothers on sexual debut for youths in *single-mother* families. The probability of sexual debut does not significantly differ between youths in never-married and those in maritally disrupted single-mother families. For both white and black adolescents, having a highly supportive mother is associated with lower odds of sexual debut, regardless of family type (model 2). However, for whites, having a strict mother is a protective factor against sexual debut in maritally disrupted households (odds ratio = .58), while for blacks, strict mothering is protective in never-married households (odds ratio = .41). Thus it appears as though strict parenting relates differently to adolescent sexual outcomes for blacks and whites in the two types of single-mother families.

Discussion

This study examined the associations between race, family structure, parenting behaviors, and adolescent sexual debut. Looking at adolescents in six family types, it was shown that the relation between family structure and sexual debut differs by race. For white youths, the odds of sexual debut were significantly greater for those in remarried stepfamilies, cohabiting households, and never-married and maritally disrupted single-parent families compared to those in two-biological-parent families. The risk of sexual debut was also higher for youths in cohabiting households compared to those in first-marriage or remarried stepfamilies. The greater risk of sexual debut for youths in cohabiting households could suggest a modeling of nonmarital sexual behavior as appropriate or acceptable. However, the meaning of living in a cohabiting family, a remarried stepfamily, or a first-marriage stepfamily varies with specific cultural or social contexts. For black adolescents, living in never-married and maritally disrupted single-parent families, but not in any of the alternative two-parent forms, was significantly related to the onset of sexual activity. Given that black children are proportionately more likely to spend time in single-parent households and to live in neighborhoods that are at least to some degree disadvantaged, the presence of an

TABLE 4.5   Logistic Regressions Predicting the Odds of Sexual Debut in Single-Parent Households, Separate Models for Whites and Blacks (Weighted)

	Whites						Blacks					
	Model 1		Model 2		Model 3		Model 1		Model 2		Model 3	
Variables	B (S.E.)	Odds Ratio	B (S.E.)	Odds Ratio	B (S.E.)	Odds Ratio	B (S.E.)	Odds Ratio	B (S.E.)	Odds Ratio	B (S.E.)	Odds Ratio
Never married Household	−.1379 (.2768)	0.87	−.1710 (.2787)	0.84	−.2001 (.5421)	0.82	−.0474 (.2761)	0.95	−.0574 (.2791)	0.94	.1654 (.6618)	1.18
Mother highly supportive	…		−.5643 (.2245)	**0.57***	−.5378 (.2434)	**0.58***	…		−.6766 (.3396)	**0.51***	−.7755 (.4438)	**0.46†**
Mother strict	…		−.3421 (.2035)	**0.71†**	−.4056 (.2194)	**0.67†**	…		−.3333 (.2662)	0.72	.0480 (.3560)	1.05
Nevermar × mother very support.	…		…		−.1922 (.6046)	0.83	…		…		.3042 (.6577)	1.36
Nevermar × mother strict	…		…		.4570 (.5689)	1.58	…		…		−.9006 (.5451)	**0.41†**
Constant	−1.2203***		−.6854†		−.6906†		−.1656		.5348		.4173	
−2LL	655.791***		646.355***		645.639***		342.531***		337.072***		334.055***	
d.f.	13		15		17		13		15		17	
Change in model chi-square			9.436**		.716				5.459†		3.017	
N	505		505		505		508		508		508	

Source: Author's compilation.
Note: Significant relations for family structure variables are in boldface types. Models control for gender, age, pubertal development, income-need ratio, and maternal education.
* $p < .05$ (two tailed). ** $p < .01$ (two tailed). *** $p < .001$ (two tailed).
† $p < .10$ (two tailed).

additional adult in the household could reduce the negative effect of a marital transition in remarried stepfamilies and act as a model of nonmarital sexual behavior in cohabiting households.

For white and black adolescents, having strict and highly supportive mothers was generally associated with a lower risk of sexual debut in both two-parent and single-parent households. In black households, having a strict mother reduced the risk of sexual debut in never-married single-parent families, while in white single-mother households, strict mothers were protective in maritally disrupted families.

Strict and highly supportive fathers were also generally associated with a lower risk of sexual debut for adolescents in both racial groups. However, for white youths, this relation was attenuated by type of father figure. While strict and supportive parenting from biological fathers was related to a lower probability of sexual debut, this same type of parenting from stepfathers in remarried stepfamilies was associated with a significantly *greater* risk of intercourse. This finding is consistent with the literature on parenting across family structures (Bray 1999). It appears as though most parenting efforts by stepfathers in remarried stepfamilies are likely to be rebuffed, at least initially, as youths adjust to the replacement of the biological father in the home. However, studies suggest that, over time, the stepfather is gradually accepted as an authority figure and his parenting efforts received more positively.

The risk of sexual debut for white adolescents in first-marriage stepfamilies was also related to father's strictness and support, but in the opposite direction. Having strict and highly supportive fathers in first-marriage stepfamilies related to a lower odds of sexual debut, although the relations were not statistically significant. That firm yet supportive parenting operates in a similarly protective way in first-marriage stepfamilies and two-biological-parent households and in a substantively different way in remarried stepfamilies provokes intriguing questions about diversity in family processes and relationship quality between the two stepfamily forms. For example, how do children perceive the arrival of a stepfather when the biological father has never lived in the home or has played a minimal role in child rearing? How might marital transitions (or the absence thereof) affect the effectiveness of the stepfather's parenting? A better understanding of the nature and the quality of the parenting provided by father figures is certainly called for.

Having a strict mother was associated with a reduced risk of sexual debut in African American two-parent households, while having a highly supportive father significantly reduced the odds of sexual debut. Interactions with father figures did not significantly improve the model. The differential effects of father's parenting between black and white youths invite further study of racial and ethnic differences in parenting styles and the relation between different parenting styles and adolescent behavior. These associations also support the further examination of *intraracial* differences in the role and meaning of father figures and parenting styles within families.

The findings of this study suggest the need for further investigations of racial and ethnic differences in the meaning and nature of social interaction in alternative two-parent households as well as of the influence of those differences on adolescent behavior. The relation between family structure and risk of teenage sexual debut may depend on the time that has elapsed since the marital transition, the community context in which the family lives, and the quality of the relationships among household members. The findings of this study also suggest the need for work that provides a better understanding of the role that the father figure plays in the lives of children in alternative two-parent households and the extent to which that role varies with the position that he occupies in the household (for example, mother's partner in a cohabiting household or stepfather in a remarried stepfamily) as well as with the types of family structure and the marital transitions that the family has experienced previously (for example, first-marriage or remarried stepfamilies).

Data from the second round of the NLSY97 will allow for the development of models that make use of family environment at time 1 as a predictor of the onset of sexual intercourse at time 2, thus establishing a more direct causal relation between household structure, parenting behaviors, and sexual debut. However, the present correlational analyses provide a preliminary if incomplete understanding of the intricate associations between family structure, parental discipline and support, and risk of sexual debut in mid-adolescence. Results from the first wave of data suggest associations between parent-child relationships and sexual activity during adolescence that are important for future study.

This research was supported by a grant from the Ford Foundation received while I was a fellow at the Program on Poverty and Social Policy at the University of Michigan and a grant from the Russell Sage Foundation in support of the NLSY97 Early Results Conference. I thank Sandra Smith for comments on an earlier draft.

Notes

1. The terms *family structure, household structure,* and *family type* are used interchangeably.

2. The ability to measure first-marriage stepfamilies and cohabiting households is a relatively unique feature of the National Longitudinal Survey of Youth, 1997 Cohort, data.

3. Twelve percent of black but only 4 percent of white unions with children are cohabiting partnerships (Manning and Lichter 1996).

4. Between 1980 and 1984, 13 percent of black nonmarital births and 10 percent of white nonmarital births were actually born into cohabiting unions (Bumpass and Raley 1995, 101, table 1 [column 5 subtracted from column 6]).

5. It should be noted that half these stepfamilies represented first marriages for the biological mother.

6. Of course, this does not apply to never-married single-parent families unless a cohabiting union preceded the single-parent state.

7. The data are weighted using the SAMPLING_WEIGHT variable, which weighs all respondents to give a national representation.

8. Differences in sample size among essays in this volume reflect differences in sample-selection criteria. For example, since I focus on black-white differences, I exclude Hispanics, but Michael and Bickert (chapter 5 in this volume) include them. Again, whereas both I and Michael and Bickert limit our samples to respondents aged fourteen and older, this being the group that was asked about sexual initiation, the age composition of samples utilized by Pierret (chapter 1 in this volume) differs depending on the outcome examined.

9. Percentages are based on weighted data.

10. Eight cases of an adoptive father in the household have been collapsed into either the *remarried family* or *first-marriage stepfamily* categories, depending on mother's marital history.

11. In neither case is the respondent's biological father in the home.

12. A parent interview was not conducted for 12 percent of youth respondents, so income information is missing for these cases. In addition, 11 percent of parents interviewed did not provide income information, bringing the total proportion of respondents for whom income information is missing to 23 percent. Regression analyses control for missing income information.

References

Amato, Paul R. 1994. "The Implications of Research Findings on Children and Stepfamilies." In *Stepfamilies: Who Benefits? Who Does Not?* edited by Alan Booth and J. Dunn. Hillsdale, N.J.: Erlbaum.

———. 1998. "More Than Money? Men's Contributions to Their Children's Lives." In *Men in Families: When Do They Get Involved? What Difference Does It Make?* edited by Alan Booth and Ann C. Crouter. Hillsdale, N.J.: Erlbaum.

Astone, Nan Marie, and Sara McLanahan. 1991. "Family Structure, Parental Practices, and High School Completion." *American Sociological Review* 56(3): 309–20.

Avenevoli, Shelli, Frances M. Sessa, and Laurence Steinberg. 1999. "Family Structure, Parenting Practices, and Adolescent Adjustment: An Ecological Examination." In *Coping with Divorce, Single Parenting, and Marriage: A Risk and Resiliency Perspective*, edited by E. Mavis Hetherington. Hillsdale, N.J.: Erlbaum.

Bray, James H. 1999. "From Marriage to Remarriage and Beyond: Findings from the Developmental Issues in Stepfamilies Research Project." In *Coping with Divorce, Single Parenting, and Marriage: A Risk and Resiliency Perspective*, edited by E. Mavis Hetherington. Hillsdale, N.J.: Erlbaum.

Brooks-Gunn, Jeanne. 1988. "Antecedents and Consequences of Variation in Girls' Maturational Timing." *Journal of Adolescent Health* 9(5): 365–73.

Bumpass, Larry. 1995. "The Declining Significance of Marriage: Changing Family Life in the United States." *National Survey of Families and Households* working paper 66. Madison: University of Wisconsin, Center for Demography and Ecology.

Bumpass, Larry, and Sara McLanahan. 1989. "Unmarried Motherhood: Recent Trends, Composition, and Black-White Differences." *Demography* 26(2): 279–86.

Bumpass, Larry, and R. Kelly Raley. 1995. "Redefining Single-Parent Families: Cohabitation and Changing Family Reality." *Demography* 32(1): 97–109.

Bumpass, Larry, R. Kelly Raley, and James Sweet. 1995. "The Changing Character of Stepfamilies: Implications of Cohabitation and Nonmarital Childbearing." *Demography* 32(4): 425–36.

Bumpass, Larry, and James Sweet. 1989. "Children's Experience in Single-Parent Families: Implications of Cohabitation and Marital Transitions." *Family Planning Perspectives* 21(6): 256–60.

Center for Human Resources. 1998. *NLSY97 User's Guide: A Guide to the Round 1 Data of the National Longitudinal Survey of Youth, 1997*. Columbus: Ohio State University.

Chase-Lansdale, P. Lindsay, Andrew Cherlin, and Kathleen E. Kiernan. 1995. "The Long-Term Effects of Parental Divorce on the Mental Health of Young Adults." *Child Development* 66(6): 1614–34.

Chase-Lansdale, P. Lindsay, and E. Mavis Hetherington. 1990. "The Impact of Divorce on Life-Span Development: Short and Long Term Effects." In *Life-Span Development and Behavior 10*, edited by P. Blates, D. Featherman, and R. Lerner. Hillsdale, N.J.: Erlbaum.

Cowan, Philip A., and E. Mavis Hetherington. 1991. *Family Transitions*. Hillsdale, N.J.: Erlbaum.

Danziger, Sandra K. 1995. "Family Life and Teenage Pregnancy in the Inner-City: Experiences of African-American Youth." *Children and Youth Services Review* 17(1/2): 183–202.

Dornbusch, S. M., J. M. Carlsmith, S. J. Bushwall, P. L. Ritter, H. Leiderman, A. H. Hastorf, and R. T. Gross. 1985. "Single Parents, Extended Households, and the Control of Adolescents." *Child Development* 56(2): 310–30.

Furstenberg, Frank, and Andrew Cherlin. 1991. *Divided Families: What Happens to Children When Parents Part.* Cambridge, Mass.: Harvard University Press.

Hetherington, E. Mavis. 1987. "Family Relations Six Years after Divorce." In *Remarriage and Stepparenting: Current Research and Theory*, edited by K. Pasley and M. Ihinger-Tallman. New York: Guilford.

———, editor. 1999. *Coping with Divorce, Single Parenting, and Marriage: A Risk and Resiliency Perspective.* Hillsdale, N.J.: Erlbaum.

Hetherington, E. Mavis, Martha Cox, and Roger Cox. 1982. "Effects of Divorce on Parents and Children." In *Nontraditional Families: Parenting and Child Development*, edited by Michael Lamb. Hillsdale, N.J.: Erlbaum.

Hogan, Dennis, and Evelyn Kitagawa. 1985. "The Impact of Social Status, Family Structure, and Neighborhood on the Fertility of Black Adolescents." *American Journal of Sociology* 90(4): 825–55.

Ihinger-Tallman, Marilyn. 1988. "Research on Stepfamilies." *American Review of Sociology* 14(1): 25–48.

Katchadourian, Herant. 1990. "Sexuality." In *At the Threshold: The Developing Adolescent*, edited by S. Feldman and G. Elliott. Cambridge, Mass.: Harvard University Press.

Landale, Nancy, and Renata Forste. 1991. "Patterns of Entry into Cohabitation and Marriage among Mainland Puerto Rican Women." *Demography* 28(4): 587–607.

Manning, Wendy, and Daniel T. Lichter. 1996. "Parental Cohabitation and Children's Economic Well-Being." *Journal of Marriage and the Family* 58(4): 998–1010.

Manning, Wendy, and Pamela Smock. 1995. "Why Marry? Race and the Transition to Marriage among Cohabitors." *Demography* 32(4): 509–20.

McLanahan, Sara. 1988. "Family Structure and Dependency: Early Transition to Female Household Headship." *Demography* 25(1): 1–16.

McLanahan, Sara, and Lynne Casper. 1995. "Growing Diversity and Inequality in the American Family." In *State of the Union: America in the 1990s*, edited by Reynolds Farley. New York: Russell Sage Foundation.

McLanahan, Sara, and Gary Sandefur. 1994. *Growing Up with a Single Parent: What Hurts, What Helps.* Cambridge, Mass.: Harvard University Press.

Moore, Mignon R., and P. Lindsay Chase-Lansdale. 2001. "Sexual Intercourse and Pregnancy among African-American Adolescent Girls in High-Poverty Neighborhoods: The Role of Family and Perceived Community Environment." *Journal of Marriage and Family* 63(4).

Mott, Frank L. 1990. "When Is a Father Really Gone? Paternal-Child Contact in Father-Absent Homes." *Demography* 27(4): 499–517.

Newcomer, Susan, and J. Richard Udry. 1984. "Mothers' Influence on the Sexual Behavior of Their Teenage Children." *Journal of Marriage and the Family* 46(2): 477–85.

Orbuch, Terri L., Joseph Veroff, and Andrea G. Hunter. 1999. "Black Couples, White Couples: The Early Years of Marriage." In *Coping with Divorce, Single-Parenting, and Marriage: A Risk and Resiliency Perspective,* edited by E. Mavis Hetherington. Hillsdale, N.J.: Erlbaum.

Pittman, Laura, and P. Lindsay Chase-Lansdale. In press. "African-American Adolescent Girls in Impoverished Communities: Parenting Styles and Adolescent Outcomes." *Journal of Research on Adolescence.*

Raley, Kelly. 1996. "A Shortage of Marriageable Men? A Note on the Role of Cohabitation in Black-White Differences in Marriage Rates." *American Sociological Review* 61(6): 973–83.

Schoen, Robert, and Dawn Owens. 1992. "A Further Look at First Unions and First Marriages." In *The Changing American Family,* edited by Scott J. South and Stewart E. Tolnay. Boulder, Colo.: Westview.

Simons, Ronald L., Les B. Whitbeck, Jay Beaman, and Rand Conger. 1994. "The Impact of Mothers' Parenting, Involvement by Nonresidential Fathers, and Parental Conflict on the Adjustment of Adolescent Children." *Journal of Marriage and the Family* 56(2): 356–74.

Smock, Pamela J. 2000. "Cohabitation in the United States: An Appraisal of Research Themes, Findings, and Implications. *Annual Review of Sociology* 26(1): 1–20.

Steinberg, L. N. Mounts, S. Lamborn, and S. Dornbusch. 1991. "Authoritative Parenting and Adolescent Adjustment across Varied Ecological Niches." *Journal of Research on Adolescence* 1(1): 19–36.

Thomson, Elizabeth, L. Hanson, and Sara McLanahan. 1994. "Family Structure and Child Well-Being: Economic Resources versus Parental Behaviors." *Social Forces* 73(1): 221–42.

Thomson, Elizabeth, Sara McLanahan, and Roberta Braun Curtin. 1992. "Family Structure, Gender, and Parental Socialization." *Journal of Marriage and the Family* 54(2): 368–78.

Thornton, Arland, and Donald Camburn. 1987. "The Influence of the Family on Premarital Sexual Attitudes and Behavior." *Demography* 24(3): 323–40.

Udry, Richard, and Benjamin C. Cambell. 1994. "Getting Started on Sexual Behavior." In *Sexuality across the Life Course,* edited by A. S. Rossi. Chicago: University of Chicago Press.

Wojtkiewicz, Roger. 1992. "Diversity in Experiences of Parental Structure during Childhood and Adolescence." *Demography* 29(1): 59–68.

Wu, Lawrence, and Brian C. Martinson. 1993. "Family Structure and the Risk of a Premarital Birth." *American Sociological Review* 58(2): 210–32.

Wu, Lawrence, and Elizabeth Thomson. 1998. "Family Change and Early Sexual Initiation." *Institute for Research on Poverty* discussion paper 1165–98. University of Wisconsin, Madison.

Zabin, Laurie, John F. Kantner, and Melvin Zelnick. 1981. "The Risk of Adolescent Pregnancy in the First Months of Intercourse." In *Teenage Sexuality, Pregnancy, and Childbearing*, edited by Frank F. Furstenberg, Richard Lincoln, and Jane A. Menken. Philadelphia: University of Pennsylvania Press.

Zabin, Laurie S., Edward A. Smith, Marilyn B. Hirsch, and Janet B. Hardy. 1986. "Ages of Physical Maturation and First Intercourse in Black Teenage Males and Females." *Demography* 23(2): 245–57.

Zelnick, Melvin, and Farida K. Shah. 1983. "First Intercourse among Youth Americans." *Family Planning Perspectives* 15(2): 64–70.

5

Exploring Determinants of Adolescents' Early Sexual Behavior

Robert T. Michael and Courtney Bickert

A young person is likely to handle the availability of alcohol, drugs and sex in a reasonable manner if there is something in his or her life at stake . . . that competes successfully with those three pursuits, each of which has the attraction of immediate gratification and the inherent flaw of not being in the end a sufficient reason all by itself for continuing to struggle with life.
—Leon Botstein, *Jefferson's Children*

A YOUTH'S SEXUAL awakening and early experiences with partnered sexual interactions are among the most salient aspects of adolescence. These experiences can be benign, healthy, and natural, but, if mishandled, they can have profound negative consequences, seriously diminishing the prospects for a healthy and productive adulthood. Consequently, they are an important arena for social policy research.

In this essay, we explore the information about the dating and sexual behavior of fourteen- to sixteen-year-olds in the National Longitudinal Survey of Youth, 1997 Cohort (NLSY97) data set. Our objectives are the following: to describe a few of the patterns of dating and sexual behavior reported in this survey; to exploit a few questions in this data set to advance our understanding of linkages between the patterns of social dating and those of sexual behavior; and to test a hypothesis suggested elsewhere about why certain family-background characteristics have the widely observed, strong influence on adolescent sexual activity that they have. Since dating may be a gateway to sexual activity, it is of interest to explore how family-background characteristics influence each. By studying the first wave of these new longitudinal data, we hope to raise more questions than we answer so that we can frame an agenda for research over the next several years as the subsequent waves of data become available.

Conceptual Issues and Framing

There are substantial literatures in sociology and developmental psychology and a small literature in economics regarding the factors surrounding the initiation of sexual activity in adolescence. An important essay on the topic from a sociological perspective is Udry and Billy (1987). These authors suggest three forces that influence the onset of partnered sexual activity: the libido, or a biologically driven motivation; the social controls imposed by parents that influence the ease or difficulty with which the youth finds the time and the place to have sex; and the youth's attractiveness, meaning pubertal development and physical appearance. Udry and Billy argue that "adolescent coitus [represents] the failure of age-graded controls" (841); in effect, they see the adolescent as hardwired to be inclined to explore sex and inhibited from doing so by "controls" imposed by parents, peers, the community, and, importantly, the adolescent himself or herself. An alternative interpretation of the parents' role in both the persuasion and the mentoring of children is found in Thornton and Camburn (1987). For an insightful essay offering a broad conceptualization of adolescent sexuality and its control, see Nathanson (1991, chapter 1).

Empirical studies have shown that young women are more likely to become sexually active at an early age if they live with only one parent, if their mother is not highly educated, or if they themselves are not performing well in school and if the family income level is relatively low (Haurin and Mott 1990; Brewster, Billy, and Grady 1993; Moore, Peterson, and Furstenberg 1984; Marsiglio and Mott 1986; Cooksey, Rindfuss, and Guilkey 1996; Michael and Joyner 2001). Parent's education is an especially important factor affecting the initiation of sexual activity, and two ways in which that influence operates have been suggested. Cooksey, Rindfuss, and Guilkey (1996) stress the role that better-educated mothers play in the schooling of their children, including their sex education. Alternatively, Michael and Joyner (2001) argue that parent's education proxies youth career aspirations and that those with strong aspirations (that is, those with more highly educated parents) have a strong motivation to avoid pregnancy and so tend to avoid sex.

Many additional factors affecting the onset of sexual activity have been documented. For example, Udry (1988) demonstrates the effect of peer influence as well as of parent's supervision on eighth and tenth graders' patterns of early coitus as well as masturbation and thinking about sex. Brewster (1994) documents the effect of neighborhood characteristics (such as occupation structure and women's labor force activity) on black women's decision to engage in sexual activity at an early age. Working with data from the 1988 National Survey of Adolescent Males, Ku, Sonenstein, and Pleck (1993) find that unemployment generally, as well as the experience of unemployment in the immediate family, affects boys' sexual behavior and the likelihood that they will get their partner pregnant. One of the broad themes found in many essays on adolescent sexuality is the notion that, when faced with an uncertain future and potential or perceived failure in school or at work, adolescents find sexual activity and pregnancy to be attractive alternatives both because they are attainable and because they are indicators of adult status (see, for example, Brewster 1994; Geronimus 1987; Anderson 1989). As we have so far undertaken analyses only of partnered sexual activity, we do not review here the considerable literature on other dimensions of sexual activity among adolescents, including exposure to risk and the use of condoms and other means of fertility control.

Similarly, since we explore dating behavior primarily in order to obtain a better understanding of the influences on sexual behavior, we provide only a very brief summary of the extensive literature on dating. Dating is an important activity, one that signals that adolescents are maturing and that their interest in members of the opposite sex is growing, and a youth's dating behavior is surely related to his or her sexual behavior. Prompted by both hormones and peers, dating allows youths to explore the social dimensions of sexuality and come to terms with the physical changes taking place in their bodies. Studies have shown that the relative timing of pubertal development has important effects on dating and sexual behavior and that those effects differ both by gender and by race-ethnicity (Brooks-Gunn and Petersen 1983; Stattin and Magnussen 1990; Michael 1999). Similarly, it has been demonstrated that both violence and drinking in a dating relationship increase the likelihood of engaging in sexual activity (Pawlby, Mills, and Quinton 1997; Cooper and Orcutt 1997; Montgomery and Sorell 1998). Typical of the literature is Donovan (1995), a San Diego–based study of 384 young men and women aged fourteen to sixteen that found a significant correlation between sexual behavior and compliance with family rules regarding dating. Hanson, Morrison, and Ginsburg (1989) determined that "men who are more popular and date more often are more likely to report that their partners became pregnant or bore their children" (583). The reason? Men who date more are "exposed to greater peer pressures and opportunities to become sexually active" (582). Attractiveness is another variable often associated with the likelihood that a youth has opportunities to engage in sexual activity (Udry and Billy 1987), and this factor is also associated with dating.

The NLSY97 Data on Dating and Sexual Behavior

The NLSY97 included an extensive self-administered questionnaire (SAQ) given to the youths. Within that SAQ were modules on the dating experiences of the youths, asking whether they had ever been "on a date with a" boyfriend or girlfriend, the age at the first date, and the number of times they had dated in the past year. Also, for those aged fourteen and older on the sample day (December 31, 1996), a series of questions was asked about the youth's experience with sexual intercourse. The youth was first asked whether he or she had ever had sexual intercourse. If the response was yes, several further questions were asked, including the youth's age the first time he or she had sex, whether any form of birth control was used that first time, the number of partners with whom the youth had ever had intercourse, the number of partners within the past year, and the number of times he or she had had sexual intercourse in the past year. The responses to these questions constitute the primary information that we use in the empirical work reported in subsequent sections. Related information on the fertility experiences of the young women in the sample is not explored here (see Walker, chapter 7 in this volume).

Factors Associated with Ever Having Had Sexual Intercourse

Michael and Joyner (2001) suggest that five factors (expressed as deterrents) influence the decision to begin partnered sexual activity: a strong conviction that sex is inappropriate at a young age; the perception that the opportunity cost of having sex is very high (that is, that engaging in sexual activity risks some other valued life goal); a relatively low hormonal impetus, gauged by the late onset of puberty; close supervision (whether by parents or the social situation in general), restricting the opportunity to have sex; and peer pressure not to become sexually active and a social atmosphere stigmatizing those who do.

Michael and Joyner test the deterrent effects of these five factors in a study utilizing data on young women from the National Health and Social Life Survey (NHSLS). They find that parent's education has a strong effect on the likelihood that a young woman will begin to have sex early and take this to be an indication of the deterrent effect of the high opportunity cost of sex relative to other important life goals. They also find strong evidence that age at puberty has a robust effect on age at first sex. Their results further indicate that family structure influences the onset of sexual activity, living with both biological parents being strongly associated with a lesser likelihood of engaging in sexual activity at an early age (the mechanism here could be either close supervision and therefore limited opportunity or social stigmatization).[1] Finally, they find no evidence (although others have done so)[2] that religious affiliation influences the onset of sexual activity.

The strong negative relation between parent's education and likelihood of young age at first sex is one of the more widespread findings in the several literatures on adolescent sexual behavior. Michael and Joyner argue that young women with a better likelihood of attending college and getting a good job will see the risks associated with sexual activity as high (that is, as affecting life chances and personal agendas) and will therefore be less likely to engage in sexual activity at an early age. Parent's education is, Michael and Joyner argue, a good proxy for life goals, which would explain the strong negative association between parent's education and early adolescent sexual activity.

That parent's education proxies life goals and in that way influences youths remains, however, a conjecture; nothing in the NHSLS allows one to prove or refute it. The NLSY97, however, permits a deeper investigation of this point. First, the NLSY97 data provide a direct indicator of grades in the eighth grade, which is one indicator of prospects for higher education. Even more directly, the survey asks respondents to estimate their chances of having earned a college degree by age 30, which speaks directly to adolescents' perceptions of their own future and thus their perceptions of the opportunity cost of sexual activity. If the NLSY97 data show a strong relation between parent's education and age at first sex, and if adding controls for grades in the eighth grade and perceived chance of college graduation weakens the observed effect, we have evidence in support of the argument that parent's education proxies life goals, which in turn influences adolescent sexual behavior.

Many of the studies that find a strong effect of parent's education on youth sexual behavior, including Michael and Joyner's, do not consider the possible effect of the peer group with which the youth interacts. It could be that parent's education is acting as a proxy, not for the adolescent's life goals, but for the peer group's attributes or attitudes. Again, it will be useful to introduce controls into the analysis, and not just for peer group, but also for neighborhood environment, for which it is also likely that parent's education proxies.

Identifying the mechanism at work here is particularly important—and worth exploring in some depth—given the current social concern regarding teenage childbearing. Teens who become parents are more likely to drop out of school to take jobs. But, because their education (training) has been thus curtailed, the employment options available to them are limited. Should evidence indeed be found that adolescents who perceive themselves as having a bright future are more likely to avoid early sexual activity and the risks to long-term happiness that it entails, and that adolescents who perceive themselves as having a bleak future are more likely to engage in early sexual activity, effective interventions could be developed targeting those less-hopeful young people.

In the statistical model to which we now turn, we measure Michael and Joyner's five target factors. First, as a measure of the youth's conviction that sex is inappropriate at a young age, we use three dummy variables indicating that the youth is Catholic, or is non-Protestant, or has no religious affiliation (the default group is those who are Protestant). Second, as a measure that the opportunity cost of having sex is high, following Michael and Joyner we initially use a set of dummies indicating the highest level of schooling attained by either parent—completed high school, completed some college, or completed college (the default group is those whose parents did not complete high school). Subsequently, we add three variables that, we argue, capture the adolescent's sense of his or her future prospects: grade-point average in the eighth grade; self-reported chance of becoming a parent by age twenty; and self-reported chance of earning a college degree by age thirty.

Third, as a measure of maturation, we use a set of single year-of-age dummies and an indication of the age at which the youth experienced puberty. Fourth, as a measure of close supervision, we use two dummies indicating that the youth did not live with the biological mother–biological father. As indicators of the social environment and culture in which the youth resides, we use dummies for race (African American) and ethnicity (Hispanic), a dummy indicating whether the youth's mother was foreign born, and a geographic indicator of region of residence (South).

Fifth, as a measure of peer pressure, we code youths' responses to a set of nine questions about peers on the basis of an index (constructed for and used in Abe and Michael [1999])[3] ranging from –7 to +7. (The questions asked about the percentage of school peers who smoke, drink, use illegal drugs, go to church/synagogue, plan to go to college, do volunteer work, and so on.) The index is calibrated so as to give a value of +1 to a response indicating that peers are ranked among the best 20 percent on a given criteria, a value of –1 to a response indicating that peers are ranked among the worst 20 percent on a given criteria, and a value of 0 otherwise.

Table 5.1 shows the (weighted) summary statistics for the several variables used in the empirical analysis reported in the following section for young men and young women separately.[4] These variables are described in the appendix.

Empirical Results
Ever Having Had Sexual Intercourse

The key behavioral variable used in this section is *eversex*, a dummy variable equal to 1 if the youth has had sexual intercourse and 0 otherwise.

TABLE 5.1   *Summary Statistics, by Gender (Weighted)*

Variable	Boys		Girls	
	Mean	S.D.	Mean	S.D.
Eversex	0.30	0.46	0.29	0.45
Everdate	0.75	0.43	0.67	0.47
Age fourteen	0.22	0.41	0.22	0.42
Age fifteen	0.33	0.47	0.34	0.47
Age sixteen	0.34	0.47	0.32	0.47
Age seventeen	0.11	0.31	0.12	0.33
Age eighteen	0.00	0.07	0.00	0.05
Pubertyage	12.48	1.29	12.59	1.41
Mispuberty age	0.03	0.18	0.11	0.31
Parent ed hs	0.28	0.45	0.29	0.45
Parent ed scol	0.25	0.43	0.25	0.43
Parent ed col	0.28	0.45	0.27	0.44
Race black	0.16	0.36	0.16	0.46
Race other	0.12	0.32	0.11	0.31
Hispanic	0.14	0.34	0.12	0.33
Rel Catholic	0.27	0.44	0.24	0.43
Rel no Protestant	0.04	0.20	0.03	0.18
Rel none	0.15	0.36	0.13	0.34
Notmom	0.12	0.33	0.12	0.33
Notdad	0.39	0.49	0.44	0.50
Foreign mom	0.10	0.30	0.09	0.28
South	0.31	0.46	0.35	0.48
Chance college	0.66	0.26	0.73	0.23
Mis chance coll	0.43	0.49	0.43	0.50
Chance notparent	0.85	0.17	0.86	0.18
Mis chance npar	0.43	0.50	0.43	0.50
Grades8	2.69	0.72	3.00	0.67
Mis grades8	0.18	0.38	0.15	0.36
Peer index	0.05	3.19	−0.52	3.30
Mis peer index	0.00	0.04	0.00	0.06
Mom strict	1.58	1.65	1.75	1.86
Dad strict	1.21	1.49	1.12	1.51
Mom not strict	1.22	1.35	1.18	1.30
Dad not strict	1.07	1.53	1.07	1.55
N	2,695		2,611	

Source: Authors' compilation.

Nearly 30 percent of the youths in our sample have had sex. Table 5.2 shows the breakdown of that variable by single year of age since it has a steep gradient by age.[5] The rates reported in table 5.2 are broadly similar to, if somewhat lower than, those found in other data.[6]

Tables 5.3 and 5.4 show the results of estimating four logistic models on *eversex*, separately for boys and girls, with the coefficients expressed as effects on the odds ratios; thus, 1.00 is the default value. Consider the boys (table 5.3) first. In model 1, the basic control variables are included. One sees the rise in incidence of sex with age. The odds of a seventeen-year-old having had sex are 6.2 times as high as those of a fourteen-year-old. (Recall that there are only ten eighteen-year-old boys in the sample; we kept that age dummy variable in the model, but its lack of precision is surely a result of the tiny number of cases.) There is a strong effect of age of puberty—if puberty occurs one year later, the odds of having had sex by the time of the interview are substantially lower: 0.83. (Throughout, since there are sizable numbers of cases of missing information on items such as age at puberty, we assign those missing cases the mean value for the gender and include in our multivariate model a dummy variable indicating that, for that youth, the value was missing. These missing dummy variables are labeled with the prefix *mis-*.)

The very strong effect of parent's education on the likelihood of ever having had sex is seen here. The odds of having had sex decline systematically as the parents' level of education rises. The odds for a boy with a college-educated parent are only 0.39 as high as for a boy whose parents dropped out of high school. This is the relation that, on the basis of the evidence in other data sets, we expected to find, and we will return to it in subsequent discussion.

TABLE 5.2   *Percentage of Youths Who Have Ever Had Sexual Intercourse, Eversex, by Single Year of Age and Gender (Weighted)*

	Boys	Girls	All
All	30.5	28.6	29.5
Age fourteen	17.4	14.0	15.7
Age fifteen	25.9	24.2	25.0
Age sixteen	37.2	35.8	36.6
Age seventeen	49.8	48.5	49.1
Age eighteen	. . .	. . .	. . .

Source: Author's compilation.

144

Black boys have an odds ratio nearly three times that of white boys; boys of other races (nonwhite and nonblack) also have significantly higher odds than white boys do. The odds of Hispanic boys were not significantly different from those of white boys. Among the religion variables tested, only *none* has a positive association, which makes sense since none of the religions specified promote early sexual activity. Living in a household with only one biological parent raises the odds of the adolescent having had sex. Living in the South does so as well.

Model 2 adds to this first model the three indicators that we use for youths' perceptions of future prospects or aspirations. As the self-assessed chance of completing college by age thirty rises (*chance college*), the likelihood of having had sex declines dramatically. As the prediction of *not* being a parent by age twenty rises (*chance not parent*), the likelihood of having had sex falls even more dramatically, although the direction of causation between these two variables is not at all clear. As grades increase (*grades8*), again the likelihood of having had sex declines quite sharply, which we suggest is a further reflection of the association between the perception of a bright future and the inclination to engage in sexual activity at an early age.

What is of particular interest is that the inclusion of these three variables does indeed reduce the influence of parent's education on the likelihood of having had sex: the coefficient on *parent ed col*, the dummy variable that reflects having a college-educated parent, declines from 0.39 to 0.55 (that is, it moves closer to 1.00), while these three additional variables have no substantial influence on the coefficients for age, puberty, black, other race, or South (they do lower the effect of no religion and the presence of the biological parents somewhat). We interpret model 2, in comparison with model 1, as offering confirming evidence of our hypothesis that one primary reason parent's education inhibits youth sexual activity is its close association with self-assessment of future prospects and of the risks associated with early sexual activity.

In model 3, we add our measure of the peer group. Doing so does affect the likelihood of having had sex, and the effect is in the expected direction: boys whose peer group is one point higher on the peer-group index have lower odds of having had sex. The addition of this peer-group variable further diminishes the strength of the association between parent's education and sexual activity, but it does not greatly influence the coefficients on any of the other covariates. In model 4, we include as well four additional variables capturing the strictness of the mother and the father, measured both from the strict end of the spectrum and from the lenient (for the definitions of these dummies, see the appendix). Only one of the four—the strictness of the father—is associated with the odds of having had sex.

(*Text continues on p. 150.*)

TABLE 5.3   *Logistic Regressions: Eversex, Boys (Weighted)*

	Model 1		Model 2		Model 3		Model 4	
	Odds Ratio	Z	Odds Ratio	Z	Odds Ratio	Z	Odds Ratio	Z
Eversex								
Age fifteen	**1.80**	3.86	**1.75**	3.14	**1.99**	3.84	**1.85**	3.31
Age sixteen	**3.51**	8.08	**3.54**	6.16	**4.65**	7.33	**4.14**	6.41
Age seventeen	**6.20**	9.28	**6.07**	7.43	**8.18**	8.49	**7.29**	7.73
Age eighteen	3.98	1.84	4.48	1.70	5.07	1.72	4.19	1.57
Pubertyage	**0.83**	-4.82	**0.82**	-4.96	**0.82**	-4.68	**0.82**	-4.69
Mispubertyage	0.87	-0.48	0.91	-0.34	1.03	0.10	1.00	0.02
Parent ed hs	0.95	-0.32	0.99	-0.06	0.95	-0.33	0.96	-0.25
Parent ed scol	**0.57**	-3.51	**0.68**	-2.25	0.71	-1.98	0.73	-1.85
Parent ed col	**0.39**	-5.75	**0.55**	-3.40	**0.58**	-3.03	**0.60**	-2.86
Race black	**2.79**	7.63	**2.87**	7.57	**2.91**	7.39	**2.89**	7.33
Race other	**1.52**	2.37	**1.55**	2.40	**1.61**	2.46	**1.58**	2.36
Hispanic	1.14	0.83	1.06	0.32	1.01	0.05	1.00	0.03
Rel Catholic	0.88	-0.91	0.89	-0.87	0.94	-0.45	0.92	-0.58
Rel no Protestant	0.73	-1.02	0.86	-0.47	0.80	-0.70	0.77	-0.81
Rel none	**1.74**	3.91	**1.57**	3.03	**1.51**	2.75	**1.49**	2.66
Notmom	**1.62**	3.22	**1.52**	2.66	**1.55**	2.74	**1.55**	2.63
Notdad	**1.40**	3.17	**1.28**	2.20	1.22	1.74	1.06	0.45

	Summary Model 1		Summary Model 2		Summary Model 3		Summary Model 4	
Foreign mom	0.93	−0.35	0.93	−0.32	1.02	0.10	1.05	0.21
South	**1.41**	3.11	**1.45**	3.28	**1.48**	3.34	**1.49**	3.41
Chance college			**0.53**	−2.80	**0.59**	−2.31	**0.59**	−2.28
Mis chance coll			1.18	0.39	1.30	0.57	1.42	0.76
Chance notparent			**0.15**	−6.12	**0.17**	−5.60	**0.17**	−5.66
Mis chance npar			0.80	−0.53	0.72	−0.74	0.72	−0.72
Grades8			**0.60**	−6.43	**0.67**	−4.96	**0.67**	−4.85
Mis grades8			1.10	0.56	**1.42**	2.10	**1.46**	2.24
Peer index					**0.85**	−9.17	**0.85**	−9.12
Mis peer index					0.15	−1.68	0.13	−1.84
Mom strict							0.98	−0.39
Dad strict							**0.88**	−2.56
Mom not strict							1.00	0.01
Dad not strict							0.96	−1.09

Summary Model 1	Summary Model 2	Summary Model 3	Summary Model 4
No. of obs. = 2,695	No. of obs. = 2,695	No. of obs. = 2,695	No. of obs. = 2,695
Chi^2 = 307.25	Chi^2 = 405.27	Chi^2 = 460.78	Chi^2 = 464.94
Prob > Chi^2 = .000	Prob > Chi^2 = .000	Prob > Chi^2 = .000	Prob > Chi^2 = .000
Pseudo-R^2 = .14	Pseudo-R^2 = .19	Pseudo-R^2 = .22	Pseudo-R^2 = .22

Source: Authors' compilation.
Note: Boldface numbers are statistically significant at $p < .05$.

TABLE 5.4   Logistic Regressions: Eversex, Girls (Weighted)

Eversex	Model 1		Model 2		Model 3		Model 4	
	Odds Ratio	Z	Odds Ratio	Z	Odds Ratio	Z	Odds Ratio	Z
Age fifteen	**2.07**	4.51	**1.85**	2.97	**2.29**	3.96	**1.79**	2.59
Age sixteen	**3.85**	8.42	**3.57**	5.54	**5.13**	6.91	**3.61**	5.00
Age seventeen	**6.76**	9.73	**5.99**	7.03	**9.12**	8.44	**6.23**	6.45
Age eighteen	3.43	1.68	1.73	0.90	3.06	1.50	1.85	0.82
Pubertyage	**0.86**	-4.25	**0.86**	-4.06	**0.86**	-4.05	**0.84**	-4.37
Mispubertyage	**0.51**	-3.66	**0.50**	-3.56	**0.51**	-3.28	**0.49**	-3.49
Parent ed hs	**0.73**	-2.08	0.76	-1.77	**0.71**	-2.01	0.72	-1.88
Parent ed scol	**0.68**	-2.38	0.77	-1.55	0.73	-1.86	0.73	-1.82
Parent ed col	**0.41**	-5.05	**0.53**	-3.44	**0.52**	-3.38	**0.54**	-3.13
Race black	1.01	0.07	0.97	-0.24	0.96	-0.29	0.97	-0.18
Race other	1.05	0.25	1.08	0.36	1.03	0.14	1.11	0.49
Hispanic	0.90	-0.57	0.84	-0.88	0.86	-0.78	0.83	-0.97
Rel Catholic	0.96	-0.28	0.96	-0.26	0.99	-0.07	0.95	-0.36
Rel no Protestant	0.48	-1.81	0.51	-1.56	0.56	-1.49	0.56	-1.45
Rel none	**1.97**	4.38	**1.90**	3.97	**1.83**	3.65	**1.67**	3.08
Notmom	1.12	0.73	1.09	0.57	1.07	0.43	0.87	-0.77
Notdad	**1.89**	5.59	**1.66**	4.32	**1.45**	3.10	**1.41**	2.50

	Model 1		Model 2		Model 3		Model 4	
Foreign mom	0.71	−1.54	0.68	−1.60	0.71	−1.45	0.72	−1.42
South	1.17	1.37	1.26	1.95	**1.32**	2.28	**1.34**	2.35
Chance college			0.80	−0.89	1.05	0.18	1.06	0.22
Mis chance coll			0.84	−0.33	0.96	−0.07	1.25	0.40
Chance notparent			**0.12**	−7.06	**0.14**	−6.37	**0.14**	−6.46
Mis chance npar			1.09	0.16	1.03	0.05	1.08	0.13
Grades8			**0.57**	−6.64	**0.64**	−5.20	**0.64**	−4.98
Mis grades8			0.96	−0.22	1.20	0.92	1.22	0.97
Peer index					**0.83**	−9.87	**0.84**	−9.41
Mis peer index					0.49	−0.74	0.34	−0.89
Mom strict							**0.75**	−4.72
Dad strict							0.92	−1.34
Mom not strict							0.95	−0.88
Dad not strict							1.02	0.54

Summary Model 1	Summary Model 2	Summary Model 3	Summary Model 4
No. of obs. = 2,611	No. of obs. = 2,611	No. of obs. = 2,611	No. of obs. = 2,611
Chi² = 249.39	Chi² = 341.61	Chi² = 409.95	Chi² = 418.80
Prob > chi² = .000	Prob > chi² = .000	Prob > chi² = .000	Prob > chi² = .000
Pseudo-R^2 = .12	Pseudo-R^2 = .17	Pseudo-R^2 = .21	Pseudo-R^2 = .23

Source: Authors' compilation.
Note: Boldface numbers are statistically significant at $p < .05$.

Turning to table 5.4, the same four models are reported for girls. Basically, similar relations are found here. Age and puberty have strong effects on the odds of having had sex. Parent's education is again strongly correlated with the odds of having had sex: having a parent who has completed college results in odds of having had sex of 0.41. Race has no effect on the reported behavior of girls (recall the strikingly large magnitude of its effect on the behavior of boys). Those who reported their religion as *none* have odds of having sex that are about twice as high as Protestant. Not having a father at home is also associated with odds of having had sex nearly twice as high as those who do have a father at home.

In model 2, the three measures of future prospects are added, and they are strongly associated with the odds of having had sex. Self-assessment of the chance of completing college by age thirty has an imprecise effect, while the other two variables are very strongly related to sexual behavior. Self-assessment of the chance of becoming a parent by age twenty is associated with an enormously large difference in the odds of having had sex.[7] Also, grade-point average in the eighth grade is associated with an additional dramatic lowering of the odds of having had sex.

For the girls, the inclusion of these three variables has a big influence on the coefficient on parent's college education, lowering it from 0.41 to 0.53. It also eliminates the statistical significance of the coefficients on the two other parent's-education dummies. This pattern reinforces what we saw for the boys, and we suggest that it offers further supporting evidence for our argument that parent's education proxies life goals. For the girls as well as for the boys, the inclusion of these three indicators of future prospects has very little effect on the measured relation between sexual activity and age, puberty, religion, or family structure; only the parent's-education effects are altered, and this is consistent with our argument.

We explored one additional factor that strengthens the interpretation just offered. Notice that a sizable proportion of both the boys and the girls did not respond when asked about their chance of completing college by age thirty and their chance of not becoming a parent by age twenty. To account for this, we assigned the mean value to all instances of missing information when running the regressions reported in tables 5.3 and 5.4. We also included two missing-value dummies in the regressions, neither of which was statistically significant for either boys or girls. To test whether the results were affected by the missing information, we reran models 1 and 2 for both boys and girls, excluding cases with missing information. The result was as expected: when the missing cases were eliminated, the coefficient on parent's education was more substantially weakened by the introduction of the variables measuring chance of completing college and chance of not becoming a parent.

Table 5.5 shows a few of the results of the reestimated models. Although we report in table 5.5 only the results of regressions in which both variables with missing information (chance of completing college and chance of not becoming a parent) were dropped, we also dropped variables individually to test for effects separately. Also, although all the variables reported in table 5.3 for models 1 and 2 were included in the reestimated models, we report in table 5.5 only the coefficients on the three parent's-education variables and on chance of completing college, chance of not becoming a parent, and grade-point average.

For the boys, one sees that, in table 5.5, model 1, among the subset with complete information, the parent's-education effects are slightly larger than those reported in table 5.3 but that, when the controls are added, the effect of some college is no longer statistically significant and the effect of college attendance by the parents falls even more dramatically (that is, the coefficient moves closer to 1.00). In table 5.5, model 2, none of the three parent's-education effects is statistically significant. The anticipated effect is indeed greater among the cases with a more adequate control. The coefficients on the percent-chance variables and on grade point average are not weaker in in table 5.5 than they were in table 5.3; this is what we would expect. The co-efficients for the girls show the same results: the coefficients on the parent's-education variables are no longer statistically significant in table 5.5, model 2, and, in two of the three cases, the effects are substantially smaller in model 2 than in model 1.

Adding characteristics of the girl's peer group in table 5.4, model 3, has the same effect on the girls as on the boys: those with a peer group that is rated higher on the index have lower odds of having had sex. In model 4, we add the dummies reflecting strictness of parents' oversight. In an intriguing example of gender symmetry, only mother's strictness for girls and father's strictness for boys exhibit a statistically significant association with having had sex.

Most of the relations shown in model 1 of tables 5.3 and 5.4 corroborate patterns of adolescent sexual behavior found in other data—which is re-assuring since there is no reason to think that the youths in our sample are any different from those in other samples. The steep age gradient, the influence of age at puberty, the strong effect of race for boys but not for girls, the weak association with religious denomination, the suggestive relation with the absence of a parent, and the strong association of parent's education with age at first sex all are reported in the literature.

We believe, however, that, in addition to having replicated previous results, we have uncovered several new pieces of evidence that could lead to more effective policy tools. Most important, we find in the survey data evidence that sexual behavior is negatively associated with future prospects: closely so with self-reported perceptions of chance of college completion by

TABLE 5.5 Reestimated Models 1 and 2 from Tables 5.3 and 5.4, Deleting Cases of Missing Values

	Boys								Girls							
	From Table 5.3				Excluding Missing Cases[a]				From Table 5.4				Excluding Missing Cases[a]			
	Model 1		Model 2		Model 1		Model 2		Model 1		Model 2		Model 1		Model 2	
	Odds Ratio	Z	Odds Ratio	Z	Odds Ratio	Z	Odds Ratio	Z	Odds Ratio	Z	Odds Ratio	Z	Odds Ratio	Z	Odds Ratio	Z
Parent ed hs	0.95	-0.32	0.99	-0.06	0.84	-0.85	0.88	-0.59	0.73	-2.08	0.76	-1.77	0.65	-2.17	0.71	-1.63
Parent ed schol	0.57	-3.51	0.68	-2.25	0.49	-3.40	0.66	-1.80	0.68	-2.38	0.77	-1.55	0.68	-1.82	0.88	-0.57
Parent ed col	0.39	-5.75	0.55	-3.40	0.37	-4.63	0.63	-1.97	0.41	-5.05	0.53	-3.44	0.44	-3.66	0.66	-1.75
Chance college			0.53	-2.80			0.45	-3.34			0.80	-0.89			0.75	-1.11
Mis chance coll			1.18	0.39			...				0.84	-0.33			...	
Chance notparent			0.15	-6.12			0.15	-6.09			0.12	-7.06			0.12	-7.17
Mis ch npar			0.80	-0.53			...				1.09	0.16			...	
Grades 8			0.60	-6.43			0.65	-4.34			0.57	-6.64			0.56	-5.68
Mis grades 8			1.10	0.56			1.12	0.32			0.96	-0.22			1.27	0.64
N	2,695		2,695		1,483		1,483		2,611		2,611		1,444		1,444	
Pseudo-R2	0.138		0.186		0.126		0.194		0.119		0.170		0.086		0.166	

Source: Authors' compilation.
Note: All variables from models 1 and 2 are included; only selected coefficients are shown.
[a] Observations dropped if missing information on the youth's assessment of the percent chance of completing college by age thirty or the percent chance of not becoming a parent by age twenty.

age thirty and chance of not becoming a parent by age twenty, but also with grade-point average in the eighth grade, an indicator of prospects for higher education and thus life chances. Better prospects, we argue, provide a greater incentive not to engage in sexual activity and thereby risk the future. Thus, it seems likely that social policies meant to improve young people's life chances will also encourage them to avoid behaviors (such as early sexual activity) that threaten those improved life chances. Furthermore, the evidence that parent's education proxies life goals (supplied by the patterns displayed by the coefficients on the parent's-education variables across tables 5.3 to 5.5) supports our argument that parents who instill a strong sense of a bright future in their children at the same time motivate them to avoid risking that future.

The estimated models also document the importance of the youth's peer group, the nature of the peer group being strongly correlated with early sexual activity. There is also some indication of an association between parenting style (strict or lenient) and age at first sex. Clearly, further research needs to be done, but the associations reported here are sensible and believable and suggest that adolescent sexual behavior is far from arbitrary, capricious, or insensitive to incentives.

Ever Having Dated

We turn now to an examination of dating behavior, using models that are analogous to those used to examine sexual behavior in order to facilitate comparison. Since dating is not a socially stigmatized activity—as sex often is among adolescents—we anticipate that several of the personal- and family-background factors that had significant effects on having had sex will not be relevant to having dated. For example, unlike sex, dating per se does not risk future prospects; we therefore do not expect to find the same relation between parent's education (which proxies for life goals) and having dated that we found between parent's education and having had sex. Similarly, while religious affiliation and grade-point average can have an inhibiting effect on sexual activity, they should not affect dating per se. (And, if grade-point average *is* negatively associated with dating, it may be because those with good grades spend their time doing homework, not dating.) Among those factors that we *do* expect to be relevant to dating are age, puberty, race, and region.

Everdate is the dichotomous dependent variable in the logistic. It is a dummy variable equal to 1 if the youth has been on a date or an unsupervised social outing with a member of the opposite sex and 0 otherwise. While the NLSY97 does ask all respondents about dating, we have limited our analyses here to those youths eligible to answer the questions about sexual activity (that is, those fourteen years of age and older), again to facilitate comparison with the results of our analyses of sexual behavior. About 72 percent of the sample youths have been on a date (compared to the nearly 30 percent who have had sex). The figures are higher for boys (75 percent) than for girls (68 percent) and are shown in table 5.6 by single year of age. In these data there is a positive correlation between the dummy variable indicating ever having dated and ever having had sex: 0.308 for boys and 0.361 for girls. That correlation has the same magnitude whether calculated separately by age or overall.

Table 5.7 shows the results of our four logistic-regression models for boys, table 5.8 the results for girls. Taking the boys (table 5.7) first, notice that model 1 does not do as well when applied to the dating-behavior dummy variable as it did when applied to the sexual-behavior dummy variable. Neither the chi-square statistic nor the pseudo-R^2 is nearly as high. That fact is reflected in the significance of the coefficients as well. Age is an important factor in the odds of having dated, boy's age at puberty has almost exactly the same relation with having dated as it had with having had sex, and absent father shows about the same magnitude of effect and so, too, no religious affiliation does. But there the similarities end. There is no parent's-education effect or no race effect on dating. The former is what we would expect if our hypothesis that parent's education affects sexual activity by proxying life goals is correct, thus lending further support to our argument.

In model 2, we do see quite a strong linkage between dating and both grade-point average in the eighth grade and self-reported chance of becoming a parent before age twenty: boys with better grades are less likely to date, as are those who think that the chance of teen parenthood is slim. While self-reported chance of completing college before age thirty was strongly negatively associated with having had sex, it is positively associated with

TABLE 5.6 *The Percentage of Youths Who Have Ever Dated, Ever-date, by Single Year of Age and by Gender (Weighted)*

	Boys	Girls	All
All	75.1	67.7	71.5
Age fourteen	62.4	48.6	55.7
Age fifteen	71.2	62.9	67.1
Age sixteen	83.1	78.1	80.8
Age seventeen and up	88.2	88.6	88.4

Source: Authors' compilation.

having dated, although the model 2 coefficients are not significant (but note that they will become significant in models 3 and 4). The peer index added in model 3 does show a negative relation with dating, but none of the measures of parents' strictness in model 4 do so, which makes sense since dating per se is not usually discouraged.

Turning to the girls (table 5.8), the relations between the personal- and family-background factors and having dated are substantially stronger than they are for the boys. The effects of age, age at puberty, absent father, and no religious affiliation on dating all mirror those on sexual activity (see table 5.4). That hormonal maturity (age and age at puberty) affects dating behavior seems reasonable in that one would expect increasing physical maturity to be associated with increasing interest in members of the opposite sex. But, for the girls, unlike for the boys, having a college-educated parent is associated with substantially higher odds of having dated, even though it is negatively associated with the odds of having had sex. In fact, these models say that the odds of having dated are nearly one and a half times higher, while the odds of having had sex are less than half as high, for a young woman with a college-educated parent as they are for a young woman whose parents did not complete high school. Clearly, while dating and sexual activity are closely associated in terms of maturation, sequencing, and socialization, they represent dramatically different risks to future prospects, which, we suggest, explains the differential effect of parent's education.

Another interesting difference in the patterns of dating and sexual behavior is found when the effect of race is examined. The African American girls in the sample are no more or no less likely than the white girls are to have had sex, but they are far *less* likely to have dated. For the boys, the pattern is different: the African American boys are much *more* likely to have had sex but no more likely than their white counterparts to have dated.

Overall, our analyses tend to confirm previous findings in the literature pointing to a relation between popularity and dating frequency and between dating frequency and sexual activity. But our understanding of the relation between dating and sexual behavior is clearly incomplete, and further work is called for. For example, it seems likely that dating occasionally will not significantly increase the odds of engaging in sexual activity while dating frequently may do so, or that dating one person exclusively may increase the odds of engaging in sexual activity but decrease the odds of engaging in risky sexual practices (such as having sex with more than one partner). While we have not yet begun to explore such issues, the NLSY97 data set contains information (for example, age at first date, dating frequency, and number of boyfriends or girlfriends) that we plan to exploit in future research.

(*Text continues on p. 160.*)

TABLE 5.7 Logistic: Everdate, Boys (Weighted)

Everdate	Model 1		Model 2		Model 3		Model 4	
	Odds Ratio	Z	Odds Ratio	Z	Odds Ratio	Z	Odds Ratio	Z
Age fifteen	**1.58**	3.63	1.34	1.92	**1.46**	2.42	1.36	1.94
Age sixteen	**3.36**	8.52	**2.71**	5.23	**3.27**	6.01	**2.90**	5.23
Age seventeen	**5.33**	7.15	**4.30**	5.47	**5.13**	6.03	**4.56**	5.48
Age eighteen	1.52	0.53	1.36	0.36	1.40	0.39	1.16	0.17
Pubertyage	**0.86**	-3.23	**0.86**	-3.35	**0.86**	-3.16	**0.87**	-3.13
Mispubertyage	**0.51**	-2.57	**0.52**	-2.51	**0.58**	-2.04	**0.57**	-2.11
Parent ed hs	0.91	-0.65	0.92	-0.56	0.89	-0.74	0.90	-0.70
Parent ed scol	1.16	0.90	1.18	1.00	1.23	1.22	1.24	1.29
Parent ed col	1.00	0.03	1.05	0.34	1.11	0.64	1.14	0.79
Race black	0.99	-0.07	0.93	-0.49	0.92	-0.59	0.91	-0.62
Race other	0.80	-1.19	0.79	-1.22	0.81	-1.08	0.80	-1.16
Hispanic	1.13	-0.70	1.07	0.37	1.02	0.10	1.02	0.10
Rel Catholic	**1.47**	2.86	**1.48**	2.90	**1.55**	3.18	**1.53**	3.07
Rel no Protestant	0.67	-1.48	0.72	-1.23	0.68	-1.42	0.65	-1.59
Rel none	**1.46**	2.38	**1.41**	2.14	1.34	1.83	1.32	1.72
Notmom	1.08	0.47	1.08	0.47	1.06	0.39	1.01	0.08
Notdad	**1.31**	2.39	**1.26**	2.01	1.20	1.58	1.15	1.05

	Model 1		Model 2		Model 3		Model 4	
Foreign mom	0.72	−1.80	0.71	−1.88	0.75	−1.50	0.77	−1.39
South	1.20	1.55	1.23	1.70	1.22	1.66	1.23	1.70
Chance college			1.53	1.70	**1.71**	2.15	**1.68**	2.07
Mis chance coll			1.31	0.52	1.40	0.62	1.59	0.85
Chance notparent			**0.22**	−3.58	**0.25**	−3.37	**0.25**	−3.38
Mis chance npar			0.65	−0.83	0.61	−0.92	0.61	−0.92
Grades8			**0.77**	−3.12	**0.83**	−2.13	**0.84**	−2.01
Mis grades8			**0.74**	−2.05	0.90	−0.68	0.92	−0.58
Peer index					**0.90**	−6.01	**0.90**	−5.93
Mis peer index					0.29	−1.03	0.28	−1.09
Mom strict							0.94	−1.27
Dad strict							0.95	−1.26
Mom not strict							0.94	−1.11
Dad not strict							1.00	−0.01

Summary Model 1	Summary Model 2	Summary Model 3	Summary Model 4
No. of obs. = 2,695	No. of obs. = 2,695	No. of obs. = 2,695	No. of obs. = 2,695
Chi^2 = 134.04	Chi^2 = 153.12	Chi^2 = 190.88	Chi^2 = 197.58
Prob > Chi^2 = .000	Prob > Chi^2 = .000	Prob > Chi^2 = .000	Prob > Chi^2 = .000
Pseudo-R^2 = .06	Pseudo-R^2 = .08	Pseudo-R^2 = .09	Pseudo-R^2 = .09

Source: Authors' compilation.
Note: Boldface numbers are statistically significant at $p < .05$.

TABLE 5.8   Logistic: *Everdate, Girls (Weighted)*

Everdate	Model 1		Model 2		Model 3		Model 4	
	Odds Ratio	Z	Odds Ratio	Z	Odds Ratio	Z	Odds Ratio	Z
Age fifteen	**1.91**	5.19	1.37	1.95	**1.62**	2.92	1.38	1.85
Age sixteen	**4.33**	10.67	**2.94**	5.71	**4.03**	6.99	**3.11**	5.26
Age seventeen	**9.89**	10.18	**6.38**	7.18	**9.01**	8.25	**6.69**	6.77
Age eighteen	. . .	. . .	. . .	. . .	. . .	. . .	. . .	. . .
Pubertyage	**0.91**	−2.59	**0.91**	−2.41	**0.92**	−2.28	**0.91**	−2.53
Mispubertyage	**0.49**	−4.50	**0.51**	−4.13	**0.53**	−3.66	**0.52**	−3.84
Parent ed hs	1.14	0.90	1.12	0.77	1.06	0.39	1.07	0.46
Parent ed scol	1.18	1.05	1.15	0.85	1.10	0.56	1.10	0.60
Parent ed col	**1.43**	2.24	**1.42**	2.09	**1.46**	2.16	**1.54**	2.44
Race black	**0.41**	−7.03	**0.38**	−7.28	**0.36**	−7.50	**0.36**	−7.50
Race other	**0.45**	−4.20	**0.45**	−4.13	**0.43**	−4.40	**0.44**	−4.32
Hispanic	1.13	0.73	1.13	0.72	1.12	0.62	1.12	0.64
Rel Catholic	1.29	1.89	1.24	1.63	1.30	1.95	1.25	1.62
Rel no Protestant	0.98	−0.06	1.02	0.07	0.96	−0.11	1.00	0.00
Rel none	**1.98**	3.97	**1.92**	3.80	**1.85**	3.44	**1.67**	2.86
Notmom	1.11	0.64	1.15	0.81	1.11	0.60	0.93	−0.37
Notdad	**1.43**	3.29	1.39	1.26	**1.25**	2.01	1.24	1.67

	Model 1		Model 2		Model 3		Model 4	
Foreign mom	0.71	−1.89	0.76	−0.49	**0.68**	−2.14	**0.68**	−2.12
South	0.93	−0.69	0.96	−0.41	1.01	0.07	1.03	0.22
Chance college			**1.39**	3.01	**1.77**	2.11	**1.74**	2.08
Mis chance coll			0.76	−0.49	0.86	−0.27	1.10	0.17
Chance notparent			**0.20**	−4.65	**0.23**	−4.20	**0.22**	−4.34
Mis chance npar			1.04	0.07	0.95	−0.08	1.05	0.09
Grades8			0.85	−1.91	0.95	−0.63	0.98	−0.26
Mis grades8			**0.61**	−3.20	0.76	−1.69	0.75	−1.70
Peer index					**0.87**	−7.93	**0.87**	−7.60
Mis peer index					0.25	−1.47	0.21	−1.60
Mom strict							**0.82**	−4.24
Dad strict							0.95	−1.09
Mom not strict							0.94	−1.18
Dad not strict							1.03	0.70

Summary Model 1	Summary Model 2	Summary Model 3	Summary Model 4
No. of obs. = 2,600	No. of obs. = 2,600	No. of obs. = 2,600	No. of obs. = 2,600
$Chi^2 = 256.62$	$Chi^2 = 281.12$	$Chi^2 = 309.63$	$Chi^2 = 335.94$
Prob > Chi^2 = .000	Prob > Chi^2 = .000	Prob > Chi^2 = .000	Prob > Chi^2 = .000
Pseudo-R^2 = .11	Pseudo-R^2 = .13	Pseudo-R^2 = .16	Pseudo-R^2 = .17

Source: Authors' compilation.
Note: Boldface numbers are statistically significant at $p < .05$.

Further Details Regarding Sexual Behavior Among Sexually Active Adolescents

The round 1 NLSY97 interview collects information on several additional dimensions of adolescent dating and sexual behavior, including age at first sex, number of sex partners ever, number of sex partners in the last year, frequency of sexual activity, whether birth control was used at first sex, and whether birth control was used in the last year. To date, we have conducted only cursory analyses of these variables, so we report on them only briefly here.

Age at First Sex

Table 5.9 shows the distribution of reported age at first sex separately for the boys and the girls *who report having had sex.* Recall that these respondents range in age from fourteen through seventeen at the time of the interview.[8]

We created a dummy variable defined as 1 if a boy had had sex by age thirteen or a girl had had sex by age fourteen. We ran logistic regressions on this dichotomous variable, using the same set of variables as was used in models 1, 2, and 3 reported earlier. Rather than show the full models, we report in table 5.10 only the variables that had statistical significance since there were few. Recall that, unlike the *eversex* models, which distinguish

TABLE 5.9   *Age at First Sex Reported by Boys and Girls, NLSY97, Round 1 (Weighted)*

Age at First Sex	Boys		Girls	
	N	Percentage	N	Percentage
≤ Eight	33	3.6	2	.3
Nine	9	.9	2	.3
Ten	20	2.1	1	.2
Eleven	25	2.7	10	1.4
Twelve	69	7.5	34	4.6
Thirteen	155	16.8	100	13.4
Fourteen	265	28.7	237	31.9
Fifteen	231	25.1	239	32.2
Sixteen	108	11.7	108	14.5
Seventeen	7	.8	9	1.2
Total	922	100.0	743	100.0

Source: NLSY97, round 1.

those who have had sex from those who have not, these models include only those youths who had become sexually active by the time of the interview. For the boys, older age at puberty, higher level of parents' education, being Catholic, and the index of peers are associated with a lower probability of having had sex by age thirteen, while blacks and Hispanics have a much higher probability. For the girls, the same relation is seen for age at puberty, the peer index, and Hispanic ethnicity, but not for the other variables. For them, the perceived chance of completing college and their grades in the eighth grade are associated with a lower probability of having had sex by age fourteen, while their parents' education variable exhibits the "wrong" sign (that is, those with a college-educated parent were more likely to have had sex early among those girls who had had sex).

We also ran OLS (ordinary-least-squares) regressions with these same three models on the more-continuous variable age at first sexual intercourse. These results are reported in panel B of table 5.10. Again, several of the same variables surfaced as important factors. For boys, age at puberty, parent's education, Catholic religion, and peer group were associated with an older age at first sex, race (black) and ethnicity (Hispanic) with earlier. For girls, age at puberty, perceived chance of college graduation, grades in the eighth grade, and peer group were associated with an older age at first sex. Girls with no religious affiliation and those whose father was not living at home show somewhat younger age at first sex, and here, as in panel A, among these sexually active girls, those with more educated parents began having sex at an earlier age.

Number of Sex Partners

The survey asked the adolescents how many sex partners they had ever had and how many they had had within the past year. Table 5.11 shows the distributions for the boys and the girls separately, for those who reported ever having had sex. We ran comparable logistic regressions on this behavior as well, defining the dichotomous variable as 1 if number of sex partners ever ranked respondents among the top 10 percent of their peers (that is, twelve or more sex partners for boys, seven or more for girls). We also ran OLS regressions on number of sex partners reported in the past year. These were weighted regressions in all cases. We do not show these results because they are very weak. For the girls, none of the variables reached the conventional level of significance in the logistic regressions, and only a very few did in the OLS regressions. For the boys, four variables did show a significant relation in the logistic regressions—boys of "other" races (that is, nonwhite and non–African American), those not living with their father, and those whose mother was foreign born were all more likely to have had twelve or more sex partners—but these relations were not confirmed by the OLS re-

TABLE 5.10   Multivariate Analyses of Age at First Sex (Weighted)

A. Logistic Regression[a] on Dummy Variable for Having Had Sex By Age Thirteen (Boys) or Age Fourteen (Girls)

| | Boys | | | | | | Girls | | | | | |
| | Model 1 | | Model 2 | | Model 3 | | Model 1 | | Model 2 | | Model 3 | |
	Odds Ratio	Z	Odds Ratio	Z	Odds Ratio	Z	Odds Ratio	Z	Odds Ratio	Z	Odds Ratio	Z
Pubertyage	0.74	-4.22	0.73	-4.27	0.74	-4.11	0.84	-2.64	0.82	-3.00	0.81	-3.10
Paredscol	0.56	-2.08										
Paredcol	0.48	-2.25							2.27	2.37	2.22	2.33
Raceblk	2.56	4.48	2.69	4.60	2.84	4.75						
Hispanic	2.27	2.72	2.32	2.78	2.20	2.54	2.31	2.21	2.37	2.38	2.65	2.71
Rel Catholic	0.50	-2.66	0.49	-2.76	0.51	-2.59						
Chance coll									0.36	-2.62	0.43	-2.07
Grades8									0.69	-2.68	0.72	-2.24[b]
Peers					0.87	-4.50					0.89	-3.22
(No. obs)	(922)		(922)		(922)		(743)		(743)		(743)	
Chi^2	103.0		103.0		116.0		218		267		317	
Pseudo-R^2	0.14		0.15		0.17		0.17		0.21		0.23	

B. OLS Regression on Age at First Sex, for Those Who Have Had Sex, by Gender of Respondent

	Coef	t	Coef	t	Coef	t	Coef	t	Coef	t	Coef	t
Pubertyage	0.21	3.84	0.22	3.89	0.21	3.79			0.08	2.65	0.08	2.72
Paredscl									-0.34	-2.31	-0.32	-2.24
Paredcol	0.54	2.71	0.44	2.13	0.40	1.96			-0.45	-2.77	-0.43	-2.74
Raceblack	-0.70	-4.40	-0.72	-4.46	-0.74	-4.64					-0.25	-2.07
Hispanic	-0.64	-2.60	-0.65	-2.71	-0.59	-2.45						
RelCatholic	0.54	3.27	0.56	3.41	0.54	3.27						
Relnone							-0.37	-2.79	-0.33	-2.60	-0.31	-2.53
NotDad							-0.35	-3.65	-0.25	-2.82	-0.22	-2.39
Chance College									0.58	-3.23[b]	0.49	2.71[b]
Grades8									0.25	3.43[b]	0.22	3.02[b]
Peers					0.08	3.87[b]					0.05	3.01[b]
(No. obs)	(922)		(922)		(922)		(743)		(743)		(743)	
Adj.R^2	0.18		0.19		0.21		0.21		0.29		0.30	

Source: Authors' compilation.
[a] Full model identical to models in table 5.3. Only statistically significant coefficients shown here; age dummies not shown.
[b] Indicates the missing value for chance college-grades-peers was significant.

TABLE 5.11   *Percentage Distribution of Number of Sex Partners, by Gender (Weighted)*

Number	Ever		Within the Past Year	
	Boys	Girls	Boys	Girls
None	1	1	6	6
One	22	34	38	54
Two	20	21	25	18
Three	15	15	11	10
Four	8	9	4	3
Five to nine	20	12	9	6
Ten to nineteen	9	6	4	2
Twenty to forty-nine	4	1	1	0
Fifty to ninety-nine	1	1	1	0
Total	100	100	100	100
(N)	(756)	(623)	(758)	(627)

Source: Authors' compilation
Note: Includes only those who reported ever having had sex.

gressions. In general, number of sex partners ever and number of sex partners in the last year seem to be associated only with age.

Frequency of Sexual Activity

For completeness, table 5.12 shows the simple distribution of the responses to the questions regarding frequency of sexual activity among sexually active adolescents. As is typically the case, those adolescents who are sexually active generally engage in sexual activity relatively infrequently. So the median frequency was five times in the past year for boys and ten times for fewer, sexually active girls.

The Use of Birth Control

Tables 5.13 and 5.14 show figures for the responses to the questions about use of birth control at sexual debut and method of birth control most often used. Obviously, we have not yet undertaken any substantial analysis.[9] It is interesting, however, that such a large percentage of those who use contraception report using condoms. Given that the median reported frequency of sexual activity is only a few times a year, and given that the risk of pregnancy

TABLE 5.12   *Percentage Distribution of Frequency of Sex in the Past Year, by Gender (Weighted)*

	Boys	Girls
None	2	2
One	9	4
2 to 4	32	22
5 to 9	22	16
10 to 19	13	18
20 to 49	10	19
50 to 99	6	7
100 to 365	4	10
366 to 999	1	1
Total	100	100
(N)	(685)	(557)

Source: Authors' compilation.
Note: Includes only those who reported ever having had sex.

in one, randomly timed act of sexual intercourse is about 0.03, it would be reasonable for the median boy to calculate that the risk of impregnating a girl over the course of a year is only about 15 percent with no contraception and for the median girl to calculate that the risk of getting pregnant over the course of a year is about 30 percent. At these rates—especially if the sexual encounter is unanticipated—it is not difficult to understand why youths often engage in unprotected sex. We do not, of course, mean to condone risky behavior or to make light of the considerable cost of pregnancy. Our point, simply, is that, given that sexual activity among adolescents occurs relatively infrequently, it is not surprising that the condom (which requires

TABLE 5.13   *Percentage Reporting Use of Birth Control at First Sexual Intercourse (Weighted)*

Response	Boys	Girls
No	20	24
Yes	77	76
[a]	3	0
(N)	(926)	(745)

Source: Authors' compilation.
[a] Coded "didn't need to" or "one of us was unable to have a child."

TABLE 5.14   *Method of Birth Control "Most Often" Used by Those Using Any Contraception, Percentage Distribution by Gender (Weighted)*

Method	Boys	Girls
Condom	88.5	71.5
Foam, jellies, suppos.	0.3	0.2
Withdrawal	2.1	4.4
Diaphragm	0.3	0.0
Rhythm	0.5	0.2
Pill	6.8	15.3
IUD	0.2	0.5
Norplant, injection	0.5	6.9
All others	0.8	1.0
(Total)	(605)	(494)

Source: Authors' compilation.

no preplanning other than having one available) is the birth-control method of choice.

Conclusion

While the preliminary results reported in this "early results" effort are intriguing, our coverage of many of them has necessarily been brief. What we have examined at greater length is the very strong effect that parent's education has on the onset of partnered sexual activity in the NLSY97 as well as in many other data sets. Our hypothesis is that parent's education proxies youth career aspirations and that those with strong aspirations (that is, those with more highly educated parents) have a strong motivation to avoid pregnancy and so tend to avoid sex. And, while we have not completed our study of the determinants of adolescent sexual and dating behavior, we think that our analysis to date offers substantial evidence in support of this hypothesis.

Clearly, our initial efforts with these data seem to indicate that much of the data is worthy of study, although some of the reported rates of frequency and partnering at the upper tails of the distributions may reflect exaggeration while other respondents may have denied their sexual activities. In the future, we intend to expand our analysis to include an examination of the determinants of risky sexual behavior at the same time as we continue our research on the relation between dating and sexual behavior.

Appendix: The Variables Used in This Study

Behavior Variables

Eversex is a dummy: 1 if the youth has had sexual intercourse, otherwise 0.

Everdate is a dummy: 1 if the youth has ever been on a date or an unsupervised social outing with a member of the opposite sex, otherwise 0.

Age

Dummies: *age14, age15, age16, age17, age18*. Each is 1 if the youth is that age at the date of the interview, otherwise 0.

Puberty

Pubertyage is the age at puberty in years (note that the very few cases with reported age of puberty less than age eight were recoded 8 and that those with missing values for the age at puberty were assigned the mean age at puberty from the data, a value of 12.5).

Mispuberty age is a dummy: 1 if *pubertyage* was missing and set to 12.5, otherwise 0.

Race

Race black is a dummy: 1 if black, otherwise 0.

Race other is a dummy: 1 if nonblack and nonwhite race, otherwise 0.

Ethnicity

Hispanic is a dummy: 1 if Hispanic, otherwise 0.

Religion

Rel Catholic is a dummy: 1 if Catholic, otherwise 0.

Rel no Protestant is a dummy: 1 if not Protestant and not Catholic but is affiliated with a religion, otherwise 0.

Rel none is a dummy: 1 if no religion, otherwise 0.

Family Structure

Notmom is a dummy: 1 if mother figure is *not* the biological mother, otherwise 0.

Notdad is dummy: 1 if father figure is *not* the biological father, otherwise 0.

Background

Foreignm is a dummy: 1 if the mother was born elsewhere than in the United States, otherwise 0.

South is a dummy: 1 if the residence is in the South region, otherwise 0.

Parent's Education

Paredhs is a dummy: 1 if either parent completed high school, otherwise 0.

Paredscol is a dummy: 1 if either parent had "some college," otherwise 0.

Paredcol is a dummy: 1 if either parent had completed college, otherwise 0.

{The default is *parednohs,* a dummy: 1 if neither parent completed high school, otherwise 0.}

Expectations

Chancecollege: The youth was asked about the percent chance he or she would have completed college by age thirty, and that value is coded here with the missing value of 0.66 for the boys and 0.73 for the girls (these are the mean values for the two genders among those with a value).

Mischcol is a dummy: 1 if a missing value was assigned, otherwise 0.

Chancenotparent: The youth was also asked about the percent chance he or she would be a parent by age twenty, and this is coded here as the percent chance of *not* being a parent with the missing values of 84.5 for the boys and 85.1 for the girls.

Mischpar is a dummy: 1 if a missing value was assigned, otherwise 0.

Grades in the Eighth Grade

Grades8 is the youth's grade-point average in the eighth grade. (The youth was asked: "Overall, what grades did you receive in eighth grade?") The values in the code are as follows: 1 is 0.8, 2 is 1.0, 3 is 1.5, 4 is 2.0, 5 is 2.5, 6 is 3.0, 7 is 3.5, 8 is 3.8, 9 is 2.8, 10 is 2.7, 11 is 2.6, 12 is 2.9, 13 is coded missing, then the missing are coded 2.65 for the boys and 2.95 for the girls (those are the unweighted means for the boys and the girls with a grade-point average).

Misgrad8 is a dummy: 1 if a missing value was assigned for that youth, otherwise 0.

Peers

Peerindex: This index was constructed by Yasuyo Abe (see Abe and Michael 1999). It scores nine attributes of peers, giving a score of 1 or −1 as the youth's report places the peers in the top or the bottom 20 percent, so the range can be from −9 to +9 and is in fact a range from −7 to +7. A value of 0.1 was assigned to those missing.

Mispeer is a dummy: 1 if a missing value was assigned, otherwise 0.

Parenting Style

The youth was asked several questions about each parent's style of parenting, and these are used to create two indices for each parent, one identifying those who are most strict with the youth, and one identifying those who are least strict, so the two tails of the distributions are each captured here. The four questions asked of the youth about each parent separately were the following: "How much does she/he know about your close friends, that is, who they are?" "How much does she/he know about your close friends' parents, that is, who they are?" "How much does she/he know about who you are with when you are not at home?" "In general, would you say she/he is permissive or strict about making sure you did what you were supposed to do?"

The first three questions were constrained to have one of five values: 0 (knows nothing), 1 (knows just a little), 2 (knows some things), 3 (knows most things), and 4 (knows everything). The fourth question was coded 1 if permissive and 2 if strict.

The variables *momstrict* and *dadstrict* are coded from these four questions, capturing the strict or involved side of the spectrum, and *momnostc* and *dadnostc* are coded from the same four questions, capturing the not-engaged side of the spectrum. The values on the strict variable are as follows: +1 if question 1 is scored 3; +2 if question 1 is scored 4; +1 if question 2 is scored 3; +2 if question 2 is scored 4; +1 if question 3 is scored 3; +2 if question 3 is scored 4; and +2 if question 4 is scored 2. So the maximum score is 8, and the values range from 0 to 8. The values on the not-strict variable are as follows: +1 if question 1 is scored 1; +2 if question 1 is scored 0; +1 if question 2 is scored 1; +2 if question 2 is scored 0; +1 if question 3 is scored 1; +2 if question 3 is scored 0; and +2 if question 4 is scored 1. So, again, the maximum score is 8, and the values range from 0 to 8.

We thank Carolyn Hill and Yasuyo Abe for help with the data files and variables and Laura Duberstein Lindberg for comments on an earlier draft. We acknowledge with thanks the financial support of the Ford Foundation (grant 990-1402).

Notes

1. The fact that, in this data set (as in most), African Americans have much higher rates of reported early sexual debut would tend to corroborate this interpretation given that black adolescents are less likely to live with both biological parents.

2. Thornton and Camburn (1987) find an effect of religion, although the relation between religious affiliation and attitude toward sexual activity is stronger than that between religious affiliation and actual sexual activity.

3. We thank Yasuyo Abe for sharing the index with us.

4. One aspect of the summary data may seem odd: the age distribution of the youths. It should be noted that only those respondents who were fourteen years old or older on the sample date, December 31, 1996, were asked the questions about sexual intercourse. However, the survey was conducted mostly between February 1997 and September 1997, with a few interviews taking place early in 1998, so many respondents were considerably older at the survey date than they were at the sample date, a fact reflected in the age distribution shown in table 5.1. In this study, we use age at survey date, not age at sample date. The age distribution of our sample is as follows: among the boys, 596 were fourteen years old, 944 were fifteen years old, 868 were sixteen years old, 281 were seventeen years old, and 10 were eighteen years old; among the girls, 587 were fourteen years old, 896 were fifteen years old, 827 were sixteen years old, 298 were seventeen years old, and 7 were eighteen years old.

5. The quality and accuracy of the information obtained in the NLSY97 about sexual activity, or about dating for that matter, have not been assessed here in any way. Since such data are often found to be inaccurate (see, for example, Alexander et al. 1993), we acknowledge the need for such an assessment. That the motivation for asking such sensitive questions is made clear and that respondents understand that their responses will remain strictly confidential can go a long way toward ensuring accuracy; for the moment, in lieu of independent verification, we must trust that the use of the SAQ and the rapport established between the interviewer and the respondent by the time the sex questions were asked served to generate reasonably good quality information.

6. The 1997 Youth Risk Behavior Survey, reported by the Centers for Disease Control and Prevention through the *Morbidity and Mortality Weekly Reports*, shows the following rates for "ever had sexual intercourse" for young men and young women in grades nine through twelve, respectively: 41.8 and 34.0; 41.7 and 43.5; 49.3 and 50.3; and 60.1 and 61.9 (Kann et al. 1998). When these school-grade rates are adjusted so as to be more comparable to our age-specific rates, ours look a little low by comparison.

Using the 1988 National Survey of Adolescent Males, Sonenstein, Pleck, and Ku (1990) report that 21 percent of fourteen-year-old boys, 38 percent of fifteen-year-old boys, 58 percent of sixteen-year-old boys, and 67 percent of seventeen-year-old boys have ever had sex, figures much higher than our NLSY97-based rates for boys.

7. This relation is also emphasized by Walker (chapter 7 in this volume). He partitions youths by whether they are sexually active and then displays their answers to the questions about the percent chance of becoming a parent. He shows that, "among the top quartile, teenagers who are sexually active report a 50 percent chance of becoming a parent by age twenty, whereas those who are not report only a 15 percent chance" (203).

    Moore (chapter 4 in this volume) also models the odds of sexual debut. Her analysis provides greater detail about family structure than we do, she includes a few additional variables, and she stresses interactions with race, whereas we fully interact by gender and focus on the magnitudes and interpretations of the parent's-education variables in particular. From the perspective of our study, it is quite interesting to note that Moore finds strong effects of mother's education, but only for white youths. That make sense in our context if mother's education is a better index of perceived opportunity for whites than it is for blacks.

    Cawley (chapter 6 in this volume) also studies early sexual activity and dating, but he focuses on a particular set of issues about physical size and the youth's perceptions of weight. And, while he controls for many of the factors that we feature, he submerges these effects to emphasize those of interest in his analysis.

8. Because many of the youths in the NLSY97 sample have not yet engaged in sexual activity, and because many have not yet attained the age at which others report age at first sex, the distributions are potentially quite misleading. One way to make this point clear is to report the distribution of those whose first sex occurred before age fifteen separately by single year of age: that is, 100 percent of fourteen-year-old boys and 100 percent of fourteen-year-old girls, 92 percent of fifteen-year-old boys and 85 percent of fifteen-year-old girls, 61 percent of sixteen-year-old boys and 46 percent of sixteen-year-old girls, and 47 percent of seventeen-year-old boys and 40 percent of seventeen-year old girls reported first sex as occurring before age fifteen. Now, this is not behaviorally meaningful. The same concerns apply to table 5.10, which is informative only if the effects of the covariates reported there are independent of the age of the youth in the interval from fourteen through seventeen years.

9. We caution that there is much complexity in properly analyzing the use of birth control, particularly condoms. For example, Pleck, Sonenstein, and Ku (1991) find that the distribution of condom usage (in terms of percentage of times used) is W shaped, that each peak in the distribution represents a different reason for condom use, and that use also differs by number of partners.

Again, Laumann et al. (1994, table 11.20) show that men are twice as likely, and women are nearly four times as likely, to report always using a condom with a secondary sex partner as they are with their primary sex partner.

References

Abe, Yasuyo, and Robert T. Michael. 1999. "Employment, Delinquency, and Sex during Adolescence: Evidence from NLSY97." Unpublished paper. University of Chicago (July).

Alexander, Cheryl S., Mark R. Somerfield, Margaret E. Ensminger, Karin E. Johnson, and Young J. Kim. 1993. "Consistency of Adolescents' Self-Report of Sexual Behavior in a Longitudinal Study." *Journal of Youth and Adolescence* 22(5): 445–471.

Anderson, E. 1989. "Sex Codes and Family Life among Poor Inner City Youth." *Annals of the American Academy of Political and Social Science* 501(1): 59–78.

Botstein, Leon. 1997. *Jefferson's Children: Education and the Promise of American Culture*. New York: Doubleday.

Brewster, Karin L. 1994. "Neighborhood Context and the Transition to Sexual Activity among Young Black Women." *Demography* 31(4): 603–14.

Brewster, Karin L., John O. G. Billy, and William R. Grady. 1993. "Social Context and Adolescent Behavior: The Impact of Community on the Transitions to Sexual Activity." *Social Forces* 71(3): 713–40.

Brooks-Gunn, Jeanne, and Anne C. Petersen, editors. 1983. *Girls at Puberty: Biological and Psychosocial Perspectives*. New York: Plenum.

Cooksey, Elizabeth C., Ronald R. Rindfuss, and David K. Guilkey. 1996. "The Interaction of Adolescent Sexual and Contraceptive Behavior during Changing Times." *Journal of Health and Social Behavior* 37(March): 59–74.

Cooper, M. L., and H. K. Orcutt. 1997. "Drinking and Sexual Experience on First Dates among Adolescents." *Journal of Abnormal Psychology* 106(2): 191–202.

Donovan, P. 1995. "Mother's Attitudes toward Adolescent Sex, Family's Dating Rules Influence Teenagers' Sexual Behavior." *Family Planning Perspectives* 27(4): 177–78.

Geronimus, Arleen T. 1987. "On Teenage Childbearing and Neonatal Mortality in the United States." *Population and Development Review* 13(2): 245–79.

Hanson, Sandra L., Donna Ruane Morrison, and Alan L. Ginsburg. 1989. "The Antecedents of Teenage Fatherhood." *Demography* 26(4): 579–96.

Haurin, R. Jean, and Frank L. Mott. 1990. "Adolescent Sexual Activity in the Family Context: The Impact of Older Siblings." *Demography* 27(4): 537–58.

Kann, Laura, et al. 1998. "Youth Risk Behavior Surveillance: United States, 1997." *Morbidity and Mortality Weekly Review* 47, No. SS-3 (August 14): 1–92.

Ku, Leighton, Freya L. Sonenstein, and Joseph H. Pleck. 1993. "Neighborhood, Family, and Work: Influences on the Premarital Behaviors of Adolescent Males." *Social Forces* 72(December): 479–503.

Laumann, E. O., J. H. Gagnon, R. T. Michael, and S. Michaels. 1994. *The Social Organization of Sexuality: Sexual Practices in the United States.* Chicago: University of Chicago Press.

Marsiglio, W., and F. L. Mott. 1986. "The Impact of Sex Education on Sexual Activity, Contraceptive Use, and Premarital Pregnancy among American Teenagers." *Family Planning Perspectives* 18(3): 151–62.

Michael, Alice. 1999. "Coming of Age: The Timing of Transitions and Adolescent Adjustment among European American and African American Girls." Ph.D. diss., University of Michigan.

Michael, Robert T., and Kara Joyner. 2001. "Choices Leading to Teenage Births." In *Sex, Love, and Health in America: Private Choices and Public Policies,* edited by E. O. Laumann and R. T. Michael. Chicago: University of Chicago Press.

Montgomery, M. J., and G. T. Sorell. 1998. "Love and Dating Experience in Early and Middle Adolescence: Grade and Gender Comparisons." *Journal of Adolescence* 21(6): 677–89.

Moore, K. A., J. L. Peterson, and Frank F. Furstenberg. 1984. "Starting Early: The Antecedents of Early Premarital Intercourse." Presented at annual meeting of Population Association of America, Minneapolis, May 1–3.

Nathanson, Constance A. 1991. *Dangerous Passage.* Philadelphia: Temple University Press.

Pawlby, S. J., A. Mills, and D. Quinton. 1997. "Vulnerable Adolescent Girls: Opposite-Sex Relationships." *Journal of Child Psychology and Psychiatry and Allied Disciplines* 38(8): 909–20.

Plcck, Joseph H., Freya L. Sonenstein, and Leighton C. Ku. 1991. "Adolescent Males' Condom Use: Relationships between Perceived Cost-Benefits and Consistency." *Journal of Marriage and the Family* 53(August): 733–45.

Sonenstein, Freya, Joseph H. Pleck, and Leighton C. Ku. 1990. "Patterns of Sexual Activity among Adolescent Males." Paper presented at the annual meeting of the American Association for the Advancement of Science. New Orleans (February 18).

Stattin, H., and D. Magnussen. 1990. *Pubertal Maturation in Female Development.* Hillsdale, N.J.: Erlbaum.

Thornton, Arland, and D. Camburn. 1987. "The Influence of the Family on Premarital Sexual Attitudes and Behavior." *Demography* 24(3): 323–40.

Udry, J. Richard. 1988. "Biological Predispositions and Social Control in Adolescent Sexual Behavior." *American Sociological Review* 53(October): 709–22.

Udry, J. Richard, and John O. G. Billy. 1987. "Initiation of Coitus in Early Adolescence." *American Sociological Review* 52(December): 841–55.

6

Body Weight and the Dating and Sexual Behaviors of Young Adolescents

John Cawley

I N CHAPTER 5 of this volume, Michael and Bickert examine the determinants of adolescents' early sexual behaviors. In chapter 4, Moore focuses on the correlation between sexual debut and race, family structure, and parental discipline. This chapter focuses more narrowly, studying how early sexual and dating behaviors are correlated with adolescents' body weight.

It has repeatedly been found that heavier adolescents have fewer dates than healthy-weight adolescents (Halpern et al. 1999; Kallen and Doughty 1984). There are three possible explanations for this correlation. The first is that, at some point, weight reduces dating opportunities, which would be true if adolescents prefer to date those who are relatively slender. The second is that a lack of dates causes weight gain, which would be true if a lack of dates caused depression and depression caused weight gain. The third is that unobserved factors (for example, certain personality traits) cause both heaviness and a lack of dates.

Using the method of instrumental variables (IV), this essay tests the first explanation, that weight lowers the probability of dating and sexual activity. The weight of the biological father is used as an instrument for the weight of the child, exploiting the genetic variation in weight. This essay also corrects for reporting error in self-reports of height and weight; details are provided in the appendix.

Body weight may be partly a matter of choice, which makes it difficult to assess the effect of body weight on outcomes. The goal of this essay is to estimate the causal effect of body weight on the probability of dating and sexual activity among adolescents.

One way to estimate the causal effect of weight on such outcomes would be to conduct a randomized clinical trial: manipulate members of an experimental group in such a way that they gain weight and then compare their dating and sexual experiences to those of a control group. Such an experiment would be unethical, so this essay exploits a natural experiment. Specifically, the weight of the biological father is used as an instrument for the weight of the child. The identifying assumption is that the weight of the father is highly genetically correlated with the weight of the child and that, after all observable factors have been taken into account, the father's weight has no independent effect on the probability that the child dates or has sex. This assumption is supported by the literature in behavioral genetics. The IV method exploits the fact that certain people are genetically endowed with a propensity to be heavy. By examining how this unchosen variation in body weight correlates with dating and sexual activity, it is possible to derive an estimate of the causal effect of weight on dating and sexual activity.

Since World War II, increasing numbers of adolescents have reported premarital sexual activity. The proportion of men who had had intercourse by age sixteen rose from 35 percent in the 1950s and 1960s to 48 percent in the 1970s and 1980s. Likewise, the percentage of women who had had intercourse by age sixteen rose from 19 percent in the 1950s and 1960s to 37 percent in the 1970s and 1980s (Laumann et al. 1994, chapter 9). Efforts to better understand the correlates of adolescent sexual activity, such as those reported in this volume, may aid efforts to target adolescents at risk of teenage pregnancy and sexually transmitted diseases.

Relationships and Matching by Weight

This essay tests whether higher body weight reduces dating and sexual activity among adolescents. This section briefly outlines the related previous literature and notes a necessary condition for weight to reduce dating and sexual activity.

Several models of marriage (for example, Becker 1991, 1976, chapter 11; and Burdett and Coles 1997) predict assortative mating—that is, that husbands and wives will have similar characteristics. This prediction has been confirmed for certain physical attributes by, for example, Spuhler (1968) and Schafer and Keith (1990), who find a positive and statistically significant correlation between the body weights of husbands and wives.

If dating and sexual activity among adolescents are also characterized by assortative matching on physical characteristics, then one would expect heavy adolescents to date other heavy adolescents, but it is not clear that heavier adolescents should have fewer dates or sexual experiences. In order for heavy adolescents to be less likely to date or have sex, a greater fraction of heavy than light adolescents must prefer not to date than to date others like themselves. This essay makes that assumption and predicts that heavier adolescents will be less likely to report dating and sexual activity. Previous studies of this topic have found that heavier adolescents and young adults tend to have fewer dates (Halpern et al. 1999; Kallen and Doughty 1984) and sexual experiences (Halpern et al. 1999). This essay attempts to determine whether weight *causes* this discrepancy.

The difficulty in determining whether weight reduces dating and sexual activity lies in the fact that body weight may be the result of other factors correlated with relative attractiveness, such as personality and self-esteem. The next section explains how the method of instrumental variables can be used to eliminate the influence of confounding factors and produce consistent estimates of the effect of weight on dating and sexual activity.

Data

The data used in this essay are from the NLSY97, a nationally representative sample of 9,022 youths who were twelve to sixteen years old as of December 31, 1996. Round 1 of the survey took place in 1997. In that round, both the eligible youth and one of the youth's parents were interviewed.

Respondents were asked to report their own height and weight. These self-reports include some degree of reporting error, which may bias coefficient estimates. Specifically, when only one regressor is measured with error, there is attenuation bias in the estimate of the coefficient associated with that regressor. However, if there are multiple regressors measured with error, there is no consistent rule about the sign of the bias in the coefficients of the variables measured with error (Judge et al. 1985). I correct the NLSY97 measures of weight and height for reporting error using the method developed by Lee and Sepanski (1995) and Bound, Brown, and Mathiowetz (1999); see the appendix for details.[1] Excluded from the sample are 98 girls who either were currently pregnant or had ever had a live birth and may therefore have been temporarily carrying extra weight. Another 518 respondents are excluded because either height or weight reports are missing.

I use two measures of body weight: weight in pounds (controlling for height) and body mass index (BMI).[2] BMI, the standard measure of body weight in epidemiology and medicine (U.S. National Institutes of Health 1998; Epstein and Higgins 1992), is calculated as weight in kilograms divided by height in meters squared.[3] BMI is a reasonable measure with which to assess fatness in children and adolescents (Dietz and Bellizzi 1999). Whereas BMI is a measure of weight for height, entering weight and height separately allows us to examine the effect of one independent of the other. Goodness-of-fit measures for the models estimated in this essay are similar for the two measures of weight. In this essay, I will occasionally refer to the concept *weight*, meaning generically the physical trait measured by BMI or pounds. When I refer to adolescents who are *heavier,* I mean in terms of either BMI or pounds.[4]

This essay is concerned with four outcomes: whether the adolescent has ever dated, whether he or she has dated at least once a month in the past year, whether he or she has ever engaged in sexual activity, and whether he or she has engaged in sexual activity in the past year.

The first dependent variable is an indicator variable for whether the youth has ever dated a member of the opposite sex. It is set equal to 1 if the respondent reports ever having been on a date or an unsupervised social outing with a boyfriend/girlfriend and 0 otherwise. In the sample used here, 67 percent of the boys and 58 percent of the girls had ever dated.

The second dependent variable is an indicator variable for whether the respondent has dated a member of the opposite sex at least once a month in the past year. It is set equal to 1 if the respondent reports a dating frequency of once a month or more in the past year and 0 if he or she reports a dating frequency of less than once a month in the past year. It is also set equal to 0 if the respondent reports never having had a date. In the sample used here, 27 percent of the boys and 31 percent of the girls dated at least once a month in the past year.

The third dependent variable is an indicator variable for whether the respondent has "ever had sexual intercourse, that is, made love, had sex, or gone all the way with a person of the opposite sex." It is set equal to 1 if the respondent has ever engaged in sex and 0 if he or she has not. In the sample used here, 28 percent of the boys (including 39.8 percent who have dated and 5.5 percent who have never dated) and 27 percent of the girls (including 35.4 percent who have dated and 3.8 percent who have never dated) had had sex.[5]

The fourth dependent variable is an indicator for whether a respondent has engaged in sexual activity in the past year. [6] It is set equal to 1 if the respondent reports having had sex at least once in the past year and 0 if he or she reports never having had sex. (Note that same-gender sexual activity is *not* excluded here. Respondents who reported having had sex only once ever were not asked how many times they had had sex in the past year. For these respondents, the indicator variable is set equal to 1 if the age at which the respondent reports having had sex is the same as or one minus his or her current age and 0 otherwise.) In the sample used here, 25 percent of both boys and girls had had sex in the past year.

I acknowledge that these self-reports of dating and sexual activity may contain some deliberate and some accidental error, but I have no way to correct for it. Nineteen NLSY97 observations are excluded because the information required to code all four of the dependent variables is missing.

The sample used in estimating the regression models is constant for different regressions using the same dependent variable. The sample does differ across dependent variables, however. For example, the two questions about dating were asked of all respondents, whereas the two questions about sexual activity were asked only of those at least fourteen years of age.

The set of regressors includes, in addition to the weight and height variables, variables that fall into the following categories: demographic variables, household characteristics, and lifestyle variables.

The demographic variables include age, age squared, and indicator variables for enrolled in school, Hispanic, African American, and white. The household characteristics include number of people living in the household, family income, and indicator variables for living with both biological parents, lived with both biological parents at age twelve, someone other than interviewer and respondent present at time of interview, region of residence, urban residence, whether interviewer rates exterior or interior of housing unit as poorly kept, whether the respondent reports that he or she is not religious, and missing values for family income, not religious, and interviewer rating of housing unit.

The lifestyle variables include age at which puberty began and indicator variables for whether puberty has begun (boys were asked about physical changes such as developing pubic or facial hair or the voice cracking or lowering; girls were asked whether they had menstruated), ever repeated a grade in school, self-rated health at least good, parent reports that youth has a chronic condition, parent reports that youth has ever had trouble seeing, hearing, or speaking, has drunk alcohol in past thirty days, and has smoked in last thirty days.

Several potential regressors were not used because they may be endogenous. These include the characteristics of the respondents' peers, whether the respondent reports that the parent is strict, measures of depression, expectations about future college attendance, and expectations about parenthood.

In this essay, the instrument for adolescent body weight is the weight of the biological father. At most, only one biological parent of the children in the NLSY97 sample was interviewed. If the responding parent was the biological father, I use his self-report of height and weight, corrected for measurement error.[7] If the responding parent was not the biological father, the responding parent's report of the biological father's weight and height is used if available.[8] An indicator variable for whether the father's weight is obtained from a self-report is included as an instrument.[9]

In order to compare probit and probit with IV results, I include in my analyses only those forty-six hundred respondents for whom information about the weight and height of the biological father is available. To the extent that the relation between body weight and dating or sexual activity varies by family type, limiting the sample in this way may introduce selection bias into the results.

Summary statistics, computed using NLSY97 sample weights, are reported separately by gender in table 6.1. NLSY97 sample weights are used in all estimations described in this essay.

The Relation Between Weight and Dating or Sexual Activity

The goal of this section is to generate a consistent estimate of the causal effect of weight on adolescent dating and sexual activity. Dating is the outcome of interest in the example that follows, but the same logic applies to adolescent sexual activity.

Assume that an individual i will have dated if his or her overall attractiveness A exceeds a critical threshold A^*. Attractiveness is assumed to be a function of body weight W, other characteristics X, and unobservables captured by an error term u. Specifically:

$$A_i = W_i \beta + X_i \gamma + u_i.$$

Overall attractiveness A is not observed, but we do know whether a person has dated; denote $D_i = 1$ if individual i has dated and $D_i = 0$ otherwise. Formally, dating relates to attractiveness in the following way:

$$D_i = 0 \quad \text{if } A_i \leq A^*,$$
$$D_i = 1 \quad \text{if } A_i > A^*.$$

Normalizing A^* at $A = 0$, the probability that one has dated is equal to

$$\mathrm{pr}\big[D_i{=}1 \,\big|\, X_i, W_i\big] = \mathrm{pr}\big[A_i > 0\big],$$
$$\mathrm{pr}\big[D_i{=}1 \,\big|\, X_i, W_i\big] = \mathrm{pr}\big[W_i\, \beta + X_i\, \gamma + u_i > 0\big],$$
$$\mathrm{pr}\big[D_i{=}1 \,\big|\, X_i, W_i\big] = \mathrm{pr}\big[u_i > -W_i\, \beta - X_i\, \gamma\big].$$

If one assumes that u is normally distributed, the probability of having dated as a function of weight W and characteristics X can be estimated using a probit regression.

There is evidence that white females are more concerned about body weight than are black females (Averett and Korenman 1999; Halpern et al. 1999); this suggests that the relation between body weight and dating or

TABLE 6.1   *National Longitudinal Survey of Youth, 1997 Cohort, Summary Statistics*

Variable	Boys			Girls		
	Number of Observations	Mean	Standard Deviation	Number of Observations	Mean	Standard Deviation
Body mass index (corrected)	1,970	21.23	4.23	1,811	21.86	4.18
Weight in pounds (corrected)	1,970	142.9	34.97	1,811	125.12	26.65
Height in inches (corrected)	1,970	68.53	3.59	1,811	63.34	2.27
Indicator: ever dated	1,970	0.67	0.47	1,811	0.58	0.49
Indicator: dated at least monthly in past year	1,966	0.27	0.45	1,809	0.31	0.46
Indicator: ever had sex	1,308	0.28	0.45	1,210	0.27	0.44
Indicator: had sex in past year	1,251	0.25	0.43	1,183	0.25	0.43
Age in years	1,970	14.6	1.48	1,811	14.6	1.49
Indicator: black	1,970	0.13	0.34	1,811	0.13	0.33
Indicator: white	1,970	0.78	0.41	1,811	0.79	0.41
Indicator: Hispanic	1,970	0.11	0.31	1,811	0.1	0.3
Indicator: lives with both biological parents	1,970	0.62	0.49	1,811	0.59	0.49
Indicator: lived with both bio. parents at age twelve	1,970	0.58	0.49	1,811	0.56	0.5
Number living in household	1,970	4.26	1.24	1,811	4.21	1.32
Indicator: experienced puberty	1,970	0.86	0.35	1,811	0.88	0.33

Age puberty began	1,970	11.42	2.2	1,811	11.23	2.09
Self-rated health at least good	1,970	0.96	0.19	1,811	0.96	0.19
Indicator: has chronic condition	1,970	0.13	0.34	1,811	0.1	0.31
Indicator: has had sensory impairment	1,970	0.18	0.38	1,811	0.17	0.38
Indicator: enrolled in school	1,970	0.95	0.21	1,811	0.96	0.19
Indicator: repeated grade of school	1,970	0.16	0.37	1,811	0.11	0.31
Indicator: interviewer rates housing unit poorly	1,918	0.06	0.24	1,764	0.06	0.25
Indicator: adolescent not alone during interview	1,970	0.34	0.48	1,811	0.36	0.48
Indicator: smoked in last thirty days	1,970	0.21	0.41	1,811	0.21	0.41
Indicator: drank alcohol in last thirty days	1,970	0.24	0.43	1,811	0.23	0.42
Indicator: residence in Northeast U.S.	1,970	0.17	0.38	1,811	0.18	0.39
Indicator: residence in Southern U.S.	1,970	0.32	0.47	1,811	0.34	0.47
Indicator: residence in Western U.S.	1,970	0.21	0.41	1,811	0.2	0.4
Indicator: urban residence	1,970	0.5	0.5	1,811	0.5	0.5
Indicator: family not religious	1,944	0.15	0.36	1,792	0.11	0.31
Household income	1,647	56,970.26	44,302.62	1,520	57,011.18	44,519.68
BMI of biological father	1,970	27.1	4.56	1,811	27.2	4.53
Indicator: height, weight of father self-reported	1,970	0.79	0.41	1,811	0.83	0.38

Source: Summary statistics computed using NLSY97 sample weights.

sexual activity may vary by race. A probit version of the Chow (1960) test was used to test for this possibility; in thirteen of the sixteen probit regressions that are subsequently reported in this essay, the hypothesis that probit coefficients on weight are equal for blacks and whites cannot be rejected. For the sake of consistency, only results using the pooled sample of all races combined are presented.

Probit estimates of the effect of weight on the likelihood of ever having dated for girls in the NLSY97 sample appear in table 6.2. This table presents the results of four regressions, each listed in a separate column. For the sake of brevity, only the marginal probabilities and Z-statistics associated with the weight variables are reported.[10] These Z-statistics reflect robust standard errors with clustering by individual. This essay uses a significance level of 5 percent, which is associated with a Z-score of absolute value 1.96.

For now, attention will be confined to the first two columns of table 6.2, which appear under the heading *Probit*. The Z-scores in columns 1 and 2 indicate that the hypothesis that the coefficient on the weight variable is 0 can be rejected at the 1 percent significance level. The marginal probability associated with weight in pounds is such that, all else equal, an extra 10 pounds is associated with a 3 percent lower probability that a girl has ever dated. An additional unit of BMI is associated with a 1.6 percent lower probability that a girl has ever dated.

Table 6.3 presents the probit estimates of the effect of weight on the likelihood of ever having dated for boys in the NLSY97 sample. The first two columns of table 6.3 indicate that, in contrast to the results for girls, the hypothesis that the coefficients on weight are equal to 0 cannot be rejected.

The first two columns of tables 6.4 and 6.5 present, for girls and boys, respectively, the probit estimates of the effect of weight on the likelihood that the adolescent has dated at least once a month in the past year. The hypothesis that the coefficients on weight are equal to 0 can be rejected for both genders. All else equal, an extra 10 pounds is associated with a 3 percent lower probability of dating at least once a month in the past year for girls and a 1 percent lower probability for boys.

The first two columns of tables 6.6 and 6.7 present, for girls and boys, respectively, probit estimates of the effect of weight on the likelihood of ever having had sex. For both boys and girls, it is impossible to reject the hypothesis that the coefficients on weight are 0 at the 5 percent significance level.

Tables 6.8 and 6.9 present the analogous results for the dependent variable that equals 1 if the adolescent has had sex in the past year. For girls, the hypothesis that the coefficients on weight are equal to 0 cannot be rejected. For boys, it is possible to reject the hypothesis for weight in pounds but not for BMI. All else equal, an additional ten pounds is associated with a 1 percent lower probability that a boy has had sex in the past year.

TABLE 6.2   *Relation between Indicator Variable for Ever Dated and Body Weight in the NLSY 1997 Cohort, Females, Marginal Probabilities and (Z-Scores)*

	Probit		Probit IV	
	(1)	(2)	(3)	(4)
Body mass index	−0.016		−0.0558	
	(−4.53)		(−2.99)	
Weight in pounds		−0.003		−0.0098
		(−4.18)		(−3.02)
Height in inches		0.01		0.0512
		(0.99)		(2.5)
Number of observations	1,811	1,811	1,811	1,811
Log likelihood	−872.99	−874.24	−869.93	−871.04
F-statistic of instruments in first stage			19.73	19.62
Marginal R^2 of instruments in first stage			0.04	0.03
P-value of Hausman test			0	0

Source: Author's compilation.
Note: Other regressors include age, age squared, age at puberty, number of people living in household, and indicator variables for live with both biological parents, puberty, not religious, self-rated health, chronic conditions, sensory problems, school enrollment, unpleasant interior or exterior of house as rated by interviewer, urban residence, the presence of another person at the time of the interview, smoked in last thirty days, drank alcohol in last thirty days, lived with both biological parents at age twelve, black, white, Hispanic, and region of residence. BMI, weight in pounds, and height are corrected for reporting error using NHANES III as validation data. NLSY 1997 sample weights are used in all regressions. Standard errors reflect cluster corrections by individual. Probit with IV uses the method of Newey (1987). Probit with IV standard errors are corrected according to Murphy and Topel (1985).

Next, it is explained why instrumental-variables estimation is necessary. Assume that weight (either BMI or weight in pounds) has the following reduced form:

$$W_i = Z_i \pi + X_i \delta + \varepsilon_i,$$

where X_i is the same set of variables that appeared in the dating equation, Z_i is a set of variables that are correlated with weight but not with the error term in the dating equation, and ε_i is the residual.

It is likely that weight W is correlated with the error term in the probit regression for dating; there are probably unobservables (for example,

TABLE 6.3   *Relation Between Indicator Variable for Ever Dated and Body Weight Among Males in the NLSY 1997 Cohort: Marginal Probabilities and (Z-Scores)*

	Probit		Probit IV	
	(1)	(2)	(3)	(4)
Body mass index	−0.003		−0.0155	
	(−1.12)		(−1.43)	
Weight in pounds		−0.001		−0.0029
		(−1.56)		(−1.69)
Height in inches		0.013		0.0271
		(2.46)		(2.25)
Number of observations	1,970	1,970	1,970	1,970
Log likelihood	−991.04	−988.13	−990.32	−987.25
F-statistic of instruments in first stage			46.02	38
Marginal R^2 of instruments in first stage			0.06	0.03
P-value of Hausman test			0.42	0.21

Source: Author's compilation.
Note: Other regressors include age, age squared, age at puberty, number of people living in household, and indicator variables for live with both biological parents, puberty, not religious, self-rated health, chronic conditions, sensory problems, school enrollment, unpleasant interior or exterior of house as rated by interviewer, urban residence, the presence of another person at the time of the interview, smoked in last thirty days, drank alcohol in last thirty days, lived with both biological parents at age twelve, black, white, Hispanic, and region of residence. BMI, weight in pounds, and height are corrected for reporting error using NHANES III as validation data. NLSY 1997 sample weights are used in all regressions. Standard errors reflect cluster corrections by individual. Probit with IV uses the method of Newey (1987). Probit with IV standard errors are corrected according to Murphy and Topel (1985).

personality traits) that affect both weight and the likelihood of dating. If this is true, the error terms ε and *u* will be correlated.

Just as in a linear regression, a correlation between a regressor and the error term violates the assumptions behind the nonlinear regression model.[11] One can still generate a consistent estimate of the effect of body weight on dating if one can identify a set of variables Z that are correlated with weight but not *u*, the error term in the dating equation. Given Z, one can calculate an instrumental-variables estimate of the effect of weight on dating.

In this essay, instrument Z is the BMI of the biological father. The identifying assumption is that the BMI of a biological father is correlated

TABLE 6.4   *Relation Between Indicator Variable for Dated at Least Once a Month in Past Year and Body Weight Among Females in the NLSY 1997 Cohort: Marginal Probabilities and (Z-Scores)*

	Probit		Probit IV	
	(1)	(2)	(3)	(4)
Body mass index	−0.015		−0.0404	
	(−4.79)		(−2.35)	
Weight in pounds		−0.003		−0.0073
		(−4.75)		(−2.39)
Height in inches		0.014		0.0412
		(1.87)		(2.14)
Number of observations	1,809	1,809	1,809	1,809
Log likelihood	−814.47	−814.82	−812.95	−813.14
F-statistic of instruments in first stage			19.59	19.48
Marginal R^2 of instruments in first stage			0.04	0.03
P-value of Hausman test			0	0

Source: Author's compilation.
Note: Other regressors include age, age squared, age at puberty, number of people living in household, and indicator variables for live with both biological parents, puberty, not religious, self-rated health, chronic conditions, sensory problems, school enrollment, unpleasant interior or exterior of house as rated by interviewer, urban residence, the presence of another person at the time of the interview, smoked in last thirty days, drank alcohol in last thirty days, lived with both biological parents at age twelve, black, white, Hispanic, and region of residence. BMI, weight in pounds, and height are corrected for reporting error using NHANES III as validation data. NLSY 1997 sample weights are used in all regressions. Standard errors reflect cluster corrections by individual. Probit with IV uses the method of Newey (1987). Probit with IV standard errors are corrected according to Murphy and Topel (1985).

with W, the weight of the adolescent, and is uncorrelated with u, the residual probability that the adolescent has dated.[12] I estimate probit with instrumental variables according to the method of Newey (1987). Standard errors for probit with IV are corrected for estimation in the first stage (see Murphy and Topel 1985).

A series of articles has been published outlining the harmful effects of weak instruments. Bound, Jaeger, and Baker (1993) point out two problems. First, a weak correlation between the instrument and the endogenous variable will exacerbate any problems associated with a correlation

TABLE 6.5   *Relation Between Indicator Variable for Dated at Least Once a Month in Past Year and Body Weight Among Males in the NLSY 1997 Cohort: Marginal Probabilities and (Z-Scores)*

	Probit		Probit IV	
	(1)	(2)	(3)	(4)
Body mass index	−0.006		−0.0063	
	(−2.12)		(−.63)	
Weight in pounds		−0.001		−0.0012
		(−2.46)		(−0.71)
Height in inches		0.012		0.0134
		(2.52)		(1.2)
Number of observations	1,966	1,966	1,966	1,966
Log likelihood	−926.6	−924.43	−926.6	−924.43
P-statistic of instruments in first stage			45.88	37.75
Marginal R^2 of instruments in first stage			0.06	0.03
P-value of Hausman test			0.04	0.02

Source: Author's compilation.
Note: Other regressors include age, age squared, age at puberty, number of people living in household, and indicator variables for live with both biological parents, puberty, not religious, self-rated health, chronic conditions, sensory problems, school enrollment, unpleasant interior or exterior of house as rated by interviewer, urban residence, the presence of another person at the time of the interview, smoked in last thirty days, drank alcohol in last thirty days, lived with both biological parents at age twelve, black, white, Hispanic, and region of residence. BMI, weight in pounds, and height are corrected for reporting error using NHANES III as validation data. NLSY 1997 sample weights are used in all regressions. Standard errors reflect cluster corrections by individual. Probit with IV uses the method of Newey (1987). Probit with IV standard errors are corrected according to Murphy and Topel (1985).

between the instrument and the residual in the second stage regression. Second, the magnitude of finite sample bias in IV estimates approaches that of the ordinary least squares (OLS) bias as the R^2 between the endogenous explanatory variable and the instruments approaches 0. They suggest that the partial R^2 and the F-statistic associated with the instruments in the first stage of two-stage least squares be reported as approximate guides to the quality of the IV estimates. Staiger and Stock (1997) argue that 10 is the minimum acceptable value of the F-statistic associated with the hypothesis that the coefficients on the instruments in the first-stage regression are jointly equal to 0.

TABLE 6.6   *Relation Between Indicator Variable for Ever Had Sex and Body Weight Among Females in the NLSY 1997 Cohort: Marginal Probabilities and (Z-Scores)*

	Probit		Probit IV	
	(1)	(2)	(3)	(4)
Body mass index	−.002		0.0233	
	(−0.6)		(1.63)	
Weight in pounds		0		0.0039
		(−0.57)		(1.57)
Height in inches		0.003		−0.0212
		(0.37)		(1.12)
Number of observations	1,210	1,210	1,210	1,210
Log likelihood	−532.71	−532.71	−530.92	−531.08
F-statistic of instruments in first stage			16.26	16.2
Marginal R^2 of instruments in first stage			0.05	0.04
P-value of Hausman test			0.21	0.24

Source: Author's compilation.
Note: Other regressors include age, age squared, age at puberty, number of people living in household, and indicator variables for live with both biological parents, puberty, not religious, self-rated health, chronic conditions, sensory problems, school enrollment, unpleasant interior or exterior of house as rated by interviewer, urban residence, the presence of another person at the time of the interview, smoked in last thirty days, drank alcohol in last thirty days, lived with both biological parents at age twelve, black, white, Hispanic, and region of residence. BMI, weight in pounds, and height are corrected for reporting error using NHANES III as validation data. NLSY 1997 sample weights are used in all regressions. Standard errors reflect cluster corrections by individual. Probit with IV uses the method of Newey (1987). Probit with IV standard errors are corrected according to Murphy and Topel (1985).

The instrumental-variables analysis of this chapter appears to be relatively free of the problems associated with weak instruments. In the first stage of instrumental-variables estimation, I reject the hypothesis that all coefficients on instruments are jointly equal to 0; although the results vary by measure of weight (BMI or weight in pounds) and by samples that vary with the outcome variable, in each case the F-statistic is at least 20 for boys and at least 15 for girls. For both boys and girls, the partial R^2 is in the range 0.03 to 0.06.[13]

However, there are additional requirements of an instrument. In particular, it is imperative that the instrument not be correlated with the error term in the second stage of instrumental-variables estimation. If it

TABLE 6.7   *Relation Between Indicator Variable for Ever Had Sex and Body Weight Among Males in the NLSY 1997 Cohort: Marginal Probabilities and (Z-Scores)*

	Probit		Probit IV	
	(1)	(2)	(3)	(4)
Body mass index	−0.006		−0.0142	
	(−1.79)		(−1.01)	
Weight in pounds		−0.001		−0.002
		(−1.9)		(−0.97)
Height in inches		0.006		0.0131
		(1.03)		(0.95)
Number of observations	1,308	1,308	1,308	1,308
Log likelihood	−563.68	−563.42	−563.48	−563.26
F-statistic of instruments in first stage			26.44	22.58
Marginal R^2 of instruments in first stage			0.05	0.04
P-value of Hausman test			0.12	0.09

Source: Author's compilation.
Note: Other regressors include age, age squared, age at puberty, number of people living in household, and indicator variables for live with both biological parents, puberty, not religious, self-rated health, chronic conditions, sensory problems, school enrollment, unpleasant interior or exterior of house as rated by interviewer, urban residence, the presence of another person at the time of the interview, smoked in last thirty days, drank alcohol in last thirty days, lived with both biological parents at age twelve, black, white, Hispanic, and region of residence. BMI, weight in pounds, and height are corrected for reporting error using NHANES III as validation data. NLSY 1997 sample weights are used in all regressions. Standard errors reflect cluster corrections by individual. Probit with IV uses the method of Newey (1987). Probit with IV standard errors are corrected according to Murphy and Topel (1985).

is, the IV procedure has accomplished nothing and may in fact have caused harm (Bound, Jaeger, and Baker 1993) because the instrumented variable is still endogenous.

The identifying assumption of the method of instrumental variables as used in this paper is that the weight of a father is uncorrelated with the error term in the equation for the dating and sexual behavior of his biological child. Two major pieces of evidence support this identifying assumption. The first is the finding that, in developed countries, no consistent pattern is found between socioeconomic status and adult male body weight (Sobal and Stunkard 1989). This suggests that the instrument is not correlated with the error term in the adolescent's dating and sexual activity equa-

TABLE 6.8   *Relation Between Indicator Variable for Had Sex in Past Year and Body Weight Among Females in the NLSY 1997 Cohort: Marginal Probabilities and (Z-Scores)*

	Probit		Probit IV	
	(1)	(2)	(3)	(4)
Body mass index	−0.002		0.0219	
	(−0.53)		(1.6)	
Weight in pounds		0		0.0037
		(−0.55)		(1.55)
Height in inches		0.006		−0.0172
		(0.69)		(−1)
Number of observations	1,183	1,183	1,183	1,183
Log likelihood	−505.63	−505.46	−504.02	−503.99
F-statistic of instruments in first stage			15.4	15.22
Marginal R^2 of instruments in first stage			0.05	0.04
P-value of Hausman test			0.23	0.23

Source: Author's compilation.
Note: Other regressors include age, age squared, age at puberty, number of people living in household, and indicator variables for live with both biological parents, puberty, not religious, self-rated health, chronic conditions, sensory problems, school enrollment, unpleasant interior or exterior of house as rated by interviewer, urban residence, the presence of another person at the time of the interview, smoked in last thirty days, drank alcohol in last thirty days, lived with both biological parents at age twelve, black, white, Hispanic, and region of residence. BMI, weight in pounds, and height are corrected for reporting error using NHANES III as validation data. NLSY 1997 sample weights are used in all regressions. Standard errors reflect cluster corrections by individual. Probit with IV uses the method of Newey (1987). Probit with IV standard errors are corrected according to Murphy and Topel (1985).

tions through socioeconomic status. I do not use the BMI of a biological mother as an instrument because, for adult women in developed countries, there exists an inverse relation between body weight and socioeconomic status (Sobal and Stunkard 1989).

One might be concerned that father's BMI is an unsuitable instrument for child's weight because common household environment affects both the father's weight and the child's propensity to date or have sex. This concern is unfounded: a body of literature finds no measurable effect of common household environment on body weight (Stunkard et al. 1986; Price and Gottesman 1991; Sorensen et al. 1992a, 1992b, 1993; Vogler et al. 1995; and Maes et al. 1997). After a comprehensive review of studies of the ge-

TABLE 6.9   *Relation Between Indicator Variable for Had Sex in Past Year and Body Weight in the NLSY 1997 Cohort, Males: Marginal Probabilities and (Z-Scores)*

	Probit		Probit IV	
	(1)	(2)	(3)	(4)
Body mass index	−0.006		−0.0139	
	(−1.9)		(−1.01)	
Weight in pounds		−0.001		−0.0022
		(−2.12)		(−1.04)
Height in inches		0.012		0.0191
		(2.01)		(1.38)
Number of observations	1,251	1,251	1,251	1,251
Log likelihood	−508.67	−507.5	−508.47	−507.3
F-statistic of instruments in first stage			24.68	20.77
Marginal R^2 of instruments in first stage			0.05	0.04
P-value of Hausman test			0.1	0.06

Source: Author's compilation.
Note: Other regressors include age, age squared, age at puberty, number of people living in household, and indicator variables for live with both biological parents, puberty, not religious, self-rated health, chronic conditions, sensory problems, school enrollment, unpleasant interior or exterior of house as rated by interviewer, urban residence, the presence of another person at the time of the interview, smoked in last thirty days, drank alcohol in last thirty days, lived with both biological parents at age twelve, black, white, Hispanic, and region of residence. BMI, weight in pounds, and height are corrected for reporting error using NHANES III as validation data. NLSY 1997 sample weights are used in all regressions. Standard errors reflect cluster corrections by individual. Probit with IV uses the method of Newey (1987). Probit with IV standard errors are corrected according to Murphy and Topel (1985).

netic and environmental influences on body weight, Grilo and Pogue-Geile (1991) conclude that "only environmental experiences that are not shared among family members appear to be important. In contrast, experiences that are shared among family members appear largely irrelevant in determining individual differences in weight and obesity" (520). In summary, environment not shared by family members affects weight (and is the reason the probit estimates are suspect and IV may be necessary), but environment shared by family members has no detectable influence on weight.

A Hausman (1978) test is used to determine the need for the IV procedure; in this case, it represents a test for the exogeneity of weight. Specifically, this test consists of regressing the outcome of interest on the adolescent's fitted weight and residual weight, as computed in the first stage of IV. If the coefficient on the residual weight is statistically significant, the hypothesis that weight is endogenous cannot be rejected. Such a finding would imply that the IV method generates more consistent estimates and should therefore be preferred.

The p-values associated with Hausman test statistics appear in columns 3 and 4 of tables 6.2 through 6.9. A p-value less than .05 indicates that IV estimates should be preferred to probit estimates. The p-values in tables 6.2 through 6.5 indicate that IV estimates should be preferred to probit estimates for the two dating outcomes for both genders, with the exception of the probability of ever dating for boys. None of the p-values in tables 6.6 through 6.9 is less than .05, which indicates that, for the two outcomes relating to sexual activity, the probit results should be preferred.

In the first stage of IV, I use OLS to estimate BMI and weight in pounds. The second stage of IV is a probit regression of the dependent variables on instrumented BMI or weight in pounds and the other regressors.

The probit with IV results appear in columns 3 and 4 of tables 6.2 through 6.9.[14] The probit with IV regressions use the same set of regressors and the same sample as the probit regressions.

While the outcome of the Hausman test differs across samples and outcome variables, the tables present both probit and IV results in every case for the sake of comparison. However, the discussion of IV results will be confined to those situations in which the Hausman test indicates that IV is necessary; the IV results that will be discussed appear in tables 6.2, 6.4, and 6.5.

In general, the marginal probabilities associated with the IV coefficients on weight in tables 6.2 and 6.4 are greater in absolute value than are those associated with the probit coefficients. A possible explanation is that weight is often correlated with puberty and maturation, which are associated with increased dating and sexual activity. To the extent such factors are correlated with weight and excluded from the set of regressors, they may raise toward 0 the probit estimate of the effect of weight on dating and sexual activity. Because the instrument (father's weight) is uncorrelated with such unobserved factors, IV, relative to ordinary probit, estimates a more negative effect of weight on the outcomes.

The IV estimates in table 6.2 suggest that, all else equal, an extra ten pounds is associated with a roughly 10 percent decrease in the likelihood of ever having dated for girls. Those in table 6.4 suggest that, all else equal, an extra ten pounds is associated with a 7.3 percent lower probability of dating at least once a month in the past year for boys.

These IV results imply that, if two otherwise identical girls differed such that one was at the median and one was at the ninety-fifth percentile for weight in pounds (a difference of 53.3 pounds), the heavier of the two is 52.2 percent less likely ever to have dated and 39 percent less likely to have dated at least once a month in the past year. If BMI instead of weight in pounds is used as the measure of body weight, the girl at the ninety-fifth percentile is 46.6 percent less likely to have ever dated and 33.8 percent less likely to have dated at least monthly in the past year.

The finding that weight lowers the probability of dating is consistent with the findings of Halpern et al. (1999). In contrast to the results for girls, the IV coefficient on weight for boys with respect to having dated at least once a month in the past year is not statistically significant (see table 6.5).

Conclusion

This essay tests whether body weight reduces the probability of dating and engaging in sexual activity for young adolescents. In order to generate a consistent estimate of the effect of body weight on dating and sexual activity, the method of instrumental variables is used when appropriate. To avoid another source of bias, self-reports of weight and height in the NLSY97 are corrected for reporting error.

Four outcomes are examined: whether the adolescent has ever dated, whether he or she has dated at least once a month in the past year, whether he or she has ever engaged in sexual activity, and whether he or she has engaged in sexual activity in the past year. It is concluded that, for girls, weight lowers the probability of ever having dated and the probability of dating at least monthly in the past year. If two otherwise identical girls differed such that one was at the median and one was at the 95th percentile for weight in pounds, the results of this essay suggest that the heavier of the two would be 52.2 percent less likely to have ever dated and 39 percent less likely to have dated at least once a month in the past year.

The finding that heavier girls are less likely to date is consistent with previous research. However, the relation between weight and dating found here is three times greater when estimated using probit with the method of instrumental variables than when using simple probit. In other words, previous studies that have not used IV have understated the effect of weight on dating for girls.

As for the other outcomes, the preponderance of evidence suggests that we cannot reject the hypotheses that weight has no effect on ever having had sex, or on having had sex in the past year.

Several other findings are of interest. While previous research has concluded that, for girls, racial differences can be found in attitudes toward body weight and in average age at sexual debut, this essay generally cannot reject the hypothesis that the effects of weight on dating and sexual activity are equal for African American and white girls.

An unexpected finding is the correlation of height with dating. The height of an adolescent is positively correlated with the probability of ever having dated and the frequency of dating. One possible explanation is that height is correlated with unobserved factors (like physical maturity) that are themselves correlated with dating. One recent study found that taller adult men have greater reproductive success (see Pawlowski et al. 2000), but this essay does not find that height is positively correlated with adolescent sexual activity.

Appendix: Reporting Error in Weight and Height

Weight and height are self-reported in the NLSY97, which makes it important to know the extent of reporting error in weight and height and, indirectly, in BMI. This appendix assesses the extent of reporting error in weight and height, and corrects for it, using the Third National Health and Nutrition Examination Survey, also known as the NHANES III.

The NHANES III, conducted 1988 to 1994, was designed to obtain information on the health and nutritional status of the U.S. population through interviews and direct physical examinations. A nationally representative sample of 33,994 persons aged two months and older was surveyed; 31,311 of those respondents also underwent physical examinations. The NHANES III is useful for the purposes of this essay because it asked adolescents to report their weight and height and then immediately measured their weight and height.[15] In order to assess the extent of reporting error in the NLSY97, I examined the reported and actual weight and height of NHANES III respondents of similar age as my NLSY97 sample and their biological fathers.

On average in the NHANES III, underreporting of weight varies positively with actual weight. For example, boys who weighed less than 110 pounds overreported their weight by an average of 1.53 percent, whereas boys who weighed 145 pounds or more underreported their weight by an average of 1.17 percent. Girls who weighed less than 110 pounds overreported their weight by an average of 2.44 percent, and girls who weighed 145 pounds or more underreported their weight by an average of 5.39 percent.[16] There is no clear pattern of misreporting of height by actual height.

The fact that reporting error in weight (and, therefore, in BMI) appears to be correlated with true weight complicates the use of common corrections for reporting error (Bound, Brown, and Mathiowetz 1999). I use the NHANES III as validation data to correct estimates for reporting error. Specifically, true height and weight in the NLSY97 are predicted using information on the relation between true and reported values in the NHANES III. This strategy is outlined in Lee and Sepanski (1995) and Bound, Brown, and Mathiowetz (1999). If one has validation data, which in this case contain measures of true and reported weight and height, one can regress the true value of the variable on its noisy reported value. The OLS coefficient on the reported value that was estimated using the validation data is then used in the primary data set; specifically, it is multiplied by the reported value in the primary data set to create an estimate of the true value. (This assumes "transportability," that is, that the relation between true and reported values is the same in both the validation and the primary data sets.)

In the first step of correcting self-reported height and weight in the NLSY97, actual values of height and weight are regressed on their reported values among NLSY97-aged (that is, twelve- to seventeen-year-olds) respondents to NHANES III.[17] The regression is estimated separately by race (black, nonblack) and gender. Actual weight or height is regressed on the reported value, its square (in deviations about racial and gender group–specific means), age, and age squared (again deviated from group mean); the intercept is suppressed.

In the second step of the correction process, the reported value, its square, age, and age squared in NLSY97 is multiplied by the first-stage coefficients associated with the correct racial-gender group in the NHANES III. The sum of these variables multiplied by the associated coefficients is the predicted value of actual weight and height given reported height and weight and age. BMI is then computed using the corrected measures of height and weight. In this essay, BMI, weight in pounds, and height in inches are based on the measures corrected for reporting error. (However, I also reestimated the models using measures of weight uncorrected for reporting error and found similar results.)

The correction for reporting error is repeated for the responding biological father's self-reported height and weight. NHANES III men aged twenty-two to eighty-two are used as validation data for responding biological fathers. No correction for reporting error is made for another person's report of the biological father's height and weight because there is no appropriate validation data, which would have to include actual weight and height and height and weight reported by another person.

For helpful comments and advice, I thank Phil DeCicca, Rachel Dunifon, Robert T. Michael, Mignon Moore, David Neumark, Janet Norwood, James Walker, Larry Wu, two anonymous referees, and seminar participants at the Early Results Conference and at the Harris School of Public Policy, University of Chicago. I thank Laura Marburger for research assistance. I gratefully acknowledge financial support from the W. T. Grant Foundation.

Notes

1. Instrumental-variables estimation is often proposed as a method of generating consistent estimates of coefficients of variables measured with error (Fuller 1987; Greene 1993). However, such an approach requires one to find an instrument that is correlated with the true value of the variable measured with error and yet is independent of the reporting error. Since, as shown in the appendix, reporting error in body mass index (BMI) is a function of level in BMI, it is not reasonable to assume that an instrument correlated with true BMI is uncorrelated with the reporting error in BMI. For this reason, I must still correct self-reported height and weight for reporting error before instrumental-variables estimation.

2. A caveat: in the empirical work reported here, I examine cumulative totals of dating and sexual activity, but I know only current weight. I must assume that weight has remained constant relative to that of peers during the dating–sex-eligible years.

3. The U.S. National Institutes of Health (1998) classifies BMI as follows: below 18.5 is underweight, 18.5 to 25 is healthy, between 25 and 30 is overweight, and over 30 is obese.

4. Gibson (chapter 9 in this volume) also focuses on the weight of NLSY97 respondents. In particular, she assesses whether adolescents whose families are living in poverty or receive Food Stamps are more likely to meet the clinical definitions of underweight and overweight.

5. Among the reasons that an adolescent may report having had sex without ever having dated are that he or she considers *dating* an anachronistic term that does not adequately describe modern adolescent courtship and that hc or she was sexually abused before beginning to date.

6. It is unknown what fraction of the population of youths of NLSY97 age has participated in same-gender sexual activity. Laumann et al. (1994) report two measures of the prevalence of same-gender sexual activity since puberty among those aged eighteen to twenty-nine. Depending on the measure used, they find that either 5.1 or 6.4 percent of the men and either 2.9 or 4.2 percent of the women have engaged in same-gender sexual activity.

7. For details on how I corrected the responding parent's self-reports of height and weight for reporting error, see the appendix.

8. Since secondary reports of actual height and weight are not available, I am unable to validate a nonresponding biological father's height and weight and therefore to correct reporting error.

9. In section 3, I explain why the biological mother's weight is not used as an instrument.

10. Complete regression results are available on request.

11. In nonlinear regression, if a regressor is correlated with the error term, it is expected that the transformed regressor is also correlated with the error term (see Greene 1993).

12. In contrast, Cawley (2000) uses the BMI of a child as an instrument for the weight of the child's mother, and Cawley, Markowitz, and Tauras (2001) use the weight of a brother as an instrument.

13. Other sources confirm that the correlation between the BMI of parents and that of children is high. Most estimates from U.S. data of the correlation between the adult BMI of a parent and the childhood or adolescent BMI of a biological child are in the range 0.21 to 0.36 (Maes et al. 1997).

14. Probit with IV uses the method outlined in Newey (1987). Standard errors are corrected according to Murphy and Topel (1985).

15. The height and weight of adolescents aged twelve to sixteen (and a few seventeen-year-olds) was measured immediately after self-report. For adults (except the frail elderly), height and weight were measured within four weeks of self-report. In this essay, the corrections for reporting error are likely more accurate for adolescents than for their biological fathers.

16. The patterns of misreporting that I find in the NHANES III are similar to those found in the NHANES II by Rowland (1989).

17. The NHANES III sample consists of 754 boys and 836 girls of NLSY97 age (twelve to seventeen).

References

Averett, Susan, and Sanders Korenman. 1999. "Black-White Differences in Social and Economic Consequences of Obesity." *International Journal of Obesity and Related Metabolic Disorders* 23(2): 166–73.

Becker, Gary S. 1976. *The Economic Approach to Human Behavior.* Chicago: University of Chicago Press.

———. 1991. *A Treatise on the Family.* Cambridge, Mass.: Harvard University Press.

Bound, John, Charles Brown, and Nancy Mathiowetz. 1999. "Measurement Error in Survey Data." In *Handbook of Econometrics*, vol. 4, edited by James Heckman and Ed Leamer. New York: Springer.

Bound, John, David A. Jaeger, and Regina Baker. 1993. "The Cure Can Be Worse Than the Disease: A Cautionary Tale Regarding Instrumental Variables." *NBER* technical paper 137. Cambridge, Mass.: National Bureau of Economic Research.

Burdett, Ken, and Melvyn G. Coles. 1997. "Marriage and Class." *Quarterly Journal of Economics* 112(1): 141–68.

Cawley, John. 2000. "Body Weight and Women's Labor Market Outcomes." *NBER* working paper 7841. Cambridge, Mass.: National Bureau of Economic Research.

Cawley, John, Sara Markowitz, and John Tauras. 2001. "Body Weight and the Smoking Initiation Decision of Adolescent Girls." Paper presented at the Allied Social Science Association Meetings, New Orleans, January.

Chow, Gregory C. 1960. "Tests of Equality between Sets of Coefficients in Two Linear Regressions." *Econometrica* 28(3): 591–605.

Dietz, William H., and Mary C. Bellizzi. 1999. "Introduction: The Use of Body Mass Index to Assess Obesity in Children." *American Journal of Clinical Nutrition* 70(1): S123–S125.

Epstein, Frederick H., and Millicent Higgins. 1992. "Epidemiology of Obesity." In *Obesity*, edited by Per Bjorntorp and Bernard N. Brodoff. New York: Lippincott.

Fuller, Wayne A. 1987. *Measurement Error Models*. New York: Wiley.

Greene, William H. 1993. *Econometric Analysis*. 2d ed. New York: Macmillan.

Grilo, Carlos M., and Michael F. Pogue-Geile. 1991. "The Nature of Environmental Influences on Weight and Obesity: A Behavioral Genetic Analysis." *Psychological Bulletin* 110(3): 520–37.

Halpern, Carolyn Tucker, J. Richard Udry, Benjamin Campbell, and Chirayath Suchindran. 1999. "Effects of Body Fat on Weight Concerns, Dating, and Sexual Activity: A Longitudinal Analysis of Black and White Adolescent Girls." *Developmental Psychology* 35(3): 721–36.

Hausman, J. A. 1978. "Specification Tests in Econometrics." *Econometrica* 46(6): 1251–71.

Judge, George G., W. E. Griffiths, R. Carter Hill, Helmut Lütkepohl, Tsaung-Chao Lee. 1985. *The Theory and Practice of Econometrics*, 2d ed. New York: Wiley.

Kallen, David J., and Andrea Doughty. 1984. "The Relationship of Weight, the Self Perception of Weight, and Self Esteem with Courtship Behavior." *Marriage and Family Review* 7(1–2): 93–114.

Laumann, Edward O., John H. Gagnon, Robert T. Michael, and Stuart Michaels. 1994. *The Social Organization of Sexuality*. Chicago: University of Chicago Press.

Lee, Lung-fei, and Jungsywan H. Sepanski. 1995. "Estimation of Linear and Nonlinear Errors-in-Variables Models Using Validation Data." *Journal of the American Statistical Association* 90(429): 130–40.

Maes, Hermine H. M., Michael C. Neale, and Lindon J. Eaves. 1997. "Genetic and Environmental Factors in Relative Body Weight and Human Adiposity." *Behavior Genetics* 27(4): 325–51.

Murphy, Kevin M., and Robert H. Topel. 1985. "Estimation and Inference in Two-Step Econometric Models." *Journal of Business and Economic Statistics* 3(4): 370–79.

Newey, Whitney K. 1987. "Efficient Estimation of Limited Dependent Variable Models with Endogenous Explanatory Variables." *Journal of Econometrics* 36(3): 231–50.

Pawlowski, Boguslaw, R. I. M. Dunbar, and Anna Lipowitz. 2000. "Evolutionary Fitness: Tall Men Have More Reproductive Success." *Nature* 403(6766): 156.

Price, R. Arlen, and Irving I. Gottesman. 1991. "Body Fat in Identical Twins Reared Apart: Roles for Genes and Environment." *Behavior Genetics* 21(1): 1–7.

Rowland, Michael L. 1989. "Reporting Bias in Height and Weight Data." *Statistical Bulletin* 70(2): 2–11.

Schafer, Robert B., and Pat M. Keith. 1990. "Matching by Weight in Married Couples: A Life Cycle Perspective." *Journal of Social Psychology* 130(5): 657–64.

Sobal, Jeffery, and Albert J. Stunkard. 1989. "Socioeconomic Status and Obesity: A Review of the Literature." *Psychological Bulletin* 105(2): 260–75.

Sorensen, Thorkild I. A., Claus Holst, and Albert J. Stunkard. 1992. "Childhood Body Mass Index–Genetic and Familial Environmental Influences Assessed in a Longitudinal Adoption Study." *International Journal of Obesity* 16(9): 705–14.

Sorensen, Thorkild I. A., Claus Holst, Albert J. Stunkard, and Lene Theil. 1992. "Correlations of Body Mass Index of Adult Adoptees and Their Biological and Adoptive Relatives." *International Journal of Obesity* 16(3): 227–36.

Sorensen, Thorkild I. A., and Albert J. Stunkard. 1993. "Does Obesity Run in Families Because of Genes? An Adoption Study Using Silhouettes as a Measure of Obesity." *Acta Psychiatrica Scandinavia* 370(supplement): 67–72.

Spuhler, J. N. 1968. "Assortative Mating with Respect to Physical Characteristics." *Social Biology* 15(2): 128–40.

Staiger, Douglas, and James H. Stock. 1997. "Instrumental Variables Regression with Weak Instruments." *Econometrica* 65(3): 557–86.

Stunkard, Albert J., Thorkild I. A. Sorensen, Craig Hanis, Thomas W. Teasdale, Ranajit Chakraborty, William J. Schull, and Fini Schulsinger. 1986. "An Adoption Study of Human Obesity." *New England Journal of Medicine* 314(4): 193–8.

U.S. National Institutes of Health. National Heart, Lung, and Blood Institute. 1998. *Clinical Guidelines on the Identification, Evaluation, and Treatment of Overweight and Obesity in Adults.* Washington, D.C.: National Institutes of Health, National Heart, Lung, and Blood Institute.

Vogler, George P., Thorkild I. A. Sorensen, Albert J. Stunkard, M. R. Srinivasan, and D. C. Rao. 1995. "Influences of Genes and Shared Family Environment on Adult Body Mass Index Assessed in an Adoption Study by a Comprehensive Path Model." *International Journal of Obesity* 19(1): 40–5.

Part III

ADOLESCENTS' EXPECTATIONS AND
THEIR WELL-BEING

7

Adolescents' Expectations Regarding Birth Outcomes: A Comparison of the NLSY79 and NLSY97 Cohorts

James R. Walker

I USE DATA from the 1979 and 1997 Cohorts of the National Longitudinal Survey of Youth (NLSY79 and NLSY97, respectively) to investigate whether youths can reasonably forecast their future fertility outcomes and, if so, whether the intentions of today's youths differ from those of earlier cohorts. A factor complicating the analysis is that the fertility questions in the NLSY97 differ from traditional fertility-expectations questions appearing, for example, in the NLSY79 and the National Survey of Family Growth 1995. Thus, instead of asking those respondents who state that they expect (plan or intend) to give birth again when they expect to do so, the NLSY97 asks respondents to assess (in separate questions) the percent change they will become (or get someone) pregnant in the next year or become a parent by age twenty. A contribution of this essay is that it develops procedures that relate the fertility-expectations questions in the NLSY97 with the more traditional measures and allows comparisons across surveys.

The young ages of the NLSY97 respondents (fifteen to seventeen years of age) means that the analysis necessarily focuses on the role of expectations near the beginning of the reproductive process. And, unlike studies based on the National Survey of Family Growth, which surveys only women, my analysis also includes men.

The very young ages of the respondents may work against their ability to forecast their fertility behavior. Even among married women well into their reproductive years, traditional fertility-expectations questions perform poorly (Westoff and Ryder 1977). Teenagers face substantial uncertainty and may not be able to forecast their future fertility outcomes or fully assess the risks that they face. For example, at ages fifteen and sixteen, many respondents are not sexually active. Pregnancy and childbirth may not be salient events for these individuals, and, if they myopically extrapolate today's conditions into the future, they may underestimate the potential risks.

Before we can investigate cohort changes in fertility expectations, we must first determine whether youths can form subjective probabilities and whether fertility events are salient to them. Recent evidence (see Hurd and McGarry 1995, 1997) reveals that mature adults (those age fifty and older) are able to form reasonable and valid subjective probabilities of survivorship to later ages (seventy-five and eighty-five).[1] Results from Dominitz and Manski (1996) suggest that youths can provide meaningful responses when the events about which they are questioned are salient.

Even granting that youths can answer expectations questions reliably, why should we care? A common complaint about subjective questions in the economics literature is that "talk is cheap"; we should care (only) about actions (revealed preferences)—the choices that individuals make. Actions are of paramount importance, but many of the decisions made over the life course (regarding, for example, fertility, career, and schooling) are forward looking, and expectations of future outcomes (along with preferences and opportunities) drive current decisions.[2] The basic premise of this essay is that, to the extent to which the economic and social environments facing youths today are different than they were twenty years ago, these differences will be incorporated in the youth's expectations regarding subsequent outcomes.

Economists' skepticism about asking individuals what their perceptions are and why they behave as they do is generally translated to mean that survey measures of expectations are valuable only if they are unbiased estimates of objective probabilities. This is wrong. If such survey responses are indeed subjective probabilities (and not a personality measure of optimism-pessimism) and have predictive content, then empirical measures of expectations are unnecessary only when the assumption of rational expectations is true. In all other cases, survey measures of expectations permit the analysis to estimate the expectation process empirically instead of imposing a possibly convenient but false process on the data.

I find that youths can reliably assess (short-term) fertility outcomes. And, unlike other events (such as mortality and perhaps college graduation), fertility events are salient to them. Nevertheless, I find little difference between the fertility expectations of the members of the NLSY79 cohort and those of the NLSY97 cohort. Differences that do occur are among males, especially poor males.

Questionnaire Structure

As Mosher and Bachrach (1996) note, small differences in the application of fertility-expectations questions can translate into large differences in measured future fertility. This section briefly summarizes the wording and the context of the fertility-expectations questions in the NLSY79 and the NLSY97. The appendix presents the fertility-expectations questions from these surveys.

NLSY79

Questions about fertility expectations have been fielded ten times in the NLSY79. They were included in the first round in 1979 and appeared again for four consecutive rounds starting in 1983. Since 1988, questions regarding fertility expectations have appeared in even-numbered years (and hence in consecutive rounds when the survey switched to a biennial fielding period). In each round, respondents (both men and women) were asked about the total number of children that they expect to have, and those who anticipate having another child were asked about the timing (in months or years) of the next birth. I analyze responses to the 1979 questions.

NLSY97

Round 1 of the NLSY97 included an expectations module that elicited responses on fertility, mortality, schooling, and employment outcomes for respondents who were born in 1980 or 1981. Except for a few individuals (those contacted during the refielding effort in the spring of 1998), most of the respondents were fifteen to seventeen years old.[3] Instead of asking respondents whether they intend to have any more children and, if so, the timing of the next birth, the NLSY97 phrases all expectations questions in terms of the *percent chance* that an event will happen in the next year or by some future age. A common feature of most questions is that they are posed in terms of two time horizons—within the next year and by age twenty or age thirty. For example, respondents are asked the percent chance that they will die within the next year and the percent chance that they will die by age twenty. Two fertility questions were asked. Youths were asked the percent chance of pregnancy in the next year and the percent chance of becoming a parent by age twenty.[4]

Descriptive Results of the NLSY97 Fertility-Expectations Responses

Before analyzing the fertility-expectations responses, it is useful to assess their quality. I consider three aspects of quality: item nonresponse; heaping; and internal consistency. The notion motivating an examination of item nonresponse and heaping is that individuals may respond that they "don't know" or may concentrate their responses to questions that they find cognitively difficult on a few focal values. An analysis of internal consistency will pick up on respondents who answer related questions haphazardly.

Item Nonresponse

Table 7.1 presents a summary listing of seven questions from the 1997 expectations module. For each question, the table reports the number of respondents answering the question, the mean percent chance, the standard deviation, and several quantiles of the response distribution. Besides the two fertility-expectations questions, I select questions to cover a range of different question types—the test question about pizza consumption, two questions about another demographic event (mortality), and questions about educational outcomes. Except for the pizza question, I restrict attention to questions regarding important events that I expect will be salient to all youths.[5]

The questions about the percent chance of eating pizza and contracting the flu in the next year (see the appendix) are introductory and are intended to help respondents understand probabilities and frame their relative risk assessments. For pizza, the mean percent chance of consumption is 93 percent. This does not mean, however, that each respondent faces a (constant) 93 percent chance of eating pizza in the next year; rather, chances vary across members of the sample. The median respondent faces a virtual certainty of consuming pizza in the next year. Those in the bottom 5 percent of the distribution perceive an even chance of consuming pizza, while those in the lowest 1 percent of the distribution perceive only a 3 percent chance.

Slightly fewer than eighty respondents did not answer the fertility-expectations questions. This level of nonresponse is slightly higher than that for the questions about education but considerably lower than that for the questions about mortality. Among those who responded to the fertility-expectations questions, the perceived mean risk of pregnancy in the next year is just below 8 percent.[6] The median respondent faces no perceived risk of pregnancy within the next year. Yet 10 percent (about 350 individuals) perceive the odds of a pregnancy occurring in the next year as roughly 1 to 2 (30 percent), while the top 5 percent (175 individuals) see the chances as even. The response distribution summarizing the chance of becoming a parent by age twenty is to the right of the pregnancy-risk distribution. The median respondent perceives a 1 in 20 chance of becoming a parent by age twenty. Ten percent perceive an even chance of becoming a parent by age twenty, while the top 5 percent assess the odds as being 3 to 1. Hence, expectations of becoming pregnant and becoming a parent are concentrated among relatively few individuals in the population. Importantly, the mean risks approximate the objective risks of teenage pregnancy and childbirth. In 1996, about 10 percent of teenage girls became pregnant (Allan Guttmacher Institute 1999). Statistics on teen birthrates are widely avail-

TABLE 7.1 Frequency Distribution Expectation Questions, NLSY97, Round 1

Question	Missing	Mean	S.D.	No. at 0 Percent	Percentiles									No. at 100 Percent
					1	5	10	25	50	75	90	95	99	
1	42	93.55	18.88	0.61	3	50	75	100	100	100	100	100	100	80.58
2	70	7.88	17.54	66.83	0	0	0	0	0	5	30	50	80	0.73
3	79	17.76	25.99	43.91	0	0	0	0	5	25	50	75	100	2.71
4	113	18.62	22.48	29.07	0	0	0	0	10	40	50	50	94	0.84
5	138	20.31	22.46	25.07	0	0	0	0	10	45	50	50	90	0.78
6	45	93.38	18.83	1.43	0	50	75	100	100	100	100	100	100	76.19
7	57	72.78	31.49	5.20	0	0	20	50	85	100	100	100	100	35.05

Source: Author's compilation.
Note: Sample size = 3,578.
Questions:
1 = Percentage chance will eat pizza in the next year.
2 = Percentage chance will become (or get someone) pregnant within the next year.
3 = Percentage chance will be a parent by age twenty.
4 = Percentage chance will die in the next year.
5 = Percentage chance will die by age twenty.
6 = Percentage chance will graduate from high school by age twenty.
7 = Percentage chance will graduate from college by age thirty.

able, but estimates of the proportion of teens who become parents are not. The NLSY79 fertility histories reveal that approximately 13 to 14 percent of white women and roughly 30 to 33 percent of African American women gave birth while still teenagers.

A review of the mortality questions reveals that not all events are salient to the young respondents. Item nonresponse for these questions is about 4 percent, noticeably higher than for the other questions. The relatively high level of item nonresponse suggests that respondents found the mortality questions more difficult than the other questions. Perhaps more telling is the expected level of mortality that they reported. The mean expected chance of dying in the next year is 20 percent, with the median respondent assessing the chance as 10 percent. One percent of the sample, thirty-four individuals, reply that death within the next year is almost certain (94 percent). Responses to the question asking the percent chance of dying by age twenty are equally stark. The median respondent estimates the chance of death before age twenty to be 1 in 10. The actual mortality risk experienced by the cohort is less than a tenth of 1 percent as six of 9,022 round 1 respondents died between round 1 and round 2 (an interval spanning about eighteen months on average).[7]

The other striking observation to be made about the responses to the expectations questions concerns the college-completion question. The mean expected chance of finishing college by age thirty is 73 percent, with the median respondent assessing the chance to be 85 percent. Fully 25 percent view a college degree by age thirty as a certainty (as likely as eating pizza in the next year).[8] While 50 to 60 percent of recent high school graduates enroll in some form of postsecondary schooling, graduation rates are far lower, on the order of 25 to 30 percent.[9] The high level of expected educational attainment raises the question whether the college-completion question elicits an *expectation* or an *aspiration*.

Interestingly, the same inflated expectations appear not to be associated with high school graduation. The mean expected chance of receiving a high school diploma is 93 percent, and only 5 percent of respondents rate the chances that they will complete high school as even. In actuality, about 95 percent of the population currently complete high school, and dropout rates stand at about 8 percent for whites and 13 percent for blacks. Thus, it appears that high school completion is salient to youths but that assessments of college graduation entail more than subjective probabilities.

Is There Evidence of Heaping?

How dispersed are the subjective assessments? Do individuals with an imprecise view respond with a few focal probabilities (for example, 0, 50, and 100 percent)? Table 7.2 reports heaping for the seven expectations questions listed in table 7.1. The table distinguishes between two types of heaping, the proportion of responses assigned to certainty outcomes (0 or 100 percent) and the proportion assigned to values ending in 0 and 5. I make this distinction because heaping on the certainty events is conceptually different than heaping at other values. Table 7.2 also reports the number of distinct values recorded for each question as well as totals for three combinations of the two types of heaping.

For the pizza question, there were forty-two distinct values reported, including the twenty-one values listed in table 7.2, with 80.2 percent of responses in the certainty category, more than for any of the other questions reported in table 7.2. Of the remaining 18.8 percent, 11.4 percent are heaped on values ending in 0 or 5. The total proportion assigned to a value ending in 0 or 5 and including the certainty events is 92.6 percent. Perhaps more informative than the total proportion assigned to a value ending in 0 or 5 is the share of responses excluding the certainty events assigned to a 0/5 value—60.7 percent.

For the fertility-expectations questions (pregnant next year and parent by age 20), forty and forty-six distinct values, respectively, were reported, and the proportion assigned to a certainty value is less than it was for the pizza question, of course with the allocation to the impossible event (no chance) instead of the certain event (100 percent chance). For the pregnant-next-year question, virtually the same total proportion of responses is assigned to a 0/5 value (including the end points) as for the pizza question. Heaping on 0/5 values for the noncertain event is higher, however, than it was for the pizza question, with 76.7 percent for pregnant next year and 84.6 percent for parent by age twenty.

The mortality questions generated fifty and fifty-three distinct responses, and they exhibit the smallest proportion in the certainty group and about the same heaping on noncertain 0/5 values as do the fertility questions. The education questions exhibit different response properties. The high school–graduation question generated only thirty-four distinct values; it had the largest fraction of responses assigned to a certainty event (save the pizza question), and heaping on noncertain events is the same as for the pregnant-next-year question. On the other hand, the college-graduation-by-age-thirty question generated the most distinct values (fifty-three) and had the lowest fraction assigned to a certain event. It exhibits, however, the most heaping on the 0/5 noncertain values and the largest share assigned to values ending in 0 or 5, including the certain events.

For the seven questions summarized in table 7.2, there is more heaping (as measured by the share assigned to noncertain 0/5 values) for questions spanning a longer time frame (that is, by age twenty or by age thirty). Most of the questions generate as many responses that do not end in 0 or 5 as responses that do. My interpretation is that all questions exhibit heaping but that heaping is less severe for the fertility-expectations questions than for the education questions.

TABLE 7.2   *Summary of Heaping Within Expectation Questions*

Value	Pizza Next Year	Pregnant Next Year	Parent by Age Twenty	Die Next Year	Die by Age Twenty	High School by Age Twenty	College by Age Thirty
0	0.61	66.83	43.91	29.07	25.07	1.43	5.20
5	0.31	3.07	5.79	8.47	7.88	0.20	0.45
10	0.70	5.90	7.94	10.42	11.46	0.39	1.59
15	0.34	1.87	3.27	3.49	4.19	0.11	0.84
20	0.34	2.07	3.77	4.05	4.64	0.25	1.48
25	0.56	3.13	4.11	5.28	5.76	0.28	2.99
30	0.17	1.09	2.10	1.62	2.57	0.20	1.09
35	0.08	0.14	0.36	0.20	0.59	0.06	0.28
40	0.11	0.53	1.29	1.06	1.20	0.14	1.12
45	0.06	0.20	0.50	0.59	0.34	0.03	0.17
50	3.05	5.70	11.29	19.06	20.18	3.44	14.65
55	0.03	0.03	0.06	0.03	0.14	0.11	0.14
60	0.20	0.14	0.56	0.28	0.50	0.34	1.57
65	0.11	0.06	0.14	0.17	0.14	0.11	0.36
70	0.31	0.17	0.64	0.31	0.28	0.28	1.79
75	2.66	0.53	1.79	0.78	0.70	2.40	8.11
80	1.01	0.11	0.61	0.20	0.34	1.29	4.30
85	0.22	0.03	0.34	0.14	0.14	0.22	1.48
90	2.82	0.11	0.48	0.20	0.25	4.39	7.32
95	1.15	0.06	0.11	0.03	0.06	2.85	3.28
100	80.58	0.73	2.71	0.84	0.78	76.19	35.05
Total (0,100)	81.19	67.56	46.62	29.91	25.85	77.62	40.25
Total 0/5	11.41	24.94	45.15	56.38	61.36	17.09	53.01
Total	92.60	92.50	91.77	86.29	87.21	94.71	93.25
Percentage heap	60.7	76.7	84.6	80.4	82.8	76.4	88.7
Distinct values	42	40	46	50	52	34	53

Source: Author's compilation.
Note: The number of observations is 3,578. Total (0,100) = sum of those responding percent chance is 0 or 100. Total 0/5 = total frequency on values ending in 0 or 5 but excluding 0 and 100. Total = total probability on values ending in 0 or 5 including 0 and 100. Percentage Heap = total 0/5 ÷ [100 − total(0,100)].

Internal Consistency of Responses

This section reviews evidence on the internal consistency of the expectations questions. The primary test of internal consistency is that, as subjective probabilities of discrete events, the expectations questions must follow the three axioms of probabilities: impossible events have probability 0; certain events have probability 1; and if event A is part (or a subset) of event B, then the probability of event A is less than or equal to the probability of event B (that is, $pr[A] \leq pr[B]$).

That the first two axioms hold should be obvious. As for the validity of the third, consider the following: Given that NLSY97 respondents are fifteen to seventeen years old, should they die within the next year (event A), they also die by age twenty (event B). (Of course, the converse need not be true.) Hence, $pr[A] \leq pr[B]$.

How well do responses to the mortality questions fare by this test? Of the 3,418 respondents who answered both mortality questions, 432 (12.1 percent) assessed the probability of dying in the next year to be greater than that of dying by age twenty. Another 160 respondents (4.4 percent) failed to answer at least one of the two mortality questions. This test reveals that, for youths, mortality is not a salient event, a result consistent with previous analyses.

The difference in wording between the two fertility-expectations questions makes an exact test of the third axiom of probability impossible. Respondents are asked the probability of becoming pregnant in the next year and the probability of becoming a parent by age twenty. In the absence of abortion and miscarriage, the chance of becoming a parent by age twenty should be no less than the chance of becoming pregnant within the next year. However, a respondent who knows that he or she would terminate an unwanted pregnancy would assess the probability of pregnancy within the next year to be higher (and possibly much higher) than the probability of becoming a parent by age twenty. Population statistics on the rate of abortion and miscarriage confirm that this response pattern is a real possibility. According to the most recent data from the Center for Disease Control, among fifteen- to seventeen-year-olds, 28 percent of pregnancies are aborted, and another 22 percent end in miscarriage. Among eighteen- to nineteen-year-olds, 30 percent of pregnancies end in abortion, and another 10 percent are miscarried (Ventura et al. 1998). Consequently, for individuals fifteen to nineteen years of age, only about half of pregnancies end in live births. It is interesting that 92.2 percent of the 3,477 NLSY97 respondents who answered both fertility-expectations questions assess the probability of pregnancy within the next year to be less than or equal to that of becoming a parent by age twenty—the majority of these individuals reporting a probability of 0 for both events. Six percent (17 of 1,222) of fifteen-year-olds and 12 percent (68 of 585) of seventeen-year-olds report a higher chance of becoming pregnant within the next year than of becoming a parent by age twenty.

Individuals who give an inconsistent response along one demographic dimension are prone to give an inconsistent response along another. Thus, 1.7 percent of respondents give inconsistent responses to both the fertility and mortality questions, more than three times the rate predicted by the marginal distributions (and statistically significant at conventional test levels). Perhaps some respondents had difficulty assessing probabilities and gave repeatedly inconsistent responses.[9]

A look at responses broken down by subgroup provides additional evidence on the nature of responses. Twenty-eight respondents reported that they were pregnant on the round 1 interview date. Of these, seventeen (60.7 percent) report no chance of becoming pregnant in the next year, five report a 100 percent chance, and the remaining six report chances ranging from 5 to 90 percent. It is reasonable for an individual who is currently pregnant to report that there is no chance of *becoming* pregnant (again) within the next twelve months. Perhaps those who reported a 100 percent chance interpreted the question as meaning being pregnant at any time within the next year.

It is harder to understand some of the responses given by women with children. In the fertility section of the NLSY97, which asks respondents to verify the accuracy of information about children given in the household roster obtained at the start of the interview, sixty-five women reported giving birth to one or more children. Of the respondents with children, nearly half (thirty respondents, or 46 percent) reported *no* chance of becoming a parent by age twenty, ten reported a 50 percent chance, and only seven reported a 100 percent chance, with the remaining responses spread across values ranging from 1 to 70 percent.

Another way in which to assess the content of expectations questions is to review whether the cross-sectional variation in responses accords with that along other related dimensions. Table 7.3 utilizes this approach, focusing on the relation between fertility expectations and both sexual activity and contraceptive practice.

Panel A of table 7.3 reports the response frequency by whether the respondent is sexually active. For both fertility outcomes (pregnant within next year and parent by age twenty), teenagers who are sexually active (who have ever had sex) report a higher perceived risk than do those who are not (those who have never had sex). Once again, differences in expectations appear at the upper end of the distribution. For example, among the top quartile, teenagers who are sexually active report a 50 percent chance of becoming a parent by age twenty, whereas those who are not report only a 15 percent chance.

Panel B of table 7.3 reports subjective fertility risk among sexually active respondents by level of sexual activity and birth-control practices.[11] Sexual activity is defined as the number of times the respondent had intercourse during the last twelve months. I split the sample into three intensity levels corresponding to the first, the second and third, and the fourth quartiles. A dichotomous split is defined for birth control—those who always use birth

TABLE 7.3 *Fertility Expectations by Sexual Activity and Contraceptive Practice, NLSY97 Cohort*

A. Sexual Initiation								
Ever Have Sex:	Count	Mean	25	50	75	90	95	99
			Chance Pregnant Next Year[a]					
No	2,149	4.26	0	0	0	10	25	50
Yes	1,316	13.68	0	0	20	50	50	100
			Chance Parent by Age Twenty[a]					
No	2,146	11.64	0	0	15	50	50	97
Yes	1,314	27.60	0	15	50	75	100	100

B. Sexual Frequency and Contraceptive Practice (Among Sexually Active)									
Sexual Activity	Birth Control	Count	Mean	25	50	75	90	95	99
				Chance Pregnant Within Next Year[a]					
Low, 0 to 3	Always	151	9.6	0	0	10	50	50	55
	Not always	74	14.9	0	1	20	50	50	100
Medium, 4 to 20	Always	242	12.2	0	0	18	50	50	100
	Not always	201	19.1	0	5	40	50	70	100
High, 21+	Always	88	19.1	1	5	25	50	50	100
	Not always	143	19.5	0	5	50	50	50	100
				Chance Pregnant by Age Twenty[a]					
Low, 0 to 3	Always	151	24.2	0	15	50	75	90	100
	Not always	74	34.2	0	30	50	80	100	100
Medium, 4 to 20	Always	152	22.2	0	10	50	55	75	100
	Not always	201	34.7	1	28	90	90	100	100
High, 21+	Always	88	26.2	0	15	50	75	80	100
	Not always	143	42.2	10	50	75	100	100	100

Source: Author's compilation.
Note: Restricted to respondents reporting ever having sex. Sexual activity is the number of times had sex in the last twelve months. The categories *low* and *high* correspond with the first and fourth quartiles of the distribution. *Always* means reporting the same number of times using birth control as the number of times had sex (in the last twelve months).
[a] Figures represent response by percentile to the question, "What is the percent chance that you will be a parent in the next year?"

control (that is, the number of times birth control was used exactly equals the number of times sexual activity was engaged in in the last year) and those who do not. Several observations emerge. First, respondents who do not always use birth control perceive the risk of pregnancy and childbirth as being higher than do respondents who always practice birth control. This is true at all levels of sexual activity. Yet the largest gap between the two birth-control groups appears in the risk of parenthood; respondents realize that risks accumulate over time. And, finally, respondents also recognize that fertility is volitional as the percent chance of parenthood exhibits almost no variation by sexual activity among those who claim always to practice birth control.

From this descriptive evidence, I infer that becoming pregnant and giving birth are salient events to these youths. More than 90 percent of the respondents provide internally consistent responses and give responses that vary in a meaningful way with the risks of pregnancy and childbirth. The next section investigates the main issue—whether fertility expectations have changed during the nearly twenty years separating the NLSY79 and the NLSY97 cohorts.

Methodology

As noted above, the NLSY79 and the NLSY97 use different questions to elicit fertility expectations. The 1997 survey asked for the percent chance of becoming a parent by age twenty. The 1979 survey asked for the expected waiting time to the next (first) birth. Yet, despite their apparent differences, the surveys measure different aspects of a waiting-time distribution. To see the relation between the two quantities, assume that menarche occurs at age fourteen, and measure age as time since age fourteen. Let waiting time to first birth be T_1 and denote the probability of giving birth by age t conditional on not having a child by age τ as $F(t|\tau)$. The NLSY97 asked respondents to give subjective estimates of $F(t|\tau)$, evaluated at $t = \tau + 1$ and at $t = 6$.

In thinking about the 1979 responses, it is easier to start from the concept of survivorship (that is, being initially childless) and derive the proportion giving birth.[12] The probability that an individual who is childless at age τ will remain childless until age t $(t > \tau)$ is denoted as $S(t|\tau)$ and equals

$$S(t|\tau) = 1 - F(t|\tau)$$

$$= \mathrm{pr}(T_1 > t | T_1 > \tau)$$

$$= \frac{S(t)}{S(\tau)} = \frac{\exp\left(-\int_0^t h(s)ds\right)}{\exp\left(-\int_0^\tau h(s)ds\right)},$$

$$= \exp\left(-\int_\tau^t h(s)ds\right),$$

where $h(x)$ is the hazard function; that is, the conditional density function $h(x) = F(x)/(1 - F(x))$.

In modeling the expected fertility process for the NLSY79 cohort, I assume that individual responses represent alternative draws from the same subjective distribution. For example, if respondents possess rational expectations about their fertility behavior, then the subjective birth process equals the objective birth process generating teen births. This modeling strategy permits me to use readily available software to estimate the parameters of the expected birth process.[13] An important feature of the modeling strategy is that it must be flexible enough to capture responses by individuals who expect to remain childless.

To account for the fraction who expect to remain childless, I model the expected fertility process as a "mover-stayer" framework, whereby proportion $1 - P_S$ expects to have a first birth (that is, to be a mover) while proportion P_S expects to remain childless (that is, to be a stayer). The survivor function at time t of individuals who remain childless is

$$S(t) = P_S + (1 - P_S)S_M(t).$$

In previous work, James Heckman and I found that a proportional-hazard model with Weibull duration dependence describes many birth processes (see Heckman and Walker 1987, 1989). With time-invariant regressors X, Weibull duration dependence, the hazard function (for the movers) is

$$h(t \mid X) = t^{\gamma_1} \exp(\gamma_0 + X'\beta).$$

The probability of being a stayer is parameterized as[14] $P_s = (1 + e^{-\mu})^{-1}$. The force of these assumptions is to collapse the description of youth expectations into the estimation of the parameters $\theta = (\mu, \beta, \gamma_0, \gamma_1)$.

The estimated survivor function based on the expected timing of the next birth summarizes the fertility expectations for the NLSY79 cohort. I evaluate the estimated survivor function at age twenty for the NLSY79 cohort and compare the proportion estimated to have at least one birth by age twenty with the mean percent chance of being a parent by age twenty reported by the NLSY97 cohort. In what follows, I compare birth expectations for subgroups defined by race, gender, and poverty status at the interview date. To be precise, let the covariate vector X describe the subgroups within the population, and denote the estimated parameters as $\hat{\theta}$. The predicted survivor function in the childless state to age twenty for individual I at age τ_i at the round 1 interview date is

$$S(6 \mid \tau_i) = S(6 \mid \tau_i, X_i, \hat{\theta}).$$

The predicted proportion of group g (defined by race, gender, and poverty status) of the NLSY79 cohort who are childless at age twenty is

$$S_g^{79} = \frac{1}{N_g^{79}} \sum_{i \in g} S\left(6 \middle| \tau_i, X_i, \hat{\theta}\right),$$

where N_g^{79} is the number of individuals in the NLSY79 cohort in the race-gender-poverty group g. Take the complement of the survivorship probability to obtain the probability of becoming a parent by age twenty, P_g^{79},

$$P_g^{79} = 1 - S_g^{79}.$$

Let π_i denote the self-reported percent chance that individual i in the NLSY97 cohort will become a parent by age twenty. Then, the mean chance of group g of the NLSY97 cohort having a birth by age twenty is

$$P_g^{97} = \frac{1}{N_g^{97}} \sum_{i \in g} \pi_i.$$

To measure the change in fertility expectations, I compare P_g^{79} with P_g^{97}.

Empirical Analysis of Shifting Expectations

To analyze expectations for similar ages, I restrict my attention to NLSY79 respondents who were fifteen, sixteen, or seventeen years old at the 1979 interview. And, because of the low numbers of Hispanics included in the NLSY79 sample, I restrict the analysis to whites and blacks. I also exclude individuals who already had their first child before the 1979 interview or who did not give complete information on birth expectations. There are 3,689 respondents who satisfy these conditions. I measure realized birth outcomes for the NLSY79 cohort using information obtained through the 1998 interview. I use information from the most recent interview available for respondents not interviewed in 1998. Births are recorded to the month and year. Respondents without children have waiting time to first birth censored at date of last interview.

Table 7.4 presents the results of a proportional-hazard model incorporating Weibull duration dependence and mover-stayer heterogeneity. Estimates (and standard errors) for the expected fertility process and the actual fertility process are reported for four gender and racial subgroups: white women, black women, white men, and black men. Panel B (actual fertility) uses information on waiting time to first birth through the 1998 round.

Estimates for the expected fertility process show that 6.9 percent of black men and 11.9 percent of black women expect to be childless. Among whites, 6.6 percent of the women and 8.2 of the men expect to be childless. All four gender and racial subgroups exhibit positive duration dependence for expected waiting time to first birth ($\gamma_1 > 1$), implying that the hazard rate increases with age. The negative estimated coefficient on age at interview implies that older respondents anticipate longer first-birth intervals than do younger respondents. Yet only for white men is the estimated coefficient on age at interview statistically significant. Poverty (at time of interview) shortens expected waiting time to first birth for all subgroups but black men. The estimated effect is statistically significant for all groups but black women.

A review of the results for the actual fertility process reveals important differences from those for the expected fertility process. First, for all four subgroups, the proportion without children is substantially larger (about two to four times) than anticipated in 1979. Second, except for black men, duration dependence is estimated to be much less steeply sloped in the actual than in the expected fertility process. The largest difference occurs for white women, who have a much flatter hazard function than anticipated; that is, the actual fertility process is not as concentrated in young ages as is the expected fertility process. The results for age at interview are mixed: they are negative and statistically significant for whites and not precisely estimated for blacks. The estimates reported in table 7.4 reveal that poverty has a positive and statistically significant effect on the hazard rate of the actual fertility process for all groups but black women.

To illustrate the quantitative magnitude of the estimated effects, table 7.5 reports estimated mean waiting time to first birth for poor and nonpoor members of each of the four subgroups. Poverty has a small effect on expected waiting times and a larger effect on observed waiting times. Notice that the effect of poverty on expected waiting time varies little, about three to five months, across the four demographic subgroups. The effect of poverty on observed waiting time is much larger. Poverty reduces waiting time to first birth by about two years for whites, by seven months for black men, and by eleven months for black women. Nevertheless, for all groups, observed waiting time to first birth is longer than the expected waiting time, with the largest gap among the nonpoor respondents.

Table 7.6 compares predicted and observed birthrates in the NLSY79 by poverty status for the same four racial and gender subgroups. Column 1 reports the size of each group. Two sets of predicted cell percentages appear in columns 2 and 3. The figures reported in column 2—the estimated proportion (expressed as a percentage) of respondents (by subgroup) who expected to become teen parents—were obtained using data on expected waiting time to first birth from table 7.4. The figures reported in column 3—the estimated proportion (expressed as a percentage) of respondents (by subgroup) who would actually become teen parents—were obtained using data

TABLE 7.4   Fertility Processes, Weibull Duration Dependence and Mover-Stayer Heterogeneity, NLSY79 Cohort, Individuals Aged Fifteen to Seventeen in 1979

A. Expected Fertility Process

	White Females		Black Females		White Males		Black Males	
	Estimate	S.E.	Estimate	S.E.	Estimate	S.E.	Estimate	S.E.
γ_0	0.7224	0.5332	0.8208	0.8645	1.4338	0.4085	1.1295	0.6770
γ_1	2.1810	0.0429	1.6705	0.0945	2.0221	0.0527	1.4951	0.0728
Age at interview/100	−0.1571	0.2713	−0.1795	0.4384	−0.6305	0.2071	−0.2991	0.3481
Poor	0.2308	0.0717	0.1116	0.0848	0.1243	0.0466	−0.1714	0.0732
μ	−2.6439	0.1103	−1.9996	0.1411	−2.4146	.1004	−2.6093	0.1659
Stayer probability (percentage)	6.6		11.9		8.2		6.9	
Log likelihood	−831.1		−395.2		−1,006.7		−448.7	
No. of observations	1,326		478		1,316		569	

B. Actual Fertility Process

γ_0	1.9105	2.4744	1.7434	-.0712
	0.7943	1.0658	0.9360	1.0850
γ_1	1.3211	0.9763	1.8175	1.1869
	0.0893	0.1172	0.1115	0.1290
Age at interview/100	-1.1019	-1.1364	-1.1621	-0.0212
	0.4014	0.5379	0.4752	0.5434
Poor	0.6595	0.4027	0.6751	0.1656
	0.1153	0.1085	0.1122	0.1173
μ	-1.4631	-1.2856	-.9105	-1.2430
	0.1011	0.1201	0.0860	0.1254
Stayer probability (percentage)	18.8	21.7	28.7	22.4
Log likelihood	-1,269.6	-477.4	-1,191.7	-612.9
No. of observations	1,326	478	1,316	569

Source: Author's compilation.
Note: The hazard function is parameterized as $h(t) = \exp[\gamma_0 + \beta'x]t^{\gamma_1}$ and the stayer probability is $P_s = (1 + e^{-\mu})^{-1}$.

TABLE 7.5   *Mean Waiting Time to First Birth by Gender, Race, and Poverty Status, Expected and Actual Fertility Process (Months)*

	Not Poor	Poor	Difference
Expected-Waiting-Time Process			
Men			
Whites	84.0	80.6	3.4
Blacks	71.5	76.7	5.2
Women			
Whites	78.7	73.2	5.5
Blacks	74.7	71.6	3.1
Observed-Waiting-Time Process			
Males			
Whites	108.6	85.4	23.2
Blacks	93.3	86.5	6.8
Females			
Whites	99.6	75.0	24.2
Blacks	82.6	72.3	10.5

Source: Author's compilation.

on observed waiting time to first birth from table 7.4. Column 4 reports the proportion (expressed as a percentage) of the sample with at least one child by age twenty.

To illustrate how to interpret the figures reported in table 7.6, consider row 7. On the basis of respondents' expectations, it was estimated that 19.1 percent of poor black women expected to become teen parents and the proportional hazard model predicts that 25.0 percent would become teen parents; in reality, 38.9 percent of poor black women became teen parents.

The difference between the proportions given in columns 3 and 4 provide a measure of the goodness of fit of the parameterized fertility process. For poor women, and especially for poor black women, the assumed parametric representation of the first waiting distribution does not capture the proportion who become teen parents very well. Discrepancies between estimated and actual values for other groups are less severe.

A comparison of columns 2 and 3 reveals the accuracy (or the lack thereof) of the fertility expectations. Men (black and white) and white women overestimate the chance of becoming a teen parent. Men's overestimation is particularly striking. For example, the estimated proportion of black men not living in poverty at the time of the interview who expect to become teen fathers is 21.4 percent, while the estimated proportion who

TABLE 7.6   *Comparison of Predicted Versus Observed Teen Parenthood Rates, Individuals Aged Fifteen to Seventeen in 1979, NLSY79*

Group	Count	Predicted Expected (Percentage)	Predicted Actual (Percentage)	Sample Proportion (Percentage) with at Least One Child by Age Twenty
Male				
White				
Poor	240	11.7	8.0	11.8
Nonpoor	1,076	12.8	5.1	5.8
Black				
Poor	254	18.8	13.8	18.5
Nonpoor	315	21.4	12.2	13.9
Female				
White				
Poor	217	16.0	14.8	23.7
Nonpoor	1,109	13.3	10.3	13.3
Black				
Poor	200	19.1	25.0	38.9
Nonpoor	278	17.4	19.2	22.8

Source: Author's compilation.
Note: Figures in the *predicted expected* column are obtained using data on the expected time to first birth and the estimated parameters reported in panel A of table 7.4. Figures in the *predicted actual* column are obtained using data on the observed waiting time to first birth and the estimated parameters reported in panel B of table 7.4. The sample proportion is 1 minus the Kaplan Meier estimate of the proportion childless at age twenty.

actually will become teen fathers is 12.2 percent. Black women, however, underestimate the chance of becoming teen mothers. The difference between the estimated proportion of nonpoor black women who expect to become teen mothers and the estimated proportion who actually become teen mothers is small, 1.8 percentage points, whereas the difference between the estimated proportion of poor black women who expect to become teen mothers and the estimated proportion who actually become teen mothers is large, 5.9 percentage points.

Results from tables 7.4 to 7.6 suggest a subtle interpretation on the accuracy of the fertility expectations by the young members of the NLSY79. The substantial underestimation of teen parenthood by one group (for example, poor black women) suggests some members experience many more teen births than anticipated. Yet, the majority of youth overestimate their fertility. Whereas only 6 to 12 percent expected to remain childless, as of 1988 about a fifth of the sample has yet to have children (when members of the analysis sample were in the their mid-thirties). A rough characterization of the fertility expectations of the NLSY79 cohort is that it (modestly?) underpredicted the incidence of teen fertility and substantially overestimated the timing of their first birth. A question for future research is why poor black women underestimate their fertility. (See Akerlof et al. 1996 and Anderson 1999 for conjectures on possible mechanisms.)

Comparison Between the NLSY79 and the NLSY97 Cohorts

Table 7.7 compares fertility expectations in the NLSY79 and the NLSY97 cohorts. Panel A lists the mean expected proportion of teen parents by race, gender, and poverty subgroup. For NLSY97 cohort, the proportions reported are the mean percent chance responses. Estimates of the proportion of teen parents are from column 2 of table 7.5. Panel B weights the 1979 estimates by the 1997 sample shares to develop estimates of the expected proportion of teen parents by larger subgroups within the population.

Reviewing the figures in panel A, more poor men (black and white) expected to become teen fathers in the NLSY97 cohort than in the NLSY79 cohort. For example, 11.7 percent of white adolescent men living in poverty expected to become teen fathers in 1979, while 18.9 percent did so in 1997, an increase of 7.2 percentage points. Again, 18.8 percent of poor black adolescent men expected to become teen fathers in 1979, while 26.8 percent did so in 1997—an increase of 8 percentage points. For the other groups, changes from 1979 to 1997 are smaller. The proportion of adolescent men not living in poverty who expected to become teen fathers increased 2 to 2.5 percentage points. And the proportion of adolescent women not living in poverty who expected to become teen mothers experienced essentially no change at all from 1979 to 1997. The summary proportions by single characteristic reported in panel B of table 7.7 show that the increase in expected teen parenthood between 1979 and 1997 is modest and concentrated among men and the poor.

Have recent programs to encourage men to act more responsibly where their children are concerned made poor adolescent men become more willing to report their expected fertility rates accurately? Do the increased fertility rates that they report reflect the harsh labor market with which they are faced? Or are they simply an artifact of the different survey instruments used in the two surveys? Perhaps the answers to these (and other) questions will emerge from analyses of future waves of the NLSY97.

Conclusion

The expectations module within the NLSY97 instrument was one of its novel features. My analysis has considered only a few of the questions contained within that module. I find that youths can provide meaningful

TABLE 7.7   *Predicted Percentage with at Least One Child by Age Twenty, 1979 and 1979, Individuals Aged Fifteen to Seventeen at Interview Date*

| | 1997 | | 1979 | |
	N	Percentage	Percentage	Change 1979 to 1997
A. Percentage of Teen Parents by Gender, Race, and Poverty Status				
Males				
White				
Poor	225	18.9	11.7	7.2
Nonpoor	806	15.4	12.8	2.6
Black				
Poor	185	26.8	18.8	8.0
Nonpoor	288	23.5	21.4	2.1
Females				
White				
Poor	207	19.5	16.0	3.5
Nonpoor	800	13.4	13.3	.1
Black				
Poor	193	19.7	19.1	.6
Nonpoor	306	17.4	17.4	.0
B. Percentage of Teen Parents Using the Sample Composition of the 1997 Survey				
Overall	3,010	17.4	15.1	2.3
Males	1,504	18.9	15.0	3.9
Females	1,506	15.9	15.2	.7
White	2,038	15.4	13.2	2.2
Black	972	21.5	19.2	2.3
Poor	810	21.0	16.2	4.8
Nonpoor	2200	16.0	14.7	1.3

Source: Author's compilation.
Note: The marginal groupings listed in panel B calculate the 1979 percentage using the population shares of the 1997. Thus, the differences control for the demographic composition within each subpopulation.

probability assessments of salient events. I find that teen pregnancy, teen parenthood, and high school completion are salient events while mortality and college graduation are not.

A limited specification was used to investigate possible changes in fertility expectations across cohorts. The analysis reveals little change in teenage fertility outcomes. The limited evidence available suggests that, while young men living in poverty exhibit increased expectations of teen fatherhood, young women's expectations of teen motherhood remain essentially unchanged. Future work will investigate whether (and, if so, how) the stability of expected rates of teen parenthood accords with educational expectations (or aspirations) in the light of the changing labor market conditions facing youths at the beginning of the new century.

Appendix

The sequence of fertility-expectations questions put to all NLSY79 respondents is reproduced in the first section of this appendix, interviewer instructions and the full expectations module from round 1 of the NLSY97 in the second. (The expectations module was the last substantive module of the NLSY97 questionnaire. It was administered only to individuals born in 1980 and 1981.) Instructions to the interviewer that are not read to respondents appear in brackets. For convenience, the label and Center for Human Resource Research reference number for each question from the NLSY79 are given in parentheses.

Fertility-Expectations Questions in the NLSY79

Now I'd like to ask you your opinions and expectations about family size.

First, what do you think is the ideal number of children for a family? (S03Q01A, R131)

How many children do you want to have? (S03Q01B, R132)

[*The interviewer was instructed to obtain date of birth (month/day/year) for each child up to a maximum of five.*]

When was your first/second/etc. child born?

Altogether, how many (more) children do you expect to have? (S03Q03, R153)

[*The following question was asked only of those who expect to have more children.*]

When do you expect to have your (first/next) child—in how many months or years? (S03Q04, R154 [months], R155 [years])

Expectations Questions in Round 1 of the NLSY97

Each of the next set of questions will ask you for your best guess at the chance that something will happen in the future. You can think of the percent chance *that some event will occur as the number of* chances out of 100 *that the event will take place. If you think that something is impossible, consider it as having a 0 percent chance. If you think the event is possible but unlikely, you might say there is a 3 percent chance or a 15 percent chance. If you think the chance is pretty even, you can say there is a*

46 percent chance or perhaps a 52 percent chance. If you think the event is likely but not certain, you might say there is a 78 percent chance or a 94 percent chance. If you think it is certain to happen, give it a 100 percent chance. Just to make sure that you are comfortable with the scale, I'd like you to do a few practice questions, and explain your answer to me.

What do you think is the percent chance that you will get the flu sometime in the next year?

What do you think is the percent chance that you will eat pizza sometime in the next year?

Think about yourself one year from now. The first questions concern what you expect to be doing then, in terms of school and work.

What is the percent chance you will be a student in a regular school one year from now?

[At this point, instructions are provided to the interviewer on how to define "regular" school.]

If you are in school a year from now, what is the percent chance that you will also be working for pay more than 20 hours per week?

[At this point, instructions are provided to the interviewer on how to define "working."]

If you are not in school a year from now, what is the percent chance that you will be working for pay more than 20 hours per week?

What is the percent chance you will become pregnant within one year from now? [if female]

What is the percent chance you will get someone pregnant within the next year? [if male]

The next questions concern some risks that you might face in the next year.

What is the percent chance that you will drink enough to get seriously drunk at least once in the next year?

What is the percent chance you will be the victim of a violent crime at least once in the next year?

What is the percent chance that you will be arrested, whether rightly or wrongly, at least once in the next year?

What is the percent chance you will die from any cause—crime, illness, accident, and so on—in the next year?

The next questions ask about your school and work situation at the time of your 20th birthday.

What is the percent chance that you will have received a high school diploma by the time you turn 20?

What is the percent chance you will serve time in jail or prison between now and when you turn 20?

What is the percent chance you will become the mother/father of a baby sometime between now and when you turn 20?

What is the percent chance that you will die (from any causes—crime, illness, accident, and so on) between now and when you turn 20?

Now think ahead to when you turn 30 years old.

What is the percent chance that you will have a four-year college degree by the time you turn 30 years old?

What is the percent chance that you will be working for pay more than 20 hours per week when you turn 30?

_____

I thank Laura Lindberg, Bob Michael, and anonymous referees for helpful comments.

Notes

1. For an alternative perspective, see Viscusi and Hakes (1998).

2. Moreover, information on individuals' (subjective) assessments of future outcomes provides additional evidence of key relations, facilitating the estimation of richer specifications of dynamic behavior. For an insightful discussion of using subjective information to estimate structural models of dynamic behavior, see Rosenzweig and Wolpin (1993). Preliminary work is now emerging in which expectations enter structural models of decision making (see, for example, Manski and Straub 2000).

3. Parents were asked a subset of the expectations questions regarding the youth respondent, including the chance that the youth will be a parent by age twenty. Responses to these questions are tabulated in appendix table 7A.1.

4. Specifically, girls were asked about the chance of becoming pregnant, while boys were asked the chance of getting someone pregnant.

5. I therefore exclude the victim, arrest, and jail questions.

6. Table 7.1 combines responses to two distinct questions asked separately of boys and girls (see the appendix).

7. The lowest nonzero answer permitted by the CAPI (computer-assisted personal interview) instrument is 1 percent, which may account for some of the discrepancy between the objective and the subjective mortality risks.

TABLE 7A.1   Distribution of Expectations by Race and Gender, Youth and Parents

	Count	Mean	S.D.	Percentile						
				5	10	25	50	75	90	95
White males										
Pregnant within next yr	1015	7.25	16.12	0	0	0	0	5	25	50
Parent by age twenty	1018	16.14	23.06	0	0	0	5	25	50	60
HS grad by age twenty	1026	93.93	17.54	50	80	100	100	100	100	100
College grad age thirty	1021	67.73	32.44	0	10	50	75	99	100	100
Work 20+ hrs age thirty	1025	94.60	12.70	75	80	95	100	100	100	100
White females										
Pregnant within next yr	987	4.66	13.03	0	0	0	0	0	15	42
Parent by age twenty	991	14.66	24.17	0	0	0	0	20	50	75
HS grad by age twenty	998	96.20	17.30	75	95	100	100	100	100	100
College grad age thirty	999	78.08	29.71	3	25	60	95	100	100	100
Work 20+ hrs age thirty	992	93.42	15.36	50	75	95	100	100	100	100
Black males										
Pregnant within next yr	463	13.67	21.72	0	0	0	0	20	50	50
Parent by age twenty	461	24.65	29.23	0	0	0	10	50	75	85
HS grad by age twenty	470	91.60	20.91	50	73	100	100	100	100	100
College grad age thirty	467	71.82	31.39	5	20	50	80	100	100	100
Work 20+ hrs age thirty	468	90.52	20.09	50	70	90	100	100	100	100
Black females										
Pregnant within next yr	492	7.96	20.31	0	0	0	0	2	25	50
Parent by age twenty	488	18.30	28.99	0	0	0	0	25	56	100

(Table continues on p. 226.)

TABLE 7A.1   *Continued*

							Percentile				
	Count	Mean	S.D.	5	10	25	50	75	90	95	
HS grad by age twenty	494	94.17	18.47	50	80	100	100	100	100	100	
College grad age thirty	492	76.33	31.38	3	20	50	95	100	100	100	
Work 20+ hrs age thirty	491	90.41	20.16	50	50	90	100	100	100	100	
Other males											
Pregnant within next yr	282	10.49	18.82	0	0	0	0	10	50	50	
Parent by age twenty	282	21.40	26.45	0	0	0	10	45	50	75	
HS grad by age twenty	286	87.00	24.30	25	50	90	100	100	100	100	
College grad age thirty	284	67.09	31.33	10	20	50	75	99	100	100	
Work 20+ hrs age thirty	284	89.67	19.06	50	70	90	100	100	100	100	
Other females											
Pregnant within next yr	259	9.45	19.40	0	0	0	0	10	42	50	
Parent by age twenty	259	18.66	28.26	0	0	0	0	30	68	85	
HS grad by age twenty	259	88.81	25.28	15	50	95	100	100	100	100	
College grad age thirty	258	73.50	30.87	2	25	50	90	100	100	100	
Work 20+ hrs age thirty	258	88.22	22.16	35	50	87	100	100	100	100	
Parent's expectation for their child											
White male											
Parent by age twenty	884	13.40	22.23	0	0	0	0	20	50	50	
HS grad by age twenty	895	95.26	16.11	50	90	100	100	100	100	100	
Col grad by age thirty	894	66.05	33.88	0	2	50	75	100	100	100	
Wrk 20 hrs + age thirty	896	97.22	10.35	80	95	100	100	100	100	100	

White female										
Parent by age twenty	881	13.60	23.20	0	0	0	0	20	50	50
HS grad by age twenty	885	96.27	14.71	70	99	100	100	100	100	100
Col grad by age thirty	880	72.92	30.58	0	25	50	80	100	100	100
Wrk 20 hrs + age thirty	883	91.80	16.84	50	75	90	100	100	100	100
Black male										
Parent by age twenty	394	17.85	26.44	0	0	0	0	50	50	70
HS grad by age twenty	405	89.77	23.26	40	50	100	100	100	100	100
Col grad by age thirty	398	64.46	34.14	0	0	50	70	100	100	100
Wrk 20 hrs + age thirty	405	93.13	15.94	50	75	100	100	100	100	100
Black female										
Parent by age twenty	407	16.64	30.04	0	0	0	0	20	50	100
HS grad by age twenty	416	93.46	18.12	50	75	100	100	100	100	100
Col grad by age thirty	410	72.49	31.72	0	20	50	80	100	100	100
Wrk 20 hrs + age thirty	413	93.09	16.77	50	75	100	100	100	100	100
Other male										
Parent by age twenty	222	18.96	28.00	0	0	0	0	30	50	80
HS grad by age twenty	224	90.64	22.44	40	60	100	100	100	100	100
Col grad by age thirty	221	66.06	34.80	0	0	50	75	100	100	100
Wrk 20 hrs + age thirty	226	95.32	15.27	70	90	100	100	100	100	100
Other female										
Parent by age twenty	189	17.68	26.50	0	0	0	0	40	75	75
HS grad by age twenty	190	93.31	18.75	50	75	100	100	100	50	100
Col grad by age thirty	189	72.75	28.57	0	40	50	80	100	100	100
Wrk 20 hrs + age thirty	189	92.19	17.80	50	70	99	100	100	100	100

Source: Author's compilation.

8. Interestingly, parents have equally high expectations of college graduation for their children. (From tabulations prepared by Kenneth Wolpin in January 1999.)

9. For an analysis of educational expectations of the NLSY97 respondents, see Reynolds and Pemberton (forthcoming).

10. For a similar finding in the Health and Retirement Survey, see Bassett and Lumsdaine (2000).

11. I thank Bob Michael for suggesting that I investigate this dimension.

12. A potential problem is that only respondents who say that, yes, they except to have more children are asked the expected waiting time to the next birth. Presumably, those with less than a 50 percent chance of having another child will respond that they do not expect to have any more children. Nevertheless, these individuals still may face a nontrivial chance of having another child and of having that child at a relatively young age. The relatively low proportion expected to remain childless suggests that the bias induced by the screening question is small. For an insightful discussion of this and other problems posed by the interpretation of questions about intentions, see Manski (1990).

13. An alternative modeling strategy would be to assume that responses represent a particular feature of the subjective-waiting-time distribution, such as the mean or the median of the distribution. Future work will investigate this modeling strategy.

14. The stayer probabilities can be estimated as functions of time-invariant covariates, but the results that I go on to report adopt simple specifications that restrict μ to be a constant (common across all individuals).

References

Akerlof, George, Janet Yellen, and Michael Katz. 1996. "An Analysis of Out-of-Wedlock Childbearing in the United States." *Quarterly Journal of Economics* 111(2): 277–317.

Allan Guttmacher Institute. 1999. "U.S. Teenage Pregnancy Rate Drops Another 4% between 1995 and 1996." Press Release. New York: Allan Guttmacher Institute, April 29.

Anderson, Elijah. 1999. *Code of the Street: Decency, Violence, and the Moral Life in the Inner City.* New York: Norton.

Bassett, William F., and Robin Lumsdaine. 2000. "Probability Limits: Are Subjective Assessments Adequately Assessed?" *Journal of Human Resources* 36(2): 327–63.

Dominitz, Jeffrey, and Charles Manski. 1996. "Perceptions of Economic Insecurity: Evidence from the Survey of Economic Expectations." *IRP* discussion paper 1105–96. Madison, Wisc.: Institute for Research on Poverty.

Heckman, James J., and James R. Walker. 1987. "Using Goodness-of-Fit and Other Criteria to Choose among Competing Duration Models: A Case Study of Hutterite Data." In *Sociological Methodology 1987*, edited by C. Clogg. Washington, D.C.: American Sociological Association.

———. 1989. "The Relationship between Wages and Income and the Timing and Spacing of Births: Evidence from Swedish Longitudinal Data." *Econometrica* 58(6): 1411–41.

Hurd, Michael, and Kathleen McGarry. 1995. "Evaluation of Subjective Probability Distributions in the HRS." *Journal of Human Resources* 30(5): S268–S292.

———. 1997. "The Predictive Validity of Subjective Probabilities of Survival." *NBER* working paper 6193. Cambridge, Mass.: National Bureau of Economic Research.

Manski, Charles F. 1990. "The Use of Intentions Data to Predict Behavior: A Best-Case Analysis." *Journal of the American Statistical Association* 85(412): 934–40.

Manski, Charles F., and John Straub. 2000. "Worker Perceptions of Job Insecurity in the Mid-1980s: Evidence from the Survey of Economic Expectations." *Journal of Human Resources* 35(3): 447–79.

Mosher, William D., and Christine A. Bachrach. 1996. "Understanding U.S. Fertility: Continuity and Change in the National Survey of Family Growth, 1988–1995." *Family Planning Perspectives* 28(1): 4–11.

Reynolds, John, and Jennifer Pemberton. Forthcoming. "Rising College Expectations among Youth in the U.S.: A Comparison of 15 and 16 Year Olds in the 1979 and 1997 NLSY." *Journal of Human Resources.* (Paper first presented at the NLSY97 Early Results Conference.) Washington: Bureau of Labor Statistics [November 18–19].

Rosenzweig, Mark R., and Kenneth I. Wolpin. 1993. "Maternal expectations and Ex Post Rationalization: The Usefulness of Survey Information on the Wantedness of Children." *Journal of Human Resources* 28(2): 205–29.

Ventura, Stephanie J., Sally C. Curtin, and T. J. Mathews. 1998. "Teenage Births in the United States: National and State Trends, 1990–96." *National Vital Statistics System.* Hyattsville, Md.: National Center for Health Statistics.

Viscusi, W. Kip, and John Hakes. 1998. "Why the Health and Retirement Study Survival Probability Is Not a Probability." Unpublished paper. Harvard University.

Westoff, Charles, and Norman Ryder. 1977. "The Predictive Validity of Reproductive Intentions." *Demography* 14(4): 431–45.

8

Who Are Youth "At Risk"? Expectations Evidence in the NLSY97

Jeff Dominitz, Charles F. Manski, and Baruch Fischhoff

T HERE has long been public concern with the prospects of youth at risk of adverse socioeconomic outcomes, but identifying these youths has been a problem for policy researchers and practitioners alike. For example, recent California legislation directs state-funded employment-training programs to serve youth "who are considered to be at-risk of homelessness, crime, or welfare dependency, and who lack employment skills" (S.B. 2190, introduced February 20, 1998). The legislation does not, however, interpret the critical phrase "considered to be at-risk."

Youth have traditionally been classified as "at risk" according to demographic attributes and personal experiences believed to predict adverse outcomes. For example, Levin (1993, 11) defines youth at risk of adverse schooling outcomes as follows: "At-risk students are defined to be those who are unlikely to succeed in school as these institutions are currently constituted because they do not have the experiences in the home, family, and community on which school success is based." A complementary approach is to classify youth as at risk according to their parents' or their own expectations of future adverse outcomes. Youths and their parents may have information not expressed by the attributes and experiences that can be observed by researchers. Youths and their parents may perceive risks of adverse outcomes differently than do researchers, who base their assessments on statistical predictions. The risk perceptions that youths and their parents hold may affect youth behavior. For all these reasons, it is important to understand how youths and their parents perceive the future.

This essay analyzes data from the National Longitudinal Survey of Youth, 1997 Cohort (NLSY97), on the expectations of youths and their parents. The expectations module of the NLSY97 elicited from youths aged sixteen and seventeen subjective probabilities of events ranging from high school and college completion to arrest and incarceration, criminal victimization, pregnancy and parenthood, and mortality. The questions sought short-, medium-, and longer-term forecasts, asking about events in the year ahead and about ones that may occur by age twenty or thirty. A subset of the questions was posed to parents as well.

We examine responses to three questions, posed to both youths and their parents, eliciting expectations for medium-term adverse socioeconomic outcomes. Specifically, these questions elicit subjective probabilities of completing high school by age twenty, serving time in jail or prison by age twenty, and becoming a parent by age twenty. We summarize and compare the perceptions of youths and parents and also examine the cross-sectional variation of expectations with demographic attributes and past experiences reported in the NLSY97. Thus, we are able to learn whether youth apt to be classified as at risk by their observed characteristics perceive themselves that way.

Our criterion for classifying youth as at risk is adapted from a previous analysis of perceptions of economic insecurity among American adults (Dominitz and Manski 1997a). There, we classified respondents to the Survey of Economic Expectations (SEE) as *highly insecure* if they reported relatively high subjective probabilities of job loss, burglary victimization, and absence of health insurance. In similar fashion, we classify respondents to the NLSY97 as *at risk* if they report relatively high subjective probabilities of not completing high school, serving time in jail, and becoming a parent. We also present alternative measures that classify youth as *at risk* if they report relatively high subjective probabilities for at least one or two adverse outcomes.

An important feature of the NLSY97, one not shared by the SEE, is the wealth of data on past experiences that may be associated with a respondent's expectations. These associations may provide insight into the information that shapes expectations. Youths reported their more sensitive experiences, such as criminal and sexual activity, confidentially in the self-administered part of the NLSY97 instrument. To the extent that parents are unaware of these experiences, they must rely on other information in forming expectations for their children's futures. Comparing youth and parent expectations, conditional on self-reported experiences, may suggest differences in how youths and parents form their expectations.

Eliciting Expectations in the NLSY97

The expectations module of the NLSY97 contains seventeen questions eliciting subjective probabilities of future events. We analyze the responses to three questions asked consecutively of both youths and parents (regarding the participating youths): What is the percent chance that you will have received a high school diploma by the time you turn 20? What is the percent chance you will serve time in jail or prison between now and when you turn 20? What is the percent chance that you will become the mom/dad of a baby sometime between now and when you turn 20? The expectations module was administered to the 3,546 NLSY97 youth respondents born in 1980 and 1981. Item response rates generally exceeded 99 percent. For the three target questions (diploma, jail, parenthood), they were 99.6, 99.5, and 98.6 percent, respectively. The response rates among the 3,062 parents interviewed were 99.1, 99.2, and 97.9 percent, respectively.

Eliciting expectations in the form of subjective probabilities has recently become common in large-scale household surveys, including the Health and Retirement Study, the Panel Study of Income Dynamics, the Survey of Economic Expectations, the Bank of Italy's Survey of Household Income and Wealth, and Tilburg University's CentER Savings Survey. For discussions of these studies, see Dominitz and Manski (1997a, 1999).

Eliciting expectations in the form of subjective probabilities allows respondents to reveal their beliefs more precisely than is possible with questions using verbal quantifiers (for example, *likely, rare*) (see Budescu and Wallsten 1995; Juster 1966; Manski 1990; and Das, Dominitz, and Van Soest 1999). Probabilistic elicitation also enables analyses that are not possible with qualitative responses. For example, researchers can evaluate expectations for different events in terms of their consistency with the algebra of probability (Bayes theorem, the law of total probability, and so on) (for example, Dominitz and Manski 1997b; Fischhoff and Beyth-Marom 1983; Yates 1990). Researchers can also compare expectations with known event frequencies to reach conclusions about the correspondence between subjective beliefs and frequentist realities (for example, Lichtenstein et al. 1978). Moreover, researchers can use elicited subjective probabilities directly when estimating structural models of decision making under uncertainty (for example, Walker, chapter 7 in this volume).

The primary criticism of probability elicitation has questioned the willingness and ability of individuals to respond to the questions posed (see Zimmer 1983, 1984; Erev and Cohen 1990; and Wallsten et al. 1993). We have previously addressed this concern in our analyses of SEE data (see Dominitz and Manski 1997a, 1997b; Dominitz 1998; Manski and Straub 2000), but it must be addressed anew in the NLSY97 setting, especially given the participation of youths, whose cognitive processes might differ from those of adults.

Fischhoff et al. (2000) have previously assessed the meaningfulness of the subjective probabilities reported by NLSY97 youths. They report that expectations of schooling, fertility, and crime events appear to express respondents' beliefs in a plausible fashion, with internally consistent expectations regarding related events. The statistical associations between probability reports and responses to related NLSY97 questions appear sensible. Aggregated forecasts tend to match up to actual population event frequencies.

Perhaps the main concerns raised by Fischhoff et al. (2000) relate to mortality expectations. The elicited subjective probabilities of death are much higher than actuarial realities and, moreover, are largely insensitive to the forecast horizon (next year, by age twenty). The mortality questions were asked only of youths, not their parents. We do not analyze these responses here, although they clearly could be considered an element of youth perceptions of being at risk.

Fischhoff et al. (2000) also discuss a tendency for probability responses to some questions to bunch at the value 50 percent. On the basis of other results (Bruine de Bruine et al. 2000; Fischhoff and Bruine de Bruin 1999), they propose that using an open-ended response format in the NLSY97 (rather than, say, a graphic scale with integer tick marks and numerals identifying every tenth mark) encouraged some respondents to respond "50" as "an expression of epistemic uncertainty (i.e., 'fifty-fifty'), rather than as a quantitative probability" (Fischhoff et al. 2000, 200). Whatever the case may be for other questions, the diploma and jail questions showed little bunching at 50—only 3.3 percent of the youth and 4.4 percent of the parent responses to the diploma question and only 2.8 percent of the youth and 2.4 percent of the parent responses for the jail question. The responses to the parenthood question show somewhat more bunching at 50, with rates of 11.6 percent and 13.6 percent, respectively.

Broad Patterns of Risk Perceptions

The expectations module was administered to 3,546 youths and 3,062 parents. Our analysis uses the 2,922 cases in which both parent and youth responded to all three of the target questions. Over three-fourths of the reduction in sample size (from 3,546 to 2,922) arises from interview nonresponse among parents, whereas less than one-fourth arises from item nonresponse by the youth and/or the parent. Our assessment of the data indicates that our findings on youth expectations are not substantively affected by the sample-selection restrictions.

The discussion in this section proceeds as follows. First, we describe the marginal distributions of the responses. Next, we introduce our classification of youth at risk. Finally, we disaggregate the data by gender and race-ethnicity and examine the association between the responses of youths and those of their parents.

Marginal Response Distributions

Table 8.1 shows the frequency distributions of responses to the diploma, jail, and parenthood questions, by youths and parents. Table 8.2 extracts the most salient features of table 8.1. Observe that most youths and parents see no chance at all of an adverse schooling or incarceration outcome, 78.7 percent of youths and 84.2 percent of parents reporting a 100 percent chance of receiving a high school diploma by age twenty, and 66.7 percent of youths and 83.0 percent of parents reporting no chance of serving jail time by age twenty. The responses to the parenthood question are more varied, with 45.3 percent of youths and 56.7 percent of parents reporting no chance of the youth becoming a parent by age twenty. On all three questions, the fraction of parents seeing no chance at all of an adverse outcome for their child exceeds the fraction of youths seeing no chance at all of an adverse outcome for themselves. This result runs counter to the common wisdom of youths seeing themselves as invulnerable (see also Quadrel, Fischhoff, and Davis 1993).

Classifying Youth as at Risk

We classify youths as at risk if they reported subjective probabilities passing the following thresholds (an alternative classification uses parent reports): no more than a 90 percent chance of receiving a high school diploma by age twenty; at least a 5 percent chance of serving time in jail by age twenty; and at least a 10 percent chance of becoming a parent by age twenty.

There is inevitably some arbitrariness in choosing thresholds to determine any discrete categorization of at-risk youth. The specific thresholds chosen here (that is, 90, 5, 10) are intended to convey nonnegligible but not overwhelming risks of adverse outcomes. Table 8.1 shows that 14.7 percent of youths perceive no more than a 90 percent chance of completing high school by age twenty, that 24.8 percent perceive at least a 5 percent chance of incarceration, and that 43.5 percent perceive at least a 10 percent chance of parenthood. Analogous calculations could, of course, be performed using other thresholds.

We use the thresholds to define three increasingly stringent criteria for being at risk. Youths are classified as *At-Risk I* if they pass the threshold for at least one adverse outcome, as *At-Risk II* if they pass the threshold for at least two adverse outcomes, and as *At-Risk III* if they pass the threshold for all three adverse outcomes. Thus, all youths classified At-Risk III are necessarily At-Risk II, and all those classified At-Risk II are necessarily At-Risk I.

Applying these alternative criteria to youth self-reports resulted in classifying 53.8 percent of the sample population as At-Risk I, 23.2 percent as At-Risk II, and 6.2 percent as At-Risk III. Applying the same criteria to the

TABLE 8.1   *Frequencies of Percentage Chance Responses, Youths and Parents*

Percentage Chance	Youths			Parents		
	Diploma	Jail	Parenthood	Diploma	Jail	Parenthood
0	39	1,950	1,323	40	2,425	1,656
1	3	116	59		61	50
2		66	46		24	16
3	2	60	48		7	8
4		5	4			
5	5	183	166	4	61	115
6 to 9		4	3		2	3
10	12	189	216	5	134	211
11 to 14			3			
15	3	48	102	1	12	22
16 to 19		2	3			
20	6	64	117	4	45	124
21 to 24						
25	5	58	117	7	33	94
26 to 29			3			
30	3	33	64	6	16	42
31 to 34			1			1
35	1	3	12		1	5
36 to 39		2				
40	5	12	39	7	10	27
41 to 44		1	1			
45		4	16			3
46 to 49		1	4			
50	95	83	340	129	69	397
51 to 54	4	2	7			
55		1	2			
56 to 59		1	1			
60	10	7	17	6	4	8
61 to 64						
65	4		3		1	1
66 to 69			1			
70	7	2	19	13	1	5
71 to 74	1					
75	62	9	52	38	4	13
76 to 79	4	2	2			
80	33	2	19	49	1	22

(*Table continues on p. 236.*)

TABLE 8.1   *Continued*

Percentage Chance	Youths			Parents		
	Diploma	Jail	Parenthood	Diploma	Jail	Parenthood
81 to 84						
85	6	1	12	8	1	4
86 to 89	4					
90	118	2	14	75	1	5
91 to 94	6					
95	84	1	4	24		4
96	2					
97	3		1	1		
98	10		1	4		
99	86		3	40	1	
100	2,299	8	77	2,461	8	86
Total	2,922	2,922	2,922	2,922	2,922	2,922

Source: Authors' compilation.

TABLE 8.2   *Features of the Marginal Response Distributions (From Table 8.1)*

Percentage Chance	Youths (Percentage)			Parents (Percentage)		
	Diploma	Jail	Parenthood	Diploma	Jail	Parenthood
0	1.3	66.7	45.3	1.4	83.0	56.7
50	3.3	2.8	11.6	4.4	2.4	13.6
100	78.7	0.3	2.6	84.2	.3	2.9
Other value	16.7	30.2	40.5	10.0	14.4	26.8

Source: Authors' compilation.

parent reports resulted in classifying 43.8 percent, 15.4 percent, and 4.8 percent of youths as At-Risk I, At-Risk II, and At-Risk III, respectively. As was apparent in the marginal distributions, higher risks of adverse outcomes were reported by youths for themselves than by parents for their children.

The magnitude 6.2 percent of the At-Risk III measure based on self-reports indicates that youths perceiving high risks of one adverse outcome tend to perceive high risks of other adverse outcomes. If subjective probabilities of the three adverse outcomes were statistically independent of one another, only 1.6 percent of youths would be classified as At-Risk III

(0.016 = 0.147 × 0.248 × 0.435). The parent responses show a similar positive association of risk perceptions.

In the remainder of this essay, youths are disaggregated by gender, race-ethnicity, and other attributes. Although all three at-risk measures are reported in the tables, the text focuses on the At-Risk II and At-Risk III measures, which seem to us more interesting than the At-Risk I measure.

Responses by Gender and Race-Ethnicity

Table 8.3 disaggregates responses by the gender and race-ethnicity of the NLSY97 youths. The three race-ethnicity categories are mutually exclusive: all youths reporting Hispanic ethnicity are classified as Hispanic, while those reporting their race as African American or white are classified as such if they are not Hispanic. For each question, the table reports the mean response along with the 0.10 quantile, the 0.50 quantile (that is, the median), and the 0.90 quantile.

Table 8.3 shows that all gender and racial-ethnicity groups have high concentrations of 100 responses for high school diploma and of 0 responses for jail and parenthood. The mean probabilities, however, reveal some differences. On average, the expectations of male youth are less favorable than are those of female youth. For boys and girls, respectively, the mean percent chances are 92.7 and 95.3 for receiving a high school diploma, 7.3 and 3.5 for serving jail time, and 19.1 and 16.4 for parenthood.

Non-Hispanic white youth report higher probabilities of high school completion and lower probabilities of incarceration and parenthood than do African American and Hispanic youth of the same gender. This finding holds strictly for mean reports of both male youth and female youth, weakly for the quantiles in table 8.3.

In all the cases reported in table 8.3, the median of the difference between parent and child reports is 0. The means of the parent-child differences, however, are relatively large in some instances. For example, the mean percent chance of serving time in jail reported by young Hispanic men is almost twice as high as that reported by their parents, 10.9 versus 5.8, respectively. The mean probabilities of parenthood reported by male youth are also considerably higher than those reported by their parents; 24.5 versus 17.5 (African American, non-Hispanic), 23.5 versus 19.9 (Hispanic), and 15.1 versus 12.3 (white non-Hispanic). The magnitude of the youth-parent differentials is uniformly lower for female youth than for male youth. The largest relative differences occur for incarceration probabilities, especially among young Hispanic women (5.0 versus 1.7).

Further detail on the correspondence between youth and parent expectations is provided in tables 8.4 to 8.9, which present the responses

(Text continues on p. 246.)

TABLE 8.3   Distribution of Responses, by Gender and Race-Ethnicity

Group	Percentage Chance of Diploma					Percentage Chance of Jail					Percentage Chance of Parenthood				
	Obs.	Mean	0.10 Quantile	0.50 Quantile	0.90 Quantile	Obs.	Mean	0.10 Quantile	0.50 Quantile	0.90 Quantile	Obs.	Mean	0.10 Quantile	0.50 Quantile	0.90 Quantile
Males															
All															
Youth	1,469	92.69	75	100	100	1,469	7.26	0	0	25	1,469	19.05	0	5	75
Parent	1,469	93.35	75	100	100	1,469	4.70	0	0	15	1,469	15.15	0	0	50
Difference	1,469	0.66	-9	0	10	1,469	-2.56	-20	0	9	1,469	-3.90	-50	0	30
Hispanic															
Youth	296	89.38	50	100	100	296	10.90	0	0	40	296	23.47	0	10	50
Parent	296	91.55	70	100	100	296	5.80	0	0	20	296	19.86	0	0	50
Difference	296	2.17	-10	0	15	296	-5.10	-30	0	5	296	-3.60	-50	0	40
African American, not Hispanic															
Youth	366	91.22	65	100	100	366	7.36	0	0	25	366	24.52	0	10	75
Parent	366	89.99	50	100	100	366	6.55	0	0	25	366	17.47	0	0	50
Difference	366	-1.23	-20	0	10	366	-0.81	-15	0	10	366	-7.05	-50	0	40
White															
Youth	760	94.52	90	100	100	760	5.94	0	0	20	760	15.14	0	5	50
Parent	760	95.65	95	100	100	760	3.54	0	0	10	760	12.32	0	0	50
Difference	760	1.13	0	0	6	760	-2.41	-20	0	5	760	-2.82	-40	0	25

	N	Mean				N	Mean				N	Mean			
Females															
All															
Youth	1,453	95.32	90	100	100	1,453	3.50	0	0	10	1,453	16.35	0	0	50
Parent	1,453	95.26	90	100	100	1,453	2.06	0	0	2	1,453	14.90	0	0	50
Difference	1,453	−0.06	0	5	0	1,453	−1.45	−10	0	10	1,453	−1.45	−30	0	30
Hispanic															
Youth	258	91.96	75	100	100	258	4.98	0	0	20	258	18.32	0	0	70
Parent	258	92.62	70	100	100	258	1.65	0	0	0	258	18.61	0	0	50
Difference	258	0.66	−10	10	0	258	−3.33	−15	0	0	258	0.29	−30	0	50
African American, not Hispanic															
Youth	391	94.63	90	100	100	391	3.17	0	0	10	391	18.38	0	0	50
Parent	391	93.50	75	100	100	391	2.75	0	0	10	391	16.39	0	0	50
Difference	391	−1.13	−10	5	0	391	−0.42	−5	0	0	391	−1.99	−40	0	40
White															
Youth	757	96.91	95	100	100	757	3.04	0	0	10	757	14.58	0	0	50
Parent	757	96.94	100	100	100	757	1.64	0	0	2	757	12.78	0	0	50
Difference	757	0.03	0	1	0	757	−1.39	−5	0	0	757	−1.80	−30	0	25

Source: Authors' compilation.

TABLE 8.4 Correspondence Between Youth and Parent Responses to Diploma Question, Young Men

Parents

Youths	{0}	(0,5]	(5,10]	(10,20]	(20,30]	(30,40]	(40,50]	{50}	(50,60]	(60,70]	(70,80]	(80,90]	(90,95]	(95,100]	{100}	Total
{0}	8		1					1			2	2	1		7	22
(0,5]	2		1								1		1	1	2	8
(5,10]	2			1											1	4
(10,20]	1							2			1				2	6
(20,30]					1			3								4
(30,40]						1		2		1					1	5
(40,50]																0
{50}	7		1	2	5	2		13		1	4	2			26	63
(50,60]															1	1
(60,70]								2						1	6	9
(70,80]			1			1		11		1	4	3	1		25	47
(80,90]								3			2	7	3		15	30
(90,95]								4				2	3	5	57	71
(95,100]								1				4	7	9	87	108
{100}	3	2		1	3	1		28		1	17	16	21	27	971	1,091
Total	23	2	4	4	9	5	0	70	0	4	31	36	37	43	1,201	1,469

Source: Authors' compilation.

TABLE 8.5   Correspondence Between Youth and Parent Responses to Jail Question, Young Men

Parents

Youths	{0}	(0,5]	(5,10]	(10,20]	(20,30]	(30,40]	(40,50]	{50}	(50,60]	(60,70]	(70,80]	(80,90]	(90,95]	(95,100]	{100}	Total
{0}	717	52	36	13	15	2		20			1				4	860
(0,5]	196	26	15	5	3	1		5								251
(5,10]	78	7	13	6	4	2		6		2	1					119
(10,20]	49	2	11	8	3	1		3								77
(20,30]	41	3	3	2	2			4						1		56
(30,40]	10	1		1				1		1						14
(40,50]	4														1	5
{50}	33	4	3	5	6			8							2	61
(50,60]	2															2
(60,70]	3			1	1	1										6
(70,80]	6							1			2					9
(80,90]			1	1	1											3
(90,95]	2															2
(95,100]																0
{100}	2							1				1				4
Total	1,143	95	82	42	35	7	0	49	0	3	4	1	0	1	7	1,469

Source: Authors' Compilation.

TABLE 8.6   Correspondence Between Youth and Parent Responses to Parenthood Question, Young Men

Parents

Youths	{0}	(0,5]	(5,10]	(10,20]	(20,30]	(30,40]	(40,50]	{50}	(50,60]	(60,70]	(70,80]	(80,90]	(90,95]	(95,100]	{100}	Total
{0}	405	33	45	20	11	3	1	56		2	1	3			3	583
(0,5]	81	28	19	14	7	3		15				1	1		5	174
(5,10]	72	10	8	7	9			15		1	1			1	3	127
(10,20]	59	13	8	18	5	2		20		1	2	1			2	131
(20,30]	36	5	9	5	10	1		22				2			1	91
(30,40]	12		2	4	4	1		5			1				2	31
(40,50]	5	2			1	1		2								11
{50}	88	13	19	9	17	2		47			4	3			4	206
(50,60]	3	1		1				1								6
(60,70]	5			1		1		6			1					14
(70,80]	15	1		3	3	1		7		2		2		1	1	36
(80,90]	8		1					5				1			1	16
(90,95]	4		1		1	1		1		1					1	10
(95,100]	1					1										2
{100}	5	1	1		1		1	10				1			11	31
Total	799	107	113	82	69	17	2	212	0	7	10	14	1	2	34	1,469

Source: Authors' compilation.

TABLE 8.7   Correspondence Between Youth and Parent Responses to Diploma Question, Young Women

Youths	Parents															Total
	{0}	(0,5]	(5,10]	(10,20]	(20,30]	(30,40]	(40,50]	{50}	(50,60]	(60,70]	(70,80]	(80,90]	(90,95]	(95,100]	{100}	
{0}	6							3			1				7	17
(0,5]								1							1	2
(5,10]			1					4				1			2	8
(10,20]					1										2	3
(20,30]								1							3	4
(30,40]		1														1
(40,50]																0
{50}	3				1			6		2	4	2	1		13	32
(50,60]								1			1				1	3
(60,70]											1	2			2	5
(70,80]	2				1			4			1	3	2		14	27
(80,90]	1							2			2	1	1	1	5	13
(90,95]						1		2			2	1	6	1	40	53
(95,100]								2					5	5	65	77
{100}	5	1		1	1	1		33			8	11	23	19	1,105	1,208
Total	17	2	1	1	4	2	0	59	0	2	20	21	38	26	1,260	1,453

Source: Authors' compilation.

TABLE 8.8 *Correspondence Between Youth and Parent Responses to Jail Question, Young Women*

Youths	Parents															Total
	{0}	(0,5]	(5,10]	(10,20]	(20,30]	(30,40]	(40,50]	{50}	(50,60]	(60,70]	(70,80]	(80,90]	(90,95]	[95,100]	{100}	
{0}	993	28	33	10	6	3		14		2					1	1,090
(0,5]	146	20	11		2											179
(5,10]	54	7	7	3	2			1								74
(10,20]	31	1	2	1		1					1					37
(20,30]	27	2			3			3								35
(30,40]	3															3
(40,50]	1															1
{50}	16		1	1	1			2				1				22
(50,60]	2															2
(60,70]	1															1
(70,80]	4															4
(80,90]																0
(90,95]																0
[95,100]	1															1
{100}	3													1		4
Total	1,282	58	54	15	14	4	0	20	0	2	1	1	1	0	1	1,453

Source: Authors' compilation.

TABLE 8.9 Correspondence Between Youth and Parent Responses to Parenthood Question, Young Women

Youths								Parents								
	{0}	(0,5]	[5,10]	[10,20]	[20,30]	[30,40]	(40,50]	{50}	(50,60)	[60,70]	[70,80]	[80,90]	[90,95]	[95,100]	{100}	Total
{0}	532	34	41	19	25	6		66		1	3	3	1		9	740
(0,5]	87	22	17	3	5			15								149
(5,10]	50	7	8	9	3	1		11				1	1		1	92
(10,20]	39	6	11	11	8	2		12						1	4	94
(20,30]	46	6	8	9	6	1		14				1			2	93
(30,40]	12	1		1	1	1		3		1		1				21
(40,50]	1		1		1		1	3			1	1			1	10
{50}	53	4	11	6	12	4		34			2	3	1		4	134
(50,60)	1				2			1								4
(60,70]	3			1	1						1				1	7
(70,80]	14		2		3	1		12			1	2			2	37
(80,90]	6		1	2				6								15
(90,95]	2							1						1		4
(95,100]	2	1		2				1							1	7
{100}	9	1	1	1				6					1		27	46
Total	857	82	101	64	67	16	1	185	0	2	8	12	4	2	52	1,453

Source: Authors' compilation.

for males and females, respectively. Generally speaking, there are moderate positive associations between the responses of youths and those of their parents. For example, table 8.4 shows that 74.3 percent of the male youth and 81.8 percent of their parents assign 100 to the chance that the youth in question will receive a high school diploma. Both the youth and his parent gave this response in 66.1 percent of the cases. If the subjective probabilities of youths and their parents were statistically independent, this percentage would be 60.8 (that is, 74.3 × .818). Similar positive associations between youth and parent responses appear throughout tables 8.4 to 8.9.

Table 8.10 disaggregates the at-risk measures by gender. The rows labeled *youth* give the percentage of youth classified as at risk on the basis of self-reports, the rows labeled *parent* give the percentage of youth classified as at risk on the basis of parent assessments, and the rows labeled *both* give the percentage of cases in which both youth and parent would consider the youth to be at risk. The findings in the *both* rows are consistently higher than they would be if the subjective probabilities of youth and parents were statistically independent.

It is sometimes suggested that responses of 50 are more subject to rounding error than are other subjective probability reports or that such responses express epistemic uncertainty rather than quantitative probability assessments. The thresholds that define the at-risk measures are well away from the value of 50, so our at-risk measures should be little affected by rounding error at this value. However, we are concerned about the possibility of epistemic uncertainty. The right-hand panel of table 8.10 takes the extreme step of recalculating the at-risk measures after discarding cases where either a youth or a parent reports 50 as the percent chance of any adverse outcome. This means excluding 328 of the 1,453 female youths and 430 of the 1,469 male youths. As would be expected, discarding cases with reports of 50 systematically lowers the fractions of youth classified as at risk. However, it does not alter the pattern of findings in the left-hand panel. For example, the responses of youths and their parents remain positively associated.

Expectations Conditional on Attributes and Experiences
Expectations Conditional on Attributes

In this section, we examine the variation of expectations with observed attributes that may be used to classify youth as at risk. Treating male youth and female youth separately throughout, table 8.11 shows the variation of

(*Text continues on p. 250.*)

TABLE 8.10   *Measures of At-Risk Status*

	All Observations			Excluding Observations With A 50 (Either Youth or Parent)		
Group	Percentage At-Risk I	Percentage At-Risk II	Percentage At-Risk III	Percentage At-Risk I	Percentage At-Risk II	Percentage At-Risk III
Young Women						
Youth (percentage)	47.42	17.07	3.85	38.67	11.64	2.22
Parent (percentage)	41.09	11.91	2.89	29.24	7.73	1.87
Both (percentage)	27.60	5.09	0.69	18.40	2.84	0.36
Number of observations	1,453	1,453	1,453	1,125	1,125	1,125
Young Men						
Youth (percentage)	60.04	29.27	8.51	48.22	19.25	3.56
Parent (percentage)	46.56	18.92	6.60	33.69	12.70	4.14
Both (percentage)	34.79	10.96	1.70	21.75	5.68	0.29
Number of observations	1,469	1,469	1,469	1,039	1,039	1,039

Source: Authors' compilation.

TABLE 8.11   *Mean Responses and Percent At Risk, Conditional on Attributes, by Gender*

| | Percentage Chance of Diploma | | | Percentage Chance of Jail | | |
Group	Obs.	Mean of Youth Responses	Mean of Parent Responses	Obs.	Mean of Youth Responses	Mean of Parent Responses
Young men						
Overall	1,469	92.69	93.35	1,469	7.26	4.70
Race-ethnicity						
Hispanic	296	89.38	91.55	296	10.90	5.80
African American, not Hispanic	66	91.22	89.99	366	7.36	6.55
White, not Hispanic	760	94.52	95.65	760	5.94	3.54
Youth lives with mother (figure) and father (figure) (yes or no)						
Yes	1,006	94.22	94.74	1,006	6.30	3.53
No	463	89.35	90.36	463	9.36	7.23
Household income (thousands of dollars)						
0 to 20	286	86.92	86.80	286	10.25	8.87
20 to 40	321	91.56	93.79	321	8.03	4.77
40 to 60	247	94.55	95.55	247	6.72	2.98
60 to 80	148	97.67	98.03	148	3.70	2.84
80 and up	187	97.76	96.65	167	5.55	2.75
Income not available	299	92.55	93.15	299	6.77	4.05
Young women						
Overall	1,453	95.32	95.26	1,453	3.50	2.06
Race-ethnicity						
Hispanic	258	91.96	92.62	258	4.98	1.65
African American, not Hispanic	391	94.63	93.50	391	3.17	2.75
White, not Hispanic	757	96.91	96.94	757	3.04	1.64
Youth lives with mother (figure) and father (figure) (yes or no)						
Yes	964	96.92	97.07	964	2.81	1.65
No	489	92.16	91.70	489	4.87	2.86
Household income (thousands of dollars)						
0 to 20	317	90.34	89.29	317	5.29	3.48
20 to 40	272	96.27	95.39	272	2.83	1.88
40 to 60	246	97.41	98.28	246	2.37	1.48
60 to 80	141	98.21	97.32	141	2.94	.81
80 and up	172	98.98	98.66	172	2.00	1.77
Income not available	303	94.51	96.02	303	4.25	1.94

Source: Authors' compilation.

	Percentage Chance of Parenthood		Percentage At-Risk I		Percentage At-Risk II		Percentage At-Risk III	
Obs.	Mean of Youth Responses	Mean of Parent Responses	Based on Youth Responses	Based on Parent Responses	Based on Youth Responses	Based on Parent Responses	Based on Youth Responses	Based on Parent Responses
1,469	19.05	15.15	60.04	46.56	29.27	18.92	8.51	6.60
296	23.47	19.86	70.95	53.72	39.19	23.65	13.85	8.78
366	24.52	17.47	65.57	49.45	33.33	23.22	9.56	9.56
760	15.14	12.32	53.42	42.63	24.08	15.39	5.92	4.34
1,006	17.13	12.92	56.46	42.74	25.45	15.41	7.06	4.67
463	23.23	19.98	67.82	54.86	37.58	26.57	11.66	10.80
286	26.86	23.64	68.88	64.69	41.61	30.07	15.73	12.94
321	20.31	15.35	67.60	46.73	28.66	19.00	9.66	6.54
247	19.58	13.42	58.30	40.89	29.55	14.98	5.26	5.67
148	10.70	9.98	43.24	36.49	16.89	10.81	4.05	2.03
187	11.90	7.29	47.90	33.53	21.56	10.78	3.59	2.40
299	17.98	15.17	60.20	45.82	28.43	19.73	8.03	6.02
1,453	16.35	14.90	47.42	41.09	17.07	11.91	3.85	2.89
258	18.32	18.61	55.43	49.61	21.32	16.28	6.59	3.49
391	18.38	16.39	46.80	38.36	16.37	13.30	3.84	4.09
757	14.58	12.78	45.44	39.89	15.32	9.51	2.64	2.11
964	14.14	12.94	43.98	37.66	14.83	9.44	3.01	2.18
489	20.72	18.77	54.19	47.85	21.47	16.77	5.52	4.29
317	24.02	21.87	57.41	54.57	26.18	21.14	6.94	5.36
272	16.90	15.53	51.84	42.65	15.07	12.50	2.57	2.57
246	15.68	13.72	47.15	36.99	13.82	6.10	2.44	1.22
141	13.41	10.62	39.01	36.88	16.31	7.09	2.84	1.42
172	8.86	7.15	32.56	28.49	9.30	9.30	.58	3.49
303	14.11	14.30	45.54	37.62	16.83	10.23	5.28	2.31

mean risk perceptions and at-risk status with race-ethnicity, household structure, and household income.

On the basis of self-reports, Hispanic youth are most likely to be classified as at risk, using any of our three criteria, followed by African Americans and whites. Parent reports yield a less clear pattern of findings.

Much attention has been paid in the literature to the association between family structure and child outcomes (for example, McLanahan and Sandefur 1994), with children growing up in nonintact homes tending to experience more adverse outcomes. We find corresponding associations between family structure and expectations of adverse outcomes. Among girls not living with two parents, 5.5 percent are classified as At-Risk III on the basis of self-reports (4.3 percent on the basis of parent reports). These figures compare to 3.0 percent (and 2.2 percent) for youths living with two parents. Among boys in nonintact homes, 11.7 percent (10.8 percent) are At-Risk III. Only 7.0 percent (4.7 percent) of boys in intact homes are At-Risk III.

It has often been observed that the incidence of adverse socioeconomic outcomes among children tends to decline with household income. We find that expectations of adverse outcomes tend to decline in similar fashion in the income range of $0 to $80,000 per year. For example, the percentage of male youth classified as At-Risk III on the basis of self-reports declines from 15.7 percent (12.9 percent on the basis of parent reports) for those in households with less than $20,000 annual income to 4.1 percent (2.0 percent) for those in households with $60,000 to $80,000 annual income. The findings for female youth show a similar, generally monotone pattern. Above $80,000 per year, however, there is suggestive evidence of an upturn in risk perceptions.

Expectations Conditional on Experiences

The NLSY97 elicited from youth respondents reports of past experiences that may be associated with risks of future adverse outcomes. We focus here on responses to the self-administered part of the questionnaire, which may include experiences unknown to parents.

Table 8.12 reports mean subjective probabilities of the diploma, jail, and parenthood outcomes conditional on gender and on self-reports of the following past experiences: school suspension, grade repetition in school, sexual intercourse, cigarette smoking, marijuana smoking, carrying of a handgun, drug dealing, and arrest. The rightmost columns give the percentage of youth classified as at risk, conditional on these reported experiences. Clearly, youths with these experiences tend to have less-favorable expectations than do other youths. This pattern holds consistently for male youth and female youth, for self-reports and for parent reports.

A closer look at the data reveals some interesting subpatterns. Among male youth, the highest mean percent chance of going to jail is reported by those who have dealt drugs (15.2), followed by those who have been arrested (13.6). Among female youth, the highest mean percent chance of going to jail is reported by those who have carried a handgun (9.7), followed by those who have dealt drugs (9.3).

Among parents, however, the highest mean percent chances of incarceration are reported by those whose children have been arrested previously: 10.2 for male youth and 9.9 for female youth. Parents of children who report having dealt drugs have lower expectations of incarceration: 7.5 for male youth and 5.0 for female youth. These youth-parent differences may reflect, in part, the differential information available to them. Parents presumably know whether their children have been arrested, but their knowledge of drug dealing and handgun access may be more limited.

Table 8.12 shows large difference in expectations of parenthood between youth who have and those who have not had the experiences in question. Yet, with the exception of engaging in sexual intercourse, these experiences are not directly related to becoming a parent. It seems that many of these experiences must simply be indicators of the types of youth who believe themselves likely to have children before age twenty. These beliefs tend to be shared by their parents.

The fraction of youth classified as at risk varies considerably throughout table 8.12. The highest rate is for those who have been arrested. Fully 17.9 percent of previously arrested female youth are classified as At-Risk III on the basis of self-reports (13.4 percent on the basis of parent reports), whereas only 2.7 percent (2.0 percent) of those who have not been arrested are so classified. This pattern holds for male youth as well, but with less striking variation—16.5 percent of previously arrested male youth are classified as At-Risk III on the basis of self-reports (13.8 percent on the basis of parent reports), versus 7.1 percent (5.4 percent) of those who have not been arrested.

Conclusion

The NLSY97 expectations module yields intriguing evidence on how youth perceive their future prospects and what their parents see ahead for them. This evidence will become more valuable in the years ahead, as further waves of NLSY97 data make it possible to observe how respondents update their expectations and what outcomes they eventually experience. Within a few years, it will become possible to relate the expectations elicited at age sixteen and seventeen to events that occur by age twenty.

(*Text continues on p. 256.*)

TABLE 8.12   *Mean Responses and Percent At Risk, Conditional on Experiences, by Gender*

Group	Percentage Chance of Diploma			Percentage Chance Of Jail		
	Obs.	Mean of Youth Responses	Mean of Parent Responses	Obs.	Mean of Youth Responses	Mean of Parent Responses
Young men						
Overall	1,469	92.69	93.35	1,469	7.26	4.70
Youth has ever been suspended (yes or no)						
Yes	600	88.29	88.65	600	11.15	8.29
No	869	95.72	96.60	869	4.58	2.22
Youth has ever repeated a grade (yes or no)						
Yes	372	85.28	85.85	372	9.44	7.54
No	1,068	95.58	96.32	1,068	6.29	3.55
Youth has ever had sexual intercourse (yes or no)						
Yes	580	89.27	88.97	580	10.26	7.67
No	878	94.87	96.16	878	5.28	2.75
Youth has ever smoked a cigarette (yes or no)						
Yes	776	90.67	91.53	776	9.59	6.25
No	691	94.94	95.38	691	4.68	2.98
Youth has ever smoked marijuana (yes or no)						
Yes	498	89.74	90.70	498	11.83	7.48
No	967	94.18	94.69	967	4.94	3.25
Youth has ever carried a handgun (yes or no)						
Yes	296	88.90	89.78	296	12.34	7.15
No	1,171	93.63	94.25	1,171	5.99	4.06
Youth has ever dealt drugs (yes or no)						
Yes	199	88.95	90.68	199	15.15	7.47
No	1,269	93.27	93.77	1,269	6.03	4.27
Youth has ever been arrested (yes or no)						
Yes	218	86.56	87.12	218	13.55	10.17
No	1,249	93.75	94.43	1,249	6.18	3.72

Obs.	Percentage Chance of Parenthood		Percentage At-Risk I		Percentage At-Risk II		Percentage At-Risk III	
	Mean of Youth Responses	Mean of Parent Responses	Based on Youth Responses	Based on Parent Responses	Based on Youth Responses	Based on Parent Responses	Based on Youth Responses	Based on Parent Responses
1,469	19.05	15.15	60.04	46.56	29.27	18.92	8.51	6.60
600	26.64	20.92	72.17	59.50	42.33	28.67	14.33	12.00
869	13.81	11.16	51.67	37.63	20.25	12.20	4.49	2.88
372	24.81	20.18	69.62	58.87	39.78	28.23	16.13	13.17
1,068	17.11	13.35	56.37	41.76	25.09	14.98	5.81	3.75
580	27.37	22.76	72.93	61.55	40.17	29.31	12.07	11.90
878	13.47	10.20	51.48	36.90	22.10	12.19	6.15	3.19
776	22.93	17.95	68.17	52.58	37.76	23.58	11.73	9.02
691	14.68	12.04	50.94	39.94	19.83	13.75	4.92	3.91
498	25.43	20.47	71.89	58.63	43.17	27.31	13.86	10.44
967	15.71	12.38	53.98	40.23	22.23	14.58	5.79	4.65
296	26.13	18.99	71.96	54.05	41.55	24.66	14.86	9.80
1,171	17.19	14.15	56.96	44.58	26.22	17.42	6.92	5.81
199	27.86	19.54	76.38	56.28	45.73	27.14	16.08	10.55
1,269	17.68	14.47	57.53	45.07	26.71	17.65	7.33	5.99
218	31.12	25.17	79.36	68.35	44.04	38.53	16.51	13.76
1,249	16.93	13.39	56.69	42.75	26.74	15.45	7.13	5.36

TABLE 8.12   Continued

Group	Percentage Chance of Diploma			Percentage Chance of Jail		
	Obs.	Mean of Youth Responses	Mean of Parent Responses	Obs.	Mean of Youth Responses	Mean of Parent Responses
Young women						
Overall	1,453	95.32	95.26	1,453	3.50	2.06
Youth has ever been suspended (yes or no)						
Yes	359	92.61	89.55	359	5.77	4.36
No	1,091	96.37	97.20	1,091	2.76	1.28
Youth has ever repeated a grade (yes or no)						
Yes	248	89.80	87.96	248	5.96	4.33
No	1,175	96.86	97.04	1,175	3.00	1.47
Youth has ever had sexual intercourse (yes or no)						
Yes	490	91.71	92.24	490	5.40	3.59
No	946	97.10	96.74	946	2.57	1.27
Youth has ever smoked a cigarette (yes or no)						
Yes	744	94.10	94.25	744	4.49	2.47
No	705	96.58	96.30	705	2.49	1.59
Youth has ever smoked marijuana (yes or no)						
Yes	440	93.68	93.60	440	6.03	3.64
No	1,004	95.99	95.95	1,004	2.43	1.35
Youth has ever carried a handgun (yes or no)						
Yes	46	89.80	92.70	46	9.67	5.70
No	1,404	95.49	95.33	1,404	3.31	1.92
Youth has ever dealt drugs (yes or no)						
Yes	106	90.93	92.47	106	9.25	4.98
No	1,342	95.65	95.46	1,342	3.06	1.81
Youth has ever been arrested (yes or no)						
Yes	112	85.75	87.58	112	8.98	9.92
No	1,337	96.10	95.89	1,337	3.06	1.38

Source: Authors' compilation.

Obs.	Percentage Chance of Parenthood		Percentage At-Risk I		Percentage At-Risk II		Percentage At-Risk III	
	Mean of Youth Responses	Mean of Parent Responses	Based on Youth Responses	Based on Parent Responses	Based on Youth Responses	Based on Parent Responses	Based on Youth Responses	Based on Parent Responses
1,453	16.35	14.90	47.42	41.09	17.07	11.91	3.85	2.89
359	27.10	22.73	63.51	56.55	27.86	22.01	6.96	6.41
1,091	12.80	12.35	41.98	35.93	13.47	8.52	2.75	1.65
248	23.38	22.00	54.44	50.40	27.82	22.58	6.45	7.66
1,175	14.74	13.25	45.70	39.06	14.81	9.28	3.15	1.62
490	28.64	24.74	66.53	55.92	27.96	20.00	7.76	5.10
946	10.07	9.82	37.84	33.40	11.52	7.93	1.90	1.80
744	21.46	17.83	58.20	47.58	22.04	14.52	5.51	3.90
705	11.03	11.90	36.17	34.33	11.91	9.22	2.13	1.84
440	25.90	20.13	66.45	55.23	27.73	18.41	7.73	4.55
1,004	12.28	12.66	39.74	34.86	12.55	9.16	2.19	2.19
46	30.26	29.72	65.22	58.70	30.43	17.39	10.87	8.70
1,404	15.93	14.42	46.94	40.38	16.67	11.75	3.63	2.71
106	31.05	19.88	79.25	61.32	41.51	21.70	12.26	9.43
1,342	15.22	14.55	45.01	39.49	15.13	11.12	3.20	2.38
112	34.57	28.87	76.79	71.43	41.07	40.79	17.86	13.39
1,337	14.88	13.74	45.10	38.44	15.11	9.57	2.69	2.02

At that point, it will be of great interest to revisit the present analysis and determine how well youths and their parents were able to assess the risks of the adverse outcomes examined here.

The collection of these data will also allow for analysis of revisions of expectations as new information is accumulated by youths and their parents (see, for example, Dominitz 1998). Such future analysis should build on the suggestive findings presented in this essay concerning the differential information available to youths and parents and the manner in which this information is used to form expectations.

This essay has used a simple binary classification of at-risk youth in order to generate simple descriptive statistics. For the purposes of monitoring trends, predicting adverse outcomes, and designing interventions, it may be preferable to develop a continuous measure and, perhaps, multiple indicators. The expectations questions asked in the NLSY97 are well suited to such applications because they elicit reports on a continuous, interpersonally comparable scale and cover a wide range of outcomes. Much work remains to be done to develop such indicators.

We thank the Bureau of Labor Statistics and the Foundation for Child Development for providing financial assistance for this project. We are grateful to the many persons who participated with us in designing the NLSY97 expectations module, including Michael Pergamit and Kenneth Wolpin as well as the expectations research group at the School of Social and Decision Sciences, Carnegie Mellon University.

References

Bruine de Bruin, Wändi, Baruch Fischhoff, Bonnie Halpern-Felsher, and Shana Millstein. 2000. "Expressing Epistemic Uncertainty: It's a Fifty-Fifty Chance." *Organizational Behavior and Human Decision Processes* 81(1): 115–31.

Budescu, David S., and Thomas V. Wallsten. 1995. "Processing Linguistic Probabilities: General Principles and Empirical Evidence." In *Decision Making from a Cognitive Perspective*, edited by J. R. Busemeyer, R. Hastie, and D. L. Medin. New York: Academic.

Das, Marcel, Jeff Dominitz, and Arthur Van Soest. 1999. "Comparing Predictions and Outcomes: Theory and Application to Income Changes." *Journal of the American Statistical Association* 94(445): 75–85.

Dominitz, Jeff. 1998. "Earnings Expectations, Revisions, and Realizations." *Review of Economics and Statistics* 80(3): 374–88.

Dominitz, Jeff, and Charles F. Manski. 1997a. "Perceptions of Economic Insecurity: Evidence from the Survey of Economic Expectations." *Public Opinion Quarterly* 61(2): 261–87.

————. 1997b. "Using Expectations Data to Study Subjective Income Expectations." *Journal of the American Statistical Association* 92(439): 855–67.

————. 1999. "The Several Cultures of Research on Subjective Expectations." In *Wealth, Work, and Health: Essays in Honor of F. Thomas Juster,* edited by J. Smith and R. Willis. Ann Arbor: University of Michigan Press.

Erev, I., and B. Cohen. 1990. "Verbal versus Numerical Probabilities: Efficiency, Biases, and the Preference Paradox." *Organizational Behavior and Human Decision Processes* 45(1): 1–18.

Fischhoff, Baruch, and Ruth Beyth-Marom. 1983. "Hypothesis Evaluation from a Bayesian Perspective." *Psychological Review* 90: 239–60.

Fischhoff, Baruch, and Wändi Bruine de Bruin. 1999. "Fifty/Fifty = 50%?" *Journal of Behavioral Decision Making* 12: 149–63.

Fischhoff, Baruch, Andrew Parker, Wändi Bruine de Bruin, Julie Downs, Claire Palmgren, Robyn Dawes, and Charles Manski. 2000. "Teen Expectations for Significant Life Events." *Public Opinion Quarterly* 64: 189–205.

Juster, F. Thomas. 1966. "Consumer Buying Intentions and Purchase Probability: An Experiment in Survey Design." *Journal of the American Statistical Association* 61(315): 658–96.

Levin, Henry M. 1993. "The Economics of Education for at-Risk Students." In *Essays on the Economics of Education*, edited by E. Hoffman. Kalamazoo, Mich.: W. E. Upjohn Institute for Employment Research.

Lichtenstein, Sara, Paul Slovic, M. Layman, and Bernard Coombs. 1978. "Judged Frequency of Lethal Events." *Journal of Experimental Psychology: Human Learning and Memory* 4: 551–78.

Manski, Charles F. 1990. "The Use of Intentions Data to Predict Behavior: A Best Case Analysis." *Journal of the American Statistical Association* 85(412): 934–40.

Manski, Charles F., and John D. Straub. 2000. "Worker Perceptions of Job Insecurity in the Mid-1990s: Evidence from the Survey of Economic Expectations." *Journal of Human Resources* 35: 349–78.

McLanahan, Sara, and Gary Sandefur. 1994. *Growing Up with a Single Parent.* Cambridge, Mass.: Harvard University Press.

Quadrel, Marilyn, Baruch Fischhoff, and Wendy Davis. 1993. "Adolescent (In)vulnerability." *American Psychologist* 48: 102–16.

Wallsten, Thomas S., David V. Budescu, Rami Zwick, and S. Kemp. 1993. "Preferences and Reasons for Communicating Probabilistic Information in Verbal or Numerical Terms." *Bulletin of the Psychonomic Society* 31: 135–38.

Yates, J. Frank. 1990. *Judgment and Decision Making.* Englewood Cliffs, N.J.: Prentice-Hall.

Zimmer, A. 1983. "Verbal vs. Numerical Processing of Subjective Probabilities." In *Decision Making under Uncertainty,* edited by R. Scholz. Amsterdam: North-Holland.

————. 1984. "A Model for the Interpretation of Verbal Predictions." *International Journal of Man-Machine Studies* 20: 121–34.

9

Food Stamp Program Participation and Health: Estimates from the NLSY97

Diane Gibson

I n 1998, the Food Stamp Program provided vouchers worth $16.9 billion to participants and served an average of 19.8 million people per month. During 1998, children under age eighteen made up 53 percent of participants in the Food Stamp Program (Mathematica Policy Research Inc. 1999). The goal of the Food Stamp Program and other nutrition-assistance programs is to fight hunger, food insecurity, and related health problems (U.S. Department of Agriculture 1999).

The expectation that participation in the Food Stamp Program improves health can be theoretically justified on the basis of a model of the demand for health developed by Grossman (1972). In this model, current health is a function of current and past resources, education, and other variables that affect the productivity of health inputs. Higher levels of resources and education lead to better health. Therefore, this model predicts that there is a positive relation between Food Stamp Program participation and health since the Food Stamp Program provides both financial resources and nutrition education.

This essay examines the empirical relation between Food Stamp Program participation and the health of youths aged twelve to eighteen using data from the first round of the National Longitudinal Survey of Youth, 1997 Cohort (NLSY97).[1] The measures of health used here are indicators of whether a youth is underweight or obese, a youth's self-reported health status, and chronic-illness status as reported by a youth's parent. Cross-sectional logistic-regression models are estimated that represent reduced-form models of the demand for youth health. Controls are included for Food Stamp Program participation, current family income, the poverty history of a youth's family, and other youth and family characteristics that are expected to influence current health.

The empirical analyses presented in this essay suggest that, for the health outcomes considered, the relation between Food Stamp Program participation and youth health is not strong. The estimates of the coefficients on Food Stamp Program participation are almost always insignificant and, when significant, sometimes opposite the direction expected given Grossman's model. In logistic-regression models that include Food Stamp Program participation and its interaction with youth age, participation in the Food Stamp Program is significantly related to the likelihood that a youth is underweight. It is associated with a significant reduction in the likelihood of being underweight for younger youths but a significant increase in the likelihood of being underweight for older youths. Food Stamp Program participation is associated with a significant decrease in the likelihood that a youth is in good self-reported health in one specification of the model of self-reported health status. However, the significance of this relation does not persist across alternative specifications of the model.

It is difficult to control adequately for the current and past characteristics of the youths and their families that are expected to influence current youth health. This raises the possibility of biased estimates of the relation between Food Stamp Program participation and current youth health. Given this difficulty, the empirical analyses presented here are best viewed as descriptive. In this essay, I will examine how the possibility of bias may be addressed with future rounds of data from the NLSY97.

Previous Research

The health outcomes that are examined in previous research on the relation between Food Stamp Program participation, income, and health can be grouped according to whether they are measures of nutritional status. Nutritional status is usually defined in terms of either *input* or *output* indicators. Input indicators are mainly measures of food and nutrient intake. Even if perfectly measured, nutrient intake cannot be equated with nutritional status because individuals differ in the efficiency of nutrient utilization. Nutritional status can be alternatively defined in terms of output measures, including anthropometry and clinical and biochemical indicators of malnutrition.[2] An advantage of using anthropometry to measure nutritional status is that health consequences are often apparent even at low levels of malnutrition. In contrast, clinical and biochemical indicators may indicate a problem only at extreme levels of malnutrition (Martorell and Ho 1984).

Three areas of research provide background for the analyses presented in this essay. The first area of research examines the relation between family income and child health. The second area of research investigates the connection between Food Stamp Program participation and input measures of nutritional status. This research has focused on the relation between Food Stamp receipt and expenditure on food or diet quality. The third area of research analyzes the association between Food Stamp receipt and output measures of nutritional status such as weight for height and height for age.

Relation Between Income and Child Health

Empirical research on the relation between income and health is relevant for constructing hypotheses about the relation between Food Stamp Program participation and health since the Food Stamp Program provides recipients with additional financial resources. The research on the relation between income and health is extensive. For the sake of brevity, only research that examines the type of health outcomes available in the NLSY97 is discussed in this section.[3] Past research primarily uses current income and other current variables to explain current health outcomes. This is problematic since relating current health solely to current income and other current variables disregards all prior influences on current health.

Studies that control only for current characteristics find that children who are poor in the year in which their health is measured are at higher risk for poor nutritional status. This result holds when nutritional status is measured using overweight (Centers for Disease Control 1998), obesity (Bhattacharya and Currie 2000), height (Miller, Fine, and Adams-Taylor 1989; Jones, Nesheim, and Habicht 1985), height for age (Miller, Fine, and Adams-Taylor 1989), and weight and skinfold thickness (Jones, Nesheim, and Habicht 1985).[4]

The National Health Interview Survey asks parents to report whether they consider their children's health to be excellent, very good, good, fair, or poor. Adams and Benson (1990) found that families with annual incomes under $10,000 reported a significantly smaller percentage of children in excellent health than did families with annual incomes over $35,000. Chronic conditions are also more prevalent among the poor (Klerman 1991). In particular, asthma appears to be associated with socioeconomic factors (Weitzman et al. 1990; Wissow et al. 1988).

Miller and Korenman (1994) examine the nutritional status of children between birth and age seven using data from NLSY79 child sample.[5] They use two dichotomous indicators of nutritional status: stunting and wasting. These indicators are based on standards developed by the National Center for Health Statistics and the World Health Organization. Children below the tenth percentile in height for children of the same age (in months) and sex are classified as *stunted*. Children below the tenth percentile in weight for children of the same height and sex are classified as *wasted*.

Miller and Korenman estimate logistic regressions for wasting and stunting, controlling for current and long-term poverty as well as for a number of other child and family characteristics. Current poverty status is not significantly related to the likelihood that a child is wasted or stunted. In contrast, long-term poverty is positively and significantly related to the likelihood of both wasting and stunting. On the basis of their findings, Miller and Korenman conclude that estimates of the relation between current income and health will be biased unless models of child health include family poverty history as an explanatory variable.

Relation Between Food Stamp Program Participation and Input Indicators of Nutritional Status

This section reviews the previous research on the relation between Food Stamp Program participation and two related input measures of nutritional status. The first measure of nutritional status is expenditure on food, and the second is the nutrient content of the diet of or of food purchased by an individual or a household.

Almost all the available empirical evidence suggests that participation in the Food Stamp Program increases expenditure on food. This literature is summarized in Levedahl (1991) and Devaney and Fraker (1989). These studies generally find that a dollar of Food Stamp income raises expenditure on food by less than a dollar but that a dollar of Food Stamp income results in a larger increase in expenditure on food than does a dollar of non–Food Stamp income.

Another line of research investigates the relation between Food Stamp Program participation and the nutrient content of the diet of or of the food purchased by an individual or a household. Considering studies that control for current family income and family characteristics in addition to participation in the Food Stamp Program, the general finding is that participation in the Food Stamp Program is associated with higher levels of nutrient consumption or of nutrient content in food purchases. This relation holds for preschoolers (Rose, Habicht, and Devaney 1998) and for households (Basiotis et al. 1983; Basiotis et al. 1987; Devaney and Moffitt 1991). Using data from the Third National Health and Nutrition Examination Survey (NHANES III), Bhattacharya and Currie (2000) find that participation in the Food Stamp Program is associated with a significant decrease in the likelihood that youths aged twelve to sixteen overconsume sweets. However, it is not significantly related to the overall quality of a youth's diet. Butler and Raymond (1996) find that participation in the Food Stamp Program is not significantly related to nutrient intake in a sample of low-income rural households. They find that there is a significant negative relation between Food Stamp Program participation and nutrient intake for a sample of elderly participants in the Food Stamp Cashout Program. However, the level of nutrient decrease associated with participation in the Food Stamp Program is not large enough to cause individuals to fall below the recommended daily allowances of these nutrients.[6]

Relation Between Food Stamp Program Participation and Output Indicators of Nutritional Status

I am aware of only two previous studies that examine the relation between Food Stamp Program participation and output indicators of nutritional status for children or youths.[7] One study (Bhattacharya and Currie 2000) does not control for a youth's history of poverty and social-program participation, and the other (Korenman and Miller 1992) does.

Using data from the NHANES III for youths aged twelve to sixteen, Bhattacharya and Currie (2000) examine the relation between family resources, education, and nutritional status measured by anemia, vitamin deficiency, high cholesterol, and obesity. They do not find a significant relation between Food Stamp Program participation and these measures of nutritional status. However, their analyses do not control for a youth's history of poverty or social-program participation.

Korenman and Miller (1992) examine the relation between Food Stamp receipt and the likelihood that a child is wasted or stunted using data on children ranging in age from birth to seven years from the NLSY79 child sample.[8] They estimate logistic-regression models that include controls for current family income and a family's history of poverty in order to prevent biased estimates of the relation between Food Stamp receipt and health. They measure long-term poverty using the average income-to-needs ratio of the child's mother over the child's lifetime.

In models that include recent Food Stamp receipt and controls for long-term poverty, Korenman and Miller do not find a significant relation between Food Stamp receipt and the likelihood that a youth is wasted or stunted. Korenman and Miller also estimate models that replace recent Food Stamp receipt with a family's history of Food Stamp receipt. They find that children whose families received Food Stamps every year in which they were poor are significantly more likely to be stunted than otherwise identical children whose families never received Food Stamps. However, children with a positive but shorter period of Food Stamp receipt are not significantly more likely to be stunted than otherwise identical children whose families never received Food Stamps. Korenman and Miller also find that children who received Food Stamps for half but not all their years in poverty are significantly less likely to be wasted than otherwise identical children whose families never received Food Stamps. However, children whose families received Food Stamps for a period of time greater than or less than half their years in poverty are not significantly less likely to be wasted than otherwise identical children whose families never received Food Stamps. In summary, the results of Korenman and Miller (1992) suggest that the relation between Food Stamp Program participation and wasting and stunting is not strong. Korenman and Miller hypothesize that the lack of a strong relation may be due to the failure to control adequately for long-term economic deprivation.

Conclusions from Previous Research

The health outcomes examined in previous research on the relation between Food Stamp Program participation, income, and health are measures of nutritional status or measures of general health. Past research consistently finds that income is positively related to all these types of health outcomes. This suggests that, since it provides financial resources, Food Stamp Program participation would have the same relation. This has been only partly borne out by past research. Food Stamp Program participation is generally associated with better health when health is gauged using input measures of nutritional status. However, the few studies that examine output measures of nutritional status rarely find a positive and significant relation between Food Stamp Program participation and output measures of nutritional status.

Further research on Food Stamp Program participation and output measures of nutritional status is warranted because only two previous studies examine health in this manner and only one of these includes controls for long-term family resources. The previous research that includes controls for long-term family resources examines children ranging in age from birth to seven years. The research reported in this essay focuses on older children (aged twelve to eighteen), and it also controls for long-term family resources. The need to control for long-term family resources is explained in detail in the following section. No previous research has been conducted on the relation between Food Stamp Program participation and health outcomes that are not considered indicators of nutritional status. The data available in the NLSY97 offer the opportunity to examine the relation between Food Stamp Program participation and self-reported health and chronic illness.

Theory

This essay tests the hypothesis that participation in the Food Stamp Program is positively related to youth health. The theoretical model developed in Grossman (1972) can be used to support this hypothesis. Grossman's model suggests an empirical model of the demand for health that can be used to examine the relation between Food Stamp Program participation and health outcomes.

In Grossman's model, good health is demanded by consumers because it is both a consumption commodity (sick days provide disutility) and an investment commodity (being healthy reduces the time lost to illness and provides more time to do other things such as work or leisure activities). The stock of health is produced with direct inputs of market goods and time. The efficiency or productivity of these inputs differs across consumers. A consumer's productivity is influenced by personal characteristics such as age, race, ethnicity, sex, and years of schooling. Consumers start with an initial stock of health and choose a stream of health inputs in order to maximize their lifetime utility, subject to both production and resource constraints. In equilibrium, consumers choose health investments so that the present value of the marginal cost of an investment is equal to the present value of the marginal benefit of the investment.

Grossman's framework can be adapted to examine the production of youth health and the demand for youth health. The production function for the stock of health at time k can be represented by the following equation:

$$\text{health}_k = S\left(\sum \alpha_t Z_t, \sum \beta_t F_t; \sum \mu_t, \text{health}_0\right),$$

where $t =$ time, and $\sum$ is the summation from $t = 0$ to $t = k$.

Health$_k$ equals the stock of health at time k, Z_k represents market and time inputs into youth health at time k other than food, F_k represents food consumed by the youth at time k, μ_k represents the production technology at time k, and health$_0$ represents the youth's initial health endowment. Grossman views education as the most important component of μ. This production function suggests that the current stock of health depends on the initial stock of health and is influenced not only by current inputs into health but also by past health inputs. The productivity of these inputs depends on the technology available.

It is assumed that the utility of the youths and that of their parents are both positively related to youth health. Youths and parents choose inputs into youth health in order to maximize lifetime utility. The demand for the stock of youth health at time k can be represented by the following equation:

$$\text{health}_k = h\left(\sum P_{Zt}, \sum P_{Ft}, \sum P_{Ct}, \sum \text{RESOURCES}_t; e, \sum \mu_t, \text{health}_0\right),$$

where $t =$ time, and $\sum$ is the summation from $t = 0$ to $t = k$.

P_{Zk}, P_{Fk}, and P_{Ck} equal, respectively, the prices of health inputs, food, and other consumption goods at time k. RESOURCES$_k$ is a vector of variables affecting resource constraints at time k, and e represents preferences. The demand for the current stock of health is a function of current and past prices, resources, and technology. Preferences and the initial stock of health also determine the demand for the current stock of health.

Bhattacharya and Currie (2000) suggest that a health-outcome function of the following form is a reduced-form representation of the demand for health based on Grossman's model:

$$\text{health outcome}_k = \beta_0 + \sum \beta_{1t}\text{RESOURCES}_t + \sum \beta_{2t}\text{EDUCATION}_t$$
$$+ \beta_3\,\text{health}_0 + \beta_4 X_k + \varepsilon_K,$$

where t = time, and $\sum$ is the summation from $t = 0$ to $t = k$.

Health outcome$_k$ represents the stock of health at time k. EDUCATION$_k$ is a vector of variables that represent the stock of education at time k, X_k is a vector of other variables that may affect the productivity of health inputs (such as age, race-ethnicity, and gender), and ε_K is an error term that is assumed to be uncorrelated with the other right-hand-side variables in the model.

Grossman also examines the effect of wages on the demand for health. In order to simplify the analysis, he treats health solely as an investment commodity. He argues that the value of healthy time rises with a person's wage. The implication of the model is that higher wages lead to a greater demand for health. Moving beyond Grossman's model, it can reasonably be assumed that good health is a normal good. Therefore, if health is modeled as a consumption commodity, higher income should also be associated with better health.

In Grossman's model, more highly educated individuals are able to obtain a larger amount of health from a given amount of input. This effect is known as *productive efficiency.* For example, people who participate in a nutrition-education program and learn cooking techniques that maximize the nutrient content in vegetables will be able to translate a given amount of vegetables into a more productive input into health than will those who do not. In Grossman's model, productive efficiency leads those who are more highly educated to have a greater demand for good health because a higher level of education increases the marginal benefit of a given amount of an input. Elsewhere, it has been proposed that education improves health because of *allocative efficiency* (Grossman and Kaestner [1997] summarize this literature). The hypothesis is that education increases knowledge about the relation between inputs and health and leads to the selection of a better mix of inputs.

Participation in the Food Stamp Program could improve health through both the RESOURCE and the EDUCATION channels. The Food Stamp Program provides families with additional financial resources in the form of Food Stamp coupons. Food Stamp benefits might be expected to improve health if they lead to the consumption of more food and/or more nutritious food (which could not previously be afforded but was desired). Even if there is no change in the amount or type of food consumed, the Food Stamp

Program may improve health by allowing families to increase expenditures on nonfood items that may affect the health of family members (medical care, for example) (Korenman and Miller 1992).

The Food Stamp Program also provides participants with nutrition education, which can improve the health of participants if it leads to healthier preparation techniques or healthier food choices. The educational materials provided by the Food Stamp Program also stress the importance of an active lifestyle. Even if Food Stamp Program participation does not change participants' preparation methods or diets, it can improve health if it results in the adoption of other "healthy-lifestyle" prescriptions. In summary, given the resource and education benefits of the Food Stamp Program, it is hypothesized that there is a positive relation between Food Stamp Program participation and health.

Data

The analyses in this essay use data from the first round of the NLSY97. The interviews for the first round of the survey were conducted between February and October 1997 and between March and May 1998. The first round of the survey consisted of an interview with the eligible youth and an interview with one of the youth's parents if the youth lived with the parent.[9] The youths were between the ages of twelve and sixteen as of December 31, 1996, and between the ages of twelve and eighteen at the date of the first-round interview.

The parent interview collected information on Food Stamp Program participation, family income, and other family characteristics that might be expected to influence youth health. Starting with the full sample of 9,022 youths, I exclude all youths whose parents did not respond to the parent questionnaire (1,056 youths) as well as youths whose parents failed to provide information on Food Stamp Program participation (an additional 268 youths) to create the NLSY97 sample used in the empirical analyses. This sample is used to calculate the descriptive statistics presented in table 9.1 (a detailed discussion of these statistics can be found in section 6, as can the table itself). The samples that I use in estimating the logistic-regression models are somewhat smaller owing to observations with missing data for some but not all of the health outcomes under consideration.

Analyses of Youth Health

Ideally, I would like to estimate models of the form of equation (3), where current youth health is a function of past and current resources and education, the youth's initial health endowment, and other variables that affect the productivity of health inputs. The NLSY97 contains a number of variables that allow an approximation of this model. In this section, I discuss the variables that are available in the NLSY97 and how well these data match the ideal.

Dependent Variables

The NLSY97 contains a variety of variables that can be used to measure the health of respondents, such as weight, height, self-reported health status, and parent reports of whether the youth suffers from a chronic illness. All the questions used to create the health-outcome variables are phrased so that they measure health at the time of the first-round interview. Each health outcome is introduced below.

Underweight and Overweight

Weight and height are self-reported by the youths.[10] Low weight for height (underweight) and high weight for height (obesity) are used as indicators of poor nutritional status. Weight for height is measured using the body mass index (BMI).[11] BMI is calculated as weight in kilograms divided by height in meters squared.

In the United States, the official definition of underweight is a BMI under 18.5, and the official definition of obesity is a BMI over 30 (U.S. National Institutes of Health 1998). Accordingly, youths are classified as underweight if their BMI is under 18.5 and as obese if their BMI is over 30.

Low weight for height is considered to be a risk factor for poor health in children and adults (Martorell and Ho 1984; Miller, Fine, and Adams-Taylor 1989). Obese adolescents are at higher risk for such health problems as hypertension, respiratory disease, certain orthopedic disorders, and diabetes. Obesity during adolescence is also associated with increased long-term mortality among men (Gortmaker et al. 1993).[12]

Self-Reported Health Status

The youths in the NLSY97 were asked to rate their general health using one of the following categories: *excellent, very good, good, fair,* or *poor.* Youths who rated their health as good or better are classified as being in good health for the purposes of the analyses reported here.

A critique of self-reported health is that it is subjective. Currie and Gruber (1996) discuss the difficulty of interpreting the effect of Medicaid eligibility on subjective health measures. They argue that increased contact with the medical system may give rise to changes in subjective health measures because those measures capture a "true" health effect and a "reported" health effect. The reported health effect may arise because contacts with medical practitioners may affect perceptions about health. The effect of Medicaid eligibility on true health is therefore difficult to evaluate.

While there may be some contact with medical practitioners through participation in the Food Stamp Program, the reported health-effects biases should be limited in the analyses presented here. Despite the difficulty of interpreting what a subjective measure of health actually means, Gruber (2000) argues that it is still worthwhile to continue to examine subjective measures of health, primarily because very few objective measures of health are available in public-use surveys.

Chronic Illness

The NLSY97 parent questionnaire asked whether the youth has or has ever had a chronic illness. Specifically, the parent questionnaire asked whether the youth suffers or has ever suffered from asthma, a heart condition, anemia, diabetes, cancer, epilepsy, infectious disease, kidney problems, allergies, or other chronic illnesses. Asthma was the most common condition; 79 percent of the 868 youths with a chronic condition have or had asthma.

Control Variables

Following Grossman's model, the variables that are used as controls in the empirical analyses measure either family resources, education, or other personal or family characteristics that are expected to influence current youth health. The variables that are used to measure family resources include Food Stamp Program participation, family income, number of children in the family, and whether the youth primarily lives with a single parent. As explained previously, resources in the current period and resources from prior periods are expected to affect current health. Variables that assess family resources in 1996 are used as measures of current resources. Variables that assess family resources in years prior to 1996 are used as measures of long-term resources.

The empirical analyses also include controls for family education, such as the highest grade completed by the respondent's parents, Food Stamp Program participation, and whether the youth is part of a single-parent family. For example, a youth who lives with a single parent may have less parental contact and possibly less exposure to health information or less supervision of choices that affect health (Klerman 1991). Notice that this variable has been mentioned as a measure of both resources and education. The empirical models that are estimated in this essay are reduced-form models, so therefore it is not possible to separate out the resource and the education effects of variables that may exert influence through both pathways.

Other controls in the empirical models include youth characteristics such as age, gender, whether a youth has reached puberty, race, ethnicity, and whether a youth lives in an urban area.[13] Parent's BMI is used as a proxy for the initial health endowment of the youth.[14] The following sections discuss the Food Stamp Program participation, income, and poverty-history variables in more detail.

Food Stamp Program Participation

The NLSY97 contains variables that make it possible to measure both current Food Stamp Program participation and a family's history of participation in food-aid programs. Current participation in the Food Stamp Program is measured using a dummy variable for Food Stamp Program participation in 1996. The number of years between 1992 and 1996 that a youth's family received food aid is used to measure the long-term receipt of food aid. The NLSY97 question that gathers this information records responses as whole numbers between 0 and 5. The variable for the long-term receipt of food aid includes benefits from Food Stamps as well as food aid from other sources, such as the Special Supplemental Food Program for Women, Infants, and Children (WIC). Since the period over which the long-term receipt of food aid is measured overlaps with the variable that measures the receipt of Food Stamps in 1996, only one of these variables is used at a time in the empirical models.

Two dummy variables were created to indicate a youth's family history of food-aid receipt. One of the dummy variables is set equal to 1 if a youth's family received food aid every year between 1992 and 1996. The other dummy variable is set equal to 1 if a youth's family received food aid for 1 to 4 years between 1992 and 1996. The excluded category for food-aid receipt is no food aid received between 1992 and 1996. The comparison group therefore includes families who were poor over that period and never received food aid.

In some of the empirical models, the variables for current Food Stamp receipt and the long-term receipt of food aid are interacted with the age of the youth. This allows an examination of whether the relation between current Food Stamp Program participation and long-term food-aid receipt varies with the age of the youth.[15]

These variables are not ideal controls for the long-term receipt of food aid for a number of reasons. For one thing, there is no information available about what types of food aid the families received. For another, it is not possible to determine in which of the last five years a youth's family received food aid. Also, a family's participation in food-aid programs more than five years ago may be related to current youth health.

Income

Gross family income in 1996 is used to calculate the income-to-needs ratio of the youth's family.[16] The income-to-needs ratio is calculated by dividing family income by the poverty line appropriate to the size of the family and its age composition. The gross-family-income variable does not include income from Food Stamps, but it does include parent's wages and payments received from interest, Aid to Families with Dependent Children (AFDC), supplemental security income (SSI) benefits, child support, and other sources of income (not including income from Food Stamps). Gross family income also includes wages for up to nine other family members in the household (not including the youth) if the family member is older than 14. If there is information on the youth's employment, the family-income variable also includes the youth's wages, interest income, dividend income, rental income, estate income, other income, unemployment-insurance payments to the youth, AFDC benefits, SSI benefits, and other welfare (again not including Food Stamps).

Two dummy variables were created to indicate the poverty status of the youth's family. If a youth's family has an income-to-needs ratio less than or equal to 0.5, the youth is categorized as very poor. If a youth's family has an income-to-needs ratio greater than 0.5 and less than or equal to 1, the youth is categorized as less poor.[17] The excluded income category is an income-to-needs ratio greater than 1. The variables created from the 1996 gross-family-income variable are referred to as *measures of current family income*. In some of the models, these variables are interacted with the age of the youth.

Poverty History

The NLSY97 will eventually be a panel data set, but at this time only data from the first round are available, and these data contain no direct measures of long-term family income or poverty status. The number of years between 1992 and 1996 in which a youth's family received AFDC is used as an approximation of long-term poverty status.[18] Two dummy variables identical in structure to those for the long-term receipt of food aid were created to indicate the youth's family history of AFDC receipt. In some of the empirical models, these variables are interacted with the age of the youth in order to examine whether the relation between long-term poverty and health depends on the age at which the youth is poor.

These variables are imperfect controls for poverty history for several reasons. First, all poor families do not participate in AFDC. Second, the exact timing of a family's participation in AFDC cannot be determined. Participation five years ago may have very different implications for youth health than participation last year, implications that cannot be examined with these variables. Third, a history of poverty that lasts for more than five years may matter for current health.

Analytic Issues

The potential for biased estimates of the relation between Food Stamp Program participation and health outcomes exists if variables related to both Food Stamp Program participation and health are excluded from the empirical analyses. Two solutions to this problem are possible. The first is to introduce fixed effects into the empirical models, and the second is to use an instrumental variable for Food Stamp Program participation.

Food Stamp recipients may differ from nonrecipients even when individuals with the same measurable characteristics are compared. For example, unmeasured characteristics such as parent motivation may be related to the likelihood that a family receives Food Stamps as well as the health of the youth. If unobserved differences between respondents are correlated with both health and Food Stamp receipt, the estimated effects of the Food Stamp Program on health will be biased. If the unobserved characteristics of the respondents do not vary over time, one solution to the omitted-variable-bias problem is a fixed-effects model. Since the NLSY97 is a panel data set, once additional years of data become available it will be possible to use fixed-effects models because of the availability of multiple observations for each youth in the sample. The fixed-effects strategy is not adopted here since only data from round 1 are available. Therefore, the results reported later in the essay have not controlled for these potential attributes that are not measured.

Even in models that include fixed effects, participation in the Food Stamp Program might still be endogenous. Assume that current Food Stamp Program participation is a function of past income, past program participation, and past health. Since the theoretical model suggests that these variables also directly affect current health, the failure to control adequately for these variables in the health-outcome models may bias the estimate of the relation between Food Stamp Program participation and health. As discussed earlier, the variables used in the empirical analyses in this essay attempt to control for a youth's history of poverty and food-aid participation, but these variables can be criticized. Since these characteristics will vary across time for an individual, fixed effects will not solve the problem. A common way of dealing with this type of endogeneity is to use instrumental variables.

An appropriate instrument for Food Stamp Program participation must be correlated with Food Stamp Program participation but not youth health. More specifically, the instrument must be highly correlated with Food Stamp Program participation after controlling for variables that are expected to influence both Food Stamp Program participation and youth health.

Consider a variable such as grandfather's education. If you believe that it does not belong in the youth-health-outcome model, it might seem like a potential instrument for Food Stamp Program participation. However, grandfather's education is of limited usefulness as an instrument because the correlation between Food Stamp Program participation and grandfather's education is very low after conditioning on the other variables included in the first stage of the model, such as parent's education and family resources. Cawley (chapter 6 in this volume) offers a detailed discussion of the method of instrumental variables and the danger of using weak instruments. None of the variables currently available in the NLSY97 meet the criteria for use as instruments for Food Stamp Program participation.[19] In the future, the geo-coded NLSY97 data will provide the opportunity to use variables that depend on variation in location as instruments for Food Stamp receipt.

The two solutions that are suggested as methods of dealing with biased estimates of the relation between Food Stamp Program participation and youth health cannot be implemented with data from the first round of the NLSY97. The good news is that future waves of data can be used to deal with this problem. Given that the NLSY97 contains a relatively full set of youth and family characteristics and variables that can approximate a family's history of Food Stamp Program participation and poverty, it is still useful to use data from the first round of the NLSY97 to examine the relation between Food Stamp Program participation and health. However, given the analytic issues raised here, it is especially important not to treat estimates from the following empirical analyses as causal. Instead, they should be regarded as descriptive of the relation between Food Stamp use and youth health.

Sample Characteristics

Examining the poverty status of the sample, 9 percent of the youths are very poor, 9 percent are less poor, and 82 percent are not poor.[20] In terms of program participation, 13 percent of the youths received Food Stamps in 1996, 6 percent received food aid every year between 1992 and 1996, and 4 percent received AFDC each year between 1992 and 1996. In terms of health outcomes, 23 percent of the youths are underweight, 4 percent are obese, 95 percent are in good health, and 11 percent have a chronic illness.

Youths whose families are current Food Stamp Program participants are significantly more likely to be overweight, be in poor health, or have a chronic illness than are youths whose families are currently nonparticipants.[21] These comparisons do not take in to account the fact that on average, current Food Stamp Program participants are significantly poorer than non-participants.

Table 9.1 categorizes youths by the poverty status of their families in 1996 and whether their families received Food Stamps in 1996. Recall that the variable used to measure family income and determine a family's income-to-needs ratio does not include income from Food Stamps. Table 9.1 indicates that, in general, youths whose families are current Food Stamp Program participants are not in better health than youths whose families are similarly poor but are not currently participating in the Food Stamp Program. In fact, among very poor youths, Food Stamp Program participants are significantly more likely to be overweight, be in poor health, or have a chronic illness than are nonparticipants. Among less-poor youths, Food Stamp Program participants are significantly more likely to have a chronic illness than are nonparticipants.[22]

It is improper to use these statistics to argue that Food Stamp Program participation has an adverse effect on youth health. The ideal analysis would compare the health of individuals whose sole difference is Food Stamp Program participation. Table 9.1 makes it clear that comparing currently poor Food Stamp Program participants to currently poor nonparticipants does not accomplish this goal. Table 9.1 shows that youths whose families currently receive Food Stamps differ significantly in terms of other government-program participation from youths whose families do not currently receive Food Stamps, even after grouping youths into categories by family income. Among youths whose families are currently poor, youths whose families are current Food Stamp recipients are much more likely to be long-term AFDC and food-aid recipients than are youths whose families are not currently receiving Food Stamps.

On this basis, it appears to be reasonable to conclude that families who are current Food Stamp Program participants suffer from more persistent poverty than do those families who are poor but are not current participants in the Food Stamp Program.[23] Grossman's model suggests that long-term resources also affect current health; therefore, the significant differences in health across categories of Food Stamp Program participation may be explained by differences in poverty history rather than Food Stamp Program participation. The logistic-regression models of youth health discussed in the next section include controls for a youth's poverty history.

Logit Models

Logistic-regression models are estimated in order to examine the relation between health outcomes and variables that measure family resources, education, and other factors that may affect the productivity of health inputs, ceteris paribus. Four logistic-regression models that approximate equation (3) are estimated for each health outcome. Model 1 includes controls

TABLE 9.1 Characteristics of Youth, by Family Poverty Status and Food Stamp Receipt in 1996 (Values Equal the Percentage of the Subsample in Each Category Unless Otherwise Noted)

Variables	Income to Needs Ratio ≤ 0.5		Income to Needs Ratio > 0.5 and ≤1		Income to Needs Ratio > 1
	Received Food Stamps	Did Not Receive Food Stamps	Received Food Stamps	Did Not Receive Food Stamps	
Health					
Underweight	26.0	28.2	25.9	20.3	23.5
Overweight	19.9	12.0	19.6	21.4	14.9
Obese	5.0	4.3	5.8	5.3	4.1
Good health	90.5	94.7	92.4	93.2	96.3
Chronic illness	13.1	5.1	16.4	9.6	11.5
Income in 1996					
Gross family income (mean dollars)	4,808	3,300	12,358	14,124	62,220
Food Stamp income (mean dollars)	2,893	0.0	2,237	0.0	65.6
Income to needs ratio (mean ratio)	0.26	0.19	0.72	0.79	3.83
AFDC receipt 1992 to 1996					
Never	28.7	94.8	36.1	80.3	94.7
One to four years	30.8	2.5	32.7	14.1	4.4
All five years	40.5	2.7	31.2	5.5	0.9

Food Aid receipt 1992 to 1996

Never	17.4	88.1	10.8	71.2	90.2
One to four years	26.5	10.5	38.7	24.9	8.5
All five years	56.1	1.5	50.5	3.8	1.4
Other youth traits					
Age	14.7	14.6	14.6	14.9	14.8
Female	54.2	42.7	48.9	51.8	48.4
Black	46.8	25.0	32.5	19.0	11.3
Hispanic	25.3	26.5	20.6	32.6	9.4
Parent's	11.1	12.1	11.2	11.5	14.1
Education					
Reached puberty	78.5	79.8	79.2	82.1	84.5
Health insurance	83.4	68.9	85.0	57.4	91.8
Single parent	75.4	44.0	65.4	42.2	21.9
Family					
Family size	5.1	4.4	4.5	4.8	4.3
Number of children in family	3.4	2.4	2.8	2.9	2.2
Number of cases	621	346	488	435	5,808

Source: Author's compilation.

Notes: Sample characteristics are calculated using the NLSY97 sample weight. Underweight = 1 if BMI ≤ 18.5; = 0 if BMI > 18.5. Overweight = 1 if BMI ≥ 25; = 0 if BMI < 25. Obese = 1 if BMI ≥ 30; = 0 if BMI < 30. Good health status = 1 if the youth reported that his or her health was "good," "very good," or "excellent"; = 0 if the youth reported that his or her health was "fair" or "poor." Chronic illness = 1 if the responding parent of the youth reported that the youth has or has ever had a chronic illness; = 0 if the responding parent of the youth reported that the youth does not have or has never had a chronic illness.

for current poverty, current Food Stamp receipt, and poverty history. Model 2 is the same as model 1 except that it adds age interactions with current Food Stamp receipt, current poverty status, and poverty history. Model 3 is the same as model 1 except that a family's history of food-aid receipt replaces current Food Stamp receipt. Model 4 is the same as model 3 except that it adds age interactions with a family's current poverty status, history of food-aid receipt, and poverty history. The four models for each health outcome also include controls for youth's age, age squared, gender, race-ethnicity, highest grade completed by the youth's parents, number of children in the youth's family, parent's BMI, urbanization, and family structure. The statistical models of underweight and obesity also include puberty onset.

An important question is how to interpret the coefficient estimates from the logistic-regression models. Grossman's theoretical model of the demand for health predicts that larger amounts of resources and greater education lead to better health. A causal relation between the variables that measure resources and education and health outcomes is one possible explanation for coefficient estimates that are significant. However, given the analytic issues mentioned earlier, significant coefficients are not sufficient evidence of a causal relation. In the discussion of the empirical results, if it is stated that a result is consistent with Grossman's model, what is meant is that the direction of the relation matches the prediction of Grossman's model.

Underweight

Table 9.2 presents the coefficient estimates from logistic-regression models 1 to 4 for underweight. In model 1, current Food Stamp receipt, current poverty, and poverty history are not significantly related to the likelihood that a youth is underweight.[24] Model 2 adds age interactions to test whether the age at which a youth receives Food Stamps or is poor is related to youth health. In this model, the coefficient estimates on the dummy variables for current Food Stamp receipt and the interaction between Food Stamp receipt and age are statistically significant. Since the Food Stamp dummy variable has a negative coefficient and the coefficient on the Food Stamp and age interaction is positive, the reduction in the likelihood that a Food Stamp Program participant is underweight dissipates for older children. In fact, older Food Stamp Program participants are more likely to be underweight than are nonparticipants of the same age.[25]

The estimates of the coefficients from models 3 and 4 exhibit a similar pattern to the estimates of the coefficients from models 1 and 2. Current poverty and past poverty are not significantly related to the likelihood that a youth is underweight in either model 3 or model 4. A youth's history of food-aid-program participation is not significant in model 3. In model 4, the coefficient on the dummy variable for participation in food-aid programs for 1 to 4 years between 1992 and 1996 is negative and significant, and the coefficient on its interaction with age is positive and significant. The coefficient on the dummy variable for participation in food-aid programs every year between 1992 and 1996 is negative, and the coefficient on its interaction with age is positive, but the coefficients are significant at the 10 percent rather than the 5 percent level. As with the estimates from model 2, the reduction in the likelihood that a youth is underweight that is associated with food-aid-program participation diminishes for older youths.[26]

Grossman's model of the demand for health predicts that Food Stamp Program participation and health are positively related. This prediction is not consistently supported by the estimates from models 1 to 4 for underweight. Food Stamp Program participation is associated with a decrease in the likelihood of being underweight for younger youths and an increase in the likelihood of being underweight for older youths. The likelihood that a youth is underweight is not significantly related to any of the other variables used to measure resources and education.

Obesity

Table 9.3 presents the coefficient estimates from logistic-regression models 1 to 4 for obesity. Obesity is not significantly related to Food Stamp Program participation, current poverty, or a family's history of poverty in any of the models. Of the other variables that are used to control for family resources and education, single-parent-family status is positively and significantly related to the likelihood that a youth is obese. Single-parent-family status may reflect both resource limitations and reduced supervision of what a youth eats and how much exercise he or she gets. Therefore, the positive relation between single-parent-family status and obesity is consistent with Grossman's model.

Self-Reported Health

Table 9.4 presents the coefficient estimates from logistic-regression models 1 to 4 for good health status. Food Stamp Program participation is significantly related to good health status only in model 3. Youths whose families participated in food-aid programs for 1 to 4 years between 1992 and 1996 are significantly less likely to be in good health than are youths whose families never participated in food-aid programs over this time period. The significance of the coefficient on this variable disappears when age interactions are introduced in model 4. The estimates from models 1 to 4 suggest that the relation between Food Stamp Program participation and good health status is not strong, in either a positive or a negative direction.

(Text continues on p. 286.)

TABLE 9.2   Logit Estimation of Underweight by Food Stamp Program Participation, Poverty Status, and Youth Characteristics

	(1)		(2)		(3)		(4)	
	Coeff.	S.E.	Coeff.	S.E.	Coeff.	S.E.	Coeff.	S.E.
Income in 1996								
Income-to-needs ratio ≤ .5	0.19	0.15	0.31	1.48	0.20	0.14	-0.23	1.40
Income-to-needs ratio > .5 and ≤ 1	0.00	0.15	-1.26	1.54	-0.01	0.14	-1.38	1.52
Income-to-needs ratio ≤ .5 × (age)	...	...	-0.01	0.10	...	...	0.03	0.10
Income-to-needs ratio > .5 and ≤ 1 × (age)	...	...	0.09	0.11	...	...	0.10	0.11
Food Stamp Program participation								
In 1996	-0.02	0.15	-3.86*	1.58	...	...	...	...
In 1996 × (age)	...	...	0.27*	0.11	...	...	...	...
Food Aid receipt 1992 to 1996								
One to four years	...	...	...	...	0.17	0.13	-2.84*	1.39
All five years	...	...	...	...	-0.26	0.22	-3.91**	2.19
One to four years × (age)	...	...	...	...	...	...	0.21*	0.10
All five years × (age)	...	...	...	...	...	...	0.25**	0.15
AFDC receipt 1992 to 1996								
One to four years	0.22	0.15	1.15	1.58	0.13	0.17	1.80	1.82
All five years	0.12	0.20	4.02**	2.25	0.33	0.23	3.98	2.46
One to four years × (age)	...	...	-0.06	0.11	...	...	-0.12	0.13
All five years × (age)	...	...	-0.27**	0.16	...	...	-0.25	0.17

Other youth traits

	Coef.	SE	Coef.	SE	Coef.	SE	Coef.	SE
Age	1.40*	0.52	1.40*	0.53	1.39*	0.52	1.31*	0.53
Age squared	−0.06*	0.02	−0.06*	0.02	−0.06*	0.02	−0.06*	0.02
Female	−0.61*	0.07	−0.62*	0.07	−0.61*	0.07	−0.61*	0.07
Black	0.14	0.10	0.13	0.10	0.15	0.10	0.15	0.10
Hispanic	−0.06	0.12	−0.07	0.12	−0.05	0.12	−0.05	0.12
Parent's education	0.02	0.01	0.02	0.01	0.02	0.01	0.02	0.01
Reached puberty	−0.66*	0.09	−0.65*	0.09	−0.67*	0.09	−0.66*	0.09
Single-parent family	−0.06	0.09	−0.07	0.09	−0.07	0.09	−0.07	0.09
Number of children in family	0.02	0.03	0.02	0.03	0.02	0.03	0.02	0.03
Urban	0.03	0.07	0.04	0.07	0.03	0.07	0.04	0.07
Pseudo-R^2	.093		.095		.094		.095	
Number of observations	6,211		6,211		6,219		6,219	

Source: Author's compilation.

Note: Underweight = 1 if BMI ≤ 18.5; = 0 if BMI > 18.5. NLSY97 sample weights are used in all regressions. The excluded income category is an income-to-needs ratio greater than 1. The excluded long-term food-aid-receipt category is no food aid received between 1992 and 1996. The excluded long-term AFDC-receipt category is no AFDC received between 1992 and 1996. The excluded race-ethnicity category is non-Hispanic, nonblack. The models also include a set of controls for the BMI of the responding parent interacted with the gender of the responding parent and whether the responding parent was biologically related to the youth.

* Significant at the 5 percent level.
** Significant at the 10 percent level.

TABLE 9.3   Logit Estimation of Obesity by Food Stamp Program Participation, Poverty Status, and Youth Characteristics

	(1)		(2)		(3)		(4)	
	Coeff.	S.E.	Coeff.	S.E.	Coeff.	S.E.	Coeff.	S.E.
Income in 1996								
Income-to-needs ratio ≤ .5	-0.04	0.28	-2.32	2.90	-0.12	0.28	-2.23	2.85
Income-to-needs ratio > .5 and ≤ 1	-0.23	0.28	-4.04	3.32	-0.31	0.29	-3.97	3.49
Income-to-needs ratio ≤ .5 × (age)	...	...	0.15	0.19	...	...	0.14	0.19
Income-to-needs ratio > .5 and ≤ 1 × (age)	...	...	0.25	0.21	...	...	0.24	0.23
Food Stamp Program participation								
In 1996	-0.18	0.30	1.96	2.98	...	...	...	...
In 1996 × (age)	...	...	-0.14	0.19	...	...	...	...
Food Aid receipt 1992 to 1996								
One to four years	...	...	...	...	-0.05	0.26	1.80	2.57
All five years	...	...	...	...	0.17	0.32	2.68	2.97
One to four years × (age)	...	...	...	...	...	...	-0.12	0.17
All five years × (age)	...	...	...	...	...	...	-0.16	0.19
AFDC receipt 1992 to 1996								
One to four years	-0.28	0.33	-3.07	3.98	-0.32	0.32	-3.44	3.59
All five years	-0.01	0.38	-0.23	4.14	-0.23	0.37	-0.61	3.90
One to four years × (age)	...	...	0.18	0.26	...	...	0.20	0.23
All five years × (age)	...	...	0.01	0.27	...	...	0.02	0.26

Other youth traits

	(1)		(2)		(3)		(4)	
Age	−1.08	1.13	−1.17	1.14	−1.07	1.13	−1.11	1.14
Age squared	0.05	0.04	0.05	0.04	0.05	0.04	0.05	0.04
Female	0.35*	0.15	0.36*	0.15	0.36*	0.15	0.36*	0.15
Black	0.28	0.21	0.27	0.21	0.26	0.21	0.24	0.21
Hispanic	0.48*	0.19	0.47*	0.19	0.47*	0.19	0.46*	0.19
Parent's education	−0.04	0.03	−0.04	0.03	−0.04	0.03	−0.04	0.03
Reached puberty	0.10	0.26	0.13	0.27	0.11	0.26	0.14	0.27
Single-parent family	0.48*	0.17	0.48*	0.17	0.47*	0.17	0.46*	0.17
Number of children in family	−0.09	0.06	−0.09	0.06	−0.09	0.06	−0.10	0.06
Urban	−0.19	0.15	−0.19	0.15	−0.19	0.15	−0.19	0.15
Pseudo-R^2	.124		.125		.124		.125	
Number of observations	6,211		6,211		6,219		6,219	

Source: Author's compilation.
Note: Obese = 1 if BMI ≥ 30; = 0 if BMI < 30. The excluded race-ethnicity category is non-Hispanic, nonblack. See also notes to table 9.2.
* Significant at the 5 percent level.
** Significant at the 10 percent level.

TABLE 9.4 *Logit Estimation of Good Health Status by Food Stamp Program Participation, Poverty Status, and Youth Characteristics*

	(1)		(2)		(3)		(4)	
	Coeff.	S.E.	Coeff.	S.E.	Coeff.	S.E.	Coeff.	S.E.
Income in 1996								
Income-to-needs ratio ≤ .5	−0.23	0.23	2.37	2.19	−0.20	0.22	2.19	2.07
Income-to-needs ratio > .5 and ≤ 1	−0.23	0.23	0.33	2.51	−0.18	0.21	0.13	2.25
Income-to-needs ratio ≤ .5 × (age)	...	...	−0.18	0.15	...	...	−0.16	0.14
Income-to-needs ratio > .5 and ≤ 1 × (age)	...	...	−0.04	0.17	...	...	−0.02	0.15
Food Stamp Program participation								
In 1996	−0.25	0.24	−1.12	2.47	...	...	...	...
In 1996 × (age)	...	...	0.06	0.16	...	...	...	...
Food Aid receipt 1992 to 1996								
One to four years	...	...	...	...	−0.55*	0.20	0.03	2.00
All five years	...	...	...	...	−0.33	0.28	−1.35	2.64
One to four years × (age)	...	...	...	...	...	...	−0.04	0.13
All five years × (age)	...	...	...	...	...	...	0.07	0.18
AFDC receipt 1992 to 1996								
One to four years	−0.12	0.24	2.53	2.55	0.09	0.23	2.09	2.30
All five years	0.09	0.28	−0.12	2.67	0.06	0.29	0.12	2.75
One to four years × (age)	...	...	−0.18	0.17	...	...	−0.13	0.15
All five years × (age)	...	...	0.01	0.18	...	...	0.00	0.19

Other youth traits

	(1)		(2)		(3)		(4)	
Age	-0.27	0.93	-0.19	0.93	-0.22	0.93	-0.14	0.93
Age squared	0.01	0.03	0.01	0.03	0.01	0.03	0.00	0.03
Female	-0.22**	0.13	-0.22**	0.13	-0.23**	0.13	-0.23**	0.13
Black	-0.31**	0.16	-0.30**	0.16	-0.30**	0.16	-0.29**	0.16
Hispanic	-0.07	0.22	-0.07	0.22	-0.06	0.22	-0.05	0.22
Parent's education	0.06*	0.03	0.06*	0.03	0.06*	0.03	0.05*	0.03
Single-parent family	-0.40*	0.15	-0.41*	0.15	-0.40*	0.15	-0.41*	0.15
Number of children in family	-0.06	0.05	-0.06	0.05	-0.06	0.05	-0.06	0.05
Urban	0.09	0.14	0.09	0.14	0.07	0.14	0.07	0.14
Pseudo-R^2	0.036		0.038		0.039		0.040	
Number of observations	6,603		6,603		6,609		6,609	

Source: Author's compilation.
Note: Good health status = 1 if the youth reported his or her health was "good," "very good," or "excellent"; = 0 if the youth reported that his or her health was "fair or poor." See also notes to table 9.2.

TABLE 9.5   Logit Estimation of Chronic Illness by Food Stamp Program Participation, Poverty Status, and Youth Characteristics

	(1)		(2)		(3)		(4)	
	Coeff.	S.E.	Coeff.	S.E.	Coeff.	S.E.	Coeff.	S.E.
Income in 1996								
Income-to-needs ratio ≤ .5	-0.37*	0.17	-0.24	1.85	-0.39*	0.17	-0.49	1.79
Income-to-needs ratio > .5 and ≤ 1	-0.19	0.17	1.19	1.66	-0.17	0.17	0.76	1.68
Income-to-needs ratio ≤ .5 × (age)	...	...	-0.01	0.13	...	...	0.01	0.12
Income-to-needs ratio > .5 and ≤ 1 × (age)	...	...	-0.09	0.11	...	...	-0.06	0.11
Food Stamp Program participation								
In 1996	-0.08	0.16	-0.61	1.56	...	...	...	...
In 1996 × (age)	...	...	0.04	0.10	...	...	...	...
Food Aid receipt 1992 to 1996								
One to four years	...	...	...	...	0.06	0.16	1.02	1.64
All five years	...	...	...	...	-0.24	0.24	-2.19	2.42
One to four years × (age)	...	...	...	...	...	...	-0.07	0.11
All five years × (age)	...	...	...	...	...	...	0.13	0.16
AFDC receipt 1992 to 1996								
One to four years	0.53*	0.17	-0.99	1.66	0.49*	0.18	-1.49	1.86
All five years	0.78*	0.22	-0.54	2.26	0.92*	0.26	1.02	2.63
One to four years × (age)	...	...	0.10	0.11	...	...	0.14	0.13
All five years × (age)	...	...	0.09	0.15	...	...	-0.01	0.18

Other youth traits

Age	−0.35	0.61	−0.42	0.61	−0.36	0.61	−0.41	0.61
Age squared	0.01	0.02	0.01	0.02	0.01	0.02	0.01	0.02
Female	−0.18*	0.09	−0.18*	0.09	−0.18*	0.09	−0.17*	0.09
Black	−0.16	0.12	−0.17	0.12	−0.16	0.12	−0.17	0.12
Hispanic	−0.28**	0.15	−0.28**	0.15	−0.30*	0.15	−0.31*	0.15
Parent's education	0.01	0.02	0.01	0.02	0.01	0.02	0.01	0.02
Single-parent family	0.15	0.10	0.15	0.10	0.15	0.10	0.15	0.10
Number of children in family	−0.09*	0.04	−0.09*	0.04	−0.08*	0.04	−0.08*	0.04
Urban	0.20*	0.09	0.20*	0.09	0.22*	0.09	0.22*	0.09
Pseudo-R^2	0.012		0.013		0.013		0.014	
Number of observations	6,570		6,570		6,576		6,576	

Source: Author's compilation.
Note: Chronic illness = 1 if the responding parent of the youth reported that the youth has or has had a chronic illness; = 0 if the responding parent of the youth reported that the youth does not have or has never had a chronic illness. See also notes to table 9.2.
* Significant at the 5 percent level. ** Significant at the 10 percent level.

Family poverty is not significantly related to good health status in any of the models. Of the other variables that are used to control for family resources and education, parent's education and single-parent-family status are statistically significant in all the models. Parent's education is positively related to good health status, and single-parent-family status is negatively related to good health status. The signs of these coefficients match predictions based on Grossman's model.

Chronic Illness

Table 9.5 presents the coefficient estimates from logistic-regression models 1 to 4 for chronic illness. Food Stamp Program participation is not significantly related to chronic illness in any of the models. The estimates indicate a complicated relation between chronic illness and poverty. In all four models, youths whose families are currently in extreme poverty are less likely to have a chronic illness than are otherwise identical youths whose families are not currently poor. These estimates are significant in models 1 and 3, the models without the age interactions. However, in all four models, long-term poverty is associated with an increase in the likelihood that a youth has a chronic illness.[27] These estimates are significant in models 1 and 3.

Grossman's model of the demand for health predicts that both current poverty and long-term poverty are positively related to the likelihood that a youth has a chronic illness. The estimates of the coefficients on current and long-term poverty from models 1 to 4 do not consistently support this prediction.

It is possible that the empirical models are misspecified if current poverty and current Food Stamp receipt are included in models of chronic illness. The wording of the question about chronic illness in the parent-interview portion of the first round of the NLSY97 does not make it possible to determine whether the youth is ill at the time of the interview or was ill at some point in the past. It is also not possible to determine how long the youth has been or had been ill. It is expected that the relation between current poverty status, current Food Stamp receipt, and chronic illness depends on how these questions are answered.

Consider a case in which a youth had a chronic illness from which he or she has since recovered. It can be argued that current poverty status and current Food Stamp receipt do not belong in a model of past chronic illness. To examine the sensitivity of the estimates to the inclusion of current poverty status and current Food Stamp receipt, models 3 and 4 were reestimated removing current poverty status (current Food Stamp receipt is already excluded from models 3 and 4). In model 3, the coefficients on the long-term receipt of food aid remain insignificant, and the coefficients on long-term poverty remain positive and significant.[28] In model 4, the coefficients on the long-term receipt of food aid and long-term poverty remain insignificant after the removal of current poverty status.

The only other variable that measures family resources or education that is significant in the models of chronic illness is number of children in a youth's family. The number of children can be viewed as a measure of how far family resources must extend and the availability of adult supervision and attention. Given Grossman's model, the expectation is that number of children is positively related to the likelihood that a youth has a chronic illness. However, the number of children is negatively and significantly related to the likelihood a youth has a chronic illness in models 1 to 4. One possible explanation for this finding is that the chronic-illness variable is capturing diagnosed chronic illness rather than the actual incidence of chronic illness. Families with a larger number of children may pay less attention to youth health, and chronic illnesses may therefore be less likely to be diagnosed.[29] It is not possible to evaluate the validity of this hypothesis with the available data.[30]

Conclusions

This essay set out to test the hypothesis that Food Stamp Program participation is positively related to youth health. This hypothesis is based on Grossman's theoretical model of the demand for health. Past empirical research lends somewhat qualified support to this hypothesis. Past research has usually found a positive and significant relation between income and both nutritional status and general health. It has also generally found a positive and significant relation between Food Stamp Program participation and input measures of nutritional status. However, the few studies that examine the relation between Food Stamp Program participation and output measures of nutritional status have generally not found a significant relation between these health measures and Food Stamp Program participation.

The empirical analyses presented in this essay suggest that, for the health outcomes considered, Food Stamp Program participation is not strongly related to youth health. The estimates of the coefficients on Food Stamp Program participation or participation in food-aid programs are almost always insignificant and, when significant, sometimes opposite the direction expected given Grossman's model. In the empirical models with age interactions, Food Stamp Program participation is significantly related to the likelihood that a youth is underweight. Food Stamp Program participation is associated with a decrease in the likelihood of being underweight for younger youths but an increase in the likelihood of being underweight for older youths. The empirical analyses presented in this essay add support to previous findings that the relation between Food Stamp Program participation and obesity is not significant. The empirical analyses also indicate that the relation between Food Stamp Program participation and general health, measured by self-reported health status and the prevalence of chronic illness, is not strong. In one model (model 3), food-aid-program participation for one to four years between 1992 and 1996 is associated with a significant decrease in the likelihood that a youth is in good health. In all the other models of good health status and all the models of chronic illness, the coefficients on Food Stamp Program participation and participation in food-aid programs are insignificant.

A concern with the empirical analyses presented in this essay is the potential for biased estimates of the relation between Food Stamp Program participation and health. The potential for bias exists if the empirical analyses fail to control for unobserved differences across individuals or fail to control adequately for long-term poverty, past program participation, or past health. With data collected from future rounds of the NLSY97, it will be possible to deal with many of the potential causes of bias. Individual fixed effects can be used to control for omitted individual characteristics that do not vary across time. Concerns have been raised about the variables used as proxies for long-term poverty and the long-term receipt of food aid. With data collected from future rounds, a more detailed history of a youth's poverty and Food Stamp Program participation will be available. Finally, the geo-coded NLSY97 data will provide opportunities to use variables that depend on variation in location as instruments for Food Stamp Program participation.

Thanks are due to Gerald Cubbin, Carolyn J. Hill, Robert Kaestner, Sanders Korenman, Robert Michael, and Tom Miles for helpful conversations and comments on earlier drafts of this essay. Thanks are also due to John Cawley, Carolyn J. Hill, Yoonae Jo, and Robert Michael for providing some of the data used in the empirical analyses. Helpful comments and suggestions were also provided by participants at the Early Results Conference. Hale Bingol and Gregory Tzouros provided able research assistance. This research was supported by a grant from the Northwestern University/University of Chicago Joint Center for Poverty Research (JCPR). Core funding for the JCPR is provided by the Office of the Assistant Secretary for Program Evaluation, the U.S. Department of Health and Human Services.

Notes

1. The youths in the NLSY97 were twelve to sixteen years of age as of December 31, 1996, but were twelve to eighteen years of age at the time of their first NLSY97 interview.

2. Anthropometric indicators of nutritional status include physical measurements such as weight, height, weight for height, height for age, weight for age, skinfold thickness, mid-arm circumference, and head circumference.

3. This section summarizes research using data from developed countries. Research using data from developing countries may not be applicable to the United States—primarily because differences exist between developed and developing countries in the severity and duration of nutrition deprivation, disease patterns, and the quality and availability of health care (Miller and Korenman 1994).

4. Miller and Korenman (1994) discuss studies with similar research designs from the 1970s; these studies also find that current poverty status is positively related to poor nutritional status among children.

5. The child sample consists of all children born to female NLSY79 respondents who completed an interview during the even-year interviews beginning in 1986 (U.S. Department of Labor 1999).

6. Rose, Habicht, and Devaney (1998), Butler and Raymond (1996), and Devaney and Moffitt (1991) all control for self-selection into the Food Stamp Program.

7. Kafatos and Zee (1977) examine the effect of a supplementary food program on child weight and height. This program includes the provision of Food Stamps, supplementary foods, day care, and an infant feeding program. Kafatos and Zee measure the weight and height of a cross-sectional sample of low-income preschool children in Memphis before the introduction of the supplementary food program. They compare the means from this sample to the means from a different cross-sectional sample of children taken three years after the introduction of the supplementary food program. They find a significant increase in the mean weight and height of children after the introduction of the program. Since the supplementary food program contains a number of different components, it is not possible to separate out the effect of the Food Stamp Program on the health of low-income preschool children.

8. Korenman and Miller (1992) also examine the relation between Food Stamp receipt during pregnancy and the health of the infant and mother. They are concerned that cross-sectional models do not capture adequately the differences between impoverished recipients and nonrecipients. Their solution is to use fixed-effects estimates that are obtained by comparing outcomes across a woman's births or pregnancies. Their sample is restricted to women who experienced both first and second births during the survey window (1979 through 1988). Their sample is approximately twenty-five hundred children. Mothers who switch between use and nonuse of Food Stamps between their first and their second births identify the effect of Food Stamp use. Korenman and Miller find that Food Stamp use during pregnancy appears to be associated with higher birth weight, but the coefficients on these

estimates are often not significant. The fixed-effects estimates suggest an effect of about 2.5 ounces on birth weight.

9. A preordered hierarchy was used in the NLSY97 to select the responding parent, starting with the youth's biological mother. If the biological mother was not present in the household, the biological father was interviewed. Other parent figures were interviewed only if neither biological parent was available.

10. The interviewer asks the respondent to approximate his or her weight and height.

11. The BMI measures used in this essay correct for measurement error in the youth height and weight reports. John Cawley provided these corrections. Cawley (chapter 6 in this volume) provides a description of the techniques used to correct these data.

12. For an analysis of the relation between body weight and dating and sexual behaviors, see also Cawley (chapter 6 in this volume).

13. Age is measured at time of interview rather than as of December 31, 1996, so that the health outcomes can be adequately age adjusted. Dummy variables for Hispanic and non-Hispanic black (hereafter referred to as black) are used to indicate race and ethnicity. Controls for puberty status are used only in the models of underweight and obesity.

    It could be argued that health insurance belongs in these models because health insurance may lead to increased utilization of the medical system and increased utilization of the medical system may lead to improved health. Gruber (2000) summarizes the research on this topic with respect to Medicaid. I decided to exclude health-insurance status for a number of reasons. First, estimates of the relation between health-insurance status and health are likely to be biased because of omitted-variable bias or the simultaneity of health and health-insurance status (Gruber 2000). Second, the few studies that examine the relation between child health and health-insurance status or eligibility and attempt to deal with the potential biases correctly find limited or no relation between child-health outcomes and health insurance (Gruber 2000; Kaestner, Racine, and Joyce 2000). Finally, other research on health outcomes, where the effect of insurance on health is not of primary interest, exclude insurance as a control (Korenman and Miller 1992; Currie and Cole 1993; Miller and Korenman 1994; Bhattacharya and Currie 2000).

14. The models include a set of dummy variables for the BMI of the responding parent interacted with the gender of the responding parent and whether the responding parent is biologically related to the youth. This approach is also used by Bhattacharya and Currie (2000), who include mother's BMI in their models of child health as a measure of the child's health endowment.

    Including parent's BMI is potentially problematic since this measure also captures elements of the parent's behavior that could be adopted by the child and therefore characterized as education rather than as a health endowment. Also, parent's BMI may be a poor proxy for a youth's initial health when dealing with health outcomes that are not related to weight and height.

15. Logistic-regression models were also run including interactions between the Food Stamp receipt variables and current poverty status. It might be assumed that Food Stamp Program participation has a different relation with health for youths who are extremely poor and youths who are less poor. The interactions between Food Stamp Program participation and current poverty status are not statistically significant in the logistic-regression models for any of the health outcomes. These results are available from the author on request.

16. The income variable used in this essay was created and provided by Carolyn J. Hill, Yoonae Jo, and Robert Michael of the Harris Graduate School of Public Policy Studies, University of Chicago.

17. If a youth's family income-to-needs ratio is less than or equal to 0.5, this is also referred to in this essay as *extreme poverty*. If a youth's family income-to-needs ratio is greater than 0.5 and less than or equal to 1, this is also referred to as *less poverty*.

18. Since AFDC receipt is likely to be highly correlated with family structure, the models of youth health include a control for whether the youth's family is headed by a single parent. This issue is discussed further in the section of the essay that describes the characteristics of the sample.

19. Korenman and Miller (1992) argue that there are no valid instruments for Food Stamp receipt in the NLSY79. They feel that all potential instruments either belong in the first stage of the model or are too weak to be of use.

20. Unless otherwise indicated, all characteristics discussed are calculated using the NLSY97 sample weight.

21. Breaking the sample into subsamples by current Food Stamp Program participation status, Pearson chi-square tests were used to test whether the unweighted percentages of each subsample in each health category are significantly different. Of the youths whose families received Food Stamps in 1996, 25 percent are underweight, 20 percent are overweight, 5.4 percent are obese, 91 percent are in good health, and 13 percent have a chronic condition. Of the youths whose families did not receive Food Stamps in 1996, 23 percent are underweight, 14 percent are overweight, 4.1 percent are obese, 96 percent are in good health, and 11 percent have a chronic condition. Chi-square statistics (d.f. = 1) are 0.78 for underweight, 22.6 for overweight, 2.1 for obesity, 55.2 for good health status, and 6.4 for chronic illness. The chi-square statistics reject the null hypothesis of equal percentages at the 5 percent significance level for overweight, good health, and chronic illness.

22. The sample is further broken down into subsamples defined by current poverty status and current Food Stamp Program participation. Within current poverty categories, Pearson chi-square tests are used to test whether the unweighted percentages of each subsample in each health category are significantly different by current Food Stamp Program participation. For extremely poor youths, chi-square statistics (d.f. = 1) are 0.38 for underweight, 5.0 for overweight, 0.27 for obesity, 5.8 for good health status, and 11.2 for chronic illness. The chi-square statistics reject the null hypothesis of equal percentages at the 5 percent significance level for overweight and good health and at the 1 percent significance level for chronic illness. For less-poor youths, chi-square statistics (d.f. = 1) are 1.7 for underweight, 0.03 for overweight, 0.54 for obesity, 0.13 for good health status, and 8.46 for chronic illness. The chi-square statistics reject the null hypothesis of equal percentages at the 5 percent significance level for chronic illness.

23. The difference in poverty history suggested by the numbers in table 9.1 may be overstated because more very poor participant families (75 percent) than very poor nonparticipant families (44 percent) are single-parent families. Poor two-parent families are very rarely eligible for AFDC (Blank 1997).

24. Only coefficients that are significant at the 5 percent level or above are referred to as *significant* in the discussion of the empirical results.

25. If a youth is twelve years old and his or her family currently participates in the Food Stamp Program, he or she is 0.51 times more likely to be underweight than is an otherwise identical twelve-year-old whose family does not currently participate in the Food Stamp Program. Using results from model 2, the effect of current Food Stamp Program participation on the log odds of underweight for twelve-year-olds is $-3.86 + 12(0.267) = (-0.656)$. Exponentiating (-0.656) gives the odds ratio. If a youth is seventeen years old and his or her family currently participates in the Food Stamp Program, he or she is 1.97 times more likely to be underweight than is an otherwise identical seventeen-year-old whose family does not currently participate in the Food Stamp Program. The age at which a youth whose family is currently participating in the Food Stamp Program is just as likely to be underweight as a youth who is otherwise identical but whose family is currently not participating in the Food Stamp Program is 14.45 years. This is found by solving for the age at which the effect of Food Stamp Program participation on the log odds of underweight equals 0.

26. If a youth is twelve years old and his or her family received food aid for one to four years between 1992 and 1996, he or she is 0.73 times more likely to be underweight than is an otherwise identical twelve-year-old whose family never received food aid between 1992 and 1996. If a youth is seventeen years old and his or her family received food aid for one to four years between 1992 and 1996, he or she is 2.11 times more likely

to be underweight than is an otherwise identical seventeen-year-old whose family never received food aid between 1992 and 1996.

27. Using the results from model 2, if a youth is twelve years old and his or her family received AFDC for one to four years between 1992 and 1996, he or she is 1.23 times more likely to be underweight than is an otherwise identical twelve-year-old whose family never received AFDC between 1992 and 1996. The effect of AFDC for one to four years between 1992 and 1996 on the log odds of underweight for twelve-year-olds is $-0.99 + 12(0.1) = 0.21$. Exponentiating 0.21 gives the odds ratio. The increase in the likelihood of chronic illness associated with long-term AFDC receipt increases with age.

28. The coefficient estimates on long-term poverty decline slightly in size and significance with the removal of current poverty status. In model 3 (without current poverty status), the coefficient on AFDC for one to four years between 1992 and 1996 is 0.44, and the p-value associated with this estimate is 0.014. The coefficient on AFDC every year between 1992 and 1996 is 0.81, and the p-value associated with this estimate is 0.001.

29. If children of families in extreme poverty are less likely to have their chronic illnesses diagnosed, this is also a possible explanation for the negative and significant coefficients on current extreme poverty in models 1 and 3.

30. This relation does not appear to be driven by whether a youth's family has insurance. In models that include insurance status, number of children is still negatively and significantly related to the likelihood that a youth has a chronic illness. These results are available from the author on request.

References

Adams, P. F., and V. Benson. 1990. "Current Estimates from the National Health Interview Survey, 1989." *Vital and Health Statistics* 10(176): 1–221.

Basiotis, Peter, Mark Brown, S. R. Johnson, and Karen Morgan. 1983. "Nutrient Availability, Food Costs, and Food Stamps." *American Journal of Agricultural Economics* 65(4): 685–93.

Basiotis, Peter, S. R. Johnson, Karen Morgan, and Jain-Shing Chen. 1987. "Food Stamps, Food Costs, Nutrient Availability, and Nutrient Intake." *Journal of Policy Modeling* 9(3): 383–404.

Bhattacharya, Jay, and Janet Currie. 2000. "Youths at Nutritional Risk: Malnourished or Misnourished." NBER working paper W7686. Cambridge, Mass.: National Bureau of Economic Research.

Blank, Rebecca. 1997. *It Takes a Nation.* New York: Russell Sage Foundation.

Butler, J. S., and Jennie Raymond. 1996. "The Effect of the Food Stamp Program on Nutrient Intake." *Economic Inquiry* 34(4): 781–92.

Centers for Disease Control. 1998. *Health, United States, 1998—Socioeconomic Status and Health Codebook.* Washington, D.C.: National Center for Health Statistics.

Currie, Janet, and Nancy Cole. 1993. "Welfare and Child Health: The Link Between AFDC Participation and Birthweight." *American Economic Review* 83(4): 971–85.

Currie, Janet, and Jonathan Gruber. 1996. "Health Insurance Eligibility, Utilization of Medical Care, and Child Health." *Quarterly Journal of Economics* 111(2): 432–66.

Devaney, Barbara, and Thomas Fraker. 1989. "The Effect of Food Stamps on Food Expenditures: An Assessment of Findings from the Nationwide Food Consumption Survey." *American Journal of Agricultural Economics* 71(1): 99–104.

Devaney, Barbara, and Robert Moffitt. 1991. "Dietary Effects of the Food Stamp Program." *American Journal of Agricultural Economics* 73(1): 202–11.

Gortmaker, Steven, Aviva Must, James Perrin, Arthur Sobol, and William Dietz. 1993. "Social and Economic Consequences of Overweight in Adolescence and Young Adulthood." *New England Journal of Medicine* 329(14): 1008–12.

Grossman, Michael. 1972. "On the Concept of Health Capital and the Demand for Health." *Journal of Political Economy* 80(2): 223–55.

Grossman, Michael, and Robert Kaestner. 1997. "Effects of Education on Health." In *The Social Benefits of Education*, edited by J. Behrman and N. Stacey. Ann Arbor: University of Michigan Press.

Gruber, Jonathan. 2000. "Means-Tested Transfer Programs in the U.S.: Medicaid." *NBER* working paper W7829. Cambridge, Mass.: National Bureau of Economic Research.

Jones, D. Yvonne, Malden Nesheim, and Jean-Pierre Habicht. 1985. "Influences in Child Growth Associated with Poverty in the 1970s: An Examination of HANESI and HANESII, Cross-Sectional US National Surveys." *American Journal of Clinical Nutrition* 42(4): 714–24.

Kaestner, Robert, Andrew Racine, and Ted Joyce. 2000. "Did Recent Expansions in Medicaid Narrow Socioeconomic Differences in Hospitalization Rates of Infants." *Medical Care* 38(2): 195–206.

Kafatos, Anthony, and Paul Zee. 1977. "Nutritional Benefits from Federal Food Assistance: A Survey of Preschool Black Children from Low-Income Families in Memphis." *American Journal of Diseases in Children* 131(3): 265–69.

Klerman, Lori. 1991. "The Health of Poor Children." In *Children in Poverty—Child Development and Public Policy*, edited by Aletha C. Huston. Cambridge: Cambridge University Press.

Korenman, Sanders, and Jane Miller. 1992. "Food Stamp Program Participation and Maternal and Child Health." Report to the U.S. Department of Agriculture, Food and Nutrition Service.

Levedahl, J. William. 1991. "The Effect of Food Stamps and Income on Household Food Expenditures." Washington: U.S. Department of Agriculture, Economic Research Service.

Martorell, Reynaldo, and Teresa Ho. 1984. "Malnutrition, Morbidity, and Mortality." *Population and Development Review* 10(supplement): 49–68.

Mathematica Policy Research Inc. 1999. "Characteristics of Food Stamp Households: Fiscal Year 1998 (Advance Report)." Report 8370-056. Washington: U.S. Department of Agriculture, Food and Nutrition Service.

Miller, C. Arden, Amy Fine, and Sharon Adams-Taylor. 1989. *Monitoring Children's Health: Key Indicators.* 2d ed. Washington, D.C.: American Public Health Association.

Miller, Jane, and Sanders Korenman. 1994. "Poverty and Children's Nutritional Status in the United States." *American Journal of Epidemiology* 40(3): 233–43.

Rose, Donald, Jean-Pierre Habicht, and Barbara Devaney. 1998. "Household Participation in the Food Stamp and WIC Programs Increases the Nutrient Intake of Preschool Children." *Journal of Nutrition* 128(3): 548–55.

U.S. Department of Agriculture. Food and Nutrition Service. 1999. "Promoting Healthy Eating: An Investment in the Future." Report to Congress. Available at *www.fns.usda.gov/oane/menu/Published/HealthyEating/PromotingHealthyEating.pdf.*

U.S. Department of Labor. 1999. *NLS Handbook, 1999.* Washington: U.S. Government Printing Office.

U.S. National Institutes of Health. National Heart, Lung, and Blood Institute. 1998. *Clinical Guidelines on the Identification, Evaluation, and Treatment of Overweight and Obesity in Adults.* Washington, D.C.: National Institutes of Health, National Heart, Lung, and Blood Institute.

Weitzman, Michael, Steven Gortmaker, Deborah Klein Walker, and Arthur Sobol. 1990. "Maternal Smoking and Childhood Asthma." *Pediatrics* 85(4): 505–11.

Wissow, Lawrence, Alan Gittelsohn, Moyses Szklo, Barbara Starfield, and M. Mussman. 1988. "Poverty, Race, and Hospitalization for Childhood Asthma." *American Journal of Public Health* 78(7): 777–82.

Part IV

Adolescents' Antisocial Behavior

10

What Determines Adolescent Demand for Alcohol and Marijuana? A Comparison of Findings from the NLSY79 and the NLSY97

Pinka Chatterji

I N 1999, 23.1 percent of high school seniors reported using marijuana in the past 30 days, and 32.9 percent admitted to having been drunk in the past 30 days (U.S. Department of Health and Human Services 1999). These high rates of substance use are troubling in the light of the potential consequences of alcohol and marijuana use during adolescence. Substance use during youth is associated with motor-vehicle accidents, mental- and physical-health problems, and reductions in educational attainment (Newcomb and Bentler 1988; Cook and Moore 1993; Hansell and Ranskin-White 1991; Newcomb and Bentler 1987; Kandel 1986). Furthermore, there is considerable evidence that adolescent alcohol and marijuana use is linked to later use of other illicit drugs and problem use during adulthood (Stein et al. 1993; Newcomb and Bentler 1988; Kandel 1986; Grant et al. 1987; Stacy and Newcomb 1999; Guy, Smith, and Bentler 1994; Golub and Johnson 1994). Preventing adolescent substance use may therefore prevent adverse outcomes during youth as well as adult substance abuse and its well-documented costs and consequences (Harwood, Fountain, and Livermore 1998). In order to create policies and programs that effectively prevent adolescent substance use, however, policy makers need up-to-date information about the determinants of adolescent substance use. In particular, they need information about the potential effect of variables over which they have some control, such as alcohol taxes and other alcohol and illicit-drug policies.

The objective of this essay is to analyze, compare, and contrast the determinants of adolescent alcohol and marijuana use using data from the National Longitudinal Survey of Youth, 1979 Cohort (NLSY79), and the recently released National Longitudinal Survey of Youth, 1997 Cohort (NLSY97). It is useful to compare and contrast the determinants of adolescent substance use using the NLSY79 and the NLSY97 for several reasons. First, the NLSY79 contains very little information on the frequency and intensity of substance use during adolescence. The use of NLSY97 data allows for significant enhancement of adolescent-substance-use measures, which in this essay are based on self-administered responses to questions about age of first use and frequency of use in the past 30 days. Second, NLSY79 respondents were adolescents during a period when state-level alcohol and illicit-drug policies were in flux. It is useful both to analyze the effect of these policy changes on substance-use behavior during the 1970s and to consider the effect of current policies. Finally, NLSY97 respondents represent a new generation of young people who, compared to NLSY79 respondents, may face different challenges and live in a distinct policy, cultural, and socioeconomic environment. A comparison of the determinants of adolescent substance use between these two cohorts may uncover interesting and useful information about the environment in which adolescents make decisions about risky behavior.

Previous Research on the Determinants of Adolescent Substance Use

Demographic Characteristics

National surveys of adolescent drug use—for example, the yearly Monitoring the Future (MTF) surveys and the Youth Risk Behavior Survey, 1997 (YRBS97)—consistently indicate that girls are less likely than boys to engage in substance use and that African American adolescents are less likely than adolescents of other races to use alcohol and marijuana (on the MTF surveys, see Johnston, O'Malley, and Bachman 1998). These survey results also suggest that, in recent years, there were only small differences in marijuana and alcohol use across adolescents living in large metropolitan areas, smaller metropolitan areas, and rural areas. Although regional differences in adolescent substance use do exist, the magnitude of these differences is small. (Johnston, O'Malley, and Bachman 1998).[1]

Parent Characteristics

Parent Substance Use   There is considerable evidence that parents' use of alcohol and other drugs is associated with adolescent substance use (Weinberg et al. 1994; Anderson and Henry 1994; Andrews et al. 1993; Ary et al. 1993; Colder et al. 1997; Chassin et al. 1998; Duncan, Duncan, et al. 1995). Genetic factors play a role in this relationship (Merikangas et al. 1998). Adopted children with alcohol-dependent biological parents are at least twice as likely as other adopted children to develop alcoholism (Belcher and Shinitzky 1998).

Family Structure and Socioeconomic Status   Previous research indicates that children from single-parent homes are more likely than children from two-parent homes to engage in substance use and to report having friends who use substances (Hoffmann 1993, 1994, 1995; Hoffmann and Johnson 1998). Parents' income, parents' education, and other indicators of family socioeconomic status, however, generally are not good predictors of adolescent alcohol and marijuana use (Kandel 1991; Bachman, Johnston, and O'Malley 1981).

Despite the importance of some parent characteristics, peer influence is one of the most important determinants of adolescent substance use (Kandel 1982; Walter, Vaughan, and Cohall 1993; Duncan, Tildesley et al. 1995; Ary et al. 1993; Zhang, Welte, and Wieczorek 1997; Hoffmann 1995). Additionally, researchers have found that adolescents who report that they are religious are less likely than other adolescents to engage in substance use (Kandel 1982; Bachman, Johnston, and O'Malley 1981; Hardert and Dowd 1994; Francis and Mullen 1993).

Alcohol and Marijuana Prices and Policies

State Excise Taxes   Economists have used state-excise-tax rates on alcohol to proxy price variability in beer and wine across states. Yamada, Kendix, and Yamada (1998), Kenkel (1993), Moore and Cook (1995), and Cook and Moore (1993) all find that, in samples from the NLSY79, state excise taxes on beer are negatively correlated with weekly alcohol consumption. Also using a sample from the NLSY79, Pacula (1998) finds that state excise taxes on beer are negatively associated with marijuana use. Using a variety of data sets, other researchers have reported that youth alcohol use is responsive to the price of alcohol (Grossman et al. 1994).

Illicit-Drug Prices   Because of problems finding high-quality data on marijuana prices, limited empirical evidence is available about young people's responsiveness to marijuana prices. Chaloupka and Laixuthai (1997) provide some evidence that the wholesale price of marijuana is positively related to alcohol use in a sample of young adults (Chaloupka and Laixuthai 1997). Grossman and Chaloupka (1998), Saffer and Chaloupka (1999), and Chaloupka, Grossman, and Tauras (1998) find that young adults' illicit-drug consumption is responsive to changes in cocaine prices, which are more readily available than marijuana prices.

Minimum Drinking Ages   During the 1970s and 1980s, minimum drinking ages varied across states, and many states changed their minimum drinking ages several times. Consequently, NLSY79 respondents were adolescents during a period when minimum drinking ages varied across and within states over time. In 1984, however, Congress passed a law denying some federal highway funding to states that did not set a minimum drinking age of twenty-one. All states currently have a minimum drinking age of twenty-one, and, as a result, all NLSY97 respondents live in an environment where the minimum drinking age is twenty-one.

There is evidence that a higher minimum drinking age reduces alcohol consumption and motor-vehicle accidents among youths. Although Cook and Moore (1993) and Pacula (1998) do not find a statistically significant association between minimum drinking age and youth alcohol use using the NLSY79, Chaloupka and Laixuthai (1997), Coate and Grossman (1988), and Dee and Evans (1997) all find that minimum drinking ages are statistically significantly, negatively associated with alcohol-use rates among youths.

Marijuana Decriminalization   During the 1970s and early 1980s, when NLSY79 respondents were adolescents, eleven states lowered penalties for the use and sale of marijuana. There is no conclusive evidence, however, that these policies, which decriminalized the possession of small amounts of marijuana for personal use, led to increases in marijuana use among youths. Thies and Register (1993) and Johnston, O'Malley, and Bachman (1981) report that marijuana decriminalization was not associated with increased marijuana use. Pacula (1998), using the NLSY79, finds that marijuana decriminalization was not associated with alcohol or marijuana use. Chaloupka, Grossman, and Tauras (1998) and Saffer and Chaloupka (1999), however, find that marijuana decriminalization was associated with increases in some forms of illicit-drug participation. Additionally, Model (1993) reports that marijuana decriminalization had a significant, positive effect on the number of marijuana-use drug mentions during emergency-room visits between 1975 and 1978.

Currently, marijuana is decriminalized in California, Colorado, Maine, Minnesota, Mississippi, Nebraska, New York, North Carolina, Ohio, and Oregon. No state has successfully decriminalized or recriminalized marijuana since 1981 (National Organization for the Reform of Marijuana Laws, personal communication, September 17, 1999). Consequently, unlike NLSY79 respondents, NLSY97 respondents have not experienced changes in state marijuana-decriminalization policies.

Juvenile Arrests and Sentencing   The full price of alcohol and marijuana use includes the potential legal penalties that young people face if apprehended by the authorities. Legal penalties include being fined, being imprisoned, losing certain rights (for example, the right to drive), and establishing a criminal record. Penalties and the probability of apprehension vary across states and over time.

As Chaloupka, Grossman, and Tauras (1998) point out, if the probability of apprehension and conviction is small, legal sanctions may not have an important effect on youth substance use. These researchers find that penalties for marijuana possession have a statistically significant, but very small, negative effect on marijuana use among high school seniors. Using NLSY79 data, DeSimone (1998) finds that, although maximum jail time for marijuana use is not a statistically significant predictor of marijuana use, individuals who live in states where there is no fine for marijuana use are more likely than similar individuals to use marijuana.

It may therefore be more useful to consider the effect of the enforcement rather than simply the existence of drug laws. County-level arrest rates for drug offenses have been used to proxy the degree of drug-law enforcement. Farrelly et al. (1999), however, report that marijuana use among youths aged twelve to twenty is not associated with county-level marijuana-possession arrest rates.

Conceptual Framework

This essay is motivated by a simple economic framework in which adolescents maximize a utility function that includes a commodity called *intoxication*—equation (1a), subject to constraints (1b) and (1c) (Stigler and Becker 1977; Chaloupka and Laixuthai 1997):

(1a)
$$\max U = U[I, A, e]$$

(where U = the adolescent utility function, I = intoxication, A = a composite commodity representing all other goods consumed during adolescence, and e = effects of unmeasured attributes on utility),

(1b)
$$\text{subject to } I = I[a, m; \alpha]$$

(where a = consumption of alcohol during adolescence, m = consumption of marijuana during adolescence, and α = a production-technology parameter),

(1c)
$$\text{subject to } p_1 a + p_2 m + p_3 A = W$$

(where p_1 = the price of alcohol, p_2 = the price of marijuana, p_3 = the price of the composite commodity, and W = income). Adolescents use alcohol, marijuana, and other inputs to produce intoxication, subject to a technological parameter; utility is therefore derived only indirectly from alcohol and marijuana use through intoxication. The shadow price of intoxication includes the money prices of substances, legal and other penalties for use, and other factors.

Maximization of this utility function subject to budget and production constraints yields adolescent demand functions for alcohol and marijuana. Equations (2a) and (2b) represent the demand functions that are estimated using the NLSY79 and the NLSY97 in this essay:

(2a)   adolescent alcohol use = f(sociodemographic factors, family background, personal characteristics, peer effects, prices, and policies) + $e(1)$,

(2b)   adolescent marijuana use = f(sociodemographic factors, family background, personal characteristics, peer effects, prices, and policies) + $e(2)$.

Methods
Variable Creation

Measuring Adolescent Substance Use   Using substance-use information from the NLSY79 (1980, 1983, and 1984 surveys) and the NLSY97 (1997 survey), table 10.1 displays the following binary adolescent-substance-use measures that were created for both the NLSY79 and the NLSY97 analyses: respondent reports any alcohol use before age seventeen; respondent reports any marijuana use before age seventeen; and respondent reports having used marijuana frequently before age seventeen. Although the frequent-marijuana-use measures do not match exactly, the NLSY97 frequent-marijuana-use indicator corresponds approximately to the frequent-marijuana-use indicator available for the NLSY79 analysis. The frequent-marijuana-use measure was created for two subsamples: fifteen- to sixteen-year-old NLSY97 respondents and fifteen- to sixteen-year-old NLSY79 respondents as of 1980.

Mensch and Kandel (1988), Fendrich and Vaughn (1994), and Fendrich and Mackesy-Amiti (1995) all find that NLSY79 respondents may have underreported or inconsistently reported their substance use. This problem appears to be particularly serious for users of illicit drugs other than marijuana and for population subgroups such as women, minorities, and the least-involved users. Fendrich and Vaughn (1994) find that a large proportion of cocaine and marijuana users reported inconsistent ages of first use in the 1984 and 1988 surveys.

The NLSY97 may offer better information on adolescent substance use than the NLSY79 for a number of reasons. First, NLSY97 respondents answered questions about age of first use during adolescence, while NLSY79 respondents answered questions about age of first use retrospectively, as

TABLE 10.1   *Substance-Use Measures Used in Both NLSY79 and NLSY97 Analyses*

	NLSY97	NLSY79
Respondent reports any alcohol use before age seventeen	Based on age-of-first-use information provided in 1997	Based on age-of-first-use information provided in 1983
Respondent reports any marijuana use before age seventeen	Based on age-of-first-use information provided in 1997	Based on age-of-first-use information provided in 1984
Respondent reports frequent marijuana use before age seventeen	Defined as at least four times in past month, based on information provided in 1997, created for subsample of fifteen- to sixteen-year-old respondents	Defined as more than fifty times in past year, based on information provided in 1980, created for fifteen- to sixteen-year-old respondents

Additional Substance-Use Measures Used in NLSY97 Analysis	
Whether respondent used alcohol in past month	Based on information provided in 1997
Number of alcoholic drinks respondent consumed in past month, given respondent used alcohol in past month	Based on information provided in 1997
Whether respondent had a binge drinking episode in past month	Based on information provided in 1997
Number of binge drinking episodes in past month, given respondent had a binge drinking episode in past month	Based on information provided in 1997
Whether respondent used marijuana in past month	Based on information provided in 1997
Number of days respondent used marijuana in past month, given respondent used marijuana in past month	Based on information provided in 1997

Source: NLSY79 (1980, 1983, 1984 surveys), NLSY97 (1997 survey).

adults. NLSY79 respondents therefore may be less likely than NLSY97 respondents to remember whether and, if so, when they initiated substance use during adolescence. Second, the NLSY79 has very little information on the frequency of adolescent substance use, while NLSY97 respondents answered detailed questions about the frequency of their current substance use. Finally, NLSY97 respondents completed a self-administered survey instrument, while NLSY79 respondents in 1984 were asked their age at first substance use by an interviewer. Fendrich and Vaughn (1994) find that NLSY79 respondents who provided self-reports were slightly less likely to provide inconsistent responses about marijuana and cocaine use than were respondents who completed in-person interviews.

Because the NLSY97 offers richer and potentially better information about adolescent substance use than the NLSY79, the adolescent-substance-use measures created for the NLSY97 analysis are not limited to binary indicators that simply reflect whether the respondent has ever used alcohol or marijuana during adolescence. In addition to the three substance-use measures described previously, table 10.1 also presents the following substance-use measures created for the NLSY97 analyses only: whether the respondent consumed alcohol in the past thirty days and, if so, the number of days the respondent consumed alcohol in the past thirty days; whether the respondent engaged in binge drinking (five or more drinks consumed during one occasion) in the past thirty days and, if so, the number of binge-drinking episodes in the past thirty days; and whether the respondent used marijuana in the past thirty days and, if so, the number of days the respondent used marijuana in the past thirty days.[2]

Measuring Prices and Policies   In the NLSY97 analysis, the state excise tax on a case of beer in 1997 proxies the price of alcohol. Because the NLSY79 substance-use measures do not correspond to a single year (unlike many of the NLSY97 measures, which correspond to 1997), alcohol prices in the NLSY79 analysis were captured by the state excise tax on a case of beer in the year in which the respondent was fourteen years old and in the state where the respondent lived at age fourteen. In the NLSY79 analysis, therefore, state excise taxes on beer vary by respondents' age and state of residence at age fourteen. The Beer Institute in Washington, D.C., provided these price data from various years of the *Brewer's Almanac.*

The analysis uses the standardized, real price for one pure gram of cocaine at the state level to proxy the money price of illicit drugs in each state. The method used to create these price data is described in Grossman and Chaloupka (1998) and elsewhere. Because cocaine-price data were not available for 1997, 1994 prices were used as estimates of 1997 prices in the NLSY97 analysis. The NLSY79 analysis matches cocaine prices to the state in which each respondent lived at age fourteen and in the year each respondent was fourteen, as was done with the excise taxes on beer, to the extent possible.[3]

Minimum drinking ages fluctuated within and across states during the time period when the NLSY79 respondents were adolescents. Previous researchers have used static indicators of minimum drinking ages to proxy legal constraints on adolescent alcohol use. In this analysis, the minimum-drinking-age measures incorporate policy changes. In addition to the minimum drinking age that existed in each state when the NLSY79 respondent was 14, the models also include dummy variables that indicate whether the state's minimum drinking age was increased to twenty-one years or was decreased to eighteen years when the respondent was between fourteen and sixteen years old. Many older NLSY79 respondents lived in states where the minimum drinking age was lowered during their early adolescence, while younger NLSY79 respondents were more likely to experience increases in minimum drinking ages. Minimum-drinking-age variables are not included in the NLSY97 models because every state had a minimum drinking age of twenty-one in 1997.

Because the money price of marijuana is not available, the NLSY79 and NLSY97 models include measures of legal sanctions for marijuana possession. These variables may be good proxies for part of the full price that adolescents face when using marijuana, which includes the probability of apprehension (as measured by arrest rates) and maximum jail terms and fines. This type of data is not readily available on a yearly basis for the NLSY79 cohort, who were adolescents in the 1970s and early 1980s. For this reason, the NLSY79 analysis incorporates 1977 state-level information on maximum fines for possession of one ounce or less of marijuana. The year 1977 corresponds to a time period when NLSY79 respondents were approximately twelve to nineteen years old.

The NLSY97 models include state-level maximum fines for the least-serious form of marijuana possession in 1997, state-level maximum prison sentences for the least-serious form of marijuana possession in 1997, and county-level information on juvenile drug-related arrests per thousand county adolescents in 1997.[4] Using arrest rates to measure the degree of drug-law enforcement, however, is limited by the fact that arrest rates capture both enforcement of juvenile drug offenses as well as the prevalence of juvenile crime.[5]

Most of the state policy data, such as beer taxes and marijuana decriminalization, probably were not measured with error. The price of cocaine, however, may suffer from measurement error for at least two reasons. First, cocaine prices were measured in specific urban areas in each state, and each respondent in the state was assigned the same cocaine price. Clearly, the price of cocaine might vary widely within states. Second, although cocaine prices were adjusted for the purity of the cocaine, cocaine users do not know the purity exactly. For this reason, there may be variation between the market price and the price that determines consumption (Grossman and Chaloupka 1998).

Measuring Peer Use   Researchers have identified peer influence as one of the most important determinants of adolescent substance use (Kandel 1982; Walter, Vaughan, and Cohall 1993; Duncan, Tildesley, et al. 1995). Although the NLSY97 has information about respondents' perceptions about peer substance use, these measures may be endogenous because substance-using adolescents may select substance-using peers as friends.[6] Consequently, to measure peer substance use, the NLSY79 analysis uses regional prevalence rates (available for four regions of the United States) for illicit-drug use among high school seniors from the yearly Monitoring the Future national substance-use survey. These rates were merged to respondents' records according to region of residence and respondent's age. The NLSY97 analysis takes advantage of the YRBS97 state-level thirty-day prevalence rates for adolescent binge drinking and marijuana use. These data were merged to NLSY97 respondent records by respondents' state of residence in 1997.[7]

These state- and regional-level measures of peer use are limited in that they mask variation in adolescent-substance-use rates within states and regions. Ideally, one would like to measure peer use with substance-use prevalence information at the level of cities, communities, or even neighborhoods. These data, however, are not available.

Measuring Demographic and Family-Background Characteristics
The NLSY79 and NLSY97 models also include demographic variables, family-background variables, and personal characteristics that are expected to be good predictors of adolescent substance use. The analysis uses categorical variables to represent respondent's race, respondent's gender, respondent's religion, mother's education, and father's education. Other covariates capture family income, respondent's age, and whether the respondent lived in an urban area.[8] The NLSY79 models included a single-parent-home dummy variable that indicated whether the respondent lived in a household with two parents (including stepparents) at age fourteen. The NLSY97 models included a single-parent-home dummy variable that indicated whether the respondent lived in a household with both a mother-mother figure and a father-father figure at the time of the 1997 survey. The analysis measured family size by number of siblings in the household (NLSY79) or number of household members under age eighteen (NLSY97). The NLSY79 models also incorporated a variable that indicated whether the respondent felt that his or her biological mother, biological father, or biological sibling was an alcoholic.

Finally, academic test scores were included in the NLSY79 and NLSY97 models to proxy school aptitude. Standardized, revised 1989 Armed Forces Qualification Test (AFQT) percentile scores were used in the NLSY79 models. In the NLSY97 models, Peabody Individual Achievement Test (PIAT) mathematics-assessment percentile scores were available for students who had not yet entered the tenth grade.

Missing Data Respondents were dropped from the NLSY79 sample if information was missing on religion in 1979 ($N = 53$), urban residence at age fourteen ($N = 40$), family structure at age fourteen ($N = 19$), frequency of religious-service attendance in 1979 ($N = 17$), standardized cocaine prices ($N = 256$; missing for Mississippi and South Dakota), 1980 marijuana use

($N = 171$), age at first marijuana use ($N = 753$), and age at first alcohol use ($N = 489$). Respondents were also dropped if they lived outside the United States, in Hawaii, or in Alaska at age fourteen ($N = 112$) because substance-price and policy information was not available for these areas over time. To avoid losing large numbers of observations because of missing data on covariates, missing-data indicators were created if more than 5 percent of the original sample had a missing value for the covariate. Missing-data indicators were created for parents' education, AFQT score, family income, and having a close relative who was an alcoholic. Respondents with missing data for these variables were assigned mean values and a missing-data indicator of 1. The final sample size for main NLSY79 analyses was 9,366 respondents.

Respondents were dropped from the NLSY97 analysis if information was missing on race ($N = 84$), religion ($N = 123$), family structure ($N = 16$), standardized cocaine price in 1994 ($N = 247$; missing for Mississippi and South Dakota), past-month marijuana use ($N = 41$), past-month alcohol use ($N = 23$), and past-month binge drinking ($N = 40$). Respondents who reported having consumed more than a thousand drinks in the past month ($N = 28$) were also dropped from the analysis. Finally, 38 respondents were dropped due to corrections to the NLSY97 data set. Missing-data indicators were created for covariates for which at least 5 percent of the original sample had a missing value. These covariates were YRBS state-substance-use prevalence rates, PIAT scores, parents' education, and family income. Respondents with missing data for these variables were assigned mean values and a missing-data indicator of 1. The final sample size for the NLSY97 analysis was 8,445 respondents. Table 10.2 displays variable means and standard deviations for the NLSY79 and NLSY97 analysis samples.

Estimation

The three substance-use measures used in both the NLSY79 and the NLSY97 analyses were binary variables, indicating simply whether the respondent engaged in any alcohol use, whether the respondent engaged in any marijuana use, and whether the respondent engaged in any frequent marijuana use before age seventeen. These models were estimated using logistic-regression models. The three additional substance-use measures used only in the NLSY97 analysis capture frequency of use in the past thirty days.

Most NLSY97 respondents report no alcohol use in the past month (81 percent), no binge drinking in the past month (90 percent), and no marijuana use in the past month (91 percent). Consequently, for many respondents, these continuous substance-use measures are censored at 0. The two-part model developed by Cragg (1971) is used to estimate two equations for each of these continuous substance-use measures. The two equations are the probability of engaging in the behavior in the past month and, given

TABLE 10.2   *Descriptive Statistics*

	NLSY79 Sample (N = 9,366)		NLSY97 Sample (N = 8,445)	
	Mean	S.D.	Mean	S.D.
Adolescent substance use				
Respondent reports any alcohol use before age seventeen	0.287	0.452	0.429	0.495
Respondent reports any marijuana use before age seventeen	0.110	0.313	0.200	0.400
Respondent reports frequent marijuana use during adolescence	0.080	0.272	0.062	0.241
Respondent reports alcohol use in the past thirty days	N.A.		0.187	0.390
Total number of drinks consumed in past thirty days among respondents who report alcohol use in past thirty days	N.A.		24.2	60.0
Respondent reports binge drinking in the past thirty days	N.A.		0.097	0.296
Number of binge-drinking episodes in the past thirty days among respondents who report binge drinking in the past thirty days	N.A.		4.00	4.58
Respondent reports marijuana use in the past thirty days	N.A.		0.087	0.281
Number of marijuana episodes in the past thirty days among respondents who report marijuana use in the past thirty days	N.A.		9.30	9.84
Prices (dollars)				
State excise tax on cigarettes when respondent was fourteen (NLSY79), state excise tax on cigarettes in 1997 (NLSY97)	0.127	0.048	0.357	0.204
State excise tax on beer when respondent was fourteen (NLSY79), state excise tax on beer in 1997 (NLSY97)	0.434	0.415	0.538	0.446
Standardized price of cocaine when respondent was fourteen (NLSY79), standardized price of cocaine in 1994 (NLSY97)	21.44	9.36	87.0	16.40

TABLE 10.2   *Continued*

	NLSY79 Sample (N = 9,366)		NLSY97 Sample (N = 8,445)	
	Mean	S.D.	Mean	S.D.
State and county policies				
State minimum drinking age was lowered when respondent was aged fourteen to sixteen	0.116	0.320	N.A.	
State minimum drinking age was increased when respondent was aged fourteen to sixteen	0.040	0.196	N.A.	
Respondent at age fourteen lived in a state where marijuana was decriminalized (NLSY79), respondent lives in a state where marijuana is decriminalized in 1997 (NLSY97)	0.276	0.447	0.329	0.470
Maximum jail term in years for least-serious marijuana-possession conviction in 1999	N.A.		0.364	0.401
Maximum fine in dollars for least-serious marijuana-possession conviction in 1977 (NLSY79), maximum fine in dollars for least-serious marijuana-possession charge,1999	681.76	749.15	4,502.52	23,257
County-level juvenile arrests for drug offenses per 1,000 residents	N.A.		4.17	3.48
Peer substance use (percentage)				
Regional illicit-drug-use prevalence rate for high school senior	62.00	5.54		[a]
State-level thirty-day marijuana prevalence rate for adolescents	N.A.		25.57	2.07
State-level thirty-day binge-drinking prevalence rate for adolescents	N.A.		30.07	3.17
Percentage drug-using peers as reported by respondent	N.A.		35.79	27.4
Family background				
Respondent lived with two parents at age fourteen (NLSY79), respondent lives in two-parent household in 1997	0.758	0.428	0.688	0.463

(Table continues on p. 312.)

TABLE 10.2   *Continued*

	NLSY79 Sample (N = 9,366)		NLSY97 Sample (N = 8,445)	
	Mean	S.D.	Mean	S.D.
Percentage of respondents' mothers who have at least a high school diploma	0.540	0.498	0.438	0.496
Percentage of respondents' fathers who have at least a high school diploma	0.496	0.500	0.411	0.492
Number of siblings in household (NLSY79), number of household members under age eighteen	3.81	2.59	2.45	1.28
Respondent believes mother, father, brother, or sister is an alcoholic	0.358	0.392	N.A.	
Family income (dollars)	15,174	11,329	46,720	34,974
Personal characteristics				
AFQT revised standardized percentile score (NLSY79), PIAT standardized percentile math score (NLSY97)	41.30	28.26	62.63	18.22
Demographic characteristics				
Female	0.512	0.500	0.489	0.500
Age in years	18.52	2.25	14.85	1.45
Hispanic	0.141	0.348	0.213	0.409
African American	0.254	0.435	0.258	0.438
Baptist-Methodist	0.337	0.473	0.266	0.442
Catholic	0.293	0.455	0.289	0.453
Lived in a city at age fourteen (NLSY79), lived in a city in 1997	0.779	0.415	0.578	0.494
Missing data indicators				
Mother's education missing	0.056	0.229	0.180	0.384
Father's education missing	0.136	0.343	0.245	0.430
AFQT (NLSY79) or PIAT (NLSY97) score missing	0.023	0.150	0.326	0.469
Family income missing	0.191	0.393	0.271	0.445
State adolescent marijuana prevalence rate missing	N.A.		0.401	0.490
State adolescent binge-drinking prevalence rate missing	N.A.		0.409	0.492

Source: NLSY79, NLSY97.
[a] State-level information available.

that the respondent has engaged in the behavior in the past month, the number of times the respondent engaged in the behavior in the past month. Standard errors were corrected for heteroskedasticity using White's (1980) method in all the models.

Descriptive Statistics

Table 10.3 displays a comparison between NLSY adolescent-substance-use rates and rates from two national surveys—Monitoring the Future (MTF) and the National Household Survey (NHS). NLSY rates are based on the respondents in the cross-sectional sample only to allow a valid comparison with the nationally representative MTF and NHS samples. The comparison suggests that, while the NLSY97 substance-use rates are within the range of rates from these two national substance-use surveys conducted in 1997, the NLSY79 rates are considerably lower than national rates from the same time period. This problem may suggest that systematic underreporting affected the NLSY79 substance-use measures, which are based on data that were collected retrospectively.

NHS data from years prior to 1994 were adjusted to be comparable to post-1993 data because the instrument was modified in 1994. From these data (displayed in table 10.3), it appears that both lifetime alcohol use and lifetime marijuana use dropped sharply between 1979 and 1997. MTF data indicate that marijuana use among high school seniors was at its peak in 1980, when NLSY79 respondents were approximately fifteen to twenty-two years old. After 1980, marijuana use among adolescents declined steadily until about 1992, when rates began to increase. By 1997, when the NLSY97 respondents were first surveyed, marijuana use among high school seniors had started to stabilize after several years of increases. On the other hand, unlike the NHS data, the MTF data suggest that alcohol use among high school seniors was quite common and quite stable from 1975 to 1999. Figure 10.1 (which is based on MTF data) displays these trends in adolescent alcohol and marijuana use over time.

Table 10.4 displays prevalence rates for three comparable substance-use measures for the NLSY79 and NLSY97 analysis samples. It is important to note that two of the three NLSY79 substance-use measures are based on adolescent-substance-use information provided retrospectively by NLSY79 respondents in 1984, when they were nineteen to twenty-seven years old. Given this limitation, it is interesting to note that NLSY97 respondents are considerably more likely than NLSY79 respondents to report having used alcohol and marijuana before age seventeen.

Patterns by race and gender, however, appear to be consistent across the NLSY79 and NLSY97 samples. In both the NLSY79 and the NLSY97 samples, girls are less likely than boys are to report substance use, and African

TABLE 10.3   Comparison of NLSY Substance-Use Rates and Rates from Two National Surveys (Percentage)

| | Use Before Age Seventeen | | Lifetime Use | |
	Cross-Sectional NLSY97	MTF Eighth Grade Students in 1997	MTF Tenth Grade Students in 1997	NHS Twelve- to Seventeen-Year-Olds in 1997
Alcohol	44.1	52.8	72.0	39.7
Marijuana	20.1	22.6	42.3	18.9

	Cross-Sectional NLSY79	MTF Twelfth Grade Students in 1979		NHS Twelve- to Seventeen-Year-Olds in 1979
Alcohol	31.1	71.8		70.8
Marijuana	10.9	36.5		31.0

Sources: NLSY79, NLSY97, SAMSHA Office of Applied Studies, National Household Survey on Drug Abuse, the Monitoring the Future Study, the University of Michigan.

FIGURE 10.1   *Trends in Lifetime Alcohol and Marijuana Use Among High School Seniors, 1976 to 1999.*

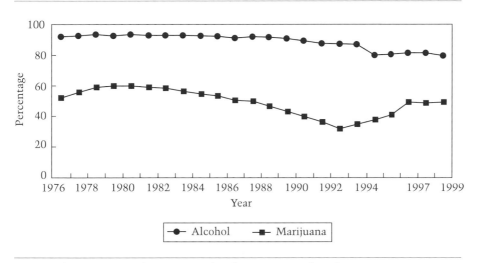

Source: The Monitoring the Future Study, The University of Michigan, 1999.

Americans are less likely than whites are to report substance use. A comparison of substance-use rates by race within gender suggests that, while African American boys and girls in both samples use alcohol at lower rates than white boys and girls do, only African American girls in the NLSY79 and NLSY97 samples are less likely to use marijuana than white girls are.

Table 10.5 displays past-month substance-use measures available only for the NLSY97 sample by age, gender, and race and by race within gender. Clearly, the NLSY97 respondent's age is positively related to both the probability of any past-month substance use and the intensity of past-month substance use. Girls are less likely than boys are to report any past-month use of marijuana, and they use both alcohol and marijuana less frequently than boys do. Although African American respondents were less likely to report any past-month alcohol or marijuana use, among those respondents who engaged in substance use in the past month the frequency of use did not vary by race.

Estimation Results

Regression results are presented in tables 10.6 to 10.9. In total, twelve models were of interest.[9] Tables 10.6 to 10.7 display estimates of odds ratios and standard errors for logistic models with the following dependent

(Text continues on p. 323.)

TABLE 10.4 Alcohol and Marijuana Use Before Age Seventeen Among NLSY79 and NLSY97 Youths

Percentage of Youths Who

	(1) Used Alcohol Before Age Seventeen		(2) Used Marijuana Before Age Seventeen		(3) Used Marijuana at Least Four Times in Past Month (Fifteen- to Sixteen-Year-Olds Only)	
	NLSY79	NLSY97	NLSY79	NLSY97	NLSY79	NLSY97
All	28.7	42.9	11.0	20.0	8.0	6.2
Male	37.2	44.1	13.1	21.4	10.2	7.5
Female	20.5***	41.7**	9.0***	18.6***	5.8***	4.9***
White	32.3	47.2	11.2	21.3	9.8	7.0
African American	20.9***	35.2***	10.1	17.7***	3.5***	4.9**
Hispanic	27.0	41.5	12.1	19.7	9.1	5.8
Males						
White	40.6	48.3	12.6	21.5	11.7	7.8
African American	29.0***	34.9***	12.7	20.9	5.7***	6.5
Hispanic	37.4	44.3	16.6***	21.5	12.1	7.9
Females						
White	24.3	46.0	9.9	21.0	7.8	6.2
African American	13.0***	35.6***	7.5**	14.6***	1.4***	3.3**
Hispanic	17.9*	38.4	8.1	17.8	6.1	3.6

Sources: NLSY97 round 1, NLSY79 rounds 2, 5, 6.
Note: *White* category includes Asian and Native American respondents.
* Denotes difference statistically significant at the .10 level relative to italicized category.
** Denotes difference statistically significant at the .05 level relative to italicized category.
*** Denotes difference statistically significant at the .01 level relative to italicized category.

TABLE 10.5 *Frequency of Alcohol and Marijuana Use Among NLSY97 Youth*

| | Percentage of Youths Who | | | Among Users in Past Month, the Mean | | |
	(1) Have Used Alcohol in Past Month	(2) Have Binged on Alcohol in Past Month	(3) Have Used Marijuana in Past Month	(4) Number of Alcohol Drinks	(5) Number of Days Had an Alcohol Binge	(6) Number of Days Used Marijuana
All	18.7	9.7	8.7	24.2	4.0	9.3
Age						
Twelve	4.4	2.0	1.4	11.8	3.3	4.4
Thirteen	8.0	3.1	3.5	13.4	3.6	5.1
Fourteen	15.1	6.7	7.0	15.5	3.7	8.0
Fifteen	24.4	12.0	10.9	19.4	4.1	9.3
Sixteen	29.5	17.2	15.0	32.9	4.3	10.8
Seventeen	36.4	21.3	16.1	32.7	4.4	10.1
Male	19.3	10.9	9.6	28.5	4.3	10.5
Female	18.2	8.4***	7.7****	19.3****	3.7**	7.7****

(Table continues on p. 318.)

TABLE 10.5   *Continued*

	Percentage of Youths Who			Among Users in Past Month, the Mean		
	(1) Have Used Alcohol in Past Month	(2) Have Binged on Alcohol in Past Month	(3) Have Used Marijuana in Past Month	(4) Number of Alcohol Drinks	(5) Number of Days Had an Alcohol Binge	(6) Number of Days Used Marijuana
White	22.0	11.3	9.6	24.1	4.1	9.1
African American	12.0***	5.2***	6.9***	20.9	4.0	10.3
Hispanic	18.9	11.1*	8.3	26.7	3.9	8.7
Males						
White	21.7	12.5	9.9	28.0	4.4	10.0
African American	12.4***	5.7***	8.7	23.0	4.1	12.6**
Hispanic	21.1*	12.7**	9.8	32.8	4.6	9.8
Females						
White	22.2	9.9	9.2	19.9	3.9	8.0
African American	11.5***	4.6***	5.1***	18.6	3.9	7.8
Hispanic	16.6	9.4	6.8	18.5	2.9	6.7

Source: NLSY97 round 1, NLSY79 rounds 2, 5, 6.
Note: White category includes Asian and Native American respondents.
* Denotes difference statistically significant at the .10 level relative to italicized category.
** Denotes difference statistically significant at the .05 level relative to italicized category.
*** Denotes difference statistically significant at the .01 level relative to italicized category.

TABLE 10.6   *NLSY97 Logistic Models—Determinants of Alcohol and Marijuana Use Before Age Seventeen, Odds Ratios and Standard Errors*

	Used Alcohol Before Age Seventeen	Used Marijuana Before Age Seventeen	Marijuana Four or More Times in Past Thirty Days (Fifteen- to Sixteen-Year-Old Sub-Sample)
Female	0.898	0.829	0.627
	(0.042)**	(0.048)**	(0.077)**
Hispanic	0.746	0.805	0.929
	(0.055)**	(0.075)**	(0.174)
African American	0.571	0.657	0.558
	(0.040)**	(0.058)**	(0.100)**
Catholic	1.179	0.889	0.722
	(0.072)**	(0.067)	(0.118)**
Baptist-Methodist	0.877	0.812	0.841
	(0.055)**	(0.063)**	(0.130)
Lives in city	0.978	1.067	1.097
	(0.051)	(0.069)	(0.148)
Age in years	1.628	1.792	2.151
	(0.038)**	(0.052)**	(0.219)**
Dad HS grad only	1.082	1.025	1.244
	(0.074)	(0.087)	(0.217
Mom HS grad only	1.007	0.975	1.089
	(0.068)	(0.083)	(0.189)
Dad some college	0.974	1.065	0.798
	(0.103)	(0.141)	(0.232)
Mom some college	1.167	1.294	1.404
	(0.124)	(0.166)**	(0.352)
Dad college grad	0.999	1.131	1.363
	(0.101)	(0.139)	(0.315)
Mom college grad	0.933	0.960	1.359
	(0.105)	(0.134)	(0.358)
Single parent household	1.416	1.673	1.883
	(0.078)**	(0.111)**	(0.257)**
Income 1996	1.000	1.000	1.000
	(0.000)	(0.000)**	(0.000)
No. of household mem under eighteen	0.887	0.938	0.884
	(0.017)**	(0.022)**	(0.045)**

TABLE 10.6   *Continued*

	Used Alcohol Before Age Seventeen	Used Marijuana Before Age Seventeen	Marijuana Four or More Times in Past Thirty Days (Fifteen- to Sixteen-Year-Old Sub-Sample)
PIAT math score	1.000	0.993	0.995
	(0.002)	(0.002)**	(0.004)
Teen drug prevalence	1.021	1.071	1.007
	(0.011)**	(0.016)**	(0.031)
Cocaine price	1.040	1.076	1.122
	(0.022)*	(0.026)**	(0.054)**
Log max sentence for mrj possession	0.984	0.933	0.955
	(0.017)	(0.019)**	(0.044)
Log max fine for mrj possession	0.981	0.998	0.937
	(0.011)*	(0.012)	(0.022)**
Cig tax	1.003	1.002	1.012
	(0.001)**	(0.002)	(0.003)**
Log beer tax	1.069	0.974	0.874
	(0.053)	(0.051)	(0.099)
County drg arrst rte	1.011	1.026	1.019
	(0.008)	(0.009)**	(0.019)
Mom educ missing	1.091	1.237	1.236
	(0.105)	(0.145)	(0.286)
Dad educ missing	1.039	1.026	1.707
	(0.087)	(0.107)	(0.360)**
PIAT score missing	0.991	0.626	0.567
	(0.081)	(0.061)**	(0.109)**
Income missing	0.822	0.774	0.537
	(0.052)**	(0.061)**	(0.089)**
Teen drg missing	1.113	0.995	1.081
	(0.070)*	(0.071)	(0.162)
Observations	8,445	8,445	5,002
Pseudo-R^2	0.10	0.10	0.09

Source: NLSY79, NLSY97
Note: Robust standard errors in parentheses.
* Significant at .05 level. ** Significant at .01 level.

TABLE 10.7   *NLSY79 Logistic Models—Determinants of Alcohol and Marijuana Use Before Age Seventeen, Odds Ratios and Standard Errors*

	Used Alcohol Before Age Seventeen	Used Marijuana Before Age Seventeen	Used Marijuana More Than Fifty Times in Past Year (Fifteen- to Sixteen-Yr-Olds)
Female	0.413	0.624	0.521
	(0.020)**	(0.042)**	(0.085)**
Age in years	0.936	0.991	2.000
	(0.011)**	(0.016)	(0.346)**
Hispanic	0.645	0.743	0.746
	(0.054)**	(0.085)**	(0.195)
African American	0.537	0.750	0.341
	(0.038)**	(0.078)**	(0.089)**
Catholic	1.100	0.982	1.108
	(0.069)	(0.089)	(0.228)
Baptist-Methodist	0.765	0.803	0.651
	(0.047)**	(0.073)**	(0.147)*
Mom college grad	1.080	1.018	1.468
	(0.125)	(0.177)	(0.608)
Mom some college	1.014	1.062	0.716
	(0.103)	(0.154)	(0.282)
Mom HS grad only	0.992	1.018	1.100
	(0.062)	(0.090)	(0.248)
Mom educ missing	1.195	0.973	1.479
	(0.129)*	(0.145)	(0.493)
Dad college grad	0.969	0.867	0.920
	(0.094)	(0.131)	(0.356)
Dad some college	0.927	0.898	1.302
	(0.093)	(0.131)	(0.424)
Dad HS grad only	1.052	0.990	1.073
	(0.068)	(0.093)	(0.243)
Dad educ missing	0.915	1.149	0.842
	(0.076)	(0.126)	(0.261)
Lived in city at fourteen	1.074	1.224	1.562
	(0.065)	(0.110)**	(0.360)**
Single parent household	1.236	1.400	1.500
	(0.076)**	(0.116)**	(0.295)**
Log beer tax	1.022	0.988	1.450
	(0.041)	(0.060)	(0.208)**

(Table continues on p. 322.)

321

TABLE 10.7   *Continued*

	Used Alcohol Before Age Seventeen	Used Marijuana Before Age Seventeen	Used Marijuana More Than Fifty Times in Past Year (Fifteen- to Sixteen-Yr-Olds)
AFQT percentile 1989	0.995	0.992	0.988
	(0.001)**	(0.001)**	(0.004)**
AFQT missing	1.052	1.059	0.285
	(0.161)	(0.227)	(0.278)
Alcoholic rel	1.690	1.547	1.434
	(0.103)**	(0.128)**	(0.274)*
Income 1979	1.000	1.000	1.000
	(0.000)**	(0.000)	(0.000)
Income missing	1.032	1.033	1.289
	(0.063)	(0.089)	(0.273)
Alc rel missing	1.151	0.996	0.962
	(0.059)**	(0.073)	(0.181)
Teen drug prevalence	1.005	1.017	1.072
	(0.006)	(0.008)**	(0.025)**
Number of siblings	0.980	0.999	0.939
	(0.010)**	(0.015)	(0.034)*
Cocaine price	0.996	0.984	0.990
	(0.003)	(0.005)**	(0.011)
Cig tax at age fourteen to fifteen	0.996	1.004	1.020
	(0.005)	(0.008)*	(0.021)
Log mrj penalty 1977	1.01	1.101	.938
	(.026)	(0.037)	(0.082)
Drnk age at fourteen	0.975	1.050	1.094
	(0.019)	(0.030)*	(0.073)
Inc drnk age fourteen to sixteen	1.118	0.679	1.267
	(0.134)	(0.135)**	(0.323)
Dec drnk age fourteen to sixteen	1.060	1.021	. . .
	(0.087)	(0.121)	
Observations	9,366	9,366	2,255
Pseudo-R^2	0.06	0.04	0.10

Source: NLSY79, NLSY97
Note: Robust standard errors in parentheses.
* Significant at .05 level. ** Significant at .01 level.

variables: any alcohol use before age seventeen; any marijuana use before age seventeen; and frequent marijuana use before age seventeen. These three models were estimated using both the NLSY79 and the NLSY97 samples. The remaining tables present results that are based on NLSY97 data only. Table 10.8 displays estimates of odds ratios and standard errors for logistic models in which the dependent variables capture any alcohol use in the past month, any binge drinking in the past month, and any marijuana use in the past month. Finally, table 10.9 presents coefficient estimates from ordinary-least-squares models in which the dependent variables were natural-log versions of the following measures: number of alcoholic drinks in the past month given that the respondent reports alcohol use in the past month; number of binge-drinking episodes in the past month given that the respondent reports binge drinking in the past month; and number of days the respondent used marijuana in the past month given that the respondent reports marijuana use in the past month.

Determinants of Alcohol and Marijuana Use Before Age Seventeen: Estimates from the NLSY79 and the NLSY97

Results from the NLSY79 and NLSY97 models consistently indicate that demographic characteristics are important determinants of initiating alcohol and marijuana use before age seventeen and engaging in frequent marijuana use before age seventeen. Girls are less likely than boys are to report any alcohol or marijuana use, although the magnitude of this effect for alcohol-use initiation is considerably smaller for the NLSY97 sample than for the NLSY79 sample. This finding concurs with Abe's (chapter 11 in this volume) work, which indicates that, in both the NLSY79 and the NLSY97, girls were less likely than boys were to report delinquent behavior, such as stealing, property crime, and getting into fights.

African American and Hispanic respondents in both the NLSY79 and the NLSY97 are less likely than other respondents are to report alcohol-use initiation, marijuana-use initiation, or frequent marijuana use before age seventeen. Although this finding is consistent with national surveys of adolescent substance use, Abe (chapter 11 in this volume) reports that African American respondents in both the NLSY79 and the NLSY97 are more likely than white respondents are to report overt types of delinquent activities, such as attacking others and using force to steal from others. Moore (chapter 4 in this volume) and Michael and Bickert (chapter 5 in this volume) also find that young African American men are more likely than others are to have engaged in sexual intercourse.

Urban residence is not associated with alcohol-use initiation before age seventeen in any of the models. Residence in an urban area is associated with marijuana-use initiation and frequent marijuana use before age

TABLE 10.8   *NLSY97 Logistic Models—Determinants of Alcohol and Marijuana Use in Past Month, Odds Ratios and Standard Errors*

	Used Alcohol in Past Thirty Days	Binged in Past Thirty Days	Used Marijuana in Past Thirty Days
Female	0.944	0.754	0.788
	(0.056)	(0.059)**	(0.064)**
Hispanic	0.757	0.934	0.839
	(0.070)**	(0.112)	(0.109)
African American	0.426	0.378	0.570
	(0.039)**	(0.047)**	(0.069)**
Catholic	1.178	1.202	0.844
	(0.088)**	(0.117)*	(0.089)
Baptist-Methodist	0.892	1.011	0.855
	(0.071)	(0.105)	(0.089)
Lives in city	1.025	0.993	1.045
	(0.066)	(0.083)	(0.095)
Age in years	1.748	1.902	1.864
	(0.052)**	(0.075)**	(0.075)**
Dad HS grad only	0.998	1.147	1.096
	(0.085)	(0.130)	(0.127)
Mom HS grad only	1.154	1.032	0.949
	(0.097)*	(0.116)	(0.110)
Dad some college	0.792	0.945	1.068
	(0.106)	(0.167)	(0.191)
Mom some college	1.321	1.171	1.334
	(0.171)*	(0.200)	(0.224)*
Dad college grad	1.088	1.341	1.219
	(0.133)	(0.212)*	(0.200)
Mom college grad	0.824	0.812	1.026
	(0.119)	(0.150)	(0.189)
Single parent household	1.347	1.468	1.704
	(0.093)**	(0.130)**	(0.156)**
Income 1996	1.000	1.000	1.000
	(0.000)	(0.000)	(0.000)
No. household mem under eighteen	0.933	0.933	0.930
	(0.023)**	(0.031)**	(0.030)**
PIAT math score	1.002	0.993	0.991
	(0.002)	(0.003)**	(0.003)**

TABLE 10.8   *Continued*

	Used Alcohol in Past Thirty Days	Binged in Past Thirty Days	Used Marijuana in Past Thirty Days
Teen drug prevalence	1.027	1.035	1.024
	(0.013)**	(0.018)**	(0.020)
Cocaine price	1.047	1.071	1.053
	(0.027)*	(0.037)**	(0.036)
Log max sentence mrj	0.977	0.948	0.950
possession	(0.021)	(0.026)**	(0.028)*
Log max fine mrj possession	0.987	1.000	0.983
	(0.013)	(0.018)	(0.016)
Cig tax	1.000	1.002	1.005
	(0.002)	(0.002)	(0.002)**
Log beer tax	1.169	1.016	0.946
	(0.073)**	(0.088)	(0.069)
County drg arrst rte	1.022	1.014	1.013
	(0.010)**	(0.014)	(0.013)
Mom educ missing	1.182	1.174	1.113
	(0.145)	(0.180)	(0.185)
Fath educ missing	0.925	1.104	1.142
	(0.101)	(0.155)	(0.170)
PIAT score missing	0.907	0.624	0.467
	(0.093)	(0.079)**	(0.060)**
Income missing	0.894	0.881	0.689
	(0.070)	(0.090)	(0.076)**
Teen drg msg	1.008	1.248	1.146
	(0.080)	(0.131)**	(0.113)
Observations	8,445	8,445	8,445
Pseudo-R^2	0.10	0.11	0.09

Source: Author's compilation.
Note: Robust standard errors in parentheses.
* Significant at .05 level. ** Significant at .01 level.

seventeen in the NLSY79 models. In the NLSY97 models, however, youths living in urban areas are not more likely than other youths are to report marijuana use. This result supports Williams's (chapter 12 in this volume) work suggesting that rates of delinquency among urban and rural youths have been converging over time.

Another finding that is very consistent across both the NLSY79 and the NLSY97 relates to the effect of family structure on adolescent alcohol

TABLE 10.9   *NLSY97 OLS Models—Determinants of Alcohol and Marijuana Use Frequency, Ordinary-Least-Squares Coefficients and Standard Errors*

	Log Number of Drinks in Last Thirty Days, Given R Drank in Last Thirty Days	Log Number of Binges in Last Thirty Days, Given R Binged in Last Thirty Days	Log Number of Days Used Marijuana in Last Thirty Days, Given R Used Marijuana in Last Thirty Days
Female	−0.275	−0.096	−0.362
	(0.071)**	(0.060)	(0.089)**
Hispanic	0.028	−0.058	0.063
	(0.102)	(0.084)	(0.132)
African American	−0.491	−0.028	−0.025
	(0.115)**	(0.106)	(0.134)
Catholic	0.048	−0.061	−0.237
	(0.086)	(0.073)	(0.113)**
Baptist-Methodist	−0.002	−0.101	−0.108
	(0.103)	(0.088)	(0.126)
Lives in city	−0.066	0.052	−0.118
	(0.078)	(0.065)	(0.094)
Age in years	0.326	0.137	0.202
	(0.042)**	(0.033)**	(0.049)**
Dad HS grad only	0.030	−0.028	0.308
	(0.104)	(0.089)	(0.128)*
Mom HS grad only	−0.084	−0.152	−0.128
	(0.102)	(0.089)*	(0.126)
Dad some college	0.046	−0.038	0.047
	(0.155)	(0.132)	(0.186)
Mom some college	−0.050	−0.064	−0.225
	(0.156)	(0.122)	(0.186)
Dad college grad	0.400	0.170	0.450
	(0.152)**	(0.123)	(0.193)**
Mom college grad	−0.045	−0.073	−0.054
	(0.170)	(0.150)	(0.209)
Single parent household	0.199	0.079	0.263
	(0.081)**	(0.067)	(0.094)**
Income 1996	0.000	0.000	0.000
	(0.000)	(0.000)	(0.000)
No. household mem under eighteen	−0.034	−0.006	−0.018
	(0.031)	(0.027)	(0.037)

TABLE 10.9   *Continued*

	Log Number of Drinks in Last Thirty Days, Given R Drank in Last Thirty Days	Log Number of Binges in Last Thirty Days, Given R Binged in Last Thirty Days	Log Number of Days Used Marijuana in Last Thirty Days, Given R Used Marijuana in Last Thirty Days
PIAT math score	−0.009	−0.008	0.000
	(0.003)**	(0.003)**	(0.004)
Teen drg prev	0.020	−0.012	−0.016
	(0.016)	(0.013)	(0.024)
Cocaine price	0.051	0.041	0.036
	(0.033)	(0.027)	(0.039)
Log max sentence mrj possession	−0.053	0.012	0.016
	(0.025)**	(0.021)	(0.031)
Log max fine mrj possession	−0.002	−0.008	−0.044
	(0.015)	(0.013)	(0.019)**
Cig tax	0.001	0.003	0.004
	(0.002)	(0.002)	(0.002)**
Log beer tax	−0.047	−0.074	−0.046
	(0.079)	(0.065)	(0.076)
County drg arrst rte	−0.006	−0.011	0.018
	(0.010)	(0.008)	(0.014)
Mom educ missing	0.123	0.187	0.150
	(0.147)	(0.137)	(0.163)
Fath educ missing	0.001	−0.093	0.200
	(0.123)	(0.105)	(0.134)
PIAT score missing	−0.393	−0.263	0.004
	(0.144)**	(0.114)*	(0.150)
Income missing	0.032	−0.130	−0.165
	(0.094)	(0.080)	(0.119)
Teen drg msg	0.210	0.005	−0.003
	(0.096)**	(0.079)	(0.104)
Constant	−3.309	−0.271	−1.173
	(0.779)**	(0.647)	(1.001)
Observations	1,583	817	731
R-squared	0.11	0.07	0.12

Source: Author's compilation.
Note: Robust standard errors in parentheses.
* Significant at .05 level. ** Significant at .01 level.

and marijuana use. In every model, respondents from single-parent families are more likely than respondents from two-parent families are to report alcohol-use initiation before age seventeen, marijuana-use initiation before age seventeen, and frequent marijuana use before age seventeen. This result generally concurs with work by Hoffmann (1993), Hoffmann (1995), Hoffmann and Johnson (1998), and others who have studied the relation between family structure and substance use among children. Interestingly, this result is also consistent with the work of Pierret (chapter 1 in this volume), Moore (chapter 4 in this volume), and Michael and Bickert (chapter 5 in this volume), who find that various forms of nonintact family structure are associated with lower school grades, sexual activity, and problem behaviors among NLSY97 respondents. Moore finds that the effect of family structure on sexual activity is limited to white adolescents. Moreover, as Pierret suggests, while parents' divorce and remarriage may lead to instability for children, it is also possible that family structure instead captures some other unobserved factors that are important determinants of adolescent substance use.

Family socioeconomic status, as measured by parents' education and current family income, had no consistent effect on alcohol-use initiation before age seventeen, marijuana-use initiation before age seventeen, or frequent marijuana use before age seventeen in any of the models. These results are consistent with those of Cook and Moore (1993) and Pacula (1998), who find no consistent effect of parents' education on substance use among NLSY79 respondents. Gill and Michaels (1991) also find that, in the NLSY79, personal characteristics are much more important than socioeconomic factors are as predictors of drug use. These NLSY findings support results based on MTF data that do not show a correlation between parents' education and adolescent substance use (Bachman, Johnston, and O'Malley 1981). In both the NLSY79 and the NLSY97 analyses, respondents who are Baptists or Methodists are less likely than others are to report any type of alcohol or marijuana use. Pacula (1998) also finds that Baptist respondents are less likely than respondents of other religions are to report alcohol and marijuana use.

Family and peer substance use had an important effect on adolescent substance use in the NLSY79 and NLSY97 analyses. NLSY79 respondents who reported that they had a biological mother, biological father, or biological sibling who was an alcoholic were more likely than other respondents were to engage in substance use before age seventeen. Genetic or environmental factors may explain this strong link between parent and adolescent substance use. Alternatively, parent and adolescent substance use might be associated with unobserved factors (such as family problems or neighborhood effects) that determine both outcomes.

Both the NLSY97 and the NLSY79 models suggest that peer substance use is a statistically significant predictor of alcohol-use and marijuana-use initiation before age seventeen. In the NLSY97 models, state-substance-use prevalence rates were associated with the initiation of alcohol and marijuana use before age seventeen but not with frequent marijuana use before age seventeen. Regional illicit-drug-use prevalence rates were associated with both marijuana-use initiation and frequent marijuana use before age seventeen in the NLSY79 models. Similarly, in models that included NLSY97 reports of peer use instead of state prevalence rates as a proxy for peer use, respondents who reported drug-using peers were more likely than other respondents were to engage in substance use before age seventeen. All these effects were small in magnitude but consistently statistically significant. These results are consistent with previous research that indicates that peer substance use is an important determinant of adolescent substance use. The findings also concur with those of Abe (chapter 11 in this volume), who notes that NLSY97 respondents' reports about peers' alcohol use and class skipping were an important predictor of antisocial acts.

Results from the NLSY79 analysis support the idea that students with higher AFQT scores are slightly less likely than students with lower AFQT scores are to initiate alcohol and marijuana use before age seventeen and to engage in frequent marijuana use before age seventeen. The models estimated using NLSY97 data indicate that, while PIAT math scores are inversely associated with marijuana-use initiation before age seventeen, they are not associated with alcohol-use initiation before age seventeen and frequent marijuana use before age seventeen.[10]

Thus far, the determinants of substance use appear to be very similar across the NLSY79 and NLSY97 cohorts. This result is consistent with the idea that adolescent tastes and the risky-behavior decision-making process do not change over time. Furthermore, the findings reported here generally correspond to other work reported in this volume on adolescent risky behaviors. It is interesting, however, to consider the effects of alcohol and marijuana policies and prices that may have evolved over time. Moreover, data on state-level illicit-drug policies are more readily available for the 1990s than for the 1970s, allowing an analysis of the NLSY97 to yield an enhanced investigation of the effect of these policies.

Surprisingly, state excise taxes on beer were not associated consistently with alcohol-use initiation, marijuana-use initiation, or frequent marijuana use in the models. This result may indicate that, while beer taxes may affect current alcohol consumption by adolescents (as previous research suggests), they are not an important determinant of substance-use initiation among adolescents. The models yielded mixed evidence about the role of cocaine prices and cigarette taxes as determinants of adolescent alcohol and marijuana use. Although cocaine price was a statistically significant predictor of initiating marijuana use before age seventeen, the sign of the coefficient was not consistent across the NLSY79 and NLSY97 models. As I have already pointed out, measurement error in this variable may explain this result.

Cigarette taxes were positively associated with alcohol-use initiation and frequent marijuana use before age seventeen in the NLSY97 models. The magnitude of this effect, however, was small; moreover, cigarette taxes were not statistically significant in any of the NLSY79 models.

In the NLSY97 models, the length of jail terms for marijuana possession was inversely associated with the initiation of marijuana use before age seventeen, and the size of fines for marijuana possession was inversely associated with frequent marijuana use. Although these effect are small in magnitude, they indicate that state-level legal penalties for marijuana use are associated with lower rates of marijuana use before age seventeen among today's adolescents. This finding is consistent with the results of Chaloupka, Grossman, and Tauras (1998), who find that, among high school seniors in the 1980s, marijuana fines are negatively associated with marijuana use. In the NLSY79 marijuana models, however, the coefficient on maximum jail sentence for marijuana possession was not statistically significant at the .05 level.

Juvenile arrest rates for drug offenses were also included in the NLSY97 models to proxy the degree of county-level enforcement of drug-related crimes. Adolescents living in counties with high levels of drug-related arrests among juveniles could be viewed as living in a stringent enforcement environment where the full price of marijuana use is higher than it is in counties where juvenile arrests for drug-related offenses are less common. This measure is problematic, however, because it also captures the prevalence of juvenile drug offenses at the county level. The enforcement measure is a statistically significant, positive determinant of marijuana initiation before age seventeen, suggesting that the measure is mainly capturing prevalence of illicit-drug use rather than enforcement of drug laws. There was no association between level of enforcement and frequent marijuana use.

Many researchers have noted that minimum drinking ages are negatively associated with adolescent alcohol use. In the NLSY79 analysis, state minimum drinking ages, increases in drinking ages, and decreases in drinking ages were not statistically significant predictors of alcohol use.

Generally, results from the NLSY79 models were not consistent with other work on the effect of beer taxes on adolescent substance use. These contradictory results possibly were the result of the use of substance-use initiation rather than substance-use frequency as an outcome. The substance-use measures captured substance use before age seventeen rather than substance use in a particular year. Consequently, the prices and policies included in the NLSY79 models did not necessarily correspond to substance use in the particular year when those prices and policies held.

Determinants of Past-Month Alcohol and Marijuana Use: Estimates from the NLSY97

Generally, the effect of family-background determinants on past-month alcohol use, past-month binge drinking, and past-month marijuana use was very similar to the effect of family-background determinants on use before age seventeen. The effect of demographic characteristics on the frequency of past-month substance use, however, was somewhat different than that found in previous results. Although girls were less likely than boys were to report substance use before age seventeen and any past-month substance use, the magnitude of this effect was fairly small. Gender was a much more important determinant of frequency of use; given that past-month substance use occurred, girls reported many fewer alcoholic drinks and marijuana-use occasions in the past month than did boys. Girls and boys did not differ, however, in their reports of the number of binge-drinking episodes in the past month. It also is interesting that, while race was an important determinant of substance-use initiation before age seventeen, it was not a statistically significant determinant of frequency of binge drinking or marijuana use in the past month given that use occurred in the past month.

The results of the past-month substance-use model also further highlighted the effect of state penalties for marijuana possession on adolescent substance use. The length of maximum jail terms for marijuana possession was inversely related to any past-month binge drinking and any past-month marijuana use. Maximum fines for marijuana use were inversely related to the number of marijuana-use occasions in the past month. These findings, along with the results from the previous models, suggest that long jail terms for marijuana possession are associated with lower levels of marijuana-use initiation and that high fines for marijuana possession are associated with a lower frequency of marijuana use once use has been initiated. The results also suggest that binge drinking and marijuana use may be complements since increases in sentences for marijuana use are associated with decreases in past-month binge drinking. If binge drinking and marijuana use are complements, policies that reduce marijuana use will have the added benefit of reducing binge drinking.

Conclusions and Directions for Future Research

The effects of prices and policies on adolescent substance use are interesting from a policy perspective because policy makers can modify these factors directly. Moreover, alcohol and illicit-drug policies can have unintended effects if certain substances are substitutes for each other or complements with each other. Finally, because alcohol and marijuana are considered to be gateway drugs, one can speculate about the longer-range effects of prices and policies. For example, if higher beer taxes reduce the probability of adolescent alcohol use, they also might reduce the probability of later illicit-drug use among adolescents if the gateway theory holds true. On the other hand, if adolescents view alcohol and marijuana as substitutes, an increase in beer taxes may increase the risk of later illicit-drug use among adolescents.

The results indicate that, for adolescents living in both the policy environment of the 1970s and the policy environment of the 1990s, the monetary prices of substances as measured by beer taxes, cigarette taxes, and cocaine prices do not have a consistent effect on substance-use initiation, past-month use, or frequency of use in the past month. These findings diverge from some other research that has shown that beer taxes in particular are inversely associated with adolescent alcohol use. In the NLSY79 analysis, only lifetime-substance-use measures were available, which limited the degree to which prices and policies could be matched to adolescent records. Similarly, only 1994 cocaine prices were available for the NLSY97 analysis. This measurement error may explain the lack of findings. Even so, it is not clear why NLSY97 adolescents were not responsive to beer taxes, data which did not suffer from measurement error.

It is interesting that this study shows that legal penalties for marijuana possession are associated with binge drinking, marijuana-use initiation, past-month marijuana use, and frequency of marijuana use. These findings are consistent with the other limited research in this area that suggests that legal penalties effectively reduce marijuana use. If binge drinking and marijuana use are complements, as this analysis suggests, more severe marijuana penalties may have the unintended benefit of reducing binge drinking among adolescents. These results, however, should be interpreted with caution for several reasons.

First, one would expect that adolescents would be more responsive to the enforcement of marijuana laws than to the simple presence of laws. Enforcement, however, as measured by the county-level juvenile arrest rate for drug offenses, was not correlated with legal penalties for marijuana possession and generally was not a significant predictor of adolescent substance use. This result casts doubt on the utility of using arrest rates as a measure of enforcement and highlights the need for better measures of enforcement.

Furthermore, state policies regarding marijuana sentencing may be endogenous. States in which the population is tolerant toward marijuana use are likely to have both higher levels of marijuana use and more lax sentencing policies for marijuana possession than are states with less tolerance for marijuana. The association between marijuana-sentencing policy and adolescent marijuana use may therefore not be causal. Finally, even if the causal link between penalties and substance use were clear, the magnitude of the effects of legal penalties for marijuana possession was very small. States would have to consider the small benefits and the potentially high costs of imprisonment and the sentencing process.

Future releases of the NLSY97 will allow longitudinal analyses of the effect of changes in policies over time on changes in substance use. This type of data will help researchers understand better the causal pathways that link policies to adolescents' risk-taking behaviors. Moreover, the NLSY97 eventually will allow a detailed analysis of the educational and labor market consequences of adolescent substance use. Currently, very little is known about the long-term human capital consequences of adolescent substance use. As NLSY97 respondents move into adulthood, their survey data will provide a wealth of information that is needed to inform policy and, in turn, help prevent adolescent substance use.

This essay was funded by the the Early Results Conference and the W. T. Grant Foundation. I thank the National Bureau of Economic Research, the Beer Institute, the National Organization for the Reform of Marijuana Laws, and the Alcoholic Beverage Medical Research Foundation for useful information and data.

Notes

1. State-level differences in adolescent substance use, however, are more striking. In 1997, of the twenty-seven states participating in YRBS97 state surveys, Washington, D.C., reported the lowest rate of any past-month binge drinking among secondary school students (18.3 percent), while South Dakota reported the highest rate (45.2 percent). Thirty-day prevalence rates for marijuana use ranged from 17.5 percent in Iowa to 35.3 percent in Vermont.

2. NLSY97 respondents provided categorical responses to questions about the number of binge-drinking episodes and marijuana-use episodes in the past 30 days. For these variables, continuous measures were created by replacing the categorical responses with the midpoints of the categories.

3. Cocaine prices were not available for years earlier than 1977; as a result, cocaine prices for older NLSY79 respondents correspond to later points during adolescence rather than to age fourteen.

4. These data are not readily available for the NLSY79 cohort.

5. Marijuana-decriminalization indicators also were available for the NLSY79 and NLSY97 analyses. Not surprisingly, these measures were very highly correlated with the legal penalties for marijuana use. Marijuana-decriminalization indicators therefore were not included in models that also included the other marijuana-penalty variables.

6. Norton, Lindrooth, and Ennett (1998), however, find that, empirically, this selection problem may not be significant in a sample of sixth- to ninth-grade students.

7. One disadvantage of including these state-level variables as covariates, however, is that the models essentially control for the indirect effect of state prices and policies on youth substance use. For example, an increase in beer taxes may reduce an adolescent's beer consumption indirectly—by reducing use among peers, which in turn affects the individual adolescent's use—as well as directly. These models control for this indirect effect of substance prices and policies. For this reason, the models were estimated with and without the state-level adolescent-substance-use prevalence rates.

8. The NLSY97 analysis uses an indicator that represents whether the respondent lived in an urban area at the time of the 1997 survey. The NLSY79 analysis uses an indicator that represents whether the respondent lived in an urban area at age fourteen.

9. Each model was estimated as a short-form model and a long-form model. The short-form model excluded a set of potentially endogenous variables and variables that did not correspond exactly to the date of the survey, while the long-form model included this set. Short-form-model results were very similar to long-form-model results. For this reason, short-form regression results are not presented.

10. It is important to note that PIAT math scores test achievement in a single subject area for NLSY97 respondents who had not yet entered the tenth grade. AFQT scores reflect skills in a broad range of subjects and are available for NLSY79 respondents of all ages. Currently, AFQT scores are not available for the NLSY97 analysis. It is possible that the specialized nature of the PIAT math score and the fact that only younger respondents (who have lower substance-use rates than older respondents do) took the exam make it a less-viable proxy for general scholastic aptitude in these models than AFQT scores are.

References

Anderson, Allan, and Carolyn Henry. 1994. "Family System Characteristics and Parental Behaviors as Predictors of Adolescent Substance Use." *Adolescence* 29(114): 405–20.

Andrews, Judy, Hyman Hops, Dennis Ary, Elizabeth Tildesley, et al. 1993. "Parental Influence on Early Adolescent Substance Use: Specific and Nonspecific Effects." *Journal of Early Adolescence* 13(3): 285–310.

Ary, Dennis, Elizabeth Tildesley, Hyman Hops, and Judy Andrews. 1993. "The Influence of Parent, Sibling, and Peer Modeling and Attitudes on Adolescent Use of Alcohol." *International Journal of Addictions* 28(9): 853–80.

Bachman, Jerald, Lloyd Johnston, and Patrick O'Malley. 1981. "Smoking, Drinking, and Drug Use among American High School Students: Correlates and Trends, 1975–1979." *American Journal of Public Health* 71(1): 59–69.

Belcher, Harolyn, and Harold Shinitzky. 1998. "Substance Abuse in Children: Prediction, Protection, and Prevention." *Archives of Pediatrics and Adolescent Medicine* 152(10): 952–60.

Chaloupka, Frank, Michael Grossman, and John Tauras. 1998. "The Demand for Cocaine and Marijuana by Youth." *NBER* working paper 6411. Cambridge, Mass.: National Bureau of Economic Research.

Chaloupka, Frank, and Adit Laixuthai. 1997. "Do Youths Substitute Alcohol and Marijuana? Some Econometric Evidence." *Eastern Economic Journal* 23(3): 253–76.

Chassin, Laurie, Clark Presson, Jennifer Rose, and Steven Sherman. 1998. "Maternal Socialization of Adolescent Smoking: Intergenerational Transmission of Smoking-Related Beliefs." *Psychology of Addictive Behaviors* 12(3): 206–16.

Coate, Douglas, and Michael Grossman. 1988. "Effects of Alcoholic Beverage Prices and Legal Drinking Ages on Youth Alcohol Use." *Journal of Law and Economics* 31(1): 145–71.

Colder, Craig, Laurie Chassin, Eric Stice, and Patrick Curran. 1997. "Alcohol Expectancies as Potential Mediators of Parent Alcoholism Effects on the Development of Adolescent Heavy Drinking." *Journal of Research on Adolescence* 7(4): 349–74.

Cook, Philip, and Michael Moore. 1993. "Drinking and Schooling." *Journal of Health Economics* 12(4): 411–29.

Cragg, John. 1971. "Some Statistical Models for Limited Dependent Variables with Application to the Demand for Durable Goods." *Econometrica* 39(5): 829–44.

Dee, Thomas, and William Evans. 1997. "Teen Drinking and Educational Attainment: Evidence from Two-Sample Instrumental Variables (TSIV) Estimates." *NBER* working paper 6082. Cambridge, Mass.: National Bureau of Economic Research.

DeSimone, Jeffrey. 1998. "Is Marijuana a Gateway Drug?" *Eastern Economic Journal* 24(2): 149–64.

Duncan, Terry, Susan Duncan, Hyman Hops, and Mike Stoolmiller. 1995. "An Analysis of the Relationship between Parent and Adolescent Marijuana Use via Generalized Estimating Equation Methodology." *Multivariate Behavioral Research* 30(3): 317–39.

Duncan, Terry, Elizabeth Tildesley, Susan Duncan, and Hyman Hops. 1995. "The Consistency of Family and Peer Influences on the Development of Substance Use in Adolescence." *Addiction* 90(12): 1647–60.

Farrelly, Michael, Jeremy Bray, Gary Zarkin, Brett Wendling, and Rosalie Pacula. 1999. "The Effects of Prices and Policies on the Demand for Marijuana: Evidence from the National Household Surveys on Drug Abuse." *NBER* working paper 6940. Cambridge, Mass.: National Bureau of Economic Research.

Fendrich, Michael, and Mary Ellen Mackesy-Amiti. 1995. "Inconsistencies in Lifetime Cocaine and Marijuana Use Reports: Impact on Prevalence and Incidence." *Addiction* 90(1): 111–18.

Fendrich, Michael, and Connie Vaughn. 1994. "Diminished Lifetime Substance Use over Time: An Inquiry into Differential Underreporting." *Public Opinion Quarterly* 58(1): 96–123.

Francis, Leslie, and Kenneth Mullen. 1993. "Religiosity and Attitudes towards Drug Use among 13–15 Year Olds in England." *Addiction* 88(5): 665–72.

Gill, Andrew, and Robert Michaels. 1991. "The Determinants of Illegal Drug Use." *Contemporary Policy Issues* 9(3): 93–105.

Golub, Andrew, and Bruce Johnson. 1994. "The Shifting Importance of Alcohol and Marijuana as Gateway Substances among Serious Drug Abusers." *Journal of Studies on Alcohol* 55(5): 607–14.

Grant, Bridget, Thomas Harford, and M. Beth Grigson. 1987. "Stability of Alcohol Consumption among Youth: A National Longitudinal Survey." *Journal of Studies on Alcohol* 49(3): 253–60.

Grossman, Michael, and Frank Chaloupka. 1998. "The Demand for Cocaine by Young Adults: A Rational Addiction Approach." *Journal of Health Economics* 17(4): 427–74.

Grossman, Michael, Frank Chaloupka, Henry Saffer, and Adit Laixuthai. 1994. "Effects of Alcohol Price Policy on Youth: A Summary of Economic Research." *Journal of Research on Adolescence* 4(2): 347–64.

Guy, Sybille, Gene Smith, and Peter Bentler. 1994. "The Influences of Adolescent Substance Use and Socialization on Deviant Behavior in Young Adulthood." *Criminal Justice and Behavior* 21(2): 236–55.

Hansell, Stephen, and Helene Ranskin-White. 1991. "Adolescent Drug Use, Psychological Distress, and Physical Symptoms." *Journal of Health and Social Behaviors* 32(3): 288–301.

Hardert, Ronald, and Timothy Dowd. 1994. "Alcohol and Marijuana Use among High School and College Students in Phoenix, Arizona: A Test of Kandel's Socialization Theory." *International Journal of the Addictions* 29(7): 887–912.

Harwood, Henrick, Douglas Fountain, and Gina Livermore. 1998. *The Economic Costs of Alcohol and Drug Abuse in the United States, 1992.* Washington, D.C.: National Institute on Drug Abuse and National Institute on Alcohol Abuse and Alcoholism.

Hoffmann, John. 1993. "Exploring the Direct and Indirect Family Effects on Adolescent Drug Use." *Journal of Drug Issues* 23(3): 535–57.

———. 1994. "Investigating the Age Effects of Family Structure on Adolescent Marijuana Use." *Journal of Youth and Adolescence* 23(2): 215–35.

———. 1995. "The Effects of Family Structure and Family Relations on Adolescent Marijuana Use." *International Journal of the Addictions* 30(10): 1207–41.

Hoffmann, John, and Robert Johnson. 1998. "A National Portrait of Family Structure and Adolescent Drug Use." *Journal of Marriage and the Family* 60(3): 633–45.

Johnston, Lloyd, Patrick O'Malley, and Jerald Bachman. 1981. "Marijuana Decriminalization: The Impact on Youth, 1975–1980." *Monitoring the Future* occasional paper 13. Ann Arbor, Mich.: Institute for Social Research.

———. 1998. *National Survey Results on Drug Use from the Monitoring the Future Study, 1975–1997.* Vol. 1, *Secondary School Students.* Vol. 2, *College Students and Young Adults. NIH* publications 98–4345 and 98–4346. Rockville, Md.: National Institute on Drug Abuse.

Kandel, Denise. 1982. "Epidemiological and Psychosocial Perspectives on Adolescent Drug Use." *Journal of the American Academy of Child Psychiatry* 21(4): 328–47.

———. 1986. "The Consequences in Young Adulthood of Adolescent Drug Involvement: An Overview." *Archives of General Psychiatry* 43(3): 746–54.

———. 1991. "The Social Demography of Drug Use." *Millbank Quarterly* 69(3): 365–414.

Kenkel, Donald. 1993. "Drinking, Driving, and Deterrence: The Effectiveness and Social Costs of Alternative Policies." *Journal of Law and Economics* 36(2): 877–913.

Mensch, Barbara, and Denise Kandel. 1988. "Underreporting of Substance Use in a National Longitudinal Youth Cohort: Individual and Interviewer Effects." *Public Opinion Quarterly* 52(1): 100–24.

Merikangas, Kathleen, Marilyn Stolar, Denise Stevens, Joseph Goulet, Martin Preisig, Brenda Fenton, Heping Zhang, Stephanie O'Malley, and Bruce Rounsaville. 1998. "Familial Transmission of Substance Use Disorders." *Archives of General Psychiatry* 55(11): 973–79.

Model, Karen. 1993. "The Effect of Marijuana Decriminalization on Hospital Emergency Room Drug Episodes: 1975–1978." *Journal of the American Statistical Association* 88(423): 737–47.

Moore, Michael, and Philip Cook. 1995. "Habit and Heterogeneity in the Youthful Demand for Alcohol." *NBER* working paper 5152. Cambridge, Mass.: National Bureau of Economic Research.

Newcomb, Michael, and Peter Bentler. 1987. "The Impact of Late Adolescent Substance Use on Young Adult Health Status and Utilization of Health Services: A Structural Equation Model over Four Years." *Social Science and Medicine* 24(1): 71–82.

———. 1988. *Consequences of Adolescent Drug Use.* Newbury Park, Cal.: Sage Publications.

Norton, Edward, Richard Lindrooth, and Susan Ennett. 1998. "Controlling for the Endogeneity of Peer Substance Use on Adolescent Alcohol and Tobacco Use." *Health Economics* 7(5): 439–53.

Pacula, Rosalie. 1998. "Does Increasing the Beer Tax Reduce Marijuana Consumption?" *Journal of Health Economics* 17(5): 557–85.

Saffer, Henry, and Frank Chaloupka. 1999. "State Drug Control Spending and Illicit Drug Participation." *NBER* working paper 7114. Cambridge, Mass.: National Bureau of Economic Research.

Stacy, A. W., and Michael Newcomb. 1999. "Adolescent Drug Use and Adult Drug Problems in Women: Direct, Interactive, and Mediational Effects." *Experimental Clinical Psychopharmacology* 7(2): 160–73.

Stein, Judith, Gene Smith, Sybille Guy, and Peter Bentler. 1993. "Consequences of Adolescent Drug Use on Young Adult Job Behavior and Job Satisfaction." *Journal of Applied Psychology* 78(3): 463–74.

Stigler, George, and Gary Becker. 1977. "De Gustibus Non Est Disputandum." *American Economic Review* 67(2): 76–90.

Thies, Clifford, and Charles Register. 1993. "Decriminalization of Marijuana and the Demand for Alcohol, Marijuana, and Cocaine." *Social Science Journal* 30(4): 385–99.

U.S. Department of Health and Human Services. Public Health Service. National Institutes of Health. 1999. *National Survey Results on Drug Use from the Monitoring the Future Study, 1975–1999.* Washington: U.S. Department of Health and Human Services.

Walter, Heather, Roger Vaughan, and Alwyn Cohall. 1993. "Comparison of Three Theoretical Models of Substance Use among Minority High School Students." *Journal of the Academy of Child and Adolescent Psychiatry* 32(5): 975–81.

Weinberg, Naimah, T. E. Dielman, Wallace Mandell, and Jean Shope. 1994. "Parental Drinking and Gender Factors in the Prediction of Early Adolescent Alcohol Use." *International Journal of the Addictions* 29(1): 89–104.

Yamada, Tetsuji, Michael Kendix, and Tadashi Yamada. 1998. "The Impact of Alcohol and Marijuana Consumption on High School Graduation." *Health Economics* 5(1): 77–92.

Zhang, Lening, John Welte, and William Wieczorek. 1997. "Peer and Parental Influences on Male Adolescent Drinking." *Substance Use and Misuse* 32(14): 2121–22.

11

Changes in Gender and Racial Gaps in Adolescent Antisocial Behavior: The NLSY97 Versus the NLSY79

Yasuyo Abe

NTISOCIAL behavior during adolescence is a widespread and troubling phenomenon (U.S. DHHS 1998). Of concern should be not only the immediate damage inflicted by lawbreaking teenagers, but also the negative personal consequences of habitual unlawful behavior, consequences that could last long beyond the adolescent years. An enhanced understanding of common delinquent behaviors among youths is, therefore, an important research goal. Using data from the National Longitudinal Survey of Youth, 1997 and 1979 Cohorts (NLSY97 and NLSY79, respectively), this essay documents the frequency and types of antisocial activity among teenagers and compares findings from the two surveys in order to identify how youth behavior has changed over the last two decades.

In documenting and comparing antisocial behavior among NLSY79 and NLSY97 respondents, I am particularly interested in determining whether and in what way that behavior parallels the often-cited patterns and trends of juvenile crime found in official records. The law-enforcement records reported in the FBI's Uniform Crime Reports (UCR) provide the most widely used official measures of delinquency. The UCR suggest that, since 1980, there has been an unsteady trend in juvenile arrests, depending on type of crime. For instance, juvenile arrests for serious crime, or so-called index offenses,[1] decreased in the early 1980s and then started to increase in the mid-1980s through the early 1990s. After peaking in the first half of the 1990s, juvenile arrests started to decrease. To illustrate, the trends in arrest rates among fifteen- to seventeen-year-olds are presented in figure 11.1. The arrest rates for all index offenses increased from 4,360 arrests per 100,000 youths in 1980 to a peak of 5,076 in 1991 and then fell to 4,364 in 1997

FIGURE 11.1   *Arrest Rates Among Youths Aged Fifteen to Seventeen,*
UCR 1978 to 1998

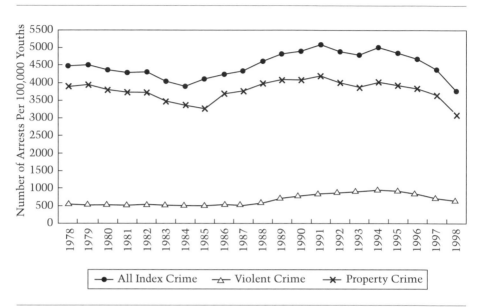

Source: Bureau of Justice Statistics. Based on FBI, Uniform Crime Reports, annual.

(Bureau of Justice Statistics 1999). This suggests that juvenile arrest rates for serious crime were at virtually the same level in 1997 and 1980.

The UCR also show that the trends in juvenile arrests vary by type of crime (Snyder 1998). Property index crime, which is far more common than violent index crime among youths, followed the overall trend described in the previous paragraph. On the other hand, as shown in figure 11.1, the arrest rate for violent index crime did not decline as fast as that for property index crime after 1994. Consequently, the 1997 level of violent-crime arrests was still higher than the 1980 level. In terms of the arrest rate among fifteen- to seventeen-year-olds, that of property index crime was 3,804 per 100,000 youths in 1980 and 3,633 in 1997, that of violent index crime 560 per 100,000 youths in 1980 and 740 in 1997 (Bureau of Justice Statistics 1999).

Although serious index crime is the most-often-cited official measure of delinquency, it should be noted that the overwhelming majority of recorded juvenile arrests have been for less-serious offenses, offenses that are not included in crime indexes (Harris, Welsh, and Butler 2000). These lesser crimes include, among other things, drug use, underage drinking, disorderly conduct, vandalism, curfew violation, and less-serious assaults. Juvenile arrests for all offenses including nonserious crimes increased steadily and at a faster rate from 1980 through the mid-1990s. They started to decline only after 1996. Accordingly, unlike that for serious crime, the arrest rate for all offenses was considerably higher in 1997 than it was in 1980. For instance, the arrest rate for all offenses among fifteen- to seventeen-year-olds was 12,387 per 100,000 youths in 1980 and 16,662 in 1997 (Bureau of Justice Statistics 1999). The arrest statistics including lesser offenses may be more relevant to antisocial-behavior measures in the NLSY, which covers a wide range of less-severe delinquent activities.

The UCR also report that, in any given year, males are more likely to be arrested than are females and African Americans than members of other racial groups. Recent studies using the UCR (Heimer 2000; O'Brien 1999; Poe-Yamagata and Butts 1996) have shown that arrests among female juvenile offenders relative to those among male juvenile offenders have increased over the last two to three decades for some types of crime, although the absolute level of arrests still remains much higher among males than among females for almost all offenses. The increase in female juvenile arrests (in terms of rates and the percentage change in the number) is relatively larger for violent crime than for property crime. Studies and reports on the trends in official juvenile arrest rates by race are scarce. For 1997, the UCR report that African Americans accounted for 26.5 percent of all arrests (including nonserious-crime arrests) among those under age eighteen, 44.2 percent of violent-index-crime arrests, and 26.6 percent of property-index-crime arrests. Thus, considering that African American youths made up about 15 percent of the U.S. juvenile population (fifteen- to nineteen-year-olds) in 1997, they were disproportionately represented in the arrest counts and particularly so in arrest counts for violent index crime.

In this study, I investigate whether commonplace teenage antisocial behavior measured in the NLSY79 and the NLSY97 mirror the patterns and trends observed in the UCR. In particular, the study attempts to examine whether antisocial behavior is more frequently observed for males and African Americans, whether the level of antisocial behavior has increased over time and how it may differ by type of activity, and whether the gender gap has narrowed and how the racial gap has changed.

While I propose to compare delinquency measures based on official arrest records with findings from the NLSY, the purpose of this study is not formally to test the validity of the NLSY data as a source of criminal-behavior measures or to explain the discrepancy between official juvenile crime records and the surveys. Rather, the scope of this study is limited to describing antisocial-behavior measures in the two NLSY studies. References to official delinquency measures are meant simply to provide a useful context in which to interpret the findings. Nonetheless, it may be worthwhile briefly to review caveats provided by previous studies comparing official records and survey results.

A host of criminological studies has examined the utility of self-report surveys as opposed to official data for measuring delinquent and criminal behavior (Thornberry and Krohn 2000). The use of self-reported data has been widely accepted since the landmark studies of Short and Nye (1957, 1958), which showed that self-reports could provide internally consistent measures of criminal behavior. The chief advantage of self-reported data is that they can capture delinquent activities that are not caught or recorded by law-enforcement agencies, avoid any potential bias due to differential treatment of subpopulations in the criminal-justice system, and provide detailed individual information that can be useful in etiological studies. On the other hand, respondents may not be willing or able to report on morally and legally sensitive issues completely and accurately, which raises questions about the reliability and validity of self-reported data.[2] Findings from various studies of the validity of self-reports indicate that, while self-reported data—especially those collected by sophisticated survey designs and instruments—are reasonably reliable and valid for most analytic purposes, underreporting still remains a concern, particularly among African American males and with respect to more serious and repeated offenses (Thornberry and Krohn 2000; Hindelang, Hirschi, and Weis 1981; Elliott and Ageton 1980; Huizinga and Elliott 1986; Weis 1986; Farrington et al. 1996). In addition, although both official records and survey data may reflect the same underlying behavioral patterns, by design they rarely measure the identical specific events or activities. Hence, one may as well expect discrepancies in results from the two types of data (Hindelang, Hirschi, and Weis 1979).

Two caveats can be derived from the previous literature. First, it is important to remember that official delinquency reports do not provide the gold standard against which the utility of NLSY antisocial-behavior measures is to be judged. Official data and survey data are probably best considered as complementary. As mentioned earlier, official records will be used here primarily to provide a relevant context. Second, when basing descriptions of behavior on survey data, one should be mindful of differential response patterns by type of activity and by subgroup. While a given set of responses may be internally consistent, generalizing from those responses may not be warranted, especially when the measures concerned are those on which subgroups are known to respond differently.

In the following sections, I first briefly discuss the data used in the analysis and then document the gender and racial patterns of antisocial behavior in 1980 and 1997 and the general trend between the two periods. Finally, results from the estimation of a multivariate model of antisocial behavior are discussed. Multivariate methods are used to control for individual and family background when examining gender and racial gaps.

Data

This study utilizes individual-level delinquent-behavior data provided by the first round of the NLSY97 and the second round (1980) of the NLSY79. The NLSY97 survey utilizes an innovative audio-CAPI (computer-assisted personal-interview) technology to collect sensitive information about antisocial behavior. Data thus collected are considered to be more accurate than those collected by other types of surveys (Tourangeau and Smith 1996; Turner et al. 1998). Nevertheless, respondents may still have underreported their own delinquent behavior, and one should be particularly cautious when making point estimates of the level of participation in illegal activity and when making comparisons between ethnic groups.[3]

Age at interview ranges from twelve to eighteen for NLSY97 respondents and from fifteen to twenty-three for NLSY79 respondents. I focus on fifteen- to seventeen-year-olds in order to make analyses comparable between the two surveys.[4] After excluding respondents who did not provide information on antisocial behavior, 4,210 NLSY97 observations and 3,831 NLSY79 observations remain.[5]

The summary statistics for the data are reported in table 11.1. While the samples used in the analysis are selected with the intention of ensuring comparability, the NLSY97 sample consists mostly of fifteen- and sixteen-year-olds, the NLSY79 sample sixteen- and seventeen-year-olds. Thus, the NLSY97 sample is slightly younger (average age = 15.7 years) than the NLSY79 sample (average age = 16.1 years). This imbalance in the age distribution could lead to overstating or understating differences between 1980 and 1997. Hence, the study presents age-specific descriptive statistics and controls for age in multivariate analyses.

Measuring Delinquency

Delinquency can be measured in several different ways. The NLSY79 asks whether in the last twelve months a youth has engaged in each of twelve antisocial activities: committing property crime; stealing less than $50; stealing more than $50; shoplifting; cheating or conning; selling stolen goods; breaking into buildings; selling illegal drugs; getting into fights; hitting or threatening to hit; attacking to hurt; or using force to get money. For this essay, youths are considered to have engaged in antisocial behavior if they report any of these twelve types of criminal activity in the past twelve months. Similarly, the NLSY97 asks whether a youth has ever engaged in each of six areas of antisocial behavior: causing property damage; stealing less than $50; stealing more than $50; committing other property crimes, such as selling stolen goods or swindling; attacking people; and

TABLE 11.1   Demographic Distributions of NLSY97 and NLSY79 Youths Who Are Fifteen to Eighteen Years Old and Reporting Delinquency Activities

| | NLSY97 (Round 1, 1997) | | | | NLSY79 (Round 2, 1980) | | | |
| | Unweighted Raw Data | | Weighted Distribution | | Unweighted Raw Data | | Weighted Distribution |
	N	Percentage	Percentage		N	Percentage	Percentage
Sample for analysis	4,210	100.0	100.0		3,831	100.0	100.0
Age							
Fifteen	1,869	44.4	43.0		936	24.4	27.8
Sixteen	1,709	40.6	41.3		1,463	38.2	37.5
Seventeen	632	15.0	15.7		1,432	37.4	34.8
		100.0	100.0			100.0	100.0
Male	2,148	51.0	51.6		1,931	50.4	50.2
Female	2,062	49.0	48.4		1,900	49.6	49.8
		100.0	100.0			100.0	100.0
Non-Hispanic white	2,040	48.5	66.2		1,926	50.3	71.7
Non-Hispanic black	1,111	26.4	15.3		981	25.6	13.7
Hispanic	905	21.5	13.5		669	17.5	6.6
Others	154	3.7	5.0		255	6.7	8.0
		100.0	100.0			100.0	100.0

Sources: NLSY97 round 1 (May 1999 release) used for 1997 statistics. NLSY79 round 2 used for 1980 statistics.
Note: For NLSY97, a small number of individuals (twenty-one) who were eighteen years old at the time of interview were included and grouped together with seventeen-year-olds.

selling illegal drugs. If any of these six areas of antisocial behavior are reported, further questioning determines the specific type of activity as well as frequency in the past twelve months. Youths are considered to have engaged in antisocial behavior if they report any of these six areas of antisocial activity in the past twelve months. Prevalence rates for these measures by age are reported in appendix B. The samples are limited to those who answered the questions in all relevant categories.

In order to distinguish between different types of antisocial activity, I borrow from developmental theory the concept of covert and overt activity (see Kelley et al. 1997; Frick et al. 1993).[6] Overt antisocial activity is characterized by aggressive or violent behavior, such as fighting, attacking, and strong-arming. Covert antisocial activity is characterized by nonaggressive or nonviolent behavior and includes committing property crime and vandalism, stealing, and selling illegal drugs. Involvement in both covert and overt criminal activity is seen as evolving over time, following a distinct pathway along which less-serious forms of delinquency precede more-serious forms. Progression along the overt pathway is also found to be interactive with progression along the covert pathway. As conceptualized here, the distinction between covert and overt antisocial activity appears to correspond closely to the FBI's distinction between property index crime and violent index crime. It will therefore be of interest to note whether the patterns observed for the latter will also be observed for the former.

Table 11.2 classifies the measures of delinquency used in the NLSY79 and the NLSY97 as either covert or overt behavior and also ranks those measures within categories according to severity. Severity rankings are based on Kelley et al. (1997) as well as on observed participation rates.

Figure 11.2 plots participation rates for all types of antisocial behavior and for covert and overt behavior by age and survey (NLSY79 and NLSY97). The figure suggests a bell-shaped pattern peaking at around age sixteen, among the oldest NLSY97 and the youngest NLSY79 respondents. It has been established in the criminal-justice and developmental-psychology literature that delinquency peaks during adolescence (Moffitt 1993; Steffensmeier et al. 1989). Data from the two NLSY surveys, shown in figure 11.2, seem to be consistent with this.

Figures 11.3 and 11.4 plot the rankings associated with different types of antisocial activity. The ordering of the prevalence rates among the different types of antisocial activity does not vary by gender, race, or age, and remains consistent between the two periods. For instance, among covert activities, property damage and shoplifting are much more common than breaking into buildings. Among overt activities, fighting is more common than using force to steal. The stable order observed is consistent with the suggestion put forward by developmental researchers that there are spe-

TABLE 11.2   Classification of Antisocial Behavior

Severity Level	NLSY97 (1997)		NLSY79 (1980)	
	Delinquency Subcategories	Percentage Youths Ever Participated	Delinquency Categories	Percentage Youths Participated in Past Year
Covert behavior:				
1	• Shoplifting	35.3	• Shoplifting	30.7
	• Property damage	30.3	• Property damage	26.3
	• Stealing less than $50[a]	4.2	• Stealing things worth less than $50	20.9
2	• Other property crime (selling stolen goods)	20.8	• Stealing things worth more than $50	5.8
	• Stealing more than $50[a]	1.9	• Cheating or trying to con	27.7
	• Selling marijuana	8.2	• Selling or holding stolen goods	13.8
3	• Selling hard drugs	5.6	• Selling marijuana	11.4
	• Breaking into a house or building to steal	3.8	• Selling other hard drugs	2.2
	• Stealing car to sell or for own use	2.0	• Breaking into building/auto to steal or look around	8.1
Overt behavior:				
1	• Attacking or getting into serious fights	20.4	• Getting into physical fights	35.0
2	• Snatching purse or pickpocketing	2.4	• Threaten to hit or hit others	10.8
3	• Using a weapon to steal	0.8	• Using force to get money or things	5.4

Source: NLSY97 (May 1999 release) and NLSY79 (1980).
Note: Participation rates are weighted and computed for fifteen- to seventeen-year-olds.
[a] These categories represent unspecified activities under the main categories of theft under $50 and theft over $50. That is, they include activities that are not categorized in any specific subcategories (shoplifting, break-ins, car theft, snatching purse, car theft, snatching purse, and pickpocketing or armed robbery).

FIGURE 11.2   *Percentage of Young Men Reporting Antisocial Activity in the Last Twelve Months, NLSY97 Versus NLSY79*

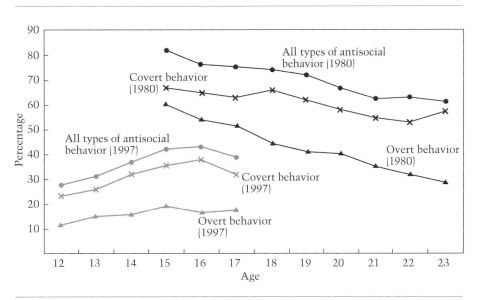

Source: Author's compilation based on NLSY97 and NLSY79.

cific pathways along which delinquency evolves, thereby providing support for the severity measures used in this study.

Because the types of antisocial activity covered as well as the questionnaire designs adopted differ somewhat between the NLSY79 and the NLSY97, the summary antisocial-behavior measures defined here (overall, covert, and overt indicators) may not be directly comparable across the surveys. In order to complement analysis using the summary measures, the study examines four specific types of antisocial activity defined in identical or closely comparable terms: committing property damage, shoplifting, selling illegal drugs, and attacking others.[7] (Indices reflecting the volume and the severity of antisocial behavior were also examined; the findings are reported in appendix A.)

Patterns of Antisocial Behavior in 1980 and 1997
Comparability of Delinquency Measures

Using the delinquency measures as defined in section 2, descriptive statistics for antisocial behavior in 1980 and 1997 are documented here. A summary of rates of antisocial behavior is given in table 11.3. It is shown

FIGURE 11.3   *Percentage of Young Men Reporting Covert Antisocial Activity, NLSY97 Versus NLSY79*

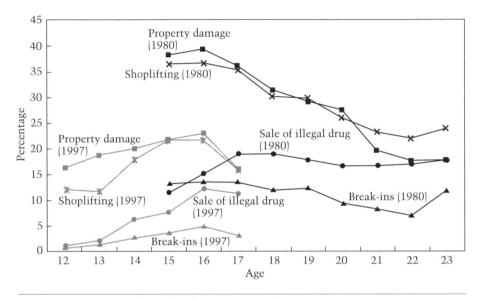

Source: Author's compilation based on NLSY97 and NLSY79.

there that participation in antisocial activity in the past twelve months was notably higher in 1980 than in 1997. Overall, 67.1 percent of fifteen- to seventeen-year-olds reported having engaged in some antisocial activity in 1980, compared to only 35.1 percent in 1997. The significant difference between the two surveys persists for all summary measures of antisocial activity (overall, covert, or overt) and is observed consistently across age, gender, and race. This difference is, however, unlikely to denote an actual shift in adolescent delinquent behavior. More likely, it reflects the fact that the summary delinquency indicators constructed from the two surveys do not measure equivalent behaviors.[8]

Cross-Sectional Gender and Racial Patterns

While the absolute levels of the 1980 and 1997 summary measures are not comparable, revealing analyses of antisocial behavior by gender and race across the survey periods can still be conducted. When between-group rates with respect to gender and race are examined within each period, consistent patterns seem to emerge. Young men are more likely than young women to participate in all types of delinquent activity in both 1980 and

FIGURE 11.4   *Percentage of Young Men Reporting Overt Antisocial Activity, NLSY97 Versus NLSY79*

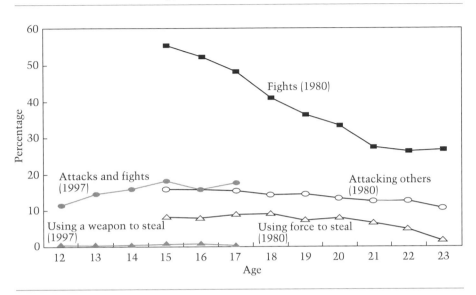

Source: Author's compilation based on NLSY97 and NLSY79.

1997. In 1980, 77.5 percent of young men and 56.5 percent of young women and, in 1997, 42.0 percent of young men and 27.8 percent of young women participated in some type of antisocial activity in the past year. Men are also found to be prone to commit antisocial activity more often and to commit more serious types of activity (see appendix A). The observed gender gap is consistent with the arrest patterns reported in the UCR.

The racial gap in antisocial behavior is more complex. Overall, white youths had a lower participation rate (66.0 percent) than African American youths (72.2 percent) in 1980, whereas white youths had a higher participation rate (36.5 percent) than African American youths (31.1 percent) in 1997. However, when participation rates are analyzed separately for covert and overt activity, the racial difference seems to be consistent across the two periods. Both surveys report that white youths are moderately more likely to participate in covert activity than are youths of other racial groups and that African American youths are more likely to participate in overt activity than are youths of other racial groups. These between-race patterns in covert and overt antisocial behavior arc observed both among young women and among young men.

In addition to participation rates, distribution by ethnicity and gender among those reporting delinquent behavior is summarized in table 11.4.

TABLE 11.3   *Antisocial Activities Committed by Fifteen- to Seventeen-*
Year-Olds in the Last Twelve Months (Weighted)

	Percentage of Youths Who					
	(1) Participated in Any Delinquent Activity		(2) Participated in Covert Antisocial Activity		(3) Participated in Overt Antisocial Activity	
	1997	1980	1997	1980	1997	1980
All	35.1	67.1	30.1	56.9	14.0	38.7
Age						
Fifteen	36.0	68.8	30.8	57.1	15.0	42.3
Sixteen	35.9	67.3	31.5	58.5	13.1	39.0
Seventeen	30.5	65.4	24.8	55.1	13.7	35.6
Male	42.0	77.5	36.0	64.8	18.0	55.3
Female	27.8	56.5	23.9	49.0	9.7	22.1
White	36.5	66.0	31.9	57.9	13.5	35.8
Black	31.1	72.2	23.9	54.6	17.3	48.8
Hispanic	34.7	67.8	29.9	55.8	13.8	44.1
Male						
White	44.4	77.6	39.2	66.1	17.9	54.3
Black	37.0	79.2	28.7	62.7	21.9	57.1
Hispanic	37.8	76.2	31.0	64.5	15.7	55.6
Female						
White	28.2	54.3	24.3	49.6	9.0	17.0
Black	24.9	65.1	18.9	46.5	12.6	40.4
Hispanic	31.0	59.2	28.5	46.9	11.4	32.2

Sources: NLSY97 round 1 (May 1999 release) used for 1997 statistics. NLSY79 round 2 used for 1980 statistics.

Young men are overrepresented in the delinquent subpopulation in both 1980 and 1997, particularly among those who participate in overt delinquent activity, reflecting the large difference in participation rate by gender. On the other hand, the overall racial distribution among the delinquent population differs only weakly from that among the general youth population. The share of African American youths among the population participating in overt criminal activity is slightly larger in both 1980 and 1997, mirroring that group's high rate of participation in overt activity, while the share of white youths among the population participating in covert criminal activity is slightly larger in 1997.

That young men are found to be more prone to antisocial behavior than young women, as observed in tables 11.3 and 11.4, is consistent with

TABLE 11.4 Gender and Race Distribution Among Delinquent Youths Aged Fifteen to Seventeen (Weighted)

| | NLSY97 (1997) | | | | NLSY79 (1980) | | | |
| | | Youth Who Participated in | | | | Youth Who Participated in | | |
	Sample Total	Any Antisocial Activity	Covert Activity	Overt Activity	Sample Total	Any Antisocial Activity	Covert Activity	Overt Activity
By gender								
Male	51.6	61.7*	61.7*	66.3*	50.2	58.0*	57.1*	71.6*
Female	48.4	38.3	38.3	33.7	49.8	42.0	42.9	28.4
	100.0	100.0	100.0	100.0	100.0	100.0	100.0	100.0
By race								
White	66.2	68.8†	70.0*	64.0†	71.7	70.6†	72.9	66.3*
Black	15.3	13.6	12.2	19.0	13.7	14.7	13.1	17.2
Hispanic	13.5	13.3	13.4	13.2	6.6	6.7	6.5	7.5
Other	5.0	4.3	4.5	3.8	8.0	8.0	7.5	8.9
	100.0	100.0	100.0	100.0	100.0	100.0	100.0	100.0

Sources: NLSY97 Round 1 (May 1999 Release) and NLSY79 Round 2 (1980).
Sample total includes non-delinquent youths.
* = Chi-square statistic for the test of independence is significant at the 1 percent confidence level.
† = significant at 10 percent level.

the gender gap found in the UCR arrest data. The marked gender difference in participation rates for overt antisocial activity in the NLSY data also parallels the highly skewed gender distribution in violent index crime. On the other hand, the findings reported here contrast with those reported in the UCR indicating that African Americans have significantly higher arrest rates than whites do and are disproportionately represented in measures of both violent and property crime. The NLSY-based antisocial-behavior measures provide little indication that African American youths are more likely than white youths are to engage in covert antisocial activity. Although these measures do indicate that, as far as overt antisocial activity is concerned, African American youths have a higher participation rate and are disproportionately represented among offenders, the magnitude of racial differentials seems far smaller than that implied in the UCR. The cross-sectional gender and racial patterns observed here for the frequency or prevalence of delinquent behavior are also commonly found in studies using other self-report data, including such large-scale national surveys as the National Youth Survey (Hindelang, Hirschi, and Weis 1981; Huizinga and Elliott 1986; Tracy 1987).

As noted earlier, the failure to detect the disproportionately high level of delinquent activity among African American youths could be a result of response patterns differing by ethnic group and, in particular, underreporting among African American youths. It is, however, unlikely that by itself underreporting can explain the failure to observe the persistently and considerably higher delinquent-activity levels among African Americans found in serious-crime statistics.[9] This discrepancy between NLSY and FBI data suggests that commonplace delinquent behavior is more equally distributed across racial groups than is serious criminal activity.

Changes Between 1980 and 1999

As discussed earlier, because of their incompatibility, the constructed summary delinquency measures are not suited to an investigation of changes in levels of antisocial behavior from 1980 to 1999. Instead, four specific types of antisocial activity defined in identical or closely comparable terms—committing property damage, shoplifting, selling illegal drugs, and attacking others—are compared. Committing property damage, shoplifting, and selling illegal drugs are categorized as covert antisocial activity, attacking others as overt antisocial activity. Because the variation in means resulting from differences in survey design is expected to be relatively small among these four activities, they should provide better measures with which to assess trends in level of participation in antisocial activity.[10]

Table 11.5 provides a summary of the participation rates for the four activities by age, gender, and race in 1980 and 1997. There are several interesting observations to be made.

TABLE 11.5   *Antisocial Activities Committed by Fifteen- to Seventeen-Year-Olds in the Last Twelve Months (Weighted)*

| | Percentage of Youths Who: | | | | | | | |
| | (1) Committed Property Damage | | (2) Shoplifted | | (3) Sold Illegal Drugs | | (4) Attacked Others to Hurt | |
	1997	1980	1997	1980	1997	1980	1997	1980
All	15.8	26.3	19.0	30.7	8.0	11.9	13.3	10.8
Age								
Fifteen	17.0	26.3	20.1	29.7	6.6	8.1	14.4	11.7
Sixteen	16.3	28.2	19.7	32.0	9.5	12.6	12.2	10.7
Seventeen	11.1	24.3	14.0	30.2	7.9	14.2	13.4	10.3
Male	21.4	38.1	21.1	36.1	10.2	15.4	17.0	15.8
Female	9.8	14.4	16.7	25.3	5.7	8.3	9.4	5.9
White	17.2	28.3	20.0	32.1	9.2	13.3	12.9	10.0
Black	12.1	19.2	14.4	25.6	4.7	6.7	16.4	12.5
Hispanic	14.8	25.6	19.0	33.7	7.6	8.4	12.9	10.9
Male								
White	23.5	41.8	22.9	38.0	11.5	17.1	16.8	14.8
Black	16.8	25.7	15.7	31.5	7.7	10.3	20.9	15.3
Hispanic	17.9	36.2	18.7	40.4	8.2	11.7	14.6	15.8
Female								
White	10.5	14.6	17.0	26.1	6.8	9.5	8.8	5.1
Black	7.2	12.7	13.0	19.5	1.6	3.1	11.7	9.7
Hispanic	11.0	14.7	19.4	26.7	6.9	5.0	10.8	5.9

Sources: NLSY97 round 1 (May 1999 release) used for 1997 statistics. NLSY79 round 2 used for 1980 statistics.

First, prevalence rates for the three covert activities—committing property damage, shoplifting, and selling illegal drugs—are significantly higher in 1980 than in 1997 across age, gender, and race. Of all youths in the sample (age range fifteen to seventeen), 26.3 percent committed property damage in 1980 and 15.8 percent in 1997, 30.7 percent shoplifted in 1980 and 19.0 percent in 1997, and 11.9 percent sold illegal drugs in 1980 and 8.0 percent in 1997. These differences are statistically significant.[11]

Since the wording of the questions assessing the commission of property damage and shoplifting is identical in the two surveys, it is unlikely that the observed decrease in prevalence rates is entirely due to measurement error. And it should again be noted that, because of the use of audio-CAPI technology in the NLSY97, illegal activity is relatively less likely to be underreported in 1997 than in 1980, suggesting an even larger gap between the two surveys. Conservatively speaking, therefore, there is little indication that the commission of property damage or shoplifting increased between 1980 and 1997. The implied reduction in the commission of property damage, shoplifting, and, to a lesser extent, the sale of illegal drugs does not precisely mirror the trend found in arrest data, which show a slight increase in the overall juvenile offense rate (including nonindex crime) and essentially no change in the rate of property index crime between 1980 and 1997. However, this may not necessarily mean that the NLSY data are at odds with the arrest data. It could be that a sharp decline in UCR juvenile arrest records since the mid-1990s is being foreshadowed by a decline in more common delinquent activity, such as committing property damage and shoplifting.

Second, in contrast to the three covert measures, attacking others increased slightly between 1980 and 1997. Of youths aged fifteen to seventeen, 10.8 percent attacked others with intent to hurt in 1980 and 13.3 percent in 1997. The difference is again statistically significant and is observed across age, gender, and race. This finding is not inconsistent with a sharp increase in arrests among violent-crime offenders. Because the questions asking about attacking others are not as closely comparable as those about committing property damage and shoplifting, intertemporal comparisons of this measure between the two surveys will not necessarily be conclusive, but they should still be informative.

Third, while the overall trend seems to vary with type of antisocial activity, consistent trends are observed within gender or racial groups. The change in participation rates for each of the four activities is smaller for young women than for young men in both absolute and relative terms. As a result, the gender gap in each activity narrowed between 1980 and 1997. As noted earlier, this relative increase in female offenders is consistent with the UCR statistics, although the magnitude of the gender gap is considerably higher in arrest statistics. African American youths are again found to be consistently less likely than whites are to commit property damage, to shoplift, or to sell illegal drugs. The participation rates for these three activities also decreased over time among African Americans, although not as quickly as participation rates for committing property damage and selling illegal drugs did among whites. The increased participation rate for attacking others seems to be greater among African American youths than among those of other races.

Multivariate Analysis

A vast literature—encompassing various disciplines (including sociology, economics, and psychology) and motivated by a wide range of theories—

has been dedicated to the etiological investigation of the effects of socio-economic- and demographic-background factors on delinquency. Elsewhere in this volume, Pierret (chapter 1), Chatterji (chapter 10), and Williams (chapter 12) use the NLSY97 (and the NLSY79) data to explore the determinants of various forms of antisocial behavior. While these researchers may adopt different theoretical perspectives, their results indicate that the incidence of antisocial behavior is indeed affected by various background factors. Thus, even though determining the causes of adolescent antisocial behavior is not within the scope of this study, it is important that background factors be taken into account when comparing prevalence rates across subpopulations.

In the rest of the essay, I investigate the gender and racial patterns as well as the time trend in antisocial behavior while holding background factors constant. Controlling socioeconomic factors may be particularly important when analyzing the racial gaps in antisocial behavior since such factors are likely to vary with race. I estimate simple multivariate logit models of the incidence of antisocial behavior in the past year among youths aged fifteen to seventeen, controlling for individual, family, and socioeconomic factors. The results of the estimation will be used to illuminate how background characteristics are associated with antisocial behavior and to examine how gender and racial gaps, controlled for the background factors, have changed between 1980 and 1997.

The same set of regressors is used for both the 1980 and the 1997 models. For each year, participation in antisocial activity is regressed on age, gender, race, (youth) employment status, school-enrollment status, family income, family size, unemployment rate, crime rate, an indicator for residence in the South, an indicator for residence in urban areas, and an indicator for whether another youth in the same household (for example, a sibling) has committed any delinquent acts. Most of these regressors are defined in highly comparable terms in the two surveys. A difference in the mean values of a covariate between the two surveys, therefore, may be attributed more to the cohort difference than to the measurement difference. However, there is a concern that family income, antisocial behavior of another youth in the household, and urban residence may not be as comparable across the surveys as the other measures are.[12] The difference in mean value between these variables is most likely to reflect the fact that they do not measure exactly the same things. A summary of variables used in the estimation is provided in table 11.6.

Several different indicators for participation in antisocial activity are used as dependent variables. They include the summary participation measures for all antisocial activity, covert activity, and overt activity. Participation in covert activity is analyzed separately from participation in overt activity since these measures are expected to vary with certain covariates.

TABLE 11.6   A Summary of Variables Used in the Estimation of
             Multivariate Models

	NLSY97 (1997)		NLSY79 (1980)	
	Mean	Std. Dev.	Mean	Std. Dev.
Committed any antisocial act last year	0.331	0.471	0.681	0.466
Committed covert antisocial last year	0.279	0.449	0.559	0.497
Committed overt antisocial last year	0.140	0.347	0.422	0.494
Worked in the past twelve months	0.668	0.471	0.658	0.474
Age sixteen	0.406	0.491	0.379	0.485
Age seventeen	0.150	0.357	0.378	0.485
Female	0.490	0.500	0.497	0.500
Non-Hispanic black	0.264	0.441	0.257	0.437
Hispanic	0.215	0.411	0.175	0.380
Other non-white ethnic	0.037	0.188	0.067	0.250
Enrolled in school	0.955	0.208	0.888	0.316
Family income (thousands)	47.073	59.521	37.500	24.766
Family size	4.448	1.571	4.115	1.961
Live in urban areas	0.581	0.493	0.750	0.433
Live in South	0.364	0.481	0.374	0.484
Other delinquent youth in household	0.155	0.362	0.446	0.497
Crime rate (no. crimes per 100,000 residents)	605.055	265.693	5142.487	3321.259
Unemployment rate	5.471	2.978	7.071	2.229
Committed property damage last year	0.147	0.354	0.242	0.428
Committed shoplifting last year	0.172	0.377	0.296	0.457
Sold illegal drugs last year	0.075	0.263	0.104	0.306
Attacked others to hurt last year	0.133	0.339	0.115	0.319
Number of observations	4210		3792	

Sources: NLSY97 (May 1999 release and geocode data) and NLSY79 (1980 survey and geocode data).
Note: For the NLSY79, thirty-nine individuals for whom the employment variable is not available are excluded from estimation. As a result, there are 3,792 observations instead of 3,831 (see table 11.1). Unemployment and crime rates are provided by NLSY geocode supplements. The NLSY79 includes 1980 MSA-level unemployment rates, and the NLSY97 includes 1998 unemployment rates. Crime rates are the numbers of crimes per 100,000 residents at the county level. NLSY79 uses the 1977 rate, and the NLSY97 uses the 1991 rate.

In addition, I use the four specific-activity measures that are more comparable between the NLSY79 and the NLSY97: committing property crime, shoplifting, selling illegal drugs, and attacking others.

Table 11.7 summarizes the logit-estimation results for participation in any antisocial behavior, participation in covert behavior, and participation in overt behavior. The estimated coefficients generally have the expected signs and are statistically significant in many cases. These results confirm that important relations exist between adolescent antisocial behavior and background factors and that such relations remain consistent over time. Other studies examining the determinants of antisocial behavior using the NLSY97 also find background factors to be important (for example, Pierret, chapter 1 in this volume; Chatterji, chapter 10 in this volume; Williams, chapter 12 in this volume; Amuedo-Dorantes and Mach 1999; Abe and Michael 1999). In both 1980 and 1997, for the model of participation in any antisocial activity, the coefficients on being female and being enrolled in school are significantly negative, while having worked in the past year and antisocial behavior of another youth in the same household are significantly positively associated with antisocial behavior. Another interesting finding is that the estimates on the background factors vary by type of antisocial behavior. For example, being enrolled in school is not significant for the covert-behavior equation but is strongly positive for the overt-behavior equation. Family income has a significantly negative coefficient for the overt-behavior equation but not for the covert-behavior equation. Discussion of the effect of a background factor on antisocial behavior, therefore, needs to be placed in the context of a specific type of antisocial behavior.

The coefficient estimates for 1980 and 1997 reported in table 11.7 appear to have the same signs and to be generally comparable in magnitude. However, because the summary measures used are not completely equivalent, neither estimated coefficients nor predicted probabilities of antisocial behavior may be directly compared across the surveys. Once again, therefore, the between-group differences are compared. To illustrate the estimated changes in gender and racial gaps, odds ratios between young women and young men and between African American and white youths are presented in table 11.8. Odds ratios here measure the relative difference in the predicted probability of delinquent incidents that can be attributed to gender or race.[13]

Consistent with the raw participation rates reported in table 11.3, one thing in table 11.8 is immediately apparent with respect to gender. The female-to-male odds ratios are less than unity across the board, indicating that, relative to young men, young women have a lower likelihood of participating in delinquent activity. That is, after controlling for background

(*Text continues on p. 360.*)

TABLE 11.7   *Logit Estimation of Participation in Antisocial Activities over Last Twelve Months Among Youth Aged Fifteen to Seventeen (Weighted)*

| | Participation in Any Antisocial Activity | | | | Participation in Covert Antisocial Activity | | | | Participation in Overt Antisocial Activity | | | |
| | 1997 | | 1980 | | 1997 | | 1980 | | 1997 | | 1980 | |
	Coef.	S.E.	Coef.	S.E.	Coef.	S.E.	Coef.	S.E.	Coef.	S.E.	Coef.	S.E.
Committed covert act	0.3180*	0.0878							1.6704*	0.1114	1.1687*	0.0933
Committed overt act					1.6734*	0.1118	1.1578*	0.0926				
Worked in last twelve months			0.4152*	0.1005	0.3166*	0.0957	0.4563*	0.0983	-0.0088	0.1255	-0.0479	0.1019
Age sixteen	-0.0707	0.0813	-0.1325	0.1158	0.0285	0.0887	0.0419	0.1099	-0.2389**	0.1174	-0.2015†	0.1127
Age seventeen	-0.3622*	0.1163	-0.2947**	0.1192	-0.3647*	0.1280	-0.1338	0.1153	-0.1196	0.1651	-0.3630*	0.1195
Female	-0.6325*	0.0759	-0.9462*	0.0895	-0.4643*	0.0828	-0.2725**	0.0891	-0.5569*	0.1112	-1.4401*	0.0906
Black	-0.1790†	0.1067	0.3425*	0.1171	-0.4402*	0.1215	-0.0650	0.1124	0.3648**	0.1537	0.4715*	0.1204
Hispanic	-0.0395	0.1193	0.0347	0.1213	0.0141	0.1311	-0.1380	0.1174	-0.1545	0.1680	0.2671**	0.1280
Other nonwhite	-0.1685	0.1936	0.1301	0.1775	-0.0968	0.2010	-0.1137	0.1655	-0.1785	0.2963	0.3826**	0.1711
Enrolled in school	-0.6985*	0.1768	-0.3686**	0.1670	-0.1731	0.1967	-0.0273	0.1557	-1.0365*	0.2178	-0.6595*	0.1471
Family income (thousands)	8.35E-06	5.94E-04	-3.08E-03†	1.76E-03	1.10E-03†	5.92E-04	8.25E-04	1.79E-03	-4.71E-03**	2.31E-03	-5.98E-03*	1.85E-03
Family size	-0.1259*	0.0268	-0.0001	0.0252	-0.1171*	0.0293	-0.0386	0.0243	-0.0362	0.0384	0.0330	0.0247

	Coef.	S.E.	Coef.	S.E.	Coef.	S.E.	Coef.	S.E.	Coef.	S.E.	Coef.	S.E.
Live in urban areas	0.1341	0.0832	0.1936	0.1256	0.2142**	0.0895	0.2595**	0.1215	0.0064	0.1207	0.0260	0.1252
Live in the South	-0.1518+	0.0860	-0.1102	0.1013	-0.1648+	0.0939	-0.4229*	0.0989	0.0211	0.1266	0.2287**	0.1033
Delinquent youths in household	0.7001*	0.1060	0.4319*	0.0943	0.4710*	0.1175	0.3538*	0.0900	0.4884*	0.1447	0.1131	0.0935
Crime rate	1.59E-04	1.67E-04	1.41E-05	1.81E-05	8.75E-05	1.80E-04	1.77E-05	1.64E-05	1.16E-04	2.45E-04	1.71E-06	1.63E-05
Unemployment rate	-0.0320**	0.0150	0.0283	0.0200	-0.0456*	0.0163	-0.0069	0.0196	0.0124	0.0219	0.0308	0.0204
Constant	0.7171*	0.2575	0.9531*	0.3025	-0.3731	0.2857	-0.3677	0.2938	-1.0964*	0.3623	-0.0237	0.2978
Obs	4206		3792		4206		3792		4206		3792	
Log likelihood	-2,609.75		-2,259.32		-2,319.52		-2,360.65		-1,468.97		-2,138.86	
Pseudo-R^2	0.0427		0.0601		0.0099		0.0891		0.1357		0.1554	
Chi-square (d.f. = 15)	171.84*		179.00*		342.98*		290.27*		345.88*		464.02*	

Source: NLSY97 (1997 survey, May 1999 release) and NLSY79 (1980 survey).

Note: Pseudo-R^2 is defined as $1 - (L1/L0)$ where L0 is the value of log likelihood with just the constant term and L1 is the value with all variables in the model. Unemployment and crime rates are provided by NLSY geocode supplements. Unemployment rate is at the MSA level, and the 1998 rates for NLSY97 and 1980 rates for NLSY79 are used. County-level crime rates are the numbers of crimes per 100,000 residents. NLSY79 uses the 1977 rate, NLSY97 the 1991 rate.

* Significant at 1 percent. ** Significant at 5 percent.

+ Significant at 10 percent.

TABLE 11.8   *Odds Ratios for Participation in Antisocial Behavior over Twelve Months: Implications from Logit Regressions (Summary Delinquency Measures)*

	(1) Participation in Any Antisocial Activity		(2) Participation in Covert Antisocial Activity		(3) Participation in Overt Antisocial Activity	
	1997	1980	1997	1980	1997	1980
By gender						
Female-to-male odds ratio	0.5313*	0.3882*	0.6285*	0.7614*	0.5730*	0.2369*
By race						
Black-to-white odds ratio	0.8361†	1.4084*	0.6439*	0.9371	1.4402**	1.6023*

Source: Author's compilation.
Note: Odds ratios are based on the estimates reported in table 11.7.
* Significant at 1 percent (H_0: odds ratio = 1). ** Significant at 5 percent.
† Significant at 10 percent.

factors, young men are still consistently more likely to have engaged in antisocial behavior than are young women across the surveys and for all summary antisocial-activity measures. The magnitude of the gender effect (the difference between unity and an odds ratio) indicates that the gender gap is somewhat smaller in 1997 than in 1980. This narrowing of the gender gap seems to be due to the narrowing of the gap among overt activities.

The racial differences are also generally consistent with the raw rates. Table 11.8 shows that, overall, African American youths are more likely than white youths are to participate in antisocial activity in 1980 (African American–to–white odds ratio of 1.4) and less likely to do so in 1997 (odds ratio of 0.8). As discussed earlier, these variations arise from different participation patterns for covert and overt antisocial activity. The African American–to–white odds ratio is less than unity for covert activity and greater than unity for overt activity in both years. In other words, African American youths are more likely to participate in overt antisocial activity than white youths are, while white youths are more likely to participate in covert antisocial activity than African American youths are. The racial gap for covert activity appears to have widened considerably between 1980 and 1997.

Table 11.9 presents the estimated odds ratios for activity measures that are more comparable between 1980 and 1997. (The corresponding logit-estimation model and results are available from the author.) The trends of the gender and racial differences observed for committing prop-

TABLE 11.9   Odds Ratios for Participation in Antisocial Behavior over Twelve Months: Implications from Logit Regressions (Property Damage, Shoplifting, Drug Sale, and Attacking)

	(1) Property Damage		(2) Shoplifting from Stores		(3) Sale of Illegal Drugs		(4) Attacking Others to Hurt	
	1997	1980	1997	1980	1997	1980	1997	1980
By gender								
Female-to-male odds ratio	0.3990*	0.2769*	0.7683*	0.6139*	0.5413*	0.4962*	0.5002*	0.3275*
By race								
Black-to-white odds ratio	0.7080**	0.7485**	0.7196**	0.9036	0.5214*	0.5113*	1.1615	1.3097

Source: Author's compilation.
Note: Odds ratios are based on estimation results available on request from the author.
* Significant at 1 percent (H_o: odds ratio = 1). ** Significant at 5 percent.

erty damage, shoplifting, selling illegal drugs, and attacking others are largely consistent with odds ratios for the summary measures reported in table 11.8 as well as with the raw rates reported in table 11.5. The differences between young men and young women in terms of odds ratios have narrowed, albeit by varying degrees, for all four target antisocial activities. On the other hand, the difference between African American and white youths seems to have widened slightly for committing property damage and shoplifting but not for selling illegal drugs or attacking others. African American–to–white odds ratios are less than unity for all three covert-activity measures for both years and are statistically significant, except shoplifting in 1980. This confirms that, even after controlling for background factors, white youths have the higher likelihood of participating in these covert activities. The odds ratios for attacking others are, in contrast, statistically insignificant in both periods. Hence, although in table 11.5 African American youths appeared to have a higher prevalence rate for attacking others, there is only weak evidence of a racial gap once the background factors are controlled for.

To recap, the logit-estimation results are largely consistent with the raw participation rates observed in tables 11.3 and 11.5. Again, the results are comparable to the trend observed in the UCR in some aspects, including the persistently higher likelihood of delinquency among young men and a hint of convergence of the gender gaps, particularly for overt activity. On the other hand, white youths were repeatedly found to have a higher likelihood of reporting covert delinquent activity than African American youths were. This racial gap between African American and white youths also appears to have widened between 1980 and 1997. The implication to be drawn from the analysis of the raw participation rates as well as from that of the multivariate models so far is that African American youths are no more likely than their white counterparts are to engage in delinquent activity. As noted earlier, this is contrary to the disproportionately high arrest incidence observed for African American youths in the UCR.

To verify the findings of the logit estimation, I further investigate whether the racial gap has narrowed or widened over time by applying a conventional decomposition. For this alternative approach, a linear-probability model for participation in antisocial behavior is first estimated separately for white and for African American youths, allowing coefficients to vary across groups. The difference in predicted probabilities between groups is then broken down into two components: one owing to the difference in group characteristics, the other owing to the difference in the coefficients (unobserved factors between the groups).[14] The latter component was approximated as the difference in intercept terms (the coefficients on dummy variables for race groups) in the logit models. Unlike the earlier logit estimation, this approach takes into account the interaction of race and other family- and socioeconomic-background variables. One may attribute the difference in predicted probabilities to the difference in coefficients to race per se, or to different rates of underreporting (or overreporting), or to group preferences, or to other factors not explained by regressors in the model. I do not speculate here on reasons for the presence of the racial difference; rather, I simply examine how the importance of the group difference that cannot be attributed to the known (controlled) background characteristics has changed over time.

Linear-probability models are estimated for two measures, committing property damage and attacking others—which respectively represent covert and overt activity—among youths aged fifteen to seventeen. (The full model and estimation results are available on request from the author.) A decomposition of the estimated racial differentials in the likelihood of participation in antisocial activity (based on the unweighted models) is reported in table 11.10. The total differential between young white men and young African American men, which by construction is equivalent to the raw differential reported earlier,[15] shows that white youths are more likely to commit property damage than African American youths are in both 1980 and 1997. The difference between African American youths and white youths in the likelihood of committing property damage was about –8.5 percentage points in 1980, of which –3.0 percentage points can be attributed to the difference in backgrounds and –5.5 percentage points to the difference in coefficient estimates. A smaller difference of about –5.7 percentage points is observed in 1997, of which 0.6 percentage points can be attributed to background differentials and –6.3 percentage points to the coefficient difference. This implies that the absolute difference between African American and white youths that can be attributed to race per se (or to some unexplained difference), therefore, may have increased slightly, from –5.5 to –6.3. The ratio of African American to white probabilities adjusted for the difference in backgrounds declined from 0.8 to 0.6, indicating a slight increase as well in relative likelihood between the two groups.

In contrast to the probability of committing property damage, the probability of attacking others increased for both white and African American youths over time. The total difference in the likelihood of attacking others is relatively small for both 1980 and 1997 (2.3 and 2.9 percentage points, respectively). Although the total racial differential is small, the decomposition shows that the difference that can be attributed to each component is nontrivial for 1980. The component that can be attributed to background characteristics is –3.2 percentage points, that to unexplained factors 5.5 percentage points. On the other hand, the total racial differential in 1997 is 2.9 percentage points, of which 1.9 percentage points can be attributed to the difference in background characteristics and 1.0 percent-

TABLE 11.10   *Decomposition of Black-White Differentials in the*
Likelihood of Participation in Antisocial Activities

	(1) Property Damage		(2) Attacking Others	
	1997	1980	1997	1980
Mean probability of white youths (X_wB_w) (percentage)	17.13	27.74	12.86	10.62
Mean probability of black youths (X_bB_b) (percentage)	11.40	19.22	15.78	12.89
Total differential in the likelihood of committing antisocial behavior $(X_bB_b - X_wB_w)$ (percentage)	−5.73	−8.52	2.92	2.27
Decomposition of total differential (percentage)				
Difference attributable to known background characteristics $(X_bB_b - X_wB_b)$	0.60	−2.99	1.89	−3.24
Difference attributable to coefficient estimates or unknown characteristics $(X_wB_b - X_wB_w)$	−6.33	−5.53	1.03	5.51
Ratio of probabilities				
Unadjusted (raw) black-white ratio of the probabilities of antisocial behavior (B_bX_b/B_wX_w)	0.67	0.69	1.23	1.21
Adjusted black-white ratio of the probabilities of antisocial behaviors (X_wB_b/X_wB_w)	0.63	0.80	1.08	1.52

Source: Based on estimation results from linear-probability models. The estimation results are available upon request from the author.

age points to unexplained factors. The absolute difference between African American and white youths that can be attributed to race per se hence decreased from 5.5 to 1.0 percentage points. Similarly, the adjusted ratio of the African American–to–white probabilities declined from 1.5 to 1.1. Thus, the (unexplained) racial gap in attacking others between African American and white youths, controlling for background characteristics, is found to have diminished in both absolute and relative terms between 1980 and 1997. As cautioned earlier, because delinquency measures and control variables in the two surveys are not completely equivalent, the implications drawn from these decomposition exercises should be considered tentative.

Conclusion

This chapter examined the patterns of antisocial behavior among youths in 1980 and 1997. While it is limited largely to within-period analysis, owing to the incomparability of key variables in the NLSY79 and the NLSY97, attempts are made to make comparisons across periods using activity measures that are similarly defined in the two surveys. The study finds that a nontrivial proportion of the youths interviewed commit various antisocial acts and that the patterns of participation vary by race and gender and by type of activity. Unlike the UCR arrests rates for all offenses (including nonindex crime), there is little evidence that the level of antisocial activity was measurably higher in 1997 than in 1980. This study finds, however, that participation patterns by gender are consistent with the official crime statistics. Young men are consistently more likely than young women are to commit any type of antisocial activity, although the difference has narrowed over time. These findings are consistent with results reported by Williams (chapter 12 in this volume), who also finds a steady trend in levels of less-serious delinquency over the past two decades and a greater propensity toward all types of antisocial activity among young men than among young women.

This essay also provided insight into the issue of race, at least insofar as it affects adolescent antisocial behavior. While there are some differences in racial patterns between the NLSY79 and the NLSY97, the overall findings are consistent. In both surveys, African American youths are more likely to engage in overt antisocial activity than white youths are. The two surveys also consistently show that, compared to white youths, African American youths are not more likely to engage in covert antisocial activity or to engage in a greater number of delinquent activities (see appendix A). The racial gap seems to have widened for covert activity while possibly narrowing for overt activity. These findings do not agree with published arrest reports, which imply a considerably higher crime rate among African American youths. As discussed in the introductory section, the discrepancy between the survey-derived delinquency measures and the UCR arrest measures does not automatically discredit the findings. It does, however, caution that certain survey-design and -implementation issues, including possible underreporting among African American youths, might affect the delinquency measures adopted in this study. Concern for these and other data-quality issues may underscore the need to address the validity of NLSY delinquency measures formally.

This study also found that background factors are correlated with participation in commonly observed antisocial behavior among adolescents. While it was not the objective of the study to explore explanations for antisocial behavior, the observed strong and consistent associations imply that an analysis of the between-group difference needs to be placed in the context of changing family and socioeconomic environments. Both the NLSY79 and the NLSY97 constitute a rich source of information about background factors that was not fully exploited in this study. Using such information, future research can further illuminate how between-group gaps found in this study arise.

Appendix A

In addition to the binary indicator for participation in delinquent activity, indices reflecting the volume and the severity of antisocial activity are also examined. The volume index is created for each survey by summing the quintile scores for the number of incidents in the last twelve months. For a given type of antisocial activity, a score of 0 is given if the reported number of incidents was 0, 1 if the reported number of incidents was greater than 0 but less than the twentieth percentile, 2 if the reported number of activities was between the twentieth and the fortieth percentiles, and so on. The scores are then summed up over all types of antisocial activity.

The created index takes a value ranging from 0 (no delinquent activity) to 25 for the NLSY97 (for the youths whose reported number of incidents is in the top or fifth quintile in five areas)[16] or from 0 to 60 for the NLSY79 (for youths whose reported number of activities is in the top or fifth quintile in all twelve areas). The measure gives equal weight to each type of antisocial activity and normalizes the "volume" across types. Since the categories of activities providing the volume are not the same in the NLSY79 and the NLSY97, the indices for the two periods are not directly comparable.

The severity index is created using the level of seriousness reported in table 11.2. The severity index was constructed separately for covert and overt antisocial activity first. The index ranges from 1 (not serious) to 3 (very serious). A composite index is then created by combining the covert- and overt-level indices, giving a score of 1 if the higher of either covert or overt severity level is 1, 2 if the higher of either covert or overt level is 2, and 3 if the higher of either covert or overt level is 3. For those who did not report any delinquent activity, a score of 0 is given.

Table 11A.1 provides the means of the volume and severity indices by age, gender, and race. Those who had a total score of 0 or who did not engage in any delinquent activity are excluded from the calculation of the means and medians. Among those who engaged in either covert or overt delinquent activity, the mean of the volume index is 4.6, and the median score 3.0, out of a maximum score of 25 in 1997. The corresponding mean

TABLE 11A.1   *Antisocial Activities Committed by Fifteen- to Seventeen-Year-Olds in the Last Twelve Months (Weighted)*

	(1) Volume Index of Delinquent Acts (Index Range)		(2) Severity Index of Delinquent Acts (Index Range)	
	1997 (1–25)	1980 (1–60)	1997 (1–3)	1980 (1–3)
All	4.59	7.70	1.59	1.93
Age				
Fifteen	4.58	7.24	1.53	1.88
Sixteen	4.63	8.13	1.65	1.96
Seventeen	4.48	7.61	1.57	1.94
Male	4.87	9.60	1.66	2.03
Female	4.03	5.09	1.47	1.80
White	4.50	8.16	1.60	1.98
Black	4.78	5.70	1.51	1.83
Hispanic	4.75	7.32	1.59	1.79
Male				
White	4.69	10.15	1.65	2.07
Black	5.52	7.02	1.64	1.94
Hispanic	4.90	9.18	1.68	1.93
Female				
White	4.14	5.26	1.51	1.85
Black	3.41	4.07	1.29	1.70
Hispanic	4.43	4.87	1.47	1.60

Sources: NLSY97 round 1 (May 1999 release) used for 1997 statistics. NLSY79 round 2 used for 1980 statistics. Only positive values are used to compute the means.

is 7.7, and the median 5.0, out of a maximum score of 60 in 1980. The relatively low mean implies that most youths who do engage in delinquent activity do not report committing many delinquent acts. As the positive skew in the distribution suggest, however, a small number of youths report having committed a large number of delinquent activities. Reported frequency of antisocial behavior also shows an unambiguous and consistent gender difference for the two surveys, while the patterns are less consistent with respect to race. As reported in table 11A.1, the mean of the volume index is higher for young men than for young women (4.9 versus 4.0 in 1997, 9.6 versus 5.1 in 1980). White youths report a slightly lower number of incidents than do African American youths (4.5 versus 4.8) in 1997 but a higher number (8.2 versus 5.7) in 1980.

The severity measures for delinquent activity are reported in the last two columns of table 11A.1. The table shows the average of the highest-ranked (most-severe) activities committed in the past twelve months. The demographic patterns of the severity measures parallel those of the volume indices. The severity rank ranges from 1 to 3, and the overall mean among those committing some antisocial activity is 1.6 in 1997 and 1.9 in 1980. In both years, young men engaged in more serious antisocial activity than young women did (2.0 versus 1.8 in 1980, 1.7 versus 1.5 in 1997). The mean of the severity index is slightly higher for whites than for African Americans in both years (2.0 versus 1.8 in 1980, 1.6 versus 1.5 in 1997).

To summarize the gender and racial differences for these indices, consistent with the results for the binary measures of delinquency, young men are more involved in antisocial activity than young women are, by both measures. However, the findings are not clear with respect to race.

Appendix B

TABLE 11B.1   Percentage of Males Who Participated in Antisocial Activity (Weighted)

Age	Any Antisocial Activity			Covert Antisocial Activity			Overt Antisocial Activity			Illegal Income Receipt	
	1997		1980		1997	1980		1997	1980	1997	1980
	Ever	Last Year	Last Year	Ever	Last Year	Last Year	Ever	Last Year	Last Year	Last Year	Last Year
12	48.8	27.9		44.6	23.2		18.2	12.1		3.8	
13	50.9	31.4		47.6	26.0		21.0	15.3		6.0	
14	57.7	36.9		55.0	31.9		23.1	16.4		9.2	
15	62.4	42.2	82.0	58.6	35.6	66.9	26.6	19.3	60.4	14.0	21.5
16	63.0	42.9	76.3	58.8	38.0	65.1	27.7	16.7	54.3	15.9	24.5
17	59.4	38.8	75.1	54.5	31.8	62.8	27.4	17.8	52.0	14.7	29.7
18			74.1			65.8			44.6		23.4
19			72.0			62.1			41.1		19.1
20			66.6			57.9			39.9		20.3
21			62.4			54.5			35.0		16.8
22			62.7			53.0			31.9		16.8
23			61.1			57.2			28.7		25.5

(Text continues on p. 370.)

TABLE 11B.1   *Continued*

| | Property Damage | | | Shoplifting | | | Theft Less than $50 | | | Theft More than $50 | | |
| | 1997 | | 1980 | 1997 | | 1980 | 1997 | | 1980 | 1997 | | 1980 |
Age	Ever	Last Year	Last Year	Ever	Last Year	Last Year	Ever	Last Year	Last Year	Ever	Last Year	Last Year
12	30.3	16.4		21.0	12.3		27.2	13.2		5.0	3.8	
13	33.5	18.8		23.9	11.9		31.0	13.8		5.0	3.7	
14	36.3	20.1		31.6	18.2		39.3	19.4		10.4	5.8	
15	40.4	21.7	38.3	36.6	21.9	36.6	41.3	21.2	28.8	13.2	9.8	8.5
16	40.7	23.0	39.4	38.7	21.8	36.8	42.9	20.8	30.1	14.7	10.1	10.9
17	35.4	15.6	36.2	37.8	16.1	35.5	41.4	14.5	25.1	12.5	8.0	9.9
18			31.4			30.4			32.4			7.9
19			29.2			29.7			26.2			7.4
20			27.5			26.1			26.4			9.7
21			19.6			23.1			24.1			5.2
22			17.7			22.0			26.3			7.3
23			18.0			23.8			19.5			6.1

	Other Property Crime				Break-Ins			Auto Theft		
	1997		1980		1997		1980	1997		1980
	Other Property Crime		Cheated or Tried to Con	Sold or Held Stolen Goods	Broke into a House or Building to Steal		Broke in House or Auto to Steal or Look	Auto Theft for Own Use or to Sell		Took a Car for Ride without Permission
Age	Ever	Last Year	Last Year	Last Year	Ever	Last Year	Last Year	Ever	Last Year	Last Year
12	7.0	2.7			1.1	0.8		.0	.0	
13	9.7	5.1			2.0	1.5		.4	.4	
14	13.4	6.9			4.0	2.8		2.2	1.2	
15	18.3	9.2	33.7	24.0	5.3	3.8	13.3	2.3	1.6	14.5
16	16.1	8.3	32.6	23.9	6.5	5.1	13.8	2.8	1.8	18.2
17	19.1	7.8	30.7	18.4	6.0	3.3	13.6	2.5	2.4	14.7
18			26.3	19.4			12.1			10.0
19			24.5	18.0			12.5			11.4
20			20.9	14.0			9.5			9.3
21			21.2	15.3			8.4			7.8
22			16.7	12.0			7.1			6.5
23			18.2	12.5			12.0			6.2

(Table continues on p. 372.)

TABLE 11B.1   *Continued*

	Sale of Illegal Drugs					Fights and Attacks					Theft with Force				
	1997		1980			1997		1980			1997				1980
	Sold Illegal Drugs		Sold Illegal Drugs	Sold Hard Drugs	Sold Marijuana	Attacked Others or Got Into Serious Fights		Hit Others	Got Into Fights	Attack Others to Hurt	Snatched Purse or Wallet or Pickpocket		Used a Weapon to Steal		Used Force to Steal
Age	Ever	Last Yr	Last Yr	Last Yr	Last Yr	Ever	Last Yr	Last Yr	Last Yr	Last Yr	Ever	Last Yr	Ever	Last Yr	Last Yr
12	1.6	1.1				17.9	11.4				1.2	0.6	0.9	0.6	
13	3.1	2.2				20.0	14.5				1.9	1.5	0.6	0.5	
14	7.7	6.3				22.7	15.8				2.1	1.5	0.7	0.4	
15	10.2	7.7	11.5	2.1	10.6	25.1	18.1	50.6	55.4	15.8	3.2	2.0	1.0	1.0	8.4
16	15.5	12.3	15.2	3.9	14.8	26.3	15.7	58.1	52.1	15.8	3.8	2.3	1.5	1.0	8.0
17	15.0	11.3	19.2	3.1	18.7	26.7	17.7	56.3	48.2	15.4	1.5	0.8	0.7	0.7	9.2
18			19.0	3.7	18.8			52.1	40.8	14.3					9.3
19			17.9	4.1	17.2			45.1	36.2	14.5					7.6
20			16.7	2.9	15.8			46.1	33.2	13.4					8.1
21			16.7	4.2	15.4			41.3	27.3	12.5					6.8
22			17.0	3.3	16.1			40.0	26.3	12.6					5.2
23			17.9	5.0	15.6			31.4	26.6	10.7					2.1

Sources: NLSY97, round 1 (May 1999 release) and NLSY79, round 2 (1980 survey). All nonmissing observations are included for each activity.

This study was funded by the Office of Assistant Secretary for Policy, U.S. Department of Labor (DOL), under purchase order OASP (B9492643). The earlier stage of this work was supported by the National Institute of Child Health and Human Development (NICHD) (5-T32-HD07302). Points of view or opinions stated in this study do not represent the official position or policy of the DOL or the NICHD. I wish to thank Early Results Conference participants, particularly Matt Stagner and Robert Michael, for their comments. I am also grateful to Ben Lahey, Robert Fairlie, and anonymous reviewers for helpful discussions and to Carolyn Hill and Yoonae Jo for their help with data. Any remaining errors are solely mine.

Notes

1. Index offenses include both serious violent and property crimes. Specifically, violent index offenses include murder and nonnegligent manslaughter, forcible rape, robbery, aggravated assault, and property index offenses include burglary, larceny-theft, and motor-vehicle theft.

2. *Reliability* concerns the consistency or repeatability of a given measure. It is the extent that a measuring instrument yields the same outcome each time it is used. *Validity* concerns the accuracy of the data. It is the extent that an instrument actually measures the concept that it purports to measure.

3. To check the extent of underreporting, I made a crude comparison of the arrest rates reported in the NLSY97 and those reported in the UCR and found the former to be lower than expected for both African American and white youths; however, the gap was relatively larger among African American youths. Hence, underreporting remains a potential problem with the NLSY97 data.

4. I included eighteen-year-olds in the NLSY97 analysis sample because a small number of individuals (twenty-one) who were between the ages twelve and sixteen at the time of sampling were eighteen when they were interviewed.

5. These observations represent those who responded to questions on all antisocial-behavior categories used to create summary measures (see subsequent discussion).

6. As originally developed, this concept clusters destructive behavior into three categories: covert behavior, overt behavior, and authority conflict. Authority conflict includes stubbornness, doing things one's own way, disobedience, staying out late, truancy, and running away. Authority conflict is not examined here partly because good measures of it are not available in the data and partly because it is not conventionally considered to be illegal activity per se.

7. The NLSY79 and the NLSY97 use the exact same wording to describe property damage ("purposely damaged or destroyed property that did

not belong to you") and shoplifting ("taking something from a store without paying for it"). (In the NLSY97, the shoplifting question is conditional on a positive response to a lead-in question about stealing; in the NLSY79, no lead-in question prefaces the shoplifting question.) The questions about attacking others and selling illegal drugs are phrased somewhat differently in the two surveys. The NLSY97 asks whether a respondent "ever attacked someone with the idea of seriously hurting or have a situation end up in a serious fight or assault of some kind" and whether a respondent "ever sold or helped sell marijuana, hashish or other hard drugs such as heroin, cocaine, or LSD," while the NLSY79 asks whether a respondent "attacked someone with the idea of seriously hurting or killing" and whether a respondent ever "sold marijuana or hashish" and ever "sold hard drugs such as heroin, cocaine, or LSD" (note that the NLSY79 asks about selling marijuana and about selling other hard drugs separately). The indicator for the sale of illegal drugs used for NLSY79 is constructed from the two separate questions.

8. To illustrate how sensitive the point estimates of the constructed measures are to the definitions used, I created an alternative indicator of delinquency for the NLSY79, excluding the three categories cheating or conning, fighting, and threatening to attack. Those three categories are relatively loosely defined and appear to include behavior that would not be considered delinquent by NLSY97 standards. When these three categories are excluded, the delinquency rates for 1980 turn out to be much lower: the overall participation rate drops from 67.1 to 52.4 percent; the covert delinquency rate drops from 56.9 to 49.4 percent; and the overt delinquency rate drops from 38.7 to 13.7 percent, very close to the 1997 rate (14.0 percent).

9. For one thing, the higher prevalence rates of covert antisocial behavior among whites relative to African Americans are consistently observed across gender, not only in the NLSY79, but also in the NLSY97, which utilized audio-CAPI technology to ask sensitive questions. Hence, one might conjecture that less-serious antisocial behaviors are indeed committed more evenly across racial groups than the serious-crime statistics suggest. It is also possible that, to the extent that minority youths are more likely to be arrested and therefore incarcerated, delinquent African American youths may be underrepresented in the sample and their prevalence rates understated. Analyses not reported here find that reported per person frequency of delinquent activity is negatively correlated with minority status, which suggests just such an imbalance in the sample.

10. The NLSY79 asks simply the number of delinquent acts committed in the past twelve months, while the NLSY97 first asks if a delinquent act has ever been committed and then, if a delinquent act has been committed, asks the number of delinquent acts committed in the past twelve months. Because the survey questions are framed in terms of different reference periods, responses may be affected even if

questions otherwise use the same or similar wording. Therefore, results discussed here should be taken with caution.

11. Pearson chi-square tests are used to test whether the participation rates in the two surveys are equivalent. For all youths in the sample (age range fifteen to seventeen), chi-square statistics (d.f. = 1) performed for unweighted participation rates are 115.90 for committing property damage, 173.01 for shoplifting, 22.75 for selling illegal drugs, and 6.47 for attacking others. The null hypothesis of the equal ratio is rejected at the 1 percent significance level for all measures except attacking others, which is rejected at the 5 percent significance level.

12. The urban-residence indicator in the NLSY97 seems to be subject to measurement error. Only 54.0 percent (weighted) of the NLSY97 youths in the study sample are found to live in urban areas, whereas 75.7 percent of all NLSY97 youths live in urban areas. More youths are in central metropolitan statistical areas (MSAs) in 1997 than in 1980, but more youths in noncentral or central-unknown MSAs are categorized as urban in 1980. The number of youths living in urban areas among the NLSY97 sample appears to be very low for a nationally representative sample, which may indicate some coding issues to be addressed. Family-income variables are constructed on the basis of differently worded income questions in each year. For the estimation, constructed net family income is used for 1980 and estimated gross family income for 1997. Similarly, the indicator for antisocial behavior committed by another youth in the same household is constructed on the basis of the summary antisocial-behavior measures defined in this study, which, as pointed out earlier in the text, may not be equivalent between the two surveys.

13. The predicted probability of a positive outcome (in this case, the probability of committing a delinquent act) for a logit model is $P = \exp(X\beta)/[1 + \exp(X\beta)]$, where X is a vector of explanatory variables, and β is a vector of corresponding coefficients. An odds ratio, $\exp(\beta_i)$, for the ith coefficient, measures the relative change in $P/(1 - P)$ that can be attributed to a unit change in X_i, the ith explanatory variable. For example, for the gender variable, the odds ratio measures the ratio of $P/(1 - P)$ for young women to $P/(1 - P)$ for young men.

14. Decomposition methods are frequently used in the discrimination literature (Oaxaca 1973; Blinder 1973; Cain 1986; Fairlie 1999). In terms of a simple estimable linear equation, where the model is written as $Y_j = X_j\,\beta_j + e_j$ (for j = group 1 or 2), the total differential in the predicted values can be written as $Y_1 - Y_2 = b_1(X_1 - X_2) + X_2(b_1 - b_2)$, where b denotes the estimate for β. The first part, $b_1(X_1 - X_2)$, is interpreted as the difference in the predicted values that can be attributed to the difference in the means of the explanatory variables (the X's). The second part, $X_2(b_1 - b_2)$, is attributed to the difference in coefficients (weighted at the means of group 2). In this study, the latter part is regarded as the difference in antisocial behavior that can be attributed to race in itself.

In this study, I adopt a simple linear-probability model to approximate the probability of participation for subgroup analyses. The use of linear-probability models is justified because their coefficient estimates are found to be comparable to those of logit models because of computational ease.

15. The total difference between the two groups may be slightly different from that reported in table 11.5 because the estimations did not use sample weights.

16. For the NLSY97, number of incidents is asked for five of the six anti-social-activity categories discussed in the text, excluding stealing less than $50. To correct for the fact that we do not know the incidence of minor theft, I assume that those who report having stolen things worth less than $50 in the past twelve months committed such an act twice in the year. Without information on the actual incidence of minor theft, the volume index for 1997 may not accurately reflect the frequency of delinquent activity among youths.

References

Abe, Yasuyo, and Robert T. Michael. 1999. "Employment, Delinquency, and Sex during Adolescence: Evidence from NLSY97." Working paper. Population Research Center, National Opinion Research Center and the University of Chicago.

Amuedo-Dorantes, Catalina, and Traci Mach. 1999. "Juvenile Crime, Delinquency, and School Quality: New Hope from the NLSY97." Paper presented at the NLSY97 Early Results Conference. Washington: Bureau of Labor Statistics (November 18–19).

Blinder, Alan S. 1973. "Wage Discrimination: Reduced Form and Structural Estimates." *Journal of Human Resources* 8(4): 436–55.

Bureau of Justice Statistics. 1999. *Crime and Justice Electronic Data Abstracts* (November 17 version). Worksheet, retrieved August 3, 2000, from *www.ojp.usdoj.gov/bjs/dtdata.htm*. (Original data source: FBI, Uniform Crime Reports.)

Cain, Glen G. 1986. "The Economic Analysis of Labor Market Discrimination: A Survey." In *Handbook of Labor Economics*, vol 1., edited by Orey Ashenfelter and Richard Layard. Amsterdam: North-Holland.

Elliott, Delbert S., and Suzanne S. Ageton. 1980. "Reconciling Race and Class Differences in Self-Reported and Official Estimates of Delinquency." *American Sociological Review* 45(February): 95–110.

Fairlie, Robert W. 1999. "The Absence of the African-American Owned Business: An Analysis of the Dynamics of Self-Employment." *Journal of Labor Economics* 17(1): 80–108.

Farrington, David P., Rolf Loeber, Magda Stouthamer-Loeber, Welmoet B. Van Kammen, and Laura Schmidt. 1996. "Self-Reported Delinquency and a Combined Delinquency Seriousness Scale Based on Boys, Mothers, and Teachers: Concurrent and Predictive Validity for African-Americans and Caucasians." *Criminology* 34(4): 493–517.

Federal Bureau of Investigation. Various years. *Crime in the United States* [Uniform Crime Reports (UCR)]. Washington: U.S. Government Printing Office.

Frick, Paul J., Benjamin B. Lahey, Rolf Loeber, Lynne Tannenbaum, Yolanda Van Horn, Mary Anne G. Christ, Elizabeth A. Hart, and Kelly Hanson. 1993. "Oppositional Defiant Disorder and Conduct Disorder: A Meta-Analytic Review of Factor Analyses and Cross-Validation in a Clinical Sample." *Clinical Psychology Review* 13(4): 319–40.

Harris, Philip W., Wayne N. Welsh, and Frank Butler. 2000. "A Century of Juvenile Justice." In *The Nature of Crime: Continuity and Change* (*Criminal Justice 2000*, vol. 1), edited by Gary LaFree. Washington, D.C.: National Institute of Justice.

Heimer, Karen. 2000. "Changes in the Gender Gap in Crime and Women's Economic Marginalization." In *The Nature of Crime: Continuity and Change* (*Criminal Justice 2000*, vol. 1), edited by Gary LaFree. Washington, D.C.: National Institute of Justice.

Hindelang, Michael J., Travis Hirschi, and Joseph G. Weis. 1979. "Correlates of Delinquency: The Illusion of Discrepancy between Self-Reports and Official Measures." *American Sociological Review* 44(6): 995–1014.

———. 1981. *Measuring Delinquency*. Beverly Hills, Calif.: Sage Publications.

Huizinga, David, and Delbert S. Elliott. 1986. Reassessing the Reliability and Validity of Self-Report Delinquent Measures." *Journal of Quantitative Criminology* 2(4): 293–327.

Kelley, Barbara Tatem, Rolf Loeber, Kate Keenan, and Mary DeLamatre. 1997. "Developmental Pathways in Boys' Disruptive and Delinquent Behavior." *OJJDP Juvenile Justice Bulletin* (December): NCJ165692.

Moffitt, Terrie. 1993 "Adolescence-Limited and Life-Course-Persistent Antisocial Behavior: A Developmental Taxonomy." *Psychological Review* 100(4): 674–701.

Oaxaca, Ronald L. 1973. "Male-Female Wage Differentials in Urban Labor Markets." *International Economic Review* 14(3): 693–709.

O'Brien, Robert M. 1999. "Measuring the Convergence/Divergence of 'Serious Crime' Arrest Rates for Males and Females: 1960–1995." *Journal of Quantitative Criminology* 5(1): 97–114.

Poe-Yamagata, Eileen, and Jeffrey A. Butts. 1996. "Female Offenders in the Juvenile Justice System." Statistics summary, NCJ 160941. Washington: U.S. Department of Justice, Office of Juvenile Justice and Delinquency Prevention.

Short, James F., and F. Ivan Nye. 1957. "Reported Behavior as a Criterion of Deviant Behavior." *Social Problems* 5(Winter): 207–13.

———. 1958. "Extent of Unrecorded Juvenile Delinquency: Tentative Conclusion." *Journal of Criminal Law and Criminology* 49(December): 296–302.

Snyder, Howard N. 1998. "Juvenile Arrests, 1997." *Juvenile Justice Bulletin*, NCJ 173938. Washington: U.S. Department of Justice, Office of Juvenile Justice and Delinquency Prevention.

Steffensmeier, Darrell J., Emilie Andersen Allan, Miles D. Harer, and Cathy Streifel. 1989. "Age and the Distribution of Crime." *American Journal of Sociology* 94(4): 803–31.

Thornberry, Terence P., and Marvin D. Krohn. 2000. "The Self-Report Method for Measuring Delinquency and Crime." In *Measurement and Analysis of Crime and Justice (Criminal Justice 2000*, vol. 4), edited by David Duffee. Washington, D.C.: National Institute of Justice.

Tourangeau, Roger, and Tom W. Smith. 1996. "Asking Sensitive Questions: The Impact of Data Collection, Mode, Question Format, and Question Context." *Public Opinion Quarterly* 60(2): 275–304.

Tracy, Paul E. 1987. "Race and Class Differences in Official and Self-Reported Delinquency." In *From Boy to Man, from Delinquency to Crime*, edited by Marvin E. Wolfgang et al. Chicago: University of Chicago Press.

Turner, C. F., L. Ku, S. M. Rogers, L. D. Lindberg, J. H. Pleck, and F. L. Sonenstein. 1998. "Adolescent Sexual Behavior, Drug Use, and Violence: Increased Reporting with Computer Survey Technology." *Science* 280(5365): 867–73.

U.S. Department of Health and Human Services. *Trends in the Well-Being of America's Children and Youth, 1998.* Washington: U.S. Department of Health and Human Services.

Weis, Joseph G. 1986. "Issues in the Measurement of Criminal Careers." In *Criminal Careers and "Career Criminal,"* vol. 2, edited by Alfred Blumstein et al. Washington, D.C.: National Academy Press.

12

City Kids and Country Cousins: Rural and Urban Youths, Deviance, and Labor Market Ties

L. Susan Williams

The creators of the suburbs did everything they could to dissociate their developments from the city. Names of developments were usually built around words like "park," "forest," "river," "hills," or "valley," mixed with "view," "park," or "estates." The resulting Forest Parks and Green Valley Estates were meant to conjure up bucolic rural imagery and only coincidentally to reflect the actual landscape.

—Edward J. Blakely and Mary Gail Snyder, *Fortress America*

AMERICANS have long maintained a romanticized view of rural life. The epigraph to this essay illustrates our obsession. Rural areas are seen as idyllic, as "God's country," as the perfect place to raise a family, free from corrupting urban influences. The thought of childhood in the country conjures images of 4-H clubs and barn dances, while the thought of childhood in the city brings images of crime and violence, perpetrated mostly by the black urban male, angry and on the prowl—a "superpredator" (Shapiro 1997). Such distorted notions of reality hinder a proper understanding of the phenomenon of juvenile delinquency in both its rural and its urban manifestations. This chapter examines ways in which the National Longitudinal Survey of Youth, 1997 Cohort (NLSY97), can contribute to our assessment of current trends in youths' illicit activities in both rural and urban areas.

Curiously, despite America's obsession with rurality and its relevance in our history, contemporary theories and empirical studies that directly address rural issues are relatively rare, especially in crime research. As the United States became less a rural, agrarian society and more an urban, industrial one, attention shifted to the lure of the city. Theory and research focused increasingly on the urban but was nevertheless assumed to be universally applicable—a phenomenon to which Weisheit (1993) refers as *urban ethnocentrism*. With technological advances and the postindustrial information age, claims of a homogenized "global village" (McLuhan and Fiore 1967)—thought to be brought about by jet transportation, television, national and international chains, and now the worldwide web—have intensified the urban bias of delinquency research. Rural areas, once the heart of American culture, seemingly vanished from researchers' radar.

Perhaps somewhat serendipitously, the recent spate of school shootings has refocused the nation's attention on rural youth violence. The first of recent rural multiple-victim shootings occurred in 1996 when a fourteen-year-old honors student from the little farm town of Moses Lake, Washington, walked into his algebra class and shot his teacher in the back and two students in the chest. In December 1997, another fourteen-year-old killed three students in West Paducah, Kentucky. In 1998, two other very young adolescents allegedly killed four students and one teacher in Jonesboro, Arkansas; one fifteen-year-old fired fifty-one rounds in a school cafeteria, killing two and injuring more than twenty after also killing his parents; and another youth was accused of killing his mother and two students in Pearl, Mississippi. Alarm escalated even further when two more teenagers launched a massive attack in Littleton, Colorado, leaving twelve students and one teacher dead and twenty-three injured, before killing themselves.

Violence is of course not unknown in American schools.[1] But earlier shootings were urban and black, taking place in areas where gang-related violence is part of everyday life and children are not strangers to death. These recent shootings were rural and white, taking place in communities once considered largely immune to the urban plague of violence. The West Paducahs and the Jonesboros were more likely to be described as places of "horse trails and tree forts where Tom Sawyer would be at home" (Johnson and Brooke 1999, 1), as "idyllic, an oasis for earlier pioneers" (Rohde 1998, 20). They are places where taxes and real estate prices are low and community ties and morals were believed to run high (VonDrehle 1999). President Clinton gave voice to a country's feelings when he said that the events in Littleton "pierced the soul of the nation" (Seelye 1999, 23). The school shootings catalyzed an underlying concern that rural America was not just disappearing but was being transformed into a fresh-faced and unpredictable doppelgänger of its evil urban twin.

The sudden focus on small-town school shootings underscores the fact that little research addresses rural youth crime and deviance. Much of the available theoretical and empirical work offers an inadequate framework within which to conceptualize rural juvenile delinquency and violence.

This chapter addresses the neglect of rural youth crime in the literature and examines ways in which *place*—here defined as rurality-urbanity—influences juvenile crime and deviance. In addition, I compare rural-urban differences between self-reported youth deviance in 1980 (the second wave of the NLSY79) and in 1997 (as reported in the NLSY97).

Geography, Culture, and Youth

Spatial organization has a well-developed theoretical base in the study of crime. Beginning with the Chicago school studies of concentric zones and social disorganization (Shaw and McKay 1942) and continuing through the more recent development of labor market theory (for example, Snipp and Bloomquist 1989; Tolbert and Killian 1987) and neighborhood studies (for example, Anderson 1992; MacLeod 1987), place long has been recognized as the basis for social organization. Some contend, however, that one meaning of place in America—rurality—has disappeared. Many claim that true rural areas today are virtually nonexistent and that, even in places geographically defined as rural, norms and social trends have become so homogenized that rurality is no longer a functional cultural construct. Weisheit, Falcone, and Wells (1999, 2) explain: "For many, the very idea of rural life seems like a historical concept with little relevance for a modern urban society. In short, contemporary American culture is considered not only homogenous, but an urban culture. Since most people have a television and a telephone, and most have access to some form of transportation, it is assumed that urban culture has permeated all parts of America, even those areas where the population is relatively sparse."

However, rural communities are more prevalent than most believe. Nearly a quarter of the U.S. population resides in rural areas (Bachman 1992); of the 3,146 counties in the United States, 76 percent are nonmetropolitan counties; and 88 percent of the incorporated communities and townships in the United States have fewer than ten thousand residents (Weisheit and Wells 1996). If one subscribes to the Durkheimian notion that less-developed areas facilitate more traditional bonds, such communities would be expected to wield a greater degree of informal social control. Indeed, much of the earlier community research supported that notion, and several researchers have found support for the idea that community change—which is more prevalent in urban areas—leads to anomie and delinquency (for example, Bursick and Grasmick 1993; Dillman and Hobbs 1982).

On the other hand, anecdotal evidence suggests, not only that a rural culture does exist, but that, perhaps as a holdover from the frontier era, it is often tied to violence: "Violence is a cultural component of many rural communities, where 'only the tough survives'" (Barlow 1993, 1). Nevertheless, whether or not a *violent* rural subculture exists, most researchers who have spent time observing rural communities agree that a *unique* rural culture persists, one that includes a "density of acquaintanceships" (Freudenberg 1986), a greater degree of face-to-face interaction, a greater emphasis on self-reliance, and a tendency to distrust outsiders (Gagne 1992; Martinez-Brawley 1990; Toomey et al. 1993; Websdale 1995; Weisheit, Falcone, and Wells 1999). Such evidence suggests a distinctly rural social structure.

The question remains, then, whether such a distinct social structure would influence the behavior of youths. Underage populations are typically subjected to social control not exerted on older age groups, and research has demonstrated that such structural constraints are especially influential among disenfranchised groups (Acker 1973; Reskin and Roos 1990; Taylor 1995; Wilson 1987). Dealing with crises may be especially difficult for youths in rural areas because of limited resources, geographic isolation, and a shortage of trained professionals (Keller and Murray 1982). Further, studies demonstrate that stressor events are different for rural youths. First, family events are more directly affected by local conditions, such as economic downturns, fluctuations in local resources, changes in population characteristics, and social trends. Second, because of the greater density of acquaintanceships in rural areas, closer interconnections among rural youths may actually intensify stressor events. Plunkett, Henry, and Knaub (1999) demonstrate that the perceived effect of farm crisis, family transition, and substance use by family members is to place the rural youths in their Nebraska sample at greater risk of serious stress; and Childs and Melton (1983) emphasize that rural culture must be considered when treating mental-health problems, including youth suicide. In sum, substantial evidence supports the idea of a distinctly rural culture that has been neglected in attempts to understand youth life processes, including crime and delinquency.

One final argument that challenges the existence of a unique rural culture is that of geographic mobility. The assumption is that, with the advent of urbanization, high-speed transportation, and high-tech industries, young people grow up in rural communities knowing that they will soon have to leave them to find jobs (Jones 1999). At the same time, businesses in some areas move farther from core urban centers, inviting commuter patterns in rural areas that were not possible two decades earlier (Treen 1999). In addition, some rural regions attract in-migration tied to lifestyle preference, tourist patterns, retirement trends, and industry building such as correctional facilities (Jobes 1999). Finally, other movement trends have altered the demographic makeup of communities as migrants follow industrial and social networks. As one example, Aponte and Siles (1994) report that Latinos account for over half the recent population growth in the Midwest, much of which can be characterized as rural, and such migrant populations tend to be younger.

At least three points underscore the importance of continuing an investigation into urban-rural differences among youths. First, not all rural areas are experiencing a population loss. In a 1996 Iowa study, for example, about half of rural counties (mostly in nonfarm areas) experienced a population increase (Day 1996). Ultimately, the growth-loss-migration pattern is too complex to assume that rural culture no longer exists. When studies can sort out migration and culture, both matter. Overall, in-migration tends to increase criminal behavior, and social cohesion depresses deviance (Jobes 1999). Second, overall geographic mobility is overestimated. One study tracked the movement of a youth population for more than fifteen years using labor market–area definitions as the home units, concluding that 65 percent of the national sample never permanently left their labor market of origin and that, of those who did, most migrated to adjacent areas (Villemez, Beggs, and Williams 1995). Finally, it is highly probable that the local culture in which one grows up is very influential during the formative decision-making years of youth, regardless of whether one ultimately migrates. It is, after all, the immediate context in which life decisions are most often conceived and articulated.

Previous Research on
Crime and Juvenile Delinquency

The earliest theories of crime and delinquency reflected the rural influence of early America. For example, Clinard (1944) found that rural offenders were less of a "criminal type" than urban offenders were, and Sorokin, Zimmerman, and Galpin (1931) noted that the rural population is more law abiding. For the most part, however, the past five decades have been dominated by a decidedly urban frame of mind (Weisheit and Wells 1996). A quick glance at criminology textbooks confirms the urban ethnocentrism, and a perusal of the last three years of *Criminology,* the discipline's leading journal, reveals virtually no studies of rural crime. Lyerly and Skipper (1981) point out that a major reason for the strong urban emphasis is the readily available heterogeneous population distribution of urban communities, which provides ample opportunity for empirical study and theory testing. And crime overall, at least by official statistics, is dramatically higher in urban areas; in 1997, city police agencies reported a rate of more than 5,200 crimes per 100,000 population, while rural counties reported just over 2,000 (Federal Bureau of Investigation 1997).

Another reason for the paucity of research on rural crime is an overemphasis on individual and psychological traits as predictors of crime, leaving explanations partial, person centered, and decontextualized. Self-control theory, named the most popular theory in a survey of criminologists (Ellis and Walsh 1999), provides few parameters for contextual influence such as community characteristics and promotes a "fallacy of autonomy" (Currie 1985)—that the influence of individual-level factors can and should be separated from the influence of outside forces. That is not to say that individual-level influences are irrelevant. In keeping with a strong empirical base of evidence, this study acknowledges the effect of factors such as family background and status (for example, Farrington 1995; Smith and Thornberry 1995), educational attainment (Farrington 1987; Winters 1997), self-esteem and efficacy (Ladd 1999), and peer influence (for example, Elliott 1994; Keenan et al. 1995; Thornberry and Krohn 1996), all of which help shape the attitudes and behavior of youth. In addition, the abuse and victimization of youth appear to be strongly associated with delinquency (Bilchik 1999; Doumas, Margolin, and John 1994; Widom 1992). However, it is the contention of this chapter that context—in this case, the rurality or urbanity of youths' immediate environment—exerts an *independent* influence and also interacts with individual-level factors in ways that are predictive of deviant behavior and social control.

A few studies have found evidence that size of community interacts with criminal behavior in several ways. For example, although overall crime rates are still higher in urban than in rural areas, differences vary by type of crime (for example, the robbery gap is much more pronounced) and reporting agency (differences are greater in the Uniform Crime Reports than in victimization data). Research demonstrates that unemployment is related to overall violent crime in urban but not rural areas (Kposowa, Breault, and Harrison 1995); violence victimization rates are higher for African Americans in the city but for whites in rural areas (Donnermeyer 1994); black arrest rates are also higher in urban than in rural areas; and, in absolute numbers, four of five rural offenders are white and only one in eight black (Donnermeyer 1994).

Some argue that a convergence effect between urban and rural areas may be occurring. Rural areas are experiencing increases in gang activity, drug trafficking, and drug production (Barlow 1993; Weisheit and Wells 1996; White 1996), and recent data suggest that violent-crime rates are down in cities and suburbs but that they are increasing in rural areas (for example, Donnermeyer 1994). Convergence is especially evident among certain types of crimes and among specific groups of people. For example, the rural elderly are just as likely as the urban elderly are to be victimized by family members or acquaintances (Bachman 1992). Among juveniles, urban teens are at a greater risk of rape and robbery, but assault rates are very similar for urban and rural youth. For example, Benson and Roehlkepartain (1993) report that 55 percent of sixth through twelfth graders in cities and small towns were involved in at least one incident of violence in the past year. Finally, fear of crime, once much lower in rural areas, is now reaching levels similar to those in urban areas (Krannich, Berry, and Greider 1989; Weisheit 1993).

Evidence suggests that omitting rurality-urbanity commits the contextual fallacy of autonomy in the study of juvenile delinquency. For example, Stark, Kent, and Doyle (1982) suggest that social ties have the greatest effect where sources of integration are strong, and Kposowa, Breault, and Harrison (1995) find that social integration, poverty, and population change are the strongest determinants of rural violence. As suggested earlier, social integration may be more salient to rural youth, who experience greater isolation and a distilled social network. Further, official, community-sanctioned forms of youth entertainment are unknown in some rural areas, giving rise to fewer deterrents and greater opportunity for deviance (Wilken 1999).

Finally, very limited information exists on differences within areas defined as rural. For example, little systematic research has been conducted on race, class, and gender differences within rural settings (but, for a study of urban arrest trends and race, class, gender, see Chilton and Datesman [1987]). From the modest but important body of literature on delinquency among girls, we know that girls are involved in more violent crime now (as perpetrators) than they were a decade ago (for example, the murder rate among girls is up 64 percent), but girls' rate of violence remains dramatically below that of boys. We also know that girls are more often objects of strict social control, both within the family and within the justice system (Chesney-Lind and Shelden 1992; Phillips 1998). But virtually no studies have appeared on rural girls in gangs or on other forms of deviance among rural girls.

Similarly, we have ample reason to suspect that race and ethnicity are social constructs that may have different meanings in rural cultures than they do in urban (Harris 1977; Weisheit and Wells 1996). For example, Messerschmidt (1997, 4), using life-history analysis, demonstrates convincingly that "gender, race, and class vary by social situation and circumstance." But no systematic studies address the multiple constructions of race, class, and gender in rural areas. One rare study of rural juvenile offending and ethnicity is that by Bond-Maupin and Maupin (1998), who find that juveniles in a largely Hispanic rural jurisdiction are subject to considerable police surveillance and extensive formal social control, contrary to folk wisdom that suggests the predominance of informal mechanisms in rural areas.

In summary, some evidence suggests a convergence between rural and urban crime, but official reports still maintain large gaps in prevalence; approximately 42 percent of violent crimes reported are in urban areas, only 16 percent in rural. Some argue that rural communities have become more homogeneous (Feld 1991) as informal bonds have weakened (Oetting and Beauvais 1986), but others claim that geography still matters. For example, low density in rural areas means a lesser chance of being caught and longer response times, and social control is often qualitatively different in a rural context than it is in an urban context (Dillman and Hobbs 1982; Weisheit and Wells 1996). Little work has examined race, class, and gender differences and criminal-deviant behavior within rural communities.

Research Questions

Given the body of evidence presented and the theoretical questions raised, this study addresses the following research questions: Do we have evidence of convergence over time between rural and urban youth delinquency? What are the effects of rurality-urbanity on current patterns of youth deviance and crime? How do gender and racial differences in offending and victimization vary by urban-rural context? How does participation in deviant acts affect youths' chances in the labor market?

Methods
Data

Most analyses reported in this chapter are based on data from the first wave of the NLSY97, a representative sample of the U.S. population born from 1980 through 1984 ($N = 9,022$), the newest survey in the National Longitudinal Survey Program. I use age at time of interview; the respondents range in age from twelve to eighteen years. Some analyses are based on various age subsets, depending on split-questionnaire design and comparison groups. The NLSY97, sponsored by the Bureau of Labor Statistics, is designed to document the transition from school to work and includes a broad range of topics: schooling, family interaction, community and family background, and self-reported attitudes and behavior, including delinquent and criminal activity, the focus of this study. Comparative data are derived from the second wave of National Longitudinal Survey of Youth, 1979 Cohort (NLSY79), a national probability sample of young men and women ($N = 12,686$) who were between the ages of fourteen and twenty-two years when first surveyed in 1979; respondents have been reinterviewed seventeen times, and the survey boasts a 90 percent retention rate. Additionally, arrest data are derived from the FBI Uniform Crime Reports.

Measures

Eleven primary variables of interest are used for the comparative analysis of the NLSY79 and the NLSY97; nine are single indicators that measure various kinds of self-reported deviant and criminal acts (*drink alcohol, smoke marijuana, destroy property, steal < $50, steal > $50, sell drugs, fight, attack* *others,* and *run away*), and two are indicators of official social control (*suspended* and *arrested*). In general, the NLSY79 survey questions asked how many times in the past year the respondent had engaged in each behavior, and the NLSY97 survey questions asked whether the respondent had ever engaged in each behavior. The 1980 (NLSY79) question about fighting included "school or work," and the NLSY97 question asked about fighting "at school." With the stated exceptions, the indicators are virtually identical. The NLSY97 measures are all binary (coded yes = 1, no = 0), and the NLSY79 measures are recoded so that "0 times" is coded 0 and all other response categories are coded 1. Other measures listed hereafter are from NLSY97 only.

The primary dependent variable used in the logistic models is *crimacts,* a composite variable that includes seven measures of self-reported deviant or criminal acts. The indicators were chosen to represent more serious kinds of deviant and criminal acts; included are *killprop* (ever purposely destroy property), *stelover* (ever steal anything worth more than $50), *hurtothr* (ever attack to hurt or fight), *selldrug* (ever sell drugs), *propcrim* (ever commit other property crime), *guncarry* (ever carry a handgun), and *gangmemb* (ever belong to gang). Because most youths have committed some kind of lower-level deviant act (for example, Kivivuori 1998; Moffitt 1993; Newburn 1998) (such as experimenting with alcohol or shoplifting), involvement in more serious types of deviance is a better test of group differences. The combined measure was tested for internal reliability, or the likelihood that the indicators reflect an underlying characteristic; the Cronbach alpha reliability coefficient for the set of variables is 0.717, indicating a strong positive correlation. *Crimacts* is then dummy-coded so that 1 = ever reporting on any one measure and 0 = reporting on no measure. I chose the dummy-coding construction so as to assess a range of behaviors into one efficient measure of serious youth crime-deviance with which to analyze broadly based effects of urban-rural context.

Urban is a major category of interest and represents the urban-rural residence distinction: respondent living in urban area = 1, and respondent living in rural area = 0. The NLSY79 defines *urban* as 50 to 100 percent urban in county, *rural* as 0 to 49 percent urban in county, with *urban* including towns-cities with a population of 2,500 or more. The NLSY97 defines *urban* as "closely settled, named, communities that generally contain a mixture of residential, commercial, and retail areas, and have a population greater than 2,500"; all other places are considered rural.[2]

Several indices were developed to reflect constructs known to be important to youth development. *Negative peers* sums responses to three questions that ask what percentage of the respondent's peers participate in drugs, gangs, and cutting classes, offering an opportunity to test the widely posited relation between peer association and delinquency. Similarly, *bad experience* totals responses about being bullied, being threatened, having seen someone shot, and having one's household burglarized; this measure will test the strongly held assumption that victimization is closely related to the commission of deviant acts. Both *negative peers* and *bad experience* are converted into dummy variables for selected models, investigating effects of negative contact versus a range of experience; in other cases, index components are examined separately to determine where group differences may lie. *Good school* includes four likert-type scales that measure positive perceptions of school environment; statements include "teachers are good," "teachers are interested in students," "grading is fair," and "discipline is fair." Responses are recoded so that high numbers reflect most positive perceptions.

Two additional indexes represent factors known to be associated with youth development and delinquency and are used as controls in regression equations. *Positive family* sums *famlyeat* (number of days per week typically eat with family), *famlyfun* (number of days per week typically have fun with family), and the respondent's positive evaluation of the mother or mother figure (think highly, mother supports respondent, mother blames respondent for trouble [coding reversed to reflect positive evaluation]), and of the father or father figure (think highly, father supports respondent, father blames respondent for trouble [coding reversed to reflect positive evaluation]). Counts are included as high if the respondent reported high on either parent or parent figure. *Prosocial competence* is constructed by including variables asked separately by gender, using likert-type scales that measure frequency of respondents' lying and sadness (coding reversed on both), two questions measuring degree of positive expectations (expecting best and optimistic about future), and two questions measuring degree of negative expectations (expecting no good and not expecting my way, both reversed).

Finally, several other single indicators are utilized. *Chance college* is the respondent's perceived percentage chance of having earned a college degree in 20 years; *poverty ratio* is the ratio of household income to the poverty level (higher scores reflect greater poverty); *black* is a dummy variable where black = 1; *minority* is a dummy variable where black + Hispanic = 1 and all others = 0; *male* is a dummy variable where male = 1 and female = 0; *single parent* is a dummy variable where 1 is coded for respondents who report living with mother only or father only; and *South* is a dummy variable.

Analysis

Differences in proportions are tested using the chi-square statistic, differences in means using the *t*-test. Logistic regression is used to model the effect of *urban*, explanatory and control variables, and dummy variables on the probability of event for the dependent variable *crimacts*. Logistic regression is the most appropriate method with which to assess a prediction model for a dichotomous dependent variable. In this case, logistic regression is especially useful because the primary theoretical question asks about the probability of an event (juvenile delinquency) in categories of interest (rural and urban) and because logistic regression allows several levels of interpretation, including direction, significance tests, strength, odds ratio, and probability of the event for categories of interest. The odds ratio is calculated by exponentiating the logit coefficient, and I am able to calculate the odds of one variable (for example, urban) on an event versus the odds for another category (for example, rural); I can also predict probabilities on the basis of a certain set of X values (Liao 1994).

Findings

I begin by presenting official arrest statistics for juveniles under age eighteen, as reported by the U.S. Federal Bureau of Investigation, Uniform Crime Reports (UCR), for 1980, 1990, and 1997. Arrest records are inherently biased toward more serious crimes and may more often reflect police practices than actual crime rates. Methodological problems include uneven reporting practices, inconsistent definitions, and incomplete or nonexistent records of multiple offenses. In addition, UCR data are imperfect for parallel comparisons with self-reported data. For example, we know from victimization and self-report studies that fewer than half of violent crimes and fewer than one-third of personal-theft crimes are reported to the police (Rennison 1999; Savitz 1982). While these alternative sources are not without limitations (such as underreporting, overreporting, and the "missing case" nature of sampling), they demonstrate the fallibility of official data. However, despite multiple problems, the UCR represent the official record of crime in the United States, and they remain the most comprehensive crime report, with more than 95 percent of all police agencies contributing (Sherman and Glick 1984). For the purposes of this study, UCR data provide a base from which to assess nationwide longitudinal trends in juvenile offending on the basis of size of place. I therefore begin the analysis with them.

The numbers reported in table 12.1 represent the percentage of juveniles under 18 among all arrests for each year, by urban-suburban-rural area and by classification as violent crime or property crime.[3] Overall, arrests for property crimes have dropped since 1980; the rate of change from 1980 to 1997 is −5.4 percent for city, −11.2 percent for suburban, and 0.5 percent for rural. Rural and suburban rank slightly below city for 1997.

Violent crime presents a different trend. Overall, city violence rates for juveniles have consistently ranked above suburban and rural violence rates; percentages for 1997 are 18.1, 15.1, and 12.2, respectively. However, in observing the percentage change, we can see that both city and sub-

TABLE 12.1   *UCR Arrest Statistics, Juveniles under Age Eighteen, Percentage of All Arrests, by Urban-Rural Area*

	Violent Crime				Property Crime			
	1980	1990	1997	Percentage Change, 1980 to 1997	1980	1990	1997	Percentage Change, 1980 to 1997
City	21.1	17.3	18.1	−3.0	40.9	32.5	35.5	−5.4
Suburban	18.4	15.1	15.1	−3.3	43.0	33.2	31.8	−11.2
Rural	7.8	7.8	12.2	4.4	31.2	27.8	31.7	0.5

Source: Author's compilation based on U.S. FBI, UCR 1980, 1990, and 1997.

urban have dropped 3 percent from 1980 to 1997 but that rural has increased 4.4 percent. The percentage differential between city and rural for 1997 is only about 4 percent. In addition, when considering the proportional change, rural juvenile violence has increased 56 percent since 1980. However, these figures reflect number of arrests, not number of persons arrested. Further, it is widely accepted that the UCR reflect a serious underreporting of crime in general, and we have reason to believe that this is especially true with regard to juvenile arrests. In addition, we cannot know whether the changes reflect a true difference in juvenile violence in rural areas or a difference in police and court processes. To address this question, I now turn to the NLSY data.

Comparative Statistics for the NLSY79 and the NLSY97 on Urban-Rural Crime and Deviance

Table 12.2 addresses the question of convergence over time for urban-rural differences in juvenile deviance. Samples of respondents fifteen to seventeen years of age at time of interview are selected from the NLSY79 (N = 4,019) and NLSY97 (N = 4,156) in order to match age groups; both young men and young women are included. NLSY79 respondents were interviewed in 1980, and NLSY97 respondents were interviewed in 1997; urban and rural definitions are reported in the respective data sets. Recall that the 1980 survey asks about behavior in the past year while the 1997 survey asks about behavior ever. Thus, total incidence between the two time periods is not directly comparable; the primary purpose is to examine differences in urban-rural behavior in 1997 as compared to urban-rural behavior in 1980.

Within the 1980 sample, we observe significant differences between the self-reported behavior of urban and rural youths in eight of the ten variables

TABLE 12.2   *Comparative Statistics for NLSY79 and NLSY97*
on Urban-Rural Differences, Self-Reported Behavior
for Youths Fifteen-to Seventeen-Years-Old, 1980
(N = 4,007) and 1997 (N = 4,156)

| | Young Men and Women, Aged Fifteen to Seventeen | | | |
| | 1980 (Percentage Reporting Each Behavior) | | 1997 (Percentage Reporting Each Behavior) | |
	Urban	Rural	Urban	Rural
Drink alcohol[a]	61.7	57.6*	57.8	59.8ns
Smoke marijuana[a]	42.2	31.9***	31.8	29.4ns
Destroy property[a]	25.2	21.6*	27.7	29.2ns
Steal < $50[a]	20.8	16.7**	36.7	35.7ns
Steal > $50[a]	7.1	4.9*	10.6	9.1ns
Sell drugs[a]	11.5	7.2***	10.3	9.2ns
Fight[b]	39.1	36.0ns	14.5	12.9ns
Attack others[a]	12.0	10.1ns	22.0	18.4**
Run away[a]	10.1	8.0*	15.6	12.5**
Suspended[d]	26.5	19.5***	35.9	31.2**
Arrested[c,d]	9.4	6.1**	12.6	9.8**
	Selected Changes, Young Women Only			
Smoke marijuana	39.4	32.7**	19.2	17.6
Steal < $50	13.2	10.4	28.0	26.6
Attack others	7.6	5.9	13.6	11.4*
Run away	11.1	7.2*	12.1	9.4**
Suspended	18.7	13.4**	23.2	17.9***
Arrested	4.1	1.9*	5.7	4.9

Source: Author's compilation based on NLSY79 and NLSY97.
Notes: All results presented here are based on the unweighted sample population. Calculations were also performed with sample weights; changes in coefficients were minimal, and no changes in statistical significance occurred. Weighted sample tables are available upon request to author.
[a] 1980 question asked about behavior in the past year; 1997 question asked about behavior "ever."
[b] 1980 survey asked about fights "at school or work"; 1997 survey asked about fights "at school."
[c] 1980 survey asked "have you ever been booked or charged"; 1997 survey asked "have you ever been arrested." Both surveys exclude minor traffic offenses.
[d] Question asks "have you ever been. . . ."
χ^2 test for difference in proportion:
* $p < .05$. ** $p < .01$. *** $p < .001$.
ns = nonsignificant.

shown. For example, 42.2 percent of urban and 31.9 percent of rural youths report using marijuana, and 7.1 percent of urban youths and 4.9 percent of rural youths report stealing something worth more than $50. Two indicators of violent crime against persons, fighting and attacking others, show no difference between urban and rural youth. With that exception, a larger percentage of urban than rural youths report all other deviant activities. In addition, urban youths are more likely than rural youths to be suspended from school and arrested.

The NLSY97 sample displays a quite different pattern. The most obvious observation is the lack of significant differences between urban and rural youths on virtually every measure; attacking others and running away are the two exceptions, with urban reporting significantly higher. Despite the general pattern of no significant differences in behavior, urban youth are still suspended and arrested at significantly higher rates than rural youth are, suggesting different levels or methods of social control.

The lower portion of table 12.2 compares selected behaviors between urban and rural young women within the two time periods. The overall pattern is not as straightforward as that demonstrated in the full sample. Some urban-rural differences in 1980 are not significant in 1997 (marijuana use, arrest rates), while attacking others is significant in 1997 but not in 1980. Running away and being suspended remain significantly higher for urban young women, and differences in petty theft remain nonsignificant. Note that rates for young women remain well below the overall average in every category except running away.

Overall, table 12.2 supports a convergence effect between 1980 and 1997 in self-reported deviant behavior for urban and rural youth but demonstrates significantly higher official processing for urban youth. The pattern is not as straightforward for young women, and their rates remain well below those of young men (with the exception of running away). We can draw few conclusions about rates of deviance over time because of nonparallel question wording; however, because the 1997 survey does ask "if ever," we can fairly safely say that marijuana use has declined significantly from 1980 to 1997.

The question of rural-to-urban and urban-to-rural migration was raised earlier in this chapter. It is possible that urban-rural convergence of offending rates observed between the 1980 and the 1997 cohorts is a result of selective migration, with particularly disadvantaged groups remaining in rural areas. I ran exploratory analyses to test whether certain urban-rural population characteristics that differed in 1980 were significantly changed in 1997. Among area characteristics, unemployment rates were higher in rural areas in 1980 (7.7 versus 6.7 percent) but lower in 1997 (5.2 versus 5.7 percent). Similarly, the percentage of families in poverty was higher in rural areas in 1980 (18.1 versus 10.4 percent) but lower in 1997 (10.6 versus

11.2 percent). Education levels were lower for rural families both in 1980 (6.5 versus 11.5 percent college educated; 51.8 versus 55.1 percent graduated high school) and in 1997 (18.6 versus 20.6 percent college educated; 73.3 versus 75.0 percent graduated high school), but the education gap between rural and urban has closed considerably. Thus, for aggregate-level indicators, rural areas (as measured in these data) have actually improved economically and as far as health is concerned compared to urban areas, suggesting that a relative increase in rural juvenile delinquency for this age group cannot be attributed solely to area economic disadvantage.

I also examined several individual-level characteristics. Rural youths in both cohorts are more likely to live with both parents (74.7 versus 67.1 percent in 1980; 53.7 versus 44.1 percent in 1997) and are more likely to report "feeling safe" (3.51 versus 3.43 on a five-point scale in 1980; 3.18 versus 3.11 in 1997). Rural youths are much less likely to be suspended in both cohorts (21.2 versus 25.6 percent in 1980; 26.3 versus 31.6 percent in 1997). In 1980, rural youths scored lower than urban youths did on self-esteem (3.46 versus 3.50 on a five-point "positive" measure; 1.61 versus 1.54 on a "negative" measure), but the scores of rural and urban youths did not differ significant on either measure in 1997 (3.03 versus 3.07 on the "positive" measure, 2.34 versus 2.35 on "negative"). Again, by comparable measures available in these two data sets, we have no indication that the composition of rural youth has changed in a way that would account for the urban-rural convergence in observed deviance measures. This evidence gives no support to migration as an explanation for urban-rural convergence. I now turn to a more in-depth look at deviance within the NLSY97 cohort.

Influence of Contextual and Situational Variables on Probability of Serious Deviant Acts

Table 12.3 reports results of logistic-regression analysis for NLSY97 youths (twelve to seventeen years, $N = 6,060$), scoring the dependent variable *crimacts* as 1 for those having ever participated in one or more criminal acts and 0 for those who have not. The criminal-deviant acts include destroying property, committing other property crimes, stealing more than $50, fighting, attacking others, selling drugs, carrying a gun, and belonging to a gang. The control variable, *poverty ratio*, represents the ratio of the respondents' household income to the federal poverty level (missing cases on this created variable account for the reduced number of respondents in the model). Higher scores on *poverty ratio* reflect a negative relation to poverty; *poverty ratio* remains nonsignificant in the multivariate model.

The odds-ratio column gives the expected change in the transformed eta, or the odds of having an event occur versus not occur, per unit change in the explanatory variable, other things being equal. Indicators that have

TABLE 12.3   *Results of Logistic Regression, Testing Influence*
of Contextual and Situational Variables on Probability
That Youth Has Engaged in Serious Criminal Acts
(N = 6,061); All Equation Variables Are Shown; Group
Differences Are Modeled for Black, Urban, and Male

DV = Crimacts[a]	Odds Ratio
Negative peers[b]	1.148
Gang in neighborhood	1.555
Good school[c]	0.869
Bad experiences[d]	2.305
Poverty ratio[e]	1.000
Black	0.775
Urban	0.879
Male	3.328

Source: Author's compilation based on NLSY97.
Notes: All results presented here are based on the unweighted sample population. Calculations were also performed with sample weights; changes in coefficients were minimal, and no changes in statistical significance occurred. Weighted sample tables are available upon request to author.
[a] Dependent variable, *crimacts*, includes self-reports of property crimes, destroying property, theft > \$50, selling drugs, carrying a handgun, gang membership, and attacking others.
[b] *Negative peers* is a percentage of peers who cut class, use drugs, and belong to gangs.
[c] *Good school* is a composite score for "teachers are good," "teachers are interested," "grading is fair," and "discipline is fair."
[d] *Bad experiences* include reports of being bullied, being threatened, seeing someone shot, and having one's house burglarized.
[e] *Poverty ratio* is a created variable that is the ratio of the respondent household's income to the poverty level; higher scores reflect a negative relation to poverty.
χ^2 test for difference in proportion ($X^2 - 2$ LOG $1 = 1,228.74$; pseudo-$R^2 = .168$):
* $p < 05$. ** $p < .01$. *** $p < 001$.

an odds ratio greater than 1 indicate an increased chance of reporting a deviant act. For example, in this model, the odds ratio for bad experience implies that those with a bad experience are more than two times as likely to report a deviant act than are those without a bad experience.

Three contextual variables exert a positive influence on the probability that a youth reports a deviant act: negative peers (range is 3 to 15, mean = 5.56, S.D. = 2.69); gang activity in the neighborhood (1 or 0); and having a bad experience. Bad experience is scored 1 if the respondent reports on any one of four indicators: being bullied, being threatened, seeing someone shot, or having his or her home burglarized. Good school (perception that teachers and teaching are positive, grading and discipline fair) reduces the probability of youths self-reporting a deviant act; the range for good school is 4 to

16, mean = 11.96, S.D. = 2.02. Three dummy-coded variables test group differences for black versus nonblack, urban versus rural, and male versus female. Note the negative coefficient and values less than 1 of the odds ratio for both black and urban. On the basis of this logit model, both black and urban youth actually have a decreased chance of a self-reported deviant act than do their counterparts, all else equal, a pattern that contradicts many societal stereotypes.

Estimated Probability of Self-Reported Deviant Acts

Table 12.4 demonstrates the usefulness of reporting probabilities from the logistic model; we can isolate the effects of one variable (for example, rural) while holding constant the effects of other conditions. Here, I report the predicted probability of self-reporting deviant acts for various groups, contexts, and situations, given a set of values in other control variables. The probabilities are obtained by using values obtained in a general logistic equation, calculating group differences and using sample means for control variables.

The NLSY97 subgroup for this analysis, aged twelve to fourteen, was selected because these individuals were asked additional self and family attitude and interaction questions. The dependent variable is again *crimacts*; negative peers, good school, and poverty ratio are the same variables as used in the previous model (table 12.3) and are evaluated at the sample mean for the group. Two additional composite variables are introduced, prosocial competence (including measures of youth's positive expectations and lying and sadness, coding reversed) and positive family (including positive attitudes toward parents and positive family interaction).

The top part of table 12.4 reports probabilities for young men, and urban/rural differences are displayed at each level. Probabilities are calculated for those living in neighborhoods with and without gangs, for blacks and for whites, and for those with and without negative life experiences. Each calculation includes the control variables, all evaluated at the sample mean. The analysis demonstrates the same general pattern as shown in table 12.3 (which includes all NLSY97 age groups); that is, negative peers and good school exert influence in the expected directions, and both black and urban are negatively associated with *crimacts*, other factors equal. In addition, prosocial competence and positive family are negatively associated with *crimacts*.[4]

Table 12.4 demonstrates the modeled associations in terms of probabilities for each subgroup. We see, for example, that the white rural young man with bad experiences who lives in a neighborhood with reported gang activity has the highest probability of self-reporting criminal acts. On the basis of the logit model, about 75 percent of youths in those circumstances are expected to report criminal behavior, given that they are average on

TABLE 12.4   *Estimated Probability That Various Groups of Youths Have Engaged in Serious Criminal Acts, Under Specified Conditions (Gangs in Neighborhood, Bad Experiences)[a]*

DV = Crimacts[b]	Urban	Rural
Young men		
Neighborhood with gangs		
Black		
With bad experience	0.6420	0.7051
Without bad experience	0.4332	0.5046
White		
With bad experience	0.6903	0.7483
Without bad experience	0.4873	0.5589
Neighborhood with no gangs		
Black		
With bad experience	0.5100	0.5812
Without bad experience	0.3073	0.3716
White		
With bad experience	0.5641	0.6331
Without bad experience	0.3555	0.4237
Selected probabilities, young women		
Neighborhood with gangs		
Black, with bad experience	0.3529	0.4209
White, with bad experience	0.4040	0.4748
Neighborhood without gangs		
Black, without bad experience	0.1189	0.1524

Source: Author's compilation based on NLSY97.
Notes: All results presented here are based on the unweighted sample population. Calculations were also performed with sample weights; changes in coefficients were minimal, and no changes in statistical significance occurred. Weighted sample tables are available upon request to author.
[a] Probabilities are based on a logistic-regression model that controls for negative peers, good school, positive family, prosocial competence, and poverty ratio. Sample means used for all control variables.
[b] Dependent variable, *crimacts*, includes self-reports of property crimes, destroying property, theft > $50, selling drugs, carrying a handgun, gang membership, and attacking others.

prosocial competence, positive family experiences, negative peers, good school, and poverty ratio. Note that the 75 percent of white rural young men with bad experiences in a gang neighborhood is higher than the 69 percent of white urban young men who are predicted to report criminal acts and the 64 percent of black urban young men in the same circumstances. The group of young men with the lowest probability of criminal acts, all else equal, is the black urban young man with no bad experiences, living in a nongang neighborhood, at about 31 percent. These predictions resonate well with what we know about the effect of victimization on the propensity to commit criminal acts, but the effects of black and urban, when controlling for other factors, are counterintuitive to what the literature suggests.

The lower portion of table 12.4 reports probabilities for selected groups of young women. The highest probability for criminal acts, all else equal, is found for the white rural young woman with bad experiences in a gang neighborhood, at 47 percent, 28 percent below her male counterpart. The lowest probability for criminal acts is found for the black urban young woman with no bad experiences, living in a nongang neighborhood, at 12 percent. Note that the black young woman with negative experiences, living in a gang neighborhood (urban or rural), is at the same probability level for criminal acts as the white young man with no negative experiences, living in a nongang neighborhood, all else equal. These comparisons are important in addressing context *within* urban-rural areas and specifying conditions that are predictors of youth deviance. These findings seriously challenge the black urban stereotypes that dominate some segments of society, and they underscore gender differences in criminal acts.

Of course, the reality is that blacks in urban areas are at greater risk for certain negative structural effects. For example, 57 percent of urban blacks report gangs in the neighborhood (versus 37 percent of rural blacks), and 56 percent of urban blacks report at least one bad experience (versus 43 percent of rural blacks). Overall, urban youths score significantly higher on negative peers (6.61) than do rural youths (5.92). Interestingly, however, the average composite score for bad experience (not dummied; a measure of a range of bad experiences) is higher for rural youths (mean = 1.54) than for urban youths (mean = 1.33); the difference is not statistically significant. In other words, while urban youths are more likely to report at least one negative experience, rural youths' range of bad experiences is not statistically different from that of urban youths. This type of analysis is important in comparing the contextual effect of urban and rural environment for specific groups of youths.

Gender Differences for Urban Youths and Rural Youths on Deviant Acts and Victimization

Table 12.5 reports gender differences in deviant acts and victimization among urban youth and among rural youth. Selected differences are shown; gender differences are few for both urban and rural youth on other reported measures of deviance such as drinking, smoking, and running away, which are not reported here.

TABLE 12.5   *Reported Differences Between Young Men and Young Women for Urban Youths and Rural Youths, Self-Reported Deviant and Criminal Acts and Victimization*

	Urban		Rural	
	Young Men	Young Women	Young Men	Young Women
Marijuana	22.6	19.2**	20.1	17.6*
Petty theft	37.0	28.0***	34.9	26.6***
Theft > $50	10.8	5.6***	9.4	4.5***
Destroy property	35.1	18.0***	33.4	19.2***
Fight	24.8	11.4***	22.4	10.8***
Attack others	23.9	13.6***	23.0	11.4***
Suspend	39.8	23.2***	34.0	17.9***
Arrested	12.7	5.7***	8.2	4.9***
Carry handgun	14.8	3.1***	17.2	2.9***
Gang member	7.6	3.3***	6.3	3.6***
Victimization				
Bad experience (dummy)	51.5	42.5***	46.2	40.5***
Bad experience (scale)	1.603	1.051***	1.733	1.331*
Threatened at school (dummy)	22.7	18.2***	22.2	20.4[ns]
Threatened at school (scale)	1.062	0.641***	1.267	1.016[ns]
See someone shot	15.5	9.8***	10.8	6.6***

Source: Author's compilation based on NLSY97.
Notes: All results presented here are based on the unweighted sample population. Calculations were also performed with sample weights; changes in coefficients were minimal, and no changes in statistical significance occurred. Weighted sample tables are available upon request to author.
* $p < .05$. ** $p < .01$. *** $p < .001$.
[ns] = nonsignificant.

    The most consistent pattern is one of similarity in gender differences between urban youth and rural youth. Overall, young men are much more likely than young women are to report deviant acts. A few other observations are noteworthy. A slightly larger percentage of urban young women than rural young women report deviant acts in virtually every category (the exception is destroying property). Interestingly, however, rural young women are just as likely as urban young women to report being a gang member, although both groups report significantly lower gang participation than young men do.
    The lower portion of table 12.5 addresses gender differences in victimization. At first glance, a larger percentage of young men than young women

report ever having a bad experience, and young men also score a higher average on the bad-experience scale, for both urban and rural groups. These findings are consistent with others in the literature that report men to be more at risk for most kinds of violent crime (sexual assault is one important exception). For example, 51.5 percent of urban young men and 46.2 percent of rural young men report ever having a bad experience, while the comparable numbers for young women are 42.5 percent and 40.5 percent, respectively. As reported earlier, however, we know that rural youth report a similar or higher average than urban youth when we consider the full range of experiences. We can now observe that rural young men average 1.733 types of bad experiences, slightly higher than the average 1.603 for urban young men (the difference is not significant).

Interactions between gender categories and urban-rural residence reveal unexpected findings. Surprisingly, rural young women score much higher (1.331) than urban young women (1.051) on types of bad experiences; the difference is statistically significant at the .05 level. Because the variable bad experience is a composite of four questions (being bullied, being threatened, being burgled, and seeing someone shot), I tested each measure separately to determine specific group differences and found that the variable threatened accounts for much of the difference. As table 12.5 demonstrates, a significantly higher percentage of urban young men (22.7 percent) than urban young women (18.2 percent) report being threatened at school (as a dummy variable), but the difference between rural young men (22.2 percent) and rural young women (20.4 percent) is not significant. I also tested the mean score on number of times threatened at school, and the same general pattern holds. That is, gender differences occur among urban youths but not among rural youths, and rural young women score higher (1.016) than urban young women do (0.641) on the mean for threatened at school. A separate chi-square test determined that the difference between urban men and rural men is not significant; the difference between urban women and rural women is significant at the .01 level. Finally, and not surprisingly, a larger percentage of urban youths report having seen someone shot; and having seen someone shot is more prevalent for both groups of young men than it is for young women.

In summary, gender differences in self-reported deviant acts remain strong, with significantly higher reporting for young men, both urban and rural. Both urban men and urban women are more likely than rural counterparts are to be suspended or arrested. Although one would assume random distribution for neighborhood characteristics by gender, young men, both urban and rural, are much more likely to report having seen someone shot (although urban is higher overall). This observation suggests different lifestyles for young men and young women, both urban and rural. Finally, victimization reports demonstrate interesting rural-urban interactions with gender differences. Rural women, but not rural men, are more likely to be threatened at school than urban counterparts are; differences on threatened are significantly higher for urban men than for urban women but not for rural men as compared to rural women.

Does a Rural Culture Still Exist?

An important question posed in light of the perceived urban-rural convergence of youth deviance is whether informal social control through family interaction has deteriorated in rural areas, especially as more women enter the workforce and as social bonds perhaps weaken. If so, a reduced level of informal social control could account for the increase in levels of rural juvenile delinquency. Or, if important differences in informal social control exist between rural and urban areas, then we would suspect that at least remnants of a rural culture remain. Table 12.6 addresses that question by regressing *run away* on several family attitude and interaction variables, controlling for poverty ratio, and modeling group differences for black, urban, and male.

The *full sample* column includes NLSY97 youths aged twelve to fourteen (*N* = 2,814; missing cases are due to poverty ratio); this age group was selected for the split questionnaire on family-interaction questions. Unstandardized parameter estimates are reported for comparison across models, and odds ratio are reported for interpreting likelihood estimates. We can see that a higher score on *thinks highly of mom* and *thinks highly of pop* (both recoded so that higher scores reflect more positive responses) is negatively associated with the probability of running away and that a higher score on *mom blames youth for trouble* is positively associated with the probability of running away. Both urban and male coefficients suggest that running away has a higher likelihood among urban youths and among young men; black is nonsignificant.

Results are then presented for separate analyses by urban and rural. The *odds ratio* column provides a relative measure of the indicators that reduce the likelihood of running away. Among urban youths, the only significant associations with running away are *think highly of pop* and *mom blames youth.* Among rural youths, all indicators are significant in the expected directions and remain so after controlling for poverty ratio. That is, the overall differences observed in the full-sample model are due in some part to the higher scores on family-interaction variables among rural youths. In this logit model among rural youths (controlling for other factors), young men are almost two times more likely than young women are to run away. Although this simple model does not include a large number of attitude and context variables, the evidence lends some support to the notion that there still exists a rural culture that exerts influence via the family on youths'

TABLE 12.6   Results of Logistic Regression, Testing Significance of Parental-Influence Variables on Youths' (Aged Twelve to Fourteen) Probability of Running Away (N = 2,814); Poverty Ratio Is Controlled, Group Differences Are Modeled for Male and Urban; Separate Analyses Are Reported for Urban and Rural

	Full Sample (N = 2,814)		Urban (N = 1,481)		Rural (N = 1,333)	
	b	Odds Ratio	b	Odds Ratio	b	Odds Ratio
Intercept	-2.0774	. . .	-1.9799	. . .	-1.5667	. . .
Thinks highly of mom[a]	-0.1434***	0.866	-0.0585ns	0.943	-0.2815**	0.755
Thinks highly of pop[a]	-0.2276**	0.796	-0.2204*	0.802	-0.2440*	0.784
Mom blames youth for trouble[b]	0.3910***	1.478	0.4270***	1.533	0.3498**	1.419
Poverty ratio	-0.0010*	0.999	-0.0007ns	0.999	-0.0018ns	0.998
Black	-0.1319ns	0.876	0.0048ns	1.005	-0.4190ns	0.658
Urban	0.4086*	1.505	. . .	. . .	. . .	. . .
Male	0.3322*	1.394	0.1735ns	1.189	0.6446*	1.905

Source: Author's compilation based on NLSY97.
Notes: All results presented here are based on the unweighted sample population. Calculations were also performed with sample weights; changes in coefficients were minimal, and no changes in statistical significance occurred. Weighted sample tables are available upon request to author.
[a] Recorded so that higher scores reflect more positive responses.
[b] Higher scores reflect greater agreement with the statement.
* $p < .05$. ** $p < .01$. *** $p < .001$.
ns = nonsignificant.

likelihood of running away and suggests that rural culture is distinctly more gender differentiated on this measure.

Influence of Deviant Acts on Probability of Arrest

Another ongoing debate in the literature is about the association between self-reported deviance and actual arrests and also about racial bias in arrest. For example, from evidence presented in table 12.2 and table 12.5, we already know that, despite similar levels of reported deviant acts, urban youths are more likely than rural youths are to report being arrested. Table 12.7 reports the effect of criminal acts on the probability of arrest, adding stepwise controls for male, urban, minority (black and Hispanic combined), and poverty ratio. The odds ratio is reported at each level.

The first column demonstrates that those who report a criminal act are more than nine times likely also to report being arrested, certainly an ex-

TABLE 12.7 *Results of Logistics Regression, Testing Significance of Self-Reported Criminal Behavior on Youths' (Aged Twelve to Seventeen) Probability of Arrest. Stepwise Controls Modeled Are Male, Urban, Minority,[a] and Poverty Ratio[b]*

DV = *arrested*	(N = 8,962)	+ Male (N = 8,962)	+ Urban (N = 8,962)	+ Minority (N = 8,962)	+ Pov. Ratio (N = 6,479)
Crimacts (odds ratio)	9.424	8.754	8.746	8.768	8.671
Male (odds ratio)	. . .	1.378	1.399	1.407	1.601
Urban (odds ratio)	. . .	. . .	1.476	1.399	1.493
Minority (odds ratio)	. . .	. . .	. . .	1.312	1.199
Poverty ratio (odds ratio)	. . .	. . .	. . .	. . .	.999

Source: Author's compilation based on NLSY97.
Notes: All results presented here are based on the unweighted sample population. Calculations were also performed with sample weights; changes in coefficients were minimal, and no changes in statistical significance occurred. Weighted sample tables are available upon request to author.
[a] Dummy variable, black and Hispanic = 1, all others = 0.
[b] All parameter estimates are significant at the .001 level with one exception: when poverty ratio is introduced into the model, minority maintains a positive effect but is not significant at the .05 level (p Wald X^2 = .0728).

pected finding. In the next column, results are reported when male is introduced into the model; the odds ratio for *crimacts* is reduced from 9.4 to 8.7, and the odds ratio for male is 1.378. In other words, controlling for reported criminal acts, young men are about 1.4 times more likely than young women are also to report arrest. Next, when urban is introduced into the model, the odds ratios for criminal acts and male remain about the same, and the odds ratio for urban is 1.476; urban youths who report criminal acts are 1.5 times more likely also to report being arrested. Similarly, minority has an odds ratio greater than 1, suggesting that minorities who report criminal acts are 1.3 times more likely than nonminorities to report being arrested. When poverty ratio is introduced, the minority odds ratio is still greater than 1 but is nonsignificant at the .05 level (p Wald $X^2 = 0.0728$).

In summary, the results of this logit model lend some support to the idea that young men and urban youths who engage in criminal acts have a greater likelihood of arrest than their counterparts do. The category minority becomes nonsignificant when poverty ratio is controlled for, suggesting that an overrepresentation of minority youths in the justice system may be due, at least in part, to their overrepresentation in poverty. A word of caution, however, is in order here. First, the measure of criminal acts is the same dummy variable used in other models and does not reflect a continuum of frequency or seriousness of crime. Second, the variable poverty ratio is missing on more than two thousand cases, and the results of the final model may therefore be biased. Third, the tendency for young men to be more involved than young women are in violent acts is not taken into account in this model and may account for their overrepresentation in reported arrests. Nevertheless, the model is useful in lending support to the suspected relation between urban and arrest, controlling for poverty ratio.

Influence of Deviant Acts on Perceived Chance of College Degree

One of the concerns about juvenile delinquency is that it may greatly inhibit life chances. In a recent analysis of NLSY79 youths, Tanner, Davies, and O'Grady (1999, 250) find that all types of youth delinquency "have consistently significant and negative impacts on educational attainment among both males and females." It is also well supported that perceptions are closely associated with outcomes and that delinquency may diminish aspirations. Thus, I test the effect of self-reported deviant acts on youths' perceived chance of a college degree for this cohort. The subsample of NLSY97 youths aged fifteen to seventeen were selected for a split questionnaire addressing expectations about the future. Along with other questions on expectations, the respondent was asked to estimate in percentage terms

TABLE 12.8   *Youths' (Aged Fifteen to Seventeen) Perceived Chance of College Degree, Regressed on Self-Reported Criminal Behavior, Controlling for Poverty Ratio, School, and Peer Influence, and Testing Group Differences for Black, Urban, and Male (N = 2,324)*

DV = *chance college*	b	β
Intercept	53.731***	
Crimacts	−4.286**	−0.066
Poverty ratio	.023***	0.172
Negative peers	−1.539***	−0.134
Good school	2.194***	0.134
Black	4.157**	0.056
Urban	2.587*	0.039
Male	−8.003***	−0.123

Source: Author's compilation based on NLSY97.
Notes: All results presented here are based on the unweighted sample population. Calculations were also performed with sample weights; changes in coefficients were minimal, and no changes in statistical significance occurred. Weighted sample tables are available upon request to author.
* $p < .05$. ** $p < .01$. *** $p < .001$.
Adj. $R^2 = 0.106$.

his or her perceived chance of obtaining a college degree by age thirty. Table 12.8 reports both the unstandardized and the standardized coefficients of an ordinary-least-squares multiple-regression model.

The primary independent variable is *crimacts*; the coefficient is negatively associated with perceived chance of a college career. Control variables include poverty ratio, negative peers, and good school, all of which are significant in the expected direction. Recall that a higher score on poverty ratio is negatively related to poverty status; thus, those youths from more affluent homes are more likely to expect a college degree. Note that blacks score higher on average than nonblacks on percentage chance of completing a college degree, other conditions equal, and urban youths are more likely than rural youths are to expect a college degree. Young men score lower than young women do on perceived chance at a college degree. Observing the standardized coefficients, poverty ratio has the strongest effect; that is, even for those who commit criminal-deviant acts, living in a high-income household may negate much of the suppressing effect of deviant acts on perceived chance at a college degree. It is also heartening to note that the variable good school exerts a strong positive effect on expecting a college degree, controlling for other conditions in the model, including deviant acts.

Conclusions

This study refocuses the study of juvenile delinquency on the importance of context and specifically addresses the salience of the rural-urban dimension. The study warrants two major conclusions: it lends partial support to rural-urban convergence in levels of serious delinquent behavior by youths; and it also finds evidence that rural areas exert a unique influence on youth deviance, often in complex, interactive ways. The data presented are creditable for advancing these conclusions in three major ways. First, self-reporting of delinquent behavior is most useful in getting at the "dark figures of crime" not reflected in official statistics (Dunford and Elliott 1983; Hindelang, Hirschi, and Weis 1981) and is especially useful in measuring youth delinquency because a great proportion of juvenile crime never reaches police records. Second, the national probability sample of youths made available through the NLSY79 and the NLSY97 is unique in that it makes available for study a large cohort not selected on the basis of delinquency. We can be confident that the representative sample reflects reporting by youths who are not institutionalized or in a juvenile system, thereby estimating behavior for the general population. Third, having two such national surveys of youths, seventeen years apart, that ask virtually identical questions about delinquent behavior affords an exemplary research opportunity.

We should not be surprised that the two major conclusions that at first glance seem contradictory—one supporting convergence, the other uniqueness—come from a careful examination of extremely complex social attitudes and behavior. That is, such complexity precludes overly simplistic portrayals. For example, we know that significant differences in self-reported delinquent behavior existed between urban youths and rural youths in 1980, but most urban-rural differences in offending have disappeared in the 1997 cohort. However, despite very similar levels of behavior, these data support the idea of differential social control in rural and urban areas. The official processing of urban youths, both for school suspension and arrests, remains significantly higher than that of rural youths. Further, the model of running away suggests that informal social control is both stronger and more gender differentiated in rural areas. Nevertheless, conclusions about urban-rural differences in the two cohorts and across time must be made with caution; more work is needed on the comparability of the rural and urban measures. Further, we cannot conclude that the overall level of juvenile delinquency has increased in the past two decades. First, levels of less-serious delinquency reflect fairly stable trends, and differences in question wording between the two surveys disallow conclusions about overall increases or decreases over time.

The significance of statistically disentangling context and interaction (artificial though this may be) becomes apparent in the prediction models.

When controlling for major factors known to be associated with delinquency (negative peers and bad experiences, family and school environment), rurality actually exerts a positive effect on youth delinquent acts—a trend opposite to that reflected in official crime rates. That is, given the same conditions, rural youths are more likely than their urban counterparts are to commit a criminal act. Statistically, the highest-probability category for criminality is the white rural young man who also reports bad experiences and living in a gang-activity neighborhood. In contrast, the stereotypical "angry young black urban male" actually has a ten-point lower probability of committing a criminal act—a direct contradiction of official statistics and common wisdom. This model specifies the most powerful conditions in which juvenile delinquency develops and underscores the need to clarify the unique contributions of race and location. Although blacks and those in urban areas are highly overrepresented in official counts of crime, whites and those in rural areas may actually be less prepared to deal with conditions conducive to crime.

One of the most striking observations about urban-rural youth crime is the similarity of gender differences. The strongest predictor of youth crime and deviance continues to be gender. While levels of alcohol and drug use are very similar between young women and young men, prevalence rates for more serious deviant acts remain much higher for young men, both in urban and in rural areas. Gender differences are particularly marked for violent incidents; more than twice as many young men as young women report fighting and gang membership. Carrying a handgun seems to be a particularly masculine marker—about five times as many young men as young women report carrying guns.

The patterns of victimization are somewhat surprising. From the literature, we know that, overall, men are more likely than women are to be victims of violent crime (Rennison 1999). And the measure bad experience confirms that young men report significantly higher levels than young women do. However, the percentage of young women who report being threatened at school (18 percent of urban women and 20 percent of rural women) was somewhat unexpected and led to the most startling observation: the mean score for threatened for rural young women is not significantly different from that for either rural or urban young men. This finding is significant and unexpected and should be the subject of future studies. It may be that rural young women are more often in close contact with young men, given the smaller number of peers in a network or school setting, or that the type of interaction between young women and young men in a rural setting is qualitatively different.

These findings are noteworthy for several reasons. First, this study addresses a popular but little-studied assumption that rural youth violence is increasing and that rural delinquency is increasingly similar to urban delinquency. Second, the study provides a baseline for several neglected areas of juvenile-delinquency research, including suspected place effects and other contextual concerns such as the increasing trend of gang activity and drug trafficking in rural areas. It also underscores the significant effect of deviant behavior on perceptions of success, a known determinant to both economic and personal achievement. Third, this research speaks to an ongoing dialogue about the changing nature of rurality, or its existence, and directs attention to the need to examine differences within rural communities. This investigation of rural youth deviance is only preliminary and has raised more questions than it has answered about the possible changing nature of social integration in some rural areas. For instance, although I included one indicator of religious influence (percentage of peers who attend church regularly), more research is needed to investigate whether religion and other types of integrative ties are weakening in rural areas (see, for example, Michael and Bickert, chapter 5 in this volume; and Chatterji, chapter 10 in this volume) and under what conditions those ties influence youth behavior. In addition, some other researchers still claim that a Southern culture exists—one that is also often characterized as distinctly rural. Although I included the Southern region as a control in certain models, I have not addressed here how rural areas may differ by region of the country. Much work is needed to disentangle structural and cultural influences that may be different for rural and urban areas and that may also be different within certain rural contexts. For example, several authors in this volume have investigated the effect of family structure on various outcomes (see especially Pierret, chapter 1, for effects on delinquency), and it may be that the influence of family structure varies by place of residence. Finally, the construction of gender and race within rural and urban areas and their interaction with delinquency is a much-neglected area of study.

In conclusion, the scant research on rural processes has enabled much speculation, idealization, and overgeneralization about rurality. When our assumptions miss the mark, ignoring important rural-urban differences and also the diversity within rural areas, our investigations are misspecified and our interpretations incomplete at best, erroneous at worst. Donnermeyer (1994, 3) spoke to the idea of a lag time in the rate at which rural processes follow urban trends, citing a Midwestern farmer who said, "We are on the same train as city people, but we're in the caboose." With the current paucity of research on rural life processes, we cannot even be sure that we are on the right train.

This project was supported by the W. T. Grant Foundation through its support of the NLSY97 Early Results Conference.

Notes

1. School-related violence peaked in 1992 to 1993, when nearly fifty were killed at school.

2. The definition of *rural* is problematic in general. Weisheit, Falcone, and Wells (1999, 182) provide a good discussion of various dimensions along which the rural-urban distinction can be characterized, including demographic, economic, social structural, and cultural. According to them, rural areas are characterized by "a lack of social resources commonly associated with large population centers—for example, mass transportation, central markets or exchanges, specialized medical facilities, newspapers, airports, television stations, museums, zoos, social services." For the purposes of this study, I assume that a rural population, as defined by the U.S. census, will be closely correlated with rural characteristics. Both data sets (NLSY79, NLSY97) utilize U.S. census definitions of urbanity-rurality, although stated in different ways (see the text). However, I cannot say with confidence that the definitions of *rural* and *urban* in the two surveys are equivalent. I am currently analyzing the two measures for comparability.

3. The UCR define *cities* as cities or towns with population over ten thousand; *suburban* includes areas covered by noncity agencies within a metropolitan statistical area (MSA); and *rural* is reported as counties that are outside MSAs and whose jurisdiction is not covered by city police agencies.

   Violent crime includes murder, forcible rape, robbery, and assault; *property crime* includes burglary, larceny theft, motor-vehicle theft, and arson.

4. In a separate analysis, I added a dummy variable for South to the logistic-regression equation to test whether the urban-rural effect might be a function of region (because the South is more rural and because some claim the existence of a Southern culture of violence). The variable *South* was positively and significantly related to *crimacts*; however, urban remained negative and significant at the .01 level (the coefficient for urban was reduced from –0.2875 to –0.2414). For clarity of interpretation, I omitted South from the model as calculated. Previous studies suggest that other aggregate-level control variables would be appropriate if one is to evaluate the Southern region for a subcultural effect.

References

Acker, Joan. 1973. "Women and Social Stratification: A Case of Intellectual Sexism." *American Journal of Sociology* 78(4): 936–46.

Anderson, Elijah. 1992. *Streetwise: Race, Class, and Change in an Urban Community.* Chicago: University of Chicago Press.

Aponte, Robert, and Marcelo Siles. 1994. "Latinos in the Heartland: The Browning of the Midwest." Research report 5. Julian Samora Research Institute, Michigan State University.

Bachman, Ronet. 1992. "Crime in Nonmetropolitan America: A National Accounting of Trends, Incidence Rates, and Idiosyncratic Vulnerabilities." *Rural Sociology* 57(4): 546–55.

Barlow, Tom. 1993. "Violence in Rural Areas: Looking beyond the View from the Highway." *Midwest Forum* 3(1). Available at *www.ncrel.org/ sdrs/areas/issues/envrnmnt/drugfree/3-1rurl.htm*

Benson, Peter L., and Eugene Roehlkepartain. 1993. "Youth Violence in Middle America." *Midwest Forum* 3(1). Available at *www.ncrel.org/sdrs/ areas/issues/envrnmnt/drugfree/3-1youth.htm.*

Bilchik, Shay. 1999. "Breaking the Cycle of Juvenile Crime." *Trial* 35(1): 36–43.

Blakely, Edward J., and Mary Gail Snyder. 1999. *Fortress America: Gated Communities in the United States.* Washington, D.C.: Brookings Institution Press.

Bond-Maupin, Lisa J., and James R. Maupin. 1998. "Juvenile Justice Decision Making in a Rural Hispanic Community." *Journal of Criminal Justice* 26(5): 373–84.

Bursick, Robert J., Jr., and Harold G. Grasmick. 1993. *Neighborhoods and Crime: The Dimensions of Effective Community Control.* New York: Lexington.

Chesney-Lind, Meda. 1997. *The Female Offender.* Thousand Oaks, Calif.: Sage Publications.

Chesney-Lind, Meda, and Randall G. Shelden. 1992. *Girls, Delinquency, and the Juvenile Justice System.* Pacific Grove, Calif.: Brooks/Cole.

Childs, Alan W., and Gary B. Melton. 1983. *Rural Psychology.* New York: Plenum.

Chilton, Roland, and Susan K. Datesman. 1987. "Gender, Race, and Crime: An Analysis of Urban Arrest Trends, 1960–1980." *Gender and Society* 1(2): 152–71.

Clinard, Marshall. 1944. "Rural Criminal Offenders." *American Journal of Sociology* 50(1): 38–45.

Connell, Robert W. 1987. *Gender and Power: Society, the Person, and Sexual Politics.* Stanford, Calif.: Stanford University Press.

Currie, Elliott. 1985. *Confronting Crime: An American Challenge.* New York: Pantheon.

Day, Bill. 1996. "Looking beyond the Numbers." *Business Record* 92(12): 4–5.

Dillman, Don A., and Daryl J. Hobbs. 1982. *Rural Society in the U.S.: Issues for the 1980's.* Boulder, Colo.: Westview.

Donnermeyer, Joseph F. 1994. "Crime and Violence in Rural Communities." Columbus: National Rural Crime Prevention Center, Ohio State University.

Dornbusch, Stanford M. 1989. "The Sociology of Adolescence." *Annual Review of Sociology* 15: 233–59.

Doumas, Diana, Gayla Margolin, and Richard S. John. 1994. "The Inter-generational Transmission of Aggression across Three Generations." *Journal of Family Violence* 9(2): 157–75.

Dunford, Franklyn, and Delbert Elliott. 1983. "Identifying Career Criminals Using Self-Reported Data." *Journal of Research in Crime and Delinquency* 21(1): 57–86.

Elliott, Delbert S. 1994. "Serious Violent Offenders: Onset, Developmental Course, and Termination." *Criminology* 32(1): 1–21.

Ellis, Lee, and Anthony Walsh. 1999. "Criminologists' Opinions about Causes and Theories of Crime and Delinquency." *Criminologist* 24(4): 1–6.

Farrington, David P. 1987. "Early Precursors of Frequent Offending." In *From Children to Citizens: Families, Schools, and Delinquency Prevention,* vol. 3, edited by James Q. Wilson and Glenn C. Loury. New York: Springer.

———. 1995. "The Development of Offending and Antisocial Behavior from Childhood: Key Findings from the Cambridge Study in Delinquency Development." *Journal of Child Psychology and Psychiatry* 36(6): 929–64.

Federal Bureau of Investigation. 1980, 1990, 1997. *Uniform Crime Reports (UCR): Crime in the United States.* Washington: U.S. Government Printing Office.

Feld, Barry. 1991. "Justice by Geography: Urban, Suburban, and Rural Variations in Juvenile Justice Administration." *Journal of Criminal Law and Criminology* 82(1): 156–210.

Freudenberg, William R. 1986. "The Density of Acquaintanceship: An Overlooked Variable in Community Research." *American Journal of Sociology* 92(1): 27–63.

Gagne, Patricia L. 1992. "Appalachian Women: Violence and Social Control." *Journal of Contemporary Ethnography* 20(4): 387–415.

Harris, Anthony R. 1977. "Sex and Theories of Deviance: Toward a Functional Theory of Deviant Type-Scripts." *American Sociological Review* 43(1): 3–17.

Hindelang, Michael, Travis Hirschi, and Joseph Weis. 1981. *Measuring Delinquency.* Thousand Oaks, Calif.: Sage Publications.

Jobes, Patrick C. 1999. "Residential Stability and Crime in Small Rural Agricultural and Recreational Towns." *Sociological Perspectives* 43(3): 499–517.

Johnson, Dirk, and James Brooke. 1999. "Portrait of Outcasts Seeking to Stand Out from Other Groups." *New York Times,* April 22: 1.

Jones, Gill. 1999. "The Same People in the Same Places? Socio-Spatial Identities and Migration of Youth." *Sociology* 33(1): 1–18.

Keenan, Kate, Rolf Loeber, Lening Zhang, Magda Stouthamer, and Welmoet B. VanKammen. 1995. "The Influence of Deviant Peers in the Development of Boys' Disruptive and Delinquent Behavior: A Temporal Analysis." *Development and Psychopathology* 7(4): 715–26.

Keller, Peter A., and J. Dennis Murray. 1982. *Handbook of Rural Community Mental Health.* New York: Human Sciences.

Kivivuori, Janne. 1998. "Delinquent Phases." *British Journal of Criminology* 38(4): 663–87.

Kposowa, Augustine J., Kevin D. Breault, and Beatrice M. Harrison. 1995. "Reassessing the Structural Covariates of Violent and Property Crimes in the USA: A County Level Analysis." *British Journal of Sociology* 46(1): 79–105.

Krannich, Richard S., E. Helen Berry, and Thomas Greider. 1989. "Fear of Crime in Rapidly Changing Rural Communities: A Longitudinal Analysis." *Rural Sociology* 54(2): 195–212.

Ladd, Gary W. 1999. "Peer Relationships and Social Competence during Early and Middle Childhood." *Annual Review of Psychology* 50(3): 333–59.

Liao, Tim Futing. 1994. *Interpreting Probability Models: Logit, Probit, and Other Generalized Linear Models.* Thousand Oaks, Calif.: Sage Publications.

Lyerly, Robert R., and James K. Skipper Jr. 1981. "Differential Rates of Rural-Urban Delinquency." *Criminology* 19(3): 385–99.

MacLeod, Jay. 1987. *Ain't No Makin' It: Leveled Aspirations in a Low-Income Neighborhood.* Boulder, Colo.: Westview.

Martinez-Brawley, Emilia E. 1990. *Perspectives on the Small Community.* Silver Spring, Md.: National Association of Social Workers Press.

McLuhan, Marshall, and Quentin Fiore. 1967. *The Medium Is the Message.* New York: Bantam.

Messerschmidt, James W. 1997. *Crime as Structured Action: Gender, Race, Class, and Crime in the Making.* Thousand Oaks, Calif.: Sage Publications.

Moffitt, Terrie. 1993. "Adolescent Limited and Life Course Persistent Antisocial Behavior: A Developmental Typology." *Psychological Review* 100(4): 674–701.

Newburn, Tim. 1998. "Young Offenders, Drugs, and Prevention." *Drugs* 5(3): 233–45.

Oetting, Earl R., and F. Beauvais. 1986. "Peer Cluster Theory: Drugs and the Adolescent." *Journal of Counseling and Development* 65(1): 17–22.

Phillips, Lynn. 1998. *The Girls Report: What We Know and Need to Know about Growing Up Female.* New York: National Council for Research on Women.

Plunkett, Scott W., Carolyn S. Henry, and Patricia K. Knaub. 1999. "Family Stressor Events, Family Coping, and Adolescent Adaptations in Farm and Ranch Families." *Adolescence* 34(133): 147–68.

Rennison, Callie M. 1999. "Changes 1997–1998 with Trends 1993–1998." Washington: Bureau of Justice, National Crime Victimization Survey.

Reskin, Barbara F., and Patricia A. Roos. 1990. *Job Queues, Gender Queues: Explaining Women's Inroads into Male Occupations.* Philadelphia: Temple University Press.

Rohde, David. 1998. "Shootings in a School: The Town; Oasis with a Dark Side." *New York Times*, May 22: 20.

Savitz, Leonard. 1982. "Official Statistics." In *Contemporary Criminology*, edited by Leonard Savitz and Norman Johnston. New York: Wiley.

Seelye, Katherine Q. 1999. "Clinton Tells Littleton Shootings 'Pierced the Soul' of the Nation." *New York Times*, May 21 (Late ed.): 23.

Shapiro, Bruce. 1997. "Behind the (Bell) Curve." *Nation* 264(1): 5.

Shaw, Clifford R., and Henry D. McKay. 1942. *Juvenile Delinquency in Urban Areas*. Boulder: University of Colorado Press.

Sherman, Lawrence, and Barry Glick. 1984. "The Quality of Arrest Statistics." *Police Foundation Reports* 2(1): 1–8.

Smith, Carolyn, and Terence P. Thornberry. 1995. "The Relationship between Childhood Maltreatment and Adolescent Involvement in Delinquency." *Criminology* 33(4): 451–81.

Snipp, C. Matthew, and Leonard E. Bloomquist. 1989. "Sociology and Labor Market Structure: A Selective Overview." In *Research in Rural Sociology and Development*, vol. 4, edited by William Falk and Thomas Lyson. Greenwich, Conn.: JAI.

Sorokin, Pitirim A., Carle C. Zimmerman, and C. J. Galpin. 1931. *A Systematic Source Book in Rural Sociology*. Minneapolis: University of Minnesota Press.

Stark, Rodney D., Lori Kent, and Daniel P. Doyle. 1982. "Religion and Delinquency: The Ecology of a 'Lost' Relationship." *Journal of Research in Crime and Delinquency* 19(1): 4–24.

Tanner, Julian, Scott Davies, and Bill O'Grady. 1999. "Whatever Happened to Yesterday's Rebels? Longitudinal Effects of Youth Delinquency." *Social Problems* 46(2): 250–74.

Taylor, Ronald L. 1995. *African-American Youth: Their Social and Economic Status in the United States*. Westport, Conn.: Praeger.

Thornberry, Terence P., and Marvin D. Krohn. 1996. "Peers, Drug Use, and Delinquency." In *Handbook of Antisocial Behavior*, edited by David M. Stoff, James Breiling, and Jack D. Maser. New York: Wiley.

Tolbert, Charles M., and Molly S. Killian. 1987. *Labor Market Areas for the United States*. Washington: U.S. Government Printing Office for U.S. Department of Agriculture.

Toomey, Beverly G., Richard J. First, Richard Greenlee, and Linda K. Cummins. 1993. "Counting the Rural Homeless Population: Methodological Dilemmas." *Social Work Research and Abstracts* 29(4): 23–27.

Treen, Dana. 1999. "Rural Florida Filling Up: People Move Out of Urban Areas." *Florida Times-Union*, no. PSA-2287, February 18 (Metro section): 1.

Villemez, Wayne J., John J. Beggs, and L. Susan Williams. 1995. "Running in Place: Mobility across Labor Market Areas." Paper presented at the annual meeting of Southern Demographic Association. Richmond, Va. (October).

VonDrehle, David. 1999. "To Killers, Model School Was Cruel." *Washington Post*, April 25, A01.

Websdale, Neil. 1995. "An Ethnographic Assessment of the Policing of Domestic Violence in Rural Eastern Kentucky." *Social Justice* 22(1): 102–22.

Weisheit, Ralph A. 1993. "Studying Drugs in Rural Areas: Notes from the Field." *Journal of Research in Crime and Delinquency* 30(2): 213–32.

Weisheit, Ralph A., David N. Falcone, and L. Edward Wells. 1999. *Crime and Policing in Rural and Small-Town America.* Prospect Heights, Ill.: Waveland.

Weisheit, Ralph A., and L. Edward Wells. 1996. "Rural Crime and Justice: Implications for Theory and Research." *Crime and Delinquency* 42(3): 379–98.

White, Michael. 1996. "Crime Brings Big City Problems to Small, Rural Towns." *Associated Press*, February 20.

Widom, Cathy S. 1992. "Childhood Victimization and Adolescent Problem Behaviors." In *Adolescent Problem Behaviors: Issues and Research*, edited by M. E. Lamb and R. D. Ketterlinus. New York: Erlbaum.

Wilken, Joy. 1999. "Sprague A4K: An Approach to Rural Substance Abuse, Crime, and Intergenerational Problems." *The Treatment Improvement Exchange.* Available at: *http://www.treatment.org/taps/tap20wilken.html.*

Wilson, William Julius. 1987. *The Truly Disadvantaged: The Inner City, the Underclass, and Public Policy.* Chicago: University of Chicago Press.

Winters, Clyde A. 1997. "Learning Disabilities, Crime, Delinquency, and Special Education Placement." *Adolescence* 32(126): 451–63.

Index

Boldface numbers refer to figures and tables.